Bergstrand

jayme pereira Pinto

jayme @

INTERNATIONAL FINANCIAL MARKETS

ABOUT THE AUTHORS

Alan L. Tucker is presently on the faculty at Temple University, Philadelphia, Pennsylvania. He holds a B.A., an M.B.A., and a Ph.D. in Finance, the latter from Florida State University. His principal research concerns domestic and foreign capital markets, derivative securities, and asset valuation. Dr. Tucker has published in the *Journal of Finance*, the *Journal of Financial and Quantitative Analysis*, the *Journal of Banking and Finance*, the *Review of Economics and Statistics*, the *Journal of International Money and Finance*, and other professional journals. He is currently the Associate Editor of the *Journal of Economics and Business* and is the author of another West textbook entitled *Financial Futures, Options, and Swaps*.

Jeff Madura is on the faculty at Florida Atlantic University. He holds a B.A., an M.A., and a Ph.D. in Finance, the latter from Florida State University. His research interests lie in international capital markets and domestic and international banking and financial institutions. Dr. Madura has written three other textbooks, and has published in numerous academic journals, including the *Journal of Money, Credit, and Banking*, the *Journal of Financial and Quantitative Analysis*, the *Journal of Banking and Finance*, the *Journal of Financial Services Research*, the *Journal of Financial Research*, and others.

Thomas C. Chiang is presently on the faculty at Drexel University, Philadelphia, Pennsylvania. He holds a B.A., an M.A., and a Ph.D. in International Finance, the latter from Pennsylvania State University. His principal research concerns international financial markets, applied time series analysis, and asset pricing. Dr. Chiang has published in the *Journal of Money, Credit, and Banking*, the *Journal of International Money and Finance*, the *Journal of Financial Research*, and other professional journals. He is currently an editorial board member of the *Journal of International Finance*, and is the coauthor of the book *Sustainable Corporate Growth: A Model and Management Planning Tool*.

INTERNATIONAL FINANCIAL MARKETS

Alan L. Tucker
Temple University

Jeff Madura
Florida Atlantic University

Thomas C. Chiang
Drexel University

WEST PUBLISHING COMPANY
St. Paul   New York   Los Angeles   San Francisco

Copyeditor Christine Thillen
Artist Tech Arts
Text Designer Lois Stanfield
Compositor Bi-Comp, Inc.

Copyright © by WEST PUBLISHING COMPANY
50 West Kellogg Boulevard
P.O. Box 64526
St. Paul, MN 55164-0526

Printed in the United States of America

98 97 96 95 94 93 92 91   8 7 6 5 4 2 1 0

Library of Congress Cataloging-in-Publication Data

Tucker, Alan L.
    International financial markets / Alan L. Tucker, Jeff Madura,
  Thomas C. Chiang.
        p.   cm.
        Includes index.
        ISBN 0-314-81721-2 (hard)
        1. International finance. I. Madura, Jeff. II. Chiang, Thomas C.
    III. Title.
  HG3881.T83 1991
  332'.042—dc20   90-19978
                                                                   CIP

CONTENTS

PREFACE

The fall of the Iron Curtain and the unification of Germany. The end of the Cold War and the marketization of the Soviet economy. The integration of the European Economic Community. The industrialization of the Pacific Rim. The progress toward the creation of a free trade zone encompassing the entire Western hemisphere. Cooperative linkages among national securities markets. The increasing number of international mergers and acquisitions. The demise of capital flow barriers. The institution of early morning and evening trading sessions at national and regional securities exchanges. Relaxed trade restrictions under the auspices of GATT. The interdependence of national economies as evidenced by the October 1987 worldwide equities market crash.

Each of these events and others clearly indicate that we are living in an increasingly integrated world market. Accordingly, the modern business student must be cognizant of the international dimension of business, both its substance and its subtleties. Indeed, the AACSB is now encouraging business schools to "internationalize" their course offerings. Included in this dimension are international financial markets such as those for Eurodollars, Eurobonds, and swaps. The purpose of *International Financial Markets* is to provide readers with a working knowledge of these markets.

This book is intended for undergraduate or MBA students, particularly those who are specializing in the study of finance, international business, or economics. We have designed this book to be the major reading source for a course devoted entirely to international financial markets. At the very least, however, the book could be employed to supplement a course devoted largely to domestic financial markets.

The materials and markets we cover in this book have been largely overlooked in the past. Courses in international economics or trade principally focus on macroeconomic issues, such as the balance of payments and its adjustment mechanisms, international reserves adequacy, and optimal monetary and fiscal policies in an open economy. On the other hand, courses in international financial management principally focus on microeconomic issues, such as capital budgeting for multinational corporations or the hedging of translation exposure. Any discussion of international financial markets in these courses and their accompanying textbooks is cursory at best. The treatment is simply too broad for students to acquire an intimate understanding of international financial markets *as markets*. This book is intended to provide such an understanding.

Chapter 1 discusses the reasons for engaging in international business, provides a brief analysis of recent and important events pertaining to international financial markets, and largely serves to motivate the study of these markets. It also provides an outline of the materials to follow, thus serving as an introduction to the rest of the book. Part I (Chapters 2 through 6) of this book addresses the foreign exchange and commodity markets, providing detailed discussion of international parity conditions that will play an important role in subsequent analyses. Part II (Chapters 7 through 11) of this book covers international securities markets, including credit and equity markets, and issues related to international banking. Part III (Chapters 12 through 16) concludes the book with an analysis of currency forward, futures, and options markets, as well as the markets for interest rate and currency swaps. This book also contains an appendix describing the ongoing integration of the European Economic Community, which is scheduled for completion in 1992.

For graduate courses, the chapters should be covered in a linear fashion. For undergraduate courses, the instructor may omit Chapters 4 through 6 (although it is not encouraged). This material is generally more advanced and its essence can be grasped by coverage contained in Chapters 2 and 3. Finally, if this book is used as a supplement for a domestic financial markets course, the most relevant chapters would be 1, 2, 3, 7, 8, 9, 12, 14, and 16.

We thank Dick Fenton, our editor, Nancy Hill-Whilton, who oversaw the book's development, and Lynette D'Amico, our production editor. We also thank numerous reviewers for their helpful comments and suggestions. We are indebted to these scholars for their insights.

Kegian Bi	Wendell H. McCulloch, Jr.
University of San Francisco	California State University— Long Beach
Robert Driskill	Lucjan T. Orlowski
Ohio State University	Sacred Heart University
Joseph E. Finnerty	S. Ghon Rhee
University of Illinois— Urbana/Champaign	University of Rhode Island
Ronald Johnson	Woodard R. Springstube
Federal Reserve Bank of New York	University of Iowa

We hope that you enjoy this book and encourage you to write to us expressing your comments.

OVERVIEW OF INTERNATIONAL FINANCIAL MARKETS

In recent years, the financial markets have become internationally integrated in many respects. The increasing internationalization is substantiated by the following trends:

- The flow of funds across countries has increased.
- Foreign investors have increased ownership of financial and real assets.
- Foreign financial institutions have increased their penetration of financial centers.
- The international investment in stocks has increased dramatically through the creation of numerous international stock mutual funds.
- Many corporations are listing their shares on foreign stock exchanges, allowing for virtual around-the-clock trading.
- International investment in bonds and money market securities has increased with the relaxation of barriers that historically discouraged cross-border transactions.

The increased volume of international transactions in these financial and real assets has caused a substantial increase in foreign exchange trading. The daily foreign exchange turnover exceeds the equivalent of $400 billion. It has been estimated that an average of 2.5% of the $400 billion is for purchases of goods and services, and the remaining 97.5% is for financial assets (Rybczynski 1988). Commercial banks that serve this market offer foreign currency for *spot* (immediate) and *forward* (future) delivery. We discuss the market for foreign exchange in detail in Part I of the text.

With the increase in international financial transactions, numerous innovative techniques have been created to hedge risk resulting from these transactions. In the following sections, we explain the motivation for participating in international financial markets, the techniques used, and the more recent developments in these markets.

IMPACT OF MARKET IMPERFECTIONS

In a typical domestic financial market, the need for either borrowed funds or equity funding is accommodated by creditors or the investors in the same country. In an extreme setting where international financial transactions were completely restricted, creditors and investors would be forced to use their available funds domestically.

At the other extreme, the existence of perfect markets with zero barriers in financial and real asset markets (including zero transaction costs or taxes) would allow creditors and investors to execute transactions in a single, integrated marketplace. Yet, under these extreme conditions, financial markets would be internationally integrated to such a degree that there would be no special opportunities in any foreign country. The existence of completely integrated real asset markets would cause economic cycles of all countries to move in tandem.

The actual setting of international financial markets lies between the two extremes just described. Several barriers prevent the markets for real or financial assets from becoming completely integrated, such as tax differentials, tariffs, quotas, labor immobility, cultural differences, financial reporting differences, and significant costs of communicating information across countries. Yet, the barriers can also create unique opportunities for specific geographic markets that will attract foreign creditors and investors. For example, barriers such as tariffs, quotas, and labor immobility can cause a given country's economic conditions to be distinctly different from others. Investors and creditors may want to do business in that country to capitalize on favorable conditions unique to that country.

MOTIVES FOR INTERNATIONAL INVESTMENT

Given the existence of imperfect markets, we now discuss some common motives for investors and creditors to penetrate foreign financial markets. These motives have precipitated the internationalization of financial markets.

Motives for Investors to Invest in Foreign Markets

Investors have one or more of the following motives for investing in foreign markets:

- *Economic conditions.* Firms in a particular foreign country may be expected to achieve more favorable performance than those in the investor's home country. For example, the loosening of restrictions in Eastern European countries in 1989 and 1990 was expected to create favorable economic conditions in West Germany, since consumers in Eastern Europe were allowed to purchase more products from West Germany. Such conditions attracted foreign investors and creditors to West German stocks.

- *Exchange rate expectations.* Some investors purchase financial securities denominated in a currency that is expected to appreciate against their own. From a foreign investor's perspective, the performance of such an investment is highly dependent on the currency movement over the investment horizon.

- *International diversification.* Investors may achieve benefits from internationally diversifying their asset portfolio. Empirical evidence indicates considerable risk reduction from international diversification. The risk-reduction benefits can be explained by cross-border differences in economic conditions, so that an investor's entire portfolio does not entirely depend on a single country's economy. Furthermore, access to foreign markets allows investors to spread their capital across a more diverse group of industries that may not be available domestically. This is especially true for investors residing in countries whose firms are concentrated in a relatively small number of industries.

Motives for Creditors to Provide Credit in Foreign Markets

Creditors have one or more of the following motives for providing credit in foreign markets:

- *High foreign interest rates.* Some countries experience a shortage of loanable funds, which can cause market interest rates to be relatively high, even after considering default risk. Foreign creditors may attempt to capitalize on the higher rates, thereby providing capital to overseas markets. We should mention that relatively high interest rates are often perceived to reflect relatively high inflationary expectations of that country. To the extent that inflation can cause depreciation of the local currency against others, high interest rates in the country may be somewhat offset by a weakening of the local currency over the time period of concern. Yet, the relation between a country's expected inflation and its local currency movements is not precise, since several other factors can influence currency movements as well. Thus, some creditors may believe that the interest rate advantage in a particular country will not be offset by a local currency depreciation over the period of concern.

- *Exchange rate expectations.* Creditors may consider supplying capital to countries whose currencies are expected to appreciate against their own. Whether the form of the transaction is a bond or a loan, the creditor benefits when the currency of denomination appreciates against the creditor's home currency.

- *International diversification.* Creditors can benefit from international diversification, which may reduce the probability of simultaneous bankruptcy across borrowers. The effectiveness of such a strategy depends on the correlation between the economic conditions of countries. If the countries of concern tend to experience somewhat similar business cycles, diversification across countries will be less effective.

Three motives for penetrating foreign markets were identified for both investors and creditors. As Exhibit 1.1 shows, there is a striking similar-

Exhibit 1

How Motives to Penetrate Foreign
Markets Relate to Risk-Return
Goals

Ultimate Goal	Related Motive for Investors	Related Motive for Creditors
Higher returns	1. Higher stock price appreciation resulting from purchasing stocks of foreign firms that are expected to experience high performance	1. Higher interest rates by serving as a creditor to firms or governments in countries with high interest rates
	2. Expected appreciation of the currency denominating the stock, which will magnify the investor's returns	2. Expected appreciation of the currency denominating the credit, which will magnify the creditor's returns
Lower risk	1. International diversification across stocks of different countries to reduce the impact of any single country's economy on the investor's returns	1. International diversification across loans or bonds of various countries to reduce the impact of any single country's economy on creditor's returns

ity between motives. Returns to investors and creditors depend on economic conditions, and on the degree of change in the value of the foreign currency denominating the transaction. To reduce risk (or the volatility of returns) over time, investors and creditors can diversify across countries, or use various hedging techniques that we discuss later in the chapter.

MOTIVES FOR FIRMS TO OBTAIN FUNDS FROM FOREIGN MARKETS

Just as investors and creditors consider foreign markets when allocating funds, firms and governments in need of funds consider foreign markets as a source of funds. Some of the more common motives follow.

Motives for Borrowing in Foreign Markets

Borrowers may have one or more of the following motives for borrowing in foreign markets:

- *Low interest rates.* Some countries have a large supply of funds available compared to the demand for funds, which can cause relatively low interest rates. Borrowers may attempt to borrow funds from creditors in these countries because the interest rate charged would be lower. However, a country with relatively low interest rates is often expected to have a relatively low rate of inflation. Since this type of inflation differential can place upward pressure on the foreign currency's value, any advantage to borrowers in the form of lower interest rates could be offset by a strengthened currency. The value of the foreign currency borrowed when converting it into the local currency would be lower than the value when repurchasing the foreign currency to repay the loan. However, since the relation between expected inflation differentials and currency movements is not precise, some borrowers will choose to borrow from a market in which nominal interest rates are low, since they do not expect an adverse currency movement to fully offset this advantage.

- *Exchange rate expectations.* Borrowers who expect a foreign currency to depreciate may consider borrowing that currency and converting it to their home currency for use. The value of the foreign currency when converted to their local currency would exceed the value when the borrowers repurchase the currency to repay the loan. This favorable currency effect can offset part or all of the interest owed on the funds borrowed.

Motives for Selling Securities in Foreign Markets

Firms and other entities may have one or more of the following motives for selling securities in foreign markets:

- *Greater access to funds.* Corporations sometimes issue securities in foreign markets to avoid flooding their local market. This practice may prevent a decline in the security price that would have occurred if the corporations had issued securities in their local market instead. In addition, the issuance in a foreign market may establish name recognition in that market, which could allow for continued access to funds from that market in the future.

- *Less price sensitivity to local market conditions.* When a corporation issues securities in another country, it can establish a secondary market for its securities in that country. By listing a stock on a foreign exchange, the corporation may reduce the stock's sensitivity to its local market index, since it is also influenced by a second force (the foreign stock index). As an example, assume that the stock of a particular U.S.-based multinational firm is listed on the Paris Stock Exchange. This stock may be affected by movements in the U.S. *and* French stock markets. Therefore, the stock is not as sensitive to U.S. market movements as it would be if it were listed only on a U.S. exchange. Some corporations would prefer reduced sensitivity to the local index because many market participants perceive the foreign listing as a reduction in the stock's systematic risk. They may be encouraged to initiate the foreign listing process by issuing stock in foreign markets.

The discussion so far suggests that foreign markets can offer investors and creditors an opportunity for higher returns. Foreign markets can also offer borrowers an opportunity for reduced borrowing costs. Whereas international diversification across financial assets can reduce risk, exposure to foreign currency movements can increase risk. Some financial market participants who expect adverse foreign currency movements may consider hedging their positions. Although hedging reduces the downside risk, it also negates potential upside returns.

INSTRUMENTS USED TO FACILITATE INTERNATIONAL TRANSACTIONS

International financial transactions can increase exposure to exchange rate or interest rate movements. A variety of techniques have been created to hedge this exposure. The most widely used techniques are currency futures, currency options, and swaps. In the following paragraphs, we introduce each of these techniques.

Currency Futures

Currency futures contracts were created to complement forward contracts in hedging international transactions. Like forward contracts, currency futures contracts allow one to lock in the price of a future purchase or sale of a foreign currency. Whereas forward contracts are negotiated with commercial banks on a personal basis, currency futures contracts are traded on an organized exchange. To facilitate foreign exchange trading, they are more standardized than forward contracts.

Futures contracts are used not only to hedge positions in foreign currencies but also to speculate on foreign currency movements. Speculators expecting appreciation of a currency consider purchasing futures contracts; speculators expecting depreciation consider selling futures contracts.

Currency Options

Currency call options provide a right to purchase a specified currency at a specified price (called the *exercise price*) within a specified period of time. Like forward and futures contracts, they can lock in the maximum price to be paid for a currency in the future, but they do not have to be exercised. In this way, they assure hedgers a maximum price to be paid for a currency but also allow them the option to purchase the currency at the spot price at the time the currency is needed. Speculators can purchase call options to capitalize on an expected appreciation of the currency. If the currency's spot rate remains below the exercise price, speculators will not be able to recover the premium initially paid for the call options. Yet, that is the most they can lose.

Speculators expecting a currency to depreciate can sell call options. If the options are not exercised, their gain is the premium received from selling the options.

Currency put options provide a right to sell a specified currency for a specified (exercise) price within a specified period of time. A put option can serve a similar purpose as the sale of a forward or futures contract, by locking in the price at which a currency can be sold. Yet, currency put options offer more flexibility in that there is no obligation. Hedgers may purchase currency put options to hedge future foreign currency receivables due to international trade or financial transactions. Speculators consider purchasing put options if they expect substantial depreciation in a foreign currency. If their expectations are correct, they will be able to buy the currency in the future at the spot rate and sell it at a higher price by exercising the option. If this difference exceeds the premium paid for the options, they will benefit. Alternatively, they consider selling currency put options if they anticipate an appreciation of the currency. If the option is not exercised, their gain is the premium received from selling the option.

Swaps

Another recent innovation is the currency swap, which allows for one party to exchange its currency for another currency at a specified time and at a specified exchange rate. Hedgers engage in a currency swap to lock in the price at which they can purchase a currency they will need in the future or sell a currency they will be receiving in the future. Speculators engage in a currency swap to capitalize on expectations about currency movements. In general, they may agree to purchase (sell) a currency if the swap rate is less (more) than the expected spot rate at that time.

A related technique is the interest rate swap, in which one party swaps a set of fixed interest payments to another party in exchange for a set of payments that are dependent on interest rates at that time. Interest rate swaps are sometimes combined with currency swaps in order to simultaneously hedge against interest rate and currency movements.

Summary of Instruments

To illustrate the use of these innovative instruments, consider a portfolio manager who has invested in bonds denominated in various currencies that provide annual coupon payments. The manager must decide whether to hedge any of these future cash inflows, and how. The alternatives include selling the currencies forward, selling futures contracts, purchasing put options, and engaging in currency and interest rate swaps. To make appropriate decisions, international portfolio managers and all other participants in international financial markets must understand the differences in these instruments. The instruments facilitate cross-border transactions by

■ Reducing the cost
■ Reducing exchange rate risk
■ Reducing exchange rate risk
■ Reducing interest rate risk
■ Redistributing risks among parties

Specific chapters of the text are devoted to each of these instruments.

MARKETS USED TO FACILITATE INTERNATIONAL TRANSACTIONS

A simplified overview of the international market transactions is illustrated in Figure 1.1. Each type of transaction is facilitated by one or more of the international financial markets. The Eurocurrency, Eurocredit, Eurobond, and international stock markets evolved to allow for the international transfer of funds from surplus units (which have excess funds) to deficit units (which have deficient funds). Each of these markets focuses on the specialized needs of surplus and deficit units.

Figure 1.1   Overview of International Financial Transactions

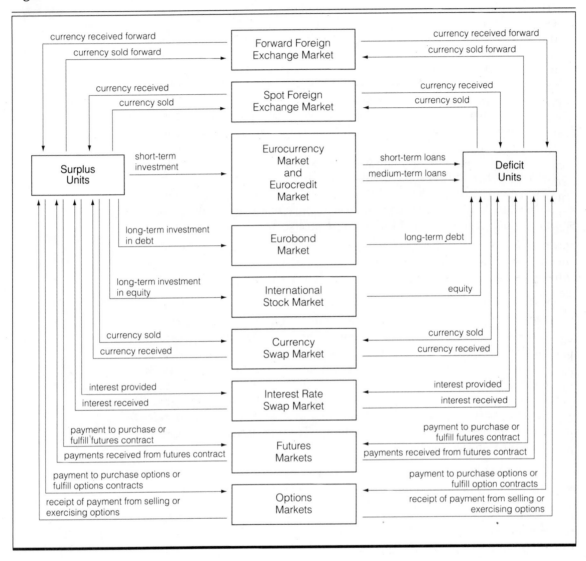

The Eurocurrency market accommodates the international transfer of short-term funds. Numerous commercial banks serve as the intermediaries in this market, accepting short-term deposits in various currencies and then using these funds to provide short-term loans. The market is wholesale in nature, with transaction amounts the equivalent of $1 million or more. The primary depositors and borrowers in this market are corporations. The volume of Eurocurrency transactions within a given area partially depends on the degree of international business in that area. Much of the growth in the Eurocurrency market has been concentrated in Asian markets, especially Hong Kong and Singapore.

The Eurocredit market services deficit units that require medium-term loans. The key difference between loans in the Eurocredit and Eurocurrency markets is the loan maturity. The commercial banks that serve as intermediaries in the Eurocurrency market also work the Eurocredit market. Corporations and governments commonly tap the Eurocredit market for funds. In many cases, the loan amount desired by a large government or corporation exceeds the amount that any individual commercial bank is willing to provide. Syndicated loans are arranged, whereby several banks participate by pooling available funds for a particular borrower. By using a syndicate of lenders, no single bank is entirely exposed to the default risk of the loan.

The Eurobond market facilitates the transfer of long-term funds from surplus units to deficit units. Like the Eurocredit and Eurocurrency markets, its transactions are in large denominations and in various currencies. Some commercial banks participate in this market by purchasing Eurobonds as an investment. However, their primary role in this market is to facilitate the placement of the bonds issued by corporations and governments. They commonly place Eurobonds with institutional investors, such as insurance companies, pension funds, and bond mutual funds.

International stock markets also facilitate the transfer of long-term funds from surplus units to deficit units. Yet, these funds reflect an equity investment instead of credit. The substantial growth in international stock transactions is largely due to international mutual funds, which have more information about foreign companies and easier access to foreign markets than individual investors. Thus, they can pool funds of individual investors to construct an international portfolio of stocks.

The international transfer of funds in international financial markets frequently exposes a surplus unit or deficit unit to exchange rate risk, interest rate risk, or market risk. The swap, futures, options, and forward markets evolved to alleviate these risks. The currency swap, options, and forward markets allow surplus or deficit units to offset exposure to exchange rate risk, and interest rate swap markets are used to mitigate interest rate risk. Some surplus and deficit units use these markets to speculate rather than hedge, which magnifies their exposure to risk.

Commercial banks and securities firms serve as the key financial intermediaries in the swap markets. They match up parties, or may even represent the counterparty in a swap transaction. Securities firms handle most futures and options transactions. We discuss the swap, futures, and options markets in detail in Part III of the text.

RECENT DEVELOPMENTS AFFECTING INTERNATIONAL FINANCIAL MARKETS

During the 1980s, several developments occurred that have affected the internationalization of financial markets. Some relevant developments are

- Bank deregulation
- Uniform capital requirements
- International debt crisis
- Thrift crisis
- EEC integration
- Eastern European enterprise

A discussion of each of these developments follows, with emphasis on their ramifications for international financial markets.

Bank Deregulation

During the 1980s, bank regulations were loosened considerably. One of the key deregulatory events was the removal of interest rate ceilings, allowing financial institutions to attract more foreign deposits by raising rates. A second key deregulatory event was the removal of barriers to entry previously imposed on foreign financial institutions, which can result in more cross-border transactions. Financial institutions were also given more freedom on the types of deposits and financial services they could offer. Yet, they were still restricted from some investment banking services. This continued to distinguish the banking and securities industries in the United States from those in Europe, where commercial banks are allowed to provide all banking and securities services. Many U.S. banks established subsidiaries in Europe to provide a full range of securities services. This strategy led to more global competition in the banking industry.

Uniform Capital Requirements

In 1988, representatives of the major industrialized countries agreed to uniform bank capital adequacy requirements, to be fully phased in by 1992. Since the 1980s, U.S. banks have been required to maintain a minimum amount of capital in order to cushion against loan losses. Yet, until the uniform capital requirements were imposed, banks in different countries were subject to different capital requirements, which gave banks from some countries a competitive advantage over others, since they could more easily meet a target return on equity by maintaining a low level of capital. These banks were able to price their services lower and still meet their profitability goals (although they may have had greater risk).

The imposition of uniform capital requirements was a major step in globalizing the banking industry because it allowed for a more level playing field. Banks will now be competing internationally under a similar set of rules. The requirements are contingent on a bank's risk, so that banks are discouraged from taking excessive risks. In addition, requirements are now also applied to off-balance-sheet items, so that banks cannot circumvent requirements. Overall, the uniform capital requirements should enhance the stability of the world financial system.

International Debt Crisis

The internationalization of credit markets was slowed by the international debt crisis, which began in August 1982 when Mexico postponed its debt payments to creditor banks. Numerous less-developed countries (LDCs) followed Mexico's lead, causing negotiations between banks and LDCs that have continued into the 1990s. Although the crisis has discouraged some types of international lending, it has resulted in the development of a secondary loan market for LDC debt. It has also enabled creditors to develop more comprehensive contingency provisions that may encourage international lending in the future. Furthermore, debt-equity swap arrangements have been developed, which may even be used in the future for highly rated foreign debt.

Thrift Crisis

During the late 1980s, the thrift industry in the United States experienced a crisis as many thrifts become insolvent. Unlike the international debt crisis, the thrift crisis was unique to the United States, since characteristics of thrift institutions in the United States differ from those in other countries. Some major problems precipitating the crisis were exposure to interest rate risk, management fraud, high default rates on real estate loans, and high default rates on junk bond investments. Moreover, as depositors learned of the crisis, they withdrew their deposits from thrifts, forcing thrifts to pay excessive rates in order to retain a sufficient deposit base.

Although this crisis was unique to the United States, it carried international implications. First, some of the large depositors of uninsured deposits at thrifts were from outside the United States. The crisis could have some impact on the willingness of non-U.S. creditors to provide credit to the United States. Second, the bailout of failed thrifts mandated by the Financial Institutions Reform, Recovery, and Enforcement (FIRRE) Act of 1989 was expected to require hundreds of billions of dollars, which could affect U.S. interest rates. To the extent that credit markets are internationally integrated, interest rates in other countries could be affected as well. Third, some of the assets of defaulted thrift institutions assumed by the U.S. government were purchased by foreign investors. In the summer of 1990, the first international auction of these assets was planned, using a satellite presentation for foreign investors.

EEC Integration

Since 1987, much progress has been made by the European Economic Community (EEC) in eliminating barriers between countries. Consequently, international trade and finance between European countries is increasing substantially. There has been some concern that the EEC will implement a "fortress Europe" policy in which new barriers are established to prevent competition outside the EEC. Yet, the highly publicized concerns appear to be exaggerated. As EEC countries become more receptive to foreign trade and financial transactions, the effects will spread throughout the world. European securities have already become more attractive to non-European investors as a result of the reduction in barriers.

Several countries in the EEC maintain the value of their currency within a narrow range of a multicurrency unit of account known as the *European Currency Unit* (ECU). As a result, these currencies are closely tied to each other. The EEC representatives are even considering the use of a single currency for international transactions between EEC countries. Meanwhile, some of the instruments already described can be used by firms wanting to mitigate exchange rate risk. As international trade between European countries increases, financial markets will grow to accommodate trade.

Eastern European Enterprise

In 1989, "the Wall" separating East and West Germany was removed. East Germans were given more freedom to travel across the border, and a new government philosophy was to encourage limited forms of capitalism. Governments of other Eastern European countries also considered some policies that would allow for more cross-border transactions and promote free enterprise. These events will have a major impact on international financial markets. As privately owned firms are developed, they will most likely attempt to access funds from Western Europe and other sources, causing a new flow of funds into Eastern Europe. Thus, some investors will attempt to capitalize on investment opportunities that were not previously available in Eastern Europe. Stock exchanges may be established over time as some firms attempt to access funds by issuing stock. For example, a stock exchange was established in Hungary in the summer of 1990. Major privatization efforts in countries such as Poland will probably result in publicly owned firms and the creation of additional stock exchanges in Eastern Europe.

Impact of Recent Developments

Overall, these developments that occurred in the late 1980s have accelerated the momentum for the globalization of financial markets in the 1990s. Although much progress has already been made, financial markets will become even more globalized once remaining cross-border barriers are eliminated. We can anticipate more intense global competition in commercial banking, investment banking, and other financial service industries.

TEXT OVERVIEW

The text following Chapter 1 is divided into three parts and one appendix:

- *Part I (Chapters 2 through 6).* We address the foreign exchange and commodity markets, discussing in detail the international parity conditions that play an important role in our subsequent analyses.
- *Part II (Chapters 7 through 11).* We cover international securities markets, including credit and equity markets, and issues related to international banking.
- *Part III (Chapters 12 through 16).* We conclude by analyzing currency forward, futures, and options markets. We also describe the markets for interest rate and currency swaps.
- *Appendix.* We describe the ongoing integration of the European Economic Community, scheduled for completion in 1992.

SUMMARY

The motives for creditors, investors, and borrowers to use international financial markets have existed for many years. However, these motives were frequently offset by explicit and implicit barriers between countries. The reduction in these barriers in recent years has led to more frequent participation in the international financial markets. The momentum toward deregulation is likely to continue, which should allow for more activity in these markets. Thus, an understanding of international financial markets has become even more important!

Questions and Problems

1. Explain how currency movements influence the return on international investments.
2. What does the empirical evidence suggest about the effect of international diversification of investments on risk?
3. Offer two reasons why the return on investment in a foreign debt security may be higher than on a domestic debt security.
4. Offer two reasons why a firm in need of funds may be able to achieve lower financing costs by issuing debt in a foreign country than in its own country.
5. Why do you suppose that currency futures were created, given that forward contracts were already available?
6. Explain how speculators could take positions in currency futures and currency options to capitalize on the expectation that the British pound will depreciate against the dollar.
7. How do the uniform capital requirements affect global competition in the banking industry?
8. How would you expect the events in Eastern Europe to influence German interest rates? What about U.S. interest rates?

9. Distinguish between the various financial markets as to whether they facilitate the international transfer of funds from surplus units to deficit units, or reduce the risk resulting from the transfer.

10. Why do you think some European countries have experienced much different economic cycles, even though they are geographically connected?

11. Your U. S. company has no business in Germany, but recently borrowed German marks (and then converted them to dollars) to take advantage of the low interest rates on marks. You have just heard a rumor that the central bank of Germany plans to intervene in the foreign exchange market to raise the value of the mark against the dollar. How will this affect your cost of financing?

12. The values of many European currencies are volatile against the U.S. dollar. Yet, they are tied to the same unit of account, and they are allowed to vary only within a narrow range against that unit of account. Would a U.S. firm that invests in European stocks be able to eliminate most of the exchange rate risk by diversifying among these currencies?

13. Several studies have found that the market price of a stock declines when a company issues more stock. Explain why issuing a stock in a foreign country may have less of an adverse effect.

14. Explain why issuing a U.S. stock on a foreign stock exchange may reduce the sensitivity of the stock's returns to the U.S. market returns.

15. A speculator expects that the Japanese yen will depreciate substantially in the near future. Should the speculator consider selling futures? Should the speculator consider buying call options? Explain.

16. Explain the differences between U.S. and non-U.S. regulations on securities activities offered by commercial banks. How might these differences cause competition in the U.S. securities industry to differ from competition in a non-U.S. securities industry?

17. Why do you think that the internationalization of financial markets may be slowed as a result of the international debt crisis?

18. How might U.S. exporting firms be affected by the integration of the EEC?

19. How might banks from a given country still maintain a competitive advantage, even with the uniform capital requirements (other than managerial superiority)?

20. Even though the thrift crisis was isolated in the U.S., it can affect the international conditions. How?

References

Adler, M., and B. Dumas. "International Portfolio Choice and Corporation Finance." *Journal of Finance* (June 1983): 925–84.

Faust, J. "U.S. Foreign Indebtedness: Are We Investing What We Borrow?" *Economic Review* (July/August 1989): 3–20.

Fieleke, N. "International Payments Imbalances in the 1980s: An Overview." *New England Economic Review* (March/April 1989): 3–14

"Future Priorities in Banking and Finances." *FRBNY Quarterly Review* (Winter 1989–1990): 1–7.

Mohl, A. "Currency Diversification in International Financial Markets." *FRBNY Quarterly Review* (Spring 1984): 31–32.

Rybczynski, T. "The Internationalization of Finance and Business." *Business Economics* (July 1988): 14–20.

Part One

FOREIGN EXCHANGE AND COMMODITY MARKETS

Part I provides a treatment of foreign exchange and commodity markets. In Chapter 2 we describe the balance of payments and its adjustment mechanisms under alternative exchange rate regimes, which are also described. In Chapter 3 we provide an overview of foreign exchange behavior under the managed-float system prevailing since 1973, and introduce the important international parity conditions that are employed throughout the remaining text. Chapter 4 is devoted to the various theories and empirical evidence regarding exchange rate determination. In Chapter 5 we consider the dynamics of currency movements, and in Chapter 6 we analyze purchasing power parity and real rates of exchange.

BALANCE OF PAYMENTS AND ADJUSTMENTS

This chapter principally concerns the *balance of payments*, which is a measurement of all transactions between domestic and foreign residents over a specified period of time. First we describe the balance of payments statement, and how there may arise a deficit or a surplus position in the statement's current account or capital account. Next we describe the various adjustment mechanisms that exist to alleviate persistent account imbalances. These adjustment mechanisms will differ across alternative exchange rate regimes, so we also provide a description of such regimes. It will be demonstrated that the balance of payments represents a measure of the strength of a nation's international economic performance when exchange rates are fixed. When exchange rates are truly flexible, changes in currency values indicate the strength of a nation's international economic performance.

The analysis of the balance of payments also affords an inspection of the international economic environment. The materials on alternative exchange rate regimes and adjustment mechanisms presented here provide an important background for the exchange rate concepts described in Chapters 3 through 6.

BALANCE OF PAYMENTS

The balance of payments is an accounting record of a nation's commercial transactions with the rest of the world. The recording of transactions is done by double-entry bookkeeping, so each transaction is recorded as both a credit and a debit. Thus, total credits and debits are identical for a nation's aggregate account balance. Still, there may be a deficit or surplus for any subset of the balance of payments statement.

There are two principal divisions of the balance of payments statement: the *current account*, which is a record of all transactions entailing goods and services, and the *capital account*, which represents the flows of financial securities (whether traded outright or in payment for goods and services). Most of these transactions involve the trading of foreign currency. For example, goods traded across national boundaries are usually priced in terms of either the importer's or exporter's currency, or perhaps a third foreign currency. We now describe current and capital accounts, and the factors affecting account balances.

Current Account

The current account typically consists of three subaccounts: the merchandise trade balance (also commonly called the balance of trade), the services balance, and the unilateral transfers balance. The sum of these three balances provides the current account balance.

Merchandise trade entails physical commodities such as grain, wine, and automobiles. *Services* include interest and dividend payments, military expenditures, and tourism. *Unilateral transfers* are gifts, either from individuals or national governments (such as foreign or military aid). In each of these three subaccounts, items are either sources of funds (e.g., merchandise trade exports) or uses of funds (e.g., merchandise trade imports). Sources of funds are denoted by plus signs (credits), and uses are denoted by minus signs (debits). Of course, the sum of such credits and debits yields the subaccount balance. Exhibit 2.1 presents the current account balance for the United States for years 1984 through 1988. The United States generally exhibited a growing current account deficit over this period, primarily owing to an increasing balance-of-trade deficit.

Capital Account

The capital account measures the flows of financial securities across national borders. These flows may be associated with the international trade of goods and services, or with portfolio shifts entailing foreign stocks, bonds, and other financial securities.

Assuming that goods and services are not traded directly via a barter system, each international transaction that entails a current account entry also yields an offsetting capital account entry. For example, a payment of $1 million for the import of French wine results in a merchandise trade (i.e., current account) debit of $1 million, and a capital account credit of $1 million to represent the transfer of a $1-million bank deposit to France. In addition, transactions affecting the capital account may occur independently of the current account. For example, the purchase of $5 million of U.K. Treasury bonds will entail two capital account entries, one representing the bond purchase and the other representing the transfer of a $5-million bank deposit to the United Kingdom.

Since the sum of all plus entries and minus entries is zero, the sum of the current and capital account transactions (ignoring other possible entries) is zero. In other words, a current account surplus equals a capital account deficit and vice versa. This implies that a current account surplus or deficit provides a measure of a net change in the ownership of

Year	Current Account Balance (millions of dollars)
1984	−107,140
1985	−115,160
1986	−138,840
1987	−152,470
1988	−134,720

Exhibit 2.1
United States Current Account Balance, 1984–1988

SOURCE: *International Financial Statistics* (1989): 142.

foreign assets. Therefore, the U.S. current account deficits of the 1980s (see Exhibit 2.1) imply that U.S. trading partners, particularly Japan, have been accumulating U.S. financial assets, such as bank deposits in New York. In turn, these deposits have been used to purchase U.S. Treasury Department securities, California real estate, and other assets. While some have suggested that the purchase of U.S. assets reflects foreign confidence in the strength and stability of the U.S. economy, others have raised concerns over the foreign control of U.S. assets and the foreign financing of the U.S. fiscal deficit. Figure 2.1 portrays the amount of U.S. federal debt held by foreign investors for the years 1979 through 1987.

Factors Affecting the Current Account Balance

Many factors affect a nation's current account balance. The most influential factors are domestic inflation, domestic income, exchange rates, and government restrictions.

Domestic Inflation   If a nation's inflation rate increases relative to that of its major trading partners, its current account balance generally decreases. This is because domestic consumers and corporations will tend to import more goods and services (because of high local inflation) and export less.

Domestic Income   If a nation's disposable income increases by a higher percent than that of its major trading partners, its current account balance generally decreases. This is because as income levels rise, so too does the consumption of goods and services, including foreign goods and services. An increase in domestic income increases the demand for foreign goods and services.

Exchange Rates   If a nation's currency starts to appreciate relative to its major trading partners, its current account balance generally decreases. This is because domestic exports become more expensive as the domestic currency strengthens. Consequently, the foreign demand for domestic exports decreases and, reciprocally, the domestic demand for foreign

Figure 2.1

U.S. Federal Debt Held by Foreign
Investors

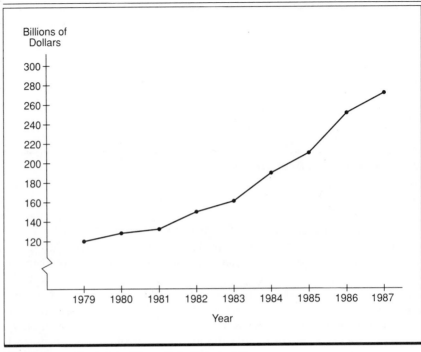

SOURCE: *Monetary Trends*, Federal Reserve Bank of St. Louis, 1989.

exports increases. This inverse relation between a nation's current account balance and currency strength is generally supported by Figure 2.2, which portrays U.S. real net exports (inflation-adjusted exports minus inflation-adjusted imports) and the real (inflation-adjusted) value of the dollar over the period 1975 through 1987. As argued previously, dollar value and real net exports tend to move in opposite directions, supporting the view that a strengthening domestic currency reduces the current account balance.

Government Restrictions Central governments can influence their current account balance by imposing *tariffs* or *quotas* on foreign-made goods. A tariff is a type of tax levied on imports. This effectively makes imports more expensive and thereby reduces domestic demand. A quota establishes an absolute limit on the number or quantity of a foreign-made good that can be imported over a prescribed time period. Obviously, imposing a quota will tend to reduce a current account deficit, ceteris paribus. Moreover, a central government can affect its current account balance by managing its currency value, a procedure discussed later in this chapter, or by providing *production subsidies* to domestic industries. Production subsidies effectively lower manufacturing costs and, thereby, finished good prices. In turn, this makes foreign manufacturers uncompetitive in price, and therefore discourages imports and encourages domestic exports.

Although most central governments tend to intervene in international trade to some extent (in recent years the Canadian government has subsidized its lumber industry, the Japanese government has subsidized

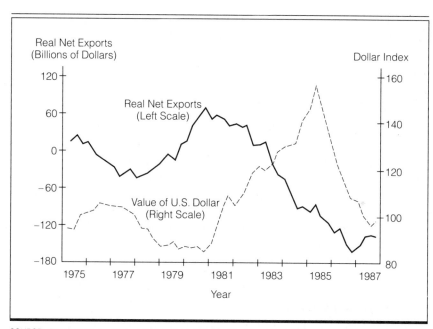

Figure 2.2
Dollar Value and U.S. Real Net Exports

SOURCE: *Economic Review*, Federal Reserve Bank of Kansas City (December 1987): p. 14; and the Board of Governors.

its steel industry, Taiwan has imposed numerous tariffs; and the United States has placed quotas on motorcycle imports), there currently exists a cooperative effort to encourage free international trade. For example, the *Trade and Tariff Act of 1984* (also known as the Omnibus Act) includes provisions to encourage free trade, and is written in the spirit of the *General Agreement on Tariffs and Trade* (GATT) provisions established in 1947. GATT allows for trade restrictions only in retaliation against the illegal trade actions of other nations. In 1989 and 1990, further progress was made in reducing trade barriers.

Factors Affecting the Capital Account Balance

As with trade flows, national governments have authority over capital (money) flows that enter or exit the country. For example, a nation's government could impose a special tax on income accrued by local investors who purchased foreign securities. Such a tax would tend to discourage the purchase of foreign securities and could therefore increase the country's capital account, at least initially. Other countries affected by this tax, however, could retaliate by imposing a similar tax on their local investors. The ultimate impact would be a reduction in aggregate foreign investment.

Over time, there has been a gradual liberalization of controls on international capital flows. Canada, Germany, and the United States have historically enforced relatively few capital controls. And other nations that have commonly imposed very restrictive controls on capital outflows in the past, such as Australia, Denmark, France, and Norway, have recently adopted more liberal laws. Moreover, sophisticated investors have developed ways and products that circumvent restrictions on capital flows. For example, currency and interest rate swaps largely developed from attempts to circumvent U.K. restrictions on capital out-flows imposed in the early 1970s (see Chapter 16).

CURRENCY ARRANGEMENTS

The factors discussed previously that influence account balances lend insight into how a persistent deficit or surplus (i.e., a balance of pay-ments disequilibrium) can be corrected. For example, imposing import tariffs or quotas may help to reduce a current account deficit, at least in the short run. The effectiveness of alternative correction mechanisms largely depends, however, on the type of exchange rate regime that the nation operates under. For this reason, we now briefly describe alterna-tive currency arrangements before turning to our discussion of balance-of-payment adjustment mechanisms.

Fixed Exchange Rate System

In a *fixed exchange rate system*, exchange rates are either held constant or are allowed to fluctuate only within very narrow boundaries. From 1944 to 1971, exchange rates were typically fixed according to a system planned at the Bretton Woods conference (in Bretton Woods, New Hampshire, 1944) by representatives from various nations. Of particular importance to these representatives was the prevention of the kind of international financial and trade breakdown that occurred after World War I. Postwar protectionism and severe hyperinflation resulted in many nations frequently altering their domestic currency values. The resulting trade wars ultimately caused a period of international isola-tionism that lasted until World War II.

A system was required that would prevent nations from changing exchange rates for competitive advantages. Also, currency reserves were required to maintain exchange rates within narrow boundaries. The *International Monetary Fund* (IMF) was established under the Bretton Woods Agreement to maintain rates of exchange. Specifically, the IMF was empowered to instruct participating central banks to buy and sell U.S. dollars and other national currencies, so that the values of these other currencies were fixed in terms of the dollar. The Bretton Woods Agreement made the dollar freely convertible into gold, and other cur-rency values were fixed in U.S. dollars. The IMF maintained exchange rates within 1% of the official parity, with intervention required to sup-port these "gold points."

This system required the United States to maintain a reserve of gold, and foreign nations to maintain a reserve of dollars. However, in order for the stock of currency reserves to finance growing world trade, the providers of reserves (primarily the United States) must run balance-of-payments deficits. In this way, other nations can accumulate dollar re-serves. The consequence is that the more reserve country deficits occur, the more foreign authorities will doubt the ability of the United States to convert dollars into gold at the official price. This paradox, often called the Triffin paradox, ultimately led to the demise of the Bretton Woods Agreement, although other contributing factors existed (Triffin 1960).

The demise of Bretton Woods first began in 1962, when France began to convert its dollar reserves into gold. Officials in France were frustrated by the seigniorage gains accruing to the United States as a result of the dollar's keystone role under the Bretton Woods Agreement. As the provider of foreign exchange reserves, the United States could ensure that foreign central banks held dollars. Most reserves, in turn, were kept in the form of U.S. Treasury securities. French officials believed that such securities were not yielding a competitive rate of interest and, thus, seigniorage gains accrued to the United States. As a result, France began to sell its dollar reserves for gold, and soon other foreign nations followed suit. Foreign officials simply thought that the dollar was overvalued.

In response to this run on gold, two actions were undertaken by participating nations. First, in 1968 a two-tier gold-pricing system was established, wherein the official dollar price of gold remained at $35 per ounce, but the private-market price of gold was allowed to be determined by free market forces. Second, in 1970 the IMF allocated *special drawing rights* (SDRs). SDRs were book entries credited to the accounts of IMF member nations, and could be used to satisfy balance-of-payments deficits. Thus, SDRs provided a net addition to the stock of reserves, theoretically allowing reserve country deficits to be avoided.

However, balance-of-trade deficits continued to plague the United States, implying that the dollar's value was still too strong, since the use of dollars for foreign purchases exceeded the demand by foreign nations for dollar-denominated goods. On August 15, 1971, the United States suspended the dollar's convertibility into gold in response to a record $30-billion trade deficit. The United States no longer subscribed to the gold standard, a 10% surcharge was placed on all imports, and President Nixon instituted a program of wage and price controls. It was obvious that currency values had to be realigned in order to restore a more balanced flow of payments between countries, and in December 1971 a conference among representatives of various nations concluded with the *Smithsonian Agreement*, which called for a devaluation of the dollar by about 8% against other currencies. In addition, boundaries for the currency values were expanded to ±2.25% of the rates initially set by the agreement. Still, international payments imbalances continued, and despite another dollar devaluation in February 1973, by March 1973 most governments of major currencies were no longer attempting to maintain their home currency value within the boundaries established by the Smithsonian Agreement. The fixed exchange rate system was in disrepair.

Floating Exchange Rate System

After the fall of the Bretton Woods and Smithsonian agreements, and the oil crises of the early 1970s, the *system of floating exchange rates* that began to appear in 1971 was adopted by many leading industrialized nations, although official ratification of the new system did not come until April 1978. Floating exchange rates were deemed acceptable by the IMF at that time, and gold was officially demonetized and sold off. Under a *freely floating exchange rate system*, exchange rates would be determined (like the prices of most commodities) by market forces and without intervention by central governments. However, the exchange rate system that exists today for the United States, Japan, and several other nations lies somewhere between fixed and freely floating. It resembles the freely floating system in that exchange rates are allowed to fluctuate on a continual basis and official boundaries do not exist. Yet, it is similar to the fixed system in that central governments can and sometimes do intervene to alter their currency's value. This type of system is known as a *managed float*, also sometimes called a dirty float. The IMF has deemed it acceptable for central banks to intervene and manage their currency's value.

The degree to which a home currency is managed varies across nations. The common reasons for central banks to intervene include smoothing exchange rate movements, establishing implicit exchange rate boundaries, and reacting to temporary disturbances. If a central bank is concerned that its economy will be affected by abrupt movements in its home currency's value, it may attempt to smooth the currency movements over time. Its actions may keep business cycles less volatile, which is generally perceived favorably by a government. Additionally, the smoothing may reduce fears in the financial markets and speculative activity that could cause a free-fall in a currency's value. Some central banks attempt to maintain their home currency rates within some unofficial boundaries. For example, the Federal Reserve periodically intervened between 1983 and 1985 in an attempt to reverse the dollar's upward momentum, and from 1986 through early 1988 to reverse the dollar's depreciation. To force a dollar depreciation, the Fed simply uses dollars to purchase foreign currency reserves. To force a dollar appreciation, the Fed purchases dollars with these reserves or with foreign currencies obtained through currency swap arrangements with other central banks.

The effectiveness of central bank intervention to alter the course of currency values has been somewhat mixed. In some cases, central bank intervention can have a very strong impact. For example, in late February of 1985, European central banks sold an estimated $1.5 billion in the foreign exchange market, causing the dollar's value to drop by more in one day than in any other day over the previous four years. However, even in cases like this where the impact of intervention is significant, it may be only temporary because of overwhelming market forces. Several studies (Trehan 1985) have found that government intervention does not permanently affect exchange rate movements.

The possibility that central bank intervention causes only transitory currency value changes has implications for the effectiveness of policy actions designed to alter balance-of-payment disequilibriums. For example, a government may reconsider depreciating its currency through selling it in the foreign exchange market in order to alleviate a domestic trade deficit. The currency's devalued state presumably should improve the deficit in the long run, although the short-run deficit may worsen (precontracted imports will cost more in domestic terms). This is the so-called *J-curve effect*, a name derived from the visual appearance of the balance of payments over time following a sudden domestic currency depreciation. However, fundamental market forces that overwhelm the intervention efforts will only result in continued long-run deficits, despite the temporary devaluation of the domestic currency. Thus, government officials may opt to pass on the intervention proposal. Some conclude that interventionism (i.e., managing the float) does not effectively alter payment balances, at least in the long run.

Pegged Exchange Rate System

A number of exchange rate arrangements exist today that involve a policy of "pegging" a currency's value to another currency or to some unit of account. For example, several currencies, including many of the Latin American nations, are pegged to the U.S. dollar. One of the most well known *pegged exchange rate systems* was established by the *European Economic Community* (EEC) in April 1972, when EEC members determined that their currencies were to be maintained within established limits of each other. This arrangement became known as the snake in the tunnel, because of the visual appearance of a time graph giving changes in the value of EEC currencies with respect to the U.S. dollar, which was still fixed. Although this arrangement had some early difficulties under the soon-to-arrive floating system, it was supported by the inception of the *European Monetary System* (EMS) in 1979. The EMS concept is similar to the original snake-in-the-tunnel arrangement, but the specific characteristics differ. Under the EMS Agreement, exchange rates of member nations are held together within specified limits and are also tied to the *European Currency Unit* (ECU). The ECU is a weighted average of exchange rates of the member nations, each weight determined by the member's relative GNP and activity in intra-European trade. The currencies of the member nations can fluctuate by no more than 2.25% (6% for Italy) from the initially established par values. To prevent currency values from moving outside their established range, member central banks must intervene within the foreign exchange markets. Like the fixed exchange rate system, intervention entails the trading of member currencies through established currency reserves. The "full" members of the EMS are Belgium, Denmark, France, Germany, Ireland, Italy, Luxembourg, the Netherlands, and the United Kingdom, which joined the EMS in late 1990. Greece, Portugal, and Spain have also signed the EMS Agreement, but chose not to participate in this exchange rate system.

The central rates of some member currencies tied to the ECU have been realigned over time. For example, in April 1986 the French franc was devalued against other currencies with the intention of increasing demand for French exports. In addition, the values of the German mark and Dutch guilder were increased against other currencies tied to the ECU. In January 1987 the member rates were realigned again. At that time, the following central rates were established in currency units per ECU:

Toward One European Currency

Cornelius J. van der Klugt, Chairman of Philips, Europe's largest consumer-electronics company, recently estimated that he could leave the Netherlands with 1,000 Dutch guilders, tour the other EEC nations, and spend 750 guilders on nothing but the cost of exchanging currencies. The cost to EEC industry alone for exchanging member currencies is currently estimated to be $10 billion a year. The cost to the entire European economy has been put at $50 billion a year.

Motivated by potential cost savings, a committee headed by European Community Commission president Jacques Delors and including the heads of all members' central banks agreed in April 1989 on a three-step process for creating a single-currency system. It would include the formation of a federated EEC central banking system independent of government influence.

The first step toward the creation of one European currency would be to have Greece, Portugal, and Spain join the EMS. The recent admission of

Britian to the EMS was a significant step toward the creation of a single European currency. The second step would be to develop a European system of central banks, similar to the U.S. Federal Reserve System, with the central banks of the member nations becoming regional branches. Related issues, such as limiting member nations' budget deficits, would also have to be ironed out. Third, exchange rates would have to be locked in and a single currency issued for the entire community.

Although the benefits derived from a single European currency would be great—both directly from reduced operating costs and indirectly through clout as a primary competitor to the dollar on global markets—a number of obstacles still remain and no specific timetable exists for currency unification. Still, an informal meeting of EEC finance ministers recently accepted the committee's report as a basis for progress toward monetary union. Currently it appears that a single European currency may soon become a reality.

Currency	Central Rate (in units per ECU)
Belgian francs	42.458200
Danish kroner	7.852120
Dutch guilders	2.319430
French francs	6.904030
Deutsche marks	2.058530
Irish pounds	0.798411
Italian lira	1483.580000

From these central rates it is possible to determine between-member currency values. For example, in January 1987 it cost 3.35386 French francs to purchase one Deutsche mark. These central rates continue to be realigned on occasion, and member central banks are obligated to maintain these central rates, again through intervention within the foreign exchange market. Although the member currencies are tied to the ECU and, thus, to each other, they float against nonmember currencies such as the U.S. dollar. For this reason, the joint EEC float is often called the snake in the lake.

Exhibit 2.2 categorizes exchange rate arrangements used by various countries today. Several small countries peg their currency to the U.S. dollar, and others peg their currency to the French franc or a currency composite. The European nations that peg their currency to the ECU are listed under the heading "Cooperative arrangements." The Mexican peso has a controlled rate that applies to international trade and a floating market rate that applies to tourism. It appears that this mixed system of managed floating rates and pegs is likely to continue in the foreseeable future.

ADJUSTMENT UNDER FIXED REGIMES

Fixed exchange rate systems exhibit a number of different but simultaneously operating mechanisms that serve to correct balance-of-payments deficits (and surpluses). The adjustment mechanisms are "automatic" and entail changes in domestic price levels, incomes, interest rates, and money supplies. The mechanisms collectively play a role analogous to that of prices in the theory of supply and demand. However, these adjustment mechanisms are not as rapid and complete as price adjustment mechanisms in a closed economy. Moreover, the adjustment mechanisms for correcting payment imbalances often adversely affect the domestic economy. For these reasons, national governments are frequently compelled to undertake policies to speed the adjustment process. This is comparable to employing fiscal and monetary policy changes to manage the domestic economy. Currently, it is debated whether such discretionary governmental policies enhance the speed and effectiveness of the adjustment mechanisms. Also, the adjustment mechanisms themselves are frequently challenged as ineffective and too costly in domestic economic consequences. These debates remain topical because of the many countries that continue to operate under a pegged exchange rate system or a managed float. The various adjustment mechanisms are discussed next.

Price Level Adjustment

In general, under a fixed exchange rate system countries tie their currencies to a central currency or unit of exchange and are required to maintain the official parity within prescribed limits. To do so, central banks must maintain reserves of domestic and foreign currencies, and to intervene to offset free-market forces that can move an exchange rate beyond the prescribed limits. This intervention takes the form of buying and selling domestic and foreign currencies, adding to or reducing central bank official reserves.

Let us use Figure 2.3 to demonstrate the intervention action and how it affects domestic price levels, and in turn the balance of payments. Begin with a "private" supply of foreign currency, $S_1(f)$, a demand for foreign currency of $D_1(f)$, and a resulting exchange rate that lies within the prescribed limits. Now let there be an increase in the demand for foreign currency to $D_2(f)$, perhaps because of changing tastes in favor of foreign imports. To maintain the exchange rate within the prescribed limits, the foreign central bank is required to increase the supply of its currency, specifically from Q_1 to, say, Q_2. This action restores the official parity.

This increase in the supply of foreign currency (eventually) has the effect of increasing the foreign nation's money supply. From the classical economic notion of the quantity theory of money, this increase in money supply causes a general increase in price levels. In its most basic form, the *quantity theory of money* holds that the

$$\text{money supply} \times \text{velocity of money}$$
$$= \text{prices} \times \text{quantity of goods and services.}$$

If we assume that money velocity and the quantity of goods and services are largely fixed, then an increase in the money supply results in higher price levels. In turn, this lowers the competitiveness of the foreign goods and services, and lowers the demand for the foreign currency. This is denoted by the demand shift back to $D_3(f)$ in Figure 2.3. Moreover, the uncompetitiveness of foreign goods also implies a general

Exhibit 2.2   Exchange Rate Arrangements

(As of September 30, 1989)[1]

Currency Pegged to					Flexibility Limited in Terms of a Single Currency or Group of Currencies		More Flexible		
U.S. Dollar	French Franc	Other Currency	SDR	Other Composite[2]	Single Currency[3]	Cooperative Arrangements[4]	Adjusted According to a Set of Indicators[5]	Other Managed Floating	Independently Floating
Afghanistan	Benin	Bhutan (Indian rupee)	Burundi	Algeria	Bahrain	Belgium	Brazil	Argentina	Australia
Angola	Burkina Faso		Iran, I.R. of	Austria	Qatar	Denmark	Chile	China, P.R.	Bolivia
Antigua and Barbuda	Cameroon	Kiribati (Australian dollar)	Libya	Bangladesh	Saudi Arabia	France	Colombia	Costa Rica	Canada
Bahamas, The	C. African Rep.		Myanmar	Botswana	United Arab Emirates	Germany	Madagascar	Dominican Rep.	Gambia, The
Barbados	Chad	Lesotho (South African rand)	Rwanda	Cape Verde		Ireland	Portugal	Ecuador	Ghana
Belize	Comoros		Seychelles	Cyprus		Italy		Egypt	Japan
Djibouti	Congo		Zambia	Fiji		Luxembourg		Greece	Lebanon
Dominica	Côte d'Ivoire	Swaziland (South African rand)		Finland		Netherlands		Guinea	Maldives
El Salvador	Equatorial Guinea			Hungary		Spain		Guinea-Bissau	New Zealand
Ethiopia	Gabon			Iceland				India	Nigeria
Grenada	Mali	Tonga (Australian dollar)		Israel				Indonesia	Paraguay
Guatemala	Niger			Jordan				Jamaica	Philippines
Guyana	Senegal			Kenya				Korea	South Africa
Haiti	Togo			Kuwait				Laos, P.D. Rep.	United Kingdom
Honduras				Malawi				Mauritania	United States
Iraq				Malaysia				Mexico	Uruguay
Liberia				Malta				Morocco	Venezuela
Nicaragua				Mauritius				Mozambique	Zaire
Oman				Nepal				Pakistan	
Panama				Norway				Singapore	
Peru				Papua New Guinea				Sri Lanka	
St. Kitts and Nevis				Poland				Tunisia	
St. Lucia				Romania				Turkey	
St. Vincent				Sao Tome and Principe				Yugoslavia	
Sierra Leone				Solomon Islands					
Sudan				Somalia					
Suriname				Sweden					
Syrian Arab Rep				Tanzania					
Trinidad and Tobago				Thailand					
Uganda				Vanuatu					
Viet Nam				Western Samoa					
Yemen Arab Rep.				Zimbabwe					
Yemen, P.D. Rep.									

Exhibit 2.2   continued

Classification Status[1]	1983	1984	1985	1986	End of Period 1987				1988				1989		
					QI	QII	QIII	QIV	QI	QII	QIII	QIV	QI	QII	QIII
Currency pegged to															
U.S. dollar	33	34	31	32	33	34	35	38	39	38	38	36	32	32	33
French franc	13	14	14	14	14	14	14	14	14	14	14	14	14	14	14
Other currency	5	5	5	5	5	5	5	5	5	5	5	5	5	5	5
of which: Pound sterling	(1)	(1)	(1)	(−)	(−)	(−)	(−)	(−)	(−)	(−)	(−)	(−)	(−)	(−)	(−)
SDR	12	11	12	10	10	10	9	8	7	7	7	8	8	7	7
Other currency composite	27	31	32	30	27	27	27	27	29	31	31	31	31	32	32
Flexibility limited vis-à-vis a single currency	9	7	5	5	5	4	4	4	4	4	4	4	4	4	4
Cooperative arrangements	8	8	8	8	8	8	8	8	8	8	8	8	8	9	9
Adjusted according to a set of indicators	5	6	5	6	6	5	5	5	5	5	5	5	5	5	5
Managed floating	25	20	21	21	22	24	24	23	21	20	21	22	24	24	24
Independently floating	8	12	15	19	20	19	19	18	18	18	17	17	19	18	18
Total[6]	146	148	149	151	151	151	151	151	151	151	151	151	151	151	152

SOURCE: *International Financial Statistics* (March 1990): p. 22.

[1] Excluding the currency of Democratic Kampuchea, for which no current information is available. For members with dual or multiple exchange markets, the arrangement shown is that in the major market.

[2] Comprises currencies which are pegged to various "baskets" of currencies of the members' own choice, as distinct from the SDR basket.

[3] Exchange rates of all currencies have shown limited flexibility in terms of the U.S. dollar.

[4] Refers to the cooperative arrangement maintained under the European Monetary System.

[5] Includes exchange arrangements under which the exchange rate is adjusted at relatively frequent intervals, on the basis of indicators determined by the respective member countries.

[6] Including the currency of Democratic Kampuchea.

increase in domestic exports, which causes a larger private supply of the foreign currency to the foreign exchange market. This is denoted by the supply shift to $S_2(f)$ in Figure 2.3.

With the new demand at $D_3(f)$ and the new supply at $S_2(f)$, the exchange rate has returned to the official parity range. Thus, central bank intervention affected money supply, local prices, and relative exporting, resulting in restored exchange rate parity. And, of course, since the original official parity was designed as to create a balance of payments equilibrium, this equilibrium is also restored. For instance, the growing balance-of-payments surplus in the foreign nation (due to the increased demand for foreign goods associated with the change in tastes) raised the foreign money supply and price levels; as a result, the domestic demand for foreign goods and services was reduced, and the foreign surplus (domestic deficit) was eliminated.

Nonsterilized versus Sterilized Intervention   When a central bank intervenes in the foreign exchange market without adjusting for the change in its money supply (as just described), it is engaging in *nonsterilized intervention*. However, if it desires to intervene while retaining the domestic money supply, it uses *sterilized intervention*, achieved by simultaneous transactions in the foreign exchange market and its Treasury securities market. For instance, if the bank desires to weaken its currency in order to alleviate a trade deficit without affecting the domestic money supply, it (1) exchanges its currency for foreign currencies, and

Figure 2.3

Central Bank Intervention to
Restore Official Parity

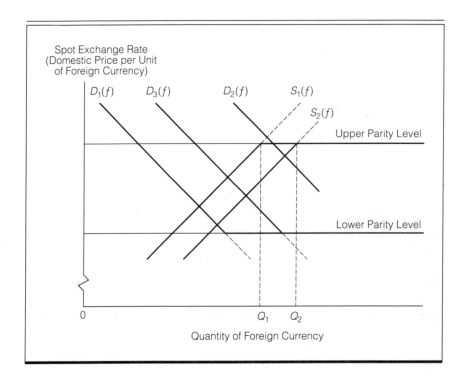

(2) sells some of its holdings of Treasury securities (for its currency). The net effect is an increase in investor holdings of Treasury securities and a decrease in bank foreign currency balances.

Eventually, sterilization results in ever-changing foreign exchange reserves and a need to revise the parity exchange rate to restore balance-of-payments equilibrium. Investors sometimes track a central bank's foreign exchange reserve statistics in order to better forecast an exchange rate realignment, with the hope of profiting from such a forecasted realignment.

Income Adjustment

An alternative adjustment mechanism to a balance-of-payments disequilibrium under a fixed regime entails changes in domestic incomes. Like the price adjustment mechanism just described, the income adjustment mechanism operates on the current account. For instance, if there is an exogenous increase in exports, domestic incomes rise. In turn, added consumption is induced, part of which involves foreign goods and services. This works to correct balance-of-payments surpluses and deficits, although it is typically argued that the income adjustment mechanism does not restore full payments equilibrium.

To better describe the specifics of the automatic income adjustment mechanism, we use the following Keynesian income-expenditure model:

2.1
$$Y = C + I_0 + (X_0 - M)$$

2.2 $$C = C_0 + cY$$

2.3 $$M = M_0 + mY,$$

where Y is national income (or GNP), C is aggregate consumption, I_0 is a given amount of aggregate investment, X_0 is a given amount of exports, and M represents imports.[1] Also, in eq. 2.2, the consumption function, C_0 is some fixed level of consumption that does not depend on income, and c is the marginal propensity to consume ($0 < c < 1$). Note further that C represents all consumption, including imports, and that the variable m in eq. 2.3 represents the marginal propensity to consume foreign foods and services.

As above, let there be some exogenous increase in exports from X_0 to $X_0 + \Delta X$. We are interested in tracing the effects of this change using our income-expenditure model. To begin, substitute eqs. 2.2 and 2.3 into 2.1 and rearrange to obtain:

2.4 $$Y = \frac{1}{1 - c + m} (C_0 + I_0 + X_0 - M_0).$$

Thus, we have expressed national income in terms of our exogenous variables, where of course $1/(1 - c + m)$ represents a type of "income multiplier" stemming from leakages in the flow of income; that is, stemming from import leakages, m, and savings, $1 - c$. The increase in exports results in a corresponding increase in income, or:

2.5 $$Y + \Delta Y = \frac{1}{1 - c + m} (C_0 + I_0 + X_0 + \Delta X - M_0).$$

Using eq. 2.4 with 2.5 to solve for ΔY yields:

2.6 $$\Delta Y = \frac{1}{1 - c + m} \Delta X.$$

As expected, the change in national income attributable to the exogenous increase in exports is given by the product of the increase and the income multiplier.

The increase in national income in turn affects the level of imports. This is the fundamental idea underlying the automatic nature of the income adjustment mechanism: increased exports increase national income, which in turn increases imports, thus working to correct payment imbalances. To see the effect of ΔY on imports, use eq. 2.3:

2.7 $$M + \Delta M = M_0 + m(Y + \Delta Y).$$

Now subtracting eq. 2.3 from 2.7 gives $\Delta M = m\Delta Y$, and substituting ΔY from eq. 2.6 yields:

2.8 $$\Delta M = \frac{m}{1 - c + m} \Delta X.$$

---

[1] We need not consider government expenditures here. Also, investment and exports are assumed to be exogenously determined.

Equation 2.8 states that imports are automatically adjusted, through national income, as exports change. Of course, the change in M for a given change in X is determined by the "import multiplier," $m/(1 - c + m)$. Since this multiplier is less than 1 (c is less than 1), it is obvious that the income adjustment process is not complete. The exogenous increase in exports here does not solicit a comparable increase in imports, and some level of trade surplus remains. This is why some argue that the automatic income adjustment mechanism cannot restore full payments equilibrium.

However, the surplus may not persist, for two additional (and related) reasons. First, under a fixed regime the central bank must supply its currency to avoid a violation of the official parity range. As previously explained, this increase in the supply of domestic currency works to reduce the surplus via the price adjustment process. Second, it is generally conceded that a money supply increase (eventually) lowers interest rates, which in turn stimulates investment and national income. Again, some of this income is used to purchase foreign goods and services, thus reducing the domestic trade surplus.

Interest Rate Adjustment

This brings us to the discussion of the automatic interest rate adjustment mechanism, which works on the capital account of the balance of payments. As noted earlier, surpluses tend to increase the money supply under a fixed regime, in turn lowering domestic interest rates. Conversely, deficits tend to cause a constriction of the money supply and thus higher interest rates.[2] Moreover, opposite interest rate changes occur in the foreign economies. The result is an interest incentive in the deficit nation, making investment in that nation's securities comparatively more attractive. Inflows in the capital account in turn improve the deficit nation's balance of payments, and increase its foreign currency position. Speculators may wager on an eventual currency devaluation of a nation that is preoccupied with maintaining low interest rates, since this can lead to deficits and declining foreign currency reserves.

It is commonly argued that in the short run the price and income adjustment mechanisms operate slowly in restoring a payments equilibrium. In the short run, the automatic interest rate adjustment mechanism is likely to be more effective, since interest rates can change rather quickly. Put another way, interest rates are less "sticky" than prices and incomes. In the long run, however, price and income adjustments should take place, implying that payment imbalances may cause only transitory changes in interest rates.

A Monetary Approach

The price, income, and interest rate adjustment mechanisms described earlier can loosely be called Keynesian in flavor. A markedly different

---

[2] This assumes that no sterilization occurs and that the demand for money is not perfectly elastic, as it is in the Keynesian liquidity trap.

approach to the balance-of-payments adjustment process under a fixed regime is the *monetary approach,* which explains the balance of payments by changes in the supply of and demand for money. Supply is determined by a nation's central bank, whereas money demand arises from the "private" sector. The monetary approach often draws drastically different conclusions than the Keynesian approach to the balance of payments. For instance, if an increase in the domestic money supply results in an excess supply, then to eliminate the excess supply the private sector purchases more domestic goods and securities. In turn, this raises domestic prices (the old adage that there are too many dollars chasing too few goods), reducing net exports and worsening a current account deficit. Moreover, securities purchases tend to bid down domestic interest rates and worsen a capital account deficit. These results are markedly different than those described earlier, in which a higher domestic money supply serves to improve a payments deficit via lower domestic interest rates. As another example, suppose that a nation's price level falls. This serves to increase the real supply of money, causing an imbalance between real money supply and real money demand. To restore equilibrium in the monetary sector, individuals purchase more domestic goods and securities. As just explained, this serves to worsen a payments deficit. Under a Keynesian approach, however, the deficit should improve.

Although attempts have been made to resolve the theoretical underpinnings of the two approaches (Frenkel et al. 1980), and empirical analyses have been conducted to ascertain the more descriptive approach (Magee 1976), the Keynesian and monetary approaches to payments equilibrium under a fixed regime remain largely at odds with each other.

ADJUSTMENT UNDER FLOATING REGIMES

With truly floating exchange rates, central governments do not intervene in the currency market to maintain explicit or implicit parity values. Instead, the exchange rate is determined by the free interplay of supply and demand forces. Exchange rate determination and dynamics under a floating system are discussed at great length in Chapters 3 through 6.

If exchange rates are not managed by government intervention, then there is no change in a nation's official reserves of foreign exchange. Consequently, the balance of payments must, by definition, be in equilibrium, since a deficit or surplus is given by a change in official reserves. Reserves remain constant, and all adjustments to payment imbalances come about through revisions in exchange rates. Thus, exchange rate changes gauge the international economic performance of a country under a truly floating regime.

Proponents of a floating system commonly argue that adjustments through exchange rate changes are more rapid and are more socially and politically acceptable than the price, income, and interest rate adjustment mechanisms that must occur under a fixed exchange regime. This and other arguments both for and against floating exchange rates are presented next.

The Case for Floating Rates

Milton Friedman and other proponents of floating exchange rates have offered at least four arguments in favor of this system:

1. *Better adjustment.* Under a floating system, a payments deficit causes a decline in the domestic currency value. The decline should be rapid, and results in more exporting and less importing, thus alleviating the deficit. A surplus imbalance is similarly corrected through a domestic currency appreciation (a foreign currency devaluation). The decline in the domestic currency value reduces the deficit by reducing domestic *real* income. Obviously, the alternative under a fixed regime is to reduce domestic *nominal* income, and consequently prices, to alleviate the deficit. Clearly it is more politically and socially acceptable to reduce the international value of a domestic currency, rather than reducing domestic incomes. Hence, the argument that a floating adjustment is superior is grounded in the ability to circumvent domestic unrest through only indirect reductions in real income.

2. *Better liquidity.* Under floating exchange rates, central banks do not have to maintain reserves of foreign currency, as they must under a fixed regime. Hence, problems associated with insufficient foreign currency reserves do not arise. Moreover, floating regimes are not subject to the Triffin paradox.

3. *Policy independence.* Under a fixed regime, it is often argued that one nation "exports" inflation or unemployment to another. For example, if a nation increases its domestic money supply, thus reducing its currency value via higher domestic prices and incomes, a foreign nation may have to increase its money supply to maintain the official parity. With flexible exchange rates, however, the increase in the money supply of the first nation serves only to move exchange rates, and not the policy actions of foreign governments. Thus, it is often argued that the domestic policies of participating nations are less interdependent under a floating regime.

4. *Freer trade.* It is commonly argued that governments are less likely to impose tariffs, quotas, and capital flow barriers under a floating regime, thereby enhancing free international trade and the associated welfare gains.

The Case against Floating Rates

Some of the criticisms that have been levied against a floating regime are as follows:

1. *Trade inhibition.* Proponents of fixed exchange rates contend that the exchange rate risk associated with a floating regime serves to inhibit international trade and investment. However, exchange rate risk can be diversified or otherwise managed through the trading of currency

forward, futures, option, and swap contracts, and empirical evidence does not support the view that the level of international trade and investment is off since the demise of Bretton Woods.

2. *Destabilizing speculation.* Some contend that floating exchange rates induce speculators to enter exchange markets and, arguably, "destabilize" the market through increasing volatility, creating speculative bubbles and the like. It is difficult to justify such an argument, since destabilizing speculation largely depends on irrational investment behavior and inefficient markets. Proponents of floating rates counter by noting that speculators increase market liquidity and serve to ensure market stability and equilibrium via arbitrage trading.

3. *LDC ineffectiveness.* It is regularly conceded that a country that is heavily dependent on imported goods cannot elicit a payments adjustment via a floating exchange rate. For instance, a currency devaluation for such a country does not entirely correct a payments deficit; it raises the prices of imports and, since imports are so vital to that country, increased import costs serve only to pressure up nominal wages, thereby counteracting the effect of the currency devaluation. For such countries, currency values are often fixed to the currency of the leading import supplier.

SUMMARY

The balance of payments is an accounting record of a nation's commercial transactions with the rest of the world. Its two principal subaccounts are the current account, which entails transactions in goods and services, and the capital account, which entails the flows of financial securities. Numerous factors affect the current and capital account balances, including relative inflation, relative income, exchange rates, and government restrictions such as tariffs, quotas, and production subsidies.

How a persistent surplus or deficit in a nation's balance of payments is corrected largely depends on the operative exchange rate regime. In general, exchange rates can be fixed, floating, or pegged, although many industrialized nations engage in a managed float. Under a fixed system, such as Bretton Woods, exchange rates are maintained to the official parity via central bank currency trading using established currency reserves. Under a truly floating regime, changes in official reserves do not occur, and exchange rates are determined by the free interplay of supply and demand forces in an open currency market. When central governments intervene in this market to alter their currency values, the system is described as a managed float. Under a pegged arrangement, a currency's value is closely tied to another currency or unit of exchange. The European Monetary System is the best-known example of this arrangement.

From a Keynesian perspective, a payments disequilibrium is automatically corrected via price, income, and interest rate adjustments under a fixed regime. A monetary prospective concludes that the adjustment instead occurs through the money market. Under a truly floating regime, a payments correction occurs through changes in currency values.

Today, the majority of economists prefer a floating arrangement, contending that such an arrangement is more acceptable than the often slow and painful mechanisms of changes in prices, nominal incomes, and interest rates.

For nations that fix exchange rates, changes in official reserves signal international economic performance. With truly flexible exchange rates, changes in currency values signal international economic performance. Performance under a managed float is more difficult to ascertain, since changes in both official reserves and currency values must be assessed. However, such changes are often reinforcing. Frequently a nation that employs its exchange reserves to stem a domestic currency depreciation is largely unsuccessful; the depreciation, fueled by overwhelming free-market forces despite the reduction in official reserves, clearly indicates worsening international economic performance.

Questions and Problems

1. Describe the balance of payments, what it measures, and its major subaccounts.

2. Distinguish between the balance of trade and the balance of payments.

3. What four major factors affect the current account balance? Describe the influence of each of these factors.

4. Distinguish between a fixed, a floating, a managed-float, and a pegged exchange rate system.

5. Describe the Triffin paradox.

6. What are SDRs, and how were they to be used to resolve the Triffin paradox?

7. Why might a government intervene in a floating regime?

8. Describe the automatic price, income, and interest rate adjustment mechanisms under a fixed regime.

9. Distinguish between sterilized and nonsterilized government intervention.

10. Why is it commonly argued that the automatic income adjustment mechanism under a fixed regime is incomplete?

11. Why is the automatic interest rate adjustment mechanism ineffective when sterilization occurs?

12. Describe the monetary approach to payments imbalances under a fixed regime.

13. Why do most economists contend that the floating exchange rate system is generally superior?

14. Why do most economists concede that a floating system is largely ineffective for correcting the trade imbalances of import-dependent nations?

15. How is the international economic performance of a nation assessed under a fixed regime? Under a truly floating regime? Under a managed float?

References

Batten, S., and M. Oh. "Five Common Myths About Floating Exchange Rates." *Review* (Federal Reserve Bank of St. Louis) (November 1983): 5–15.

Bergstrand, J. "Selected Views of Exchange Rate Determination After a Decade of 'Floating'." *New England Economic Review* (Federal Reserve Bank of Boston) (May–June 1983): 14–29.

Dornbusch, R. "Monetary Policy Under Exchange Rate Flexibility." In *Managed Exchange Rate Flexibility*, vol. 20. Boston: Federal Reserve Bank of Boston, 1979.

Frenkel, J., T. Gylfason, and J. Helliwell. "A Synthesis of Monetary and Keynesian Approaches to Short-Run Balance of Payment Theory." *Economic Journal* 90 (September 1980): 582–92.

Frenkel, J., and H. Johnson (eds.). *The Monetary Approach to the Balance of Payments.* London: Allen and Unwin, Ltd., 1976.

Friedman, M. "The Case for Flexibility Exchange Rates." In *Essays in Positive Economics.* Chicago: University of Chicago Press, 1953.

Friedman, M., and R. Roosa. "Free versus Fixed Exchange Rates: A Debate." *Journal of Portfolio Management* (Spring 1977): 68–73.

Genberg, H. "Effects of Central Bank Intervention in the Foreign Exchange Market." *International Monetary Fund Staff Papers* (September 1981): 451–76.

Houthakker, H. "The Breakdown of Bretton Woods." In *Economic Advice and Executive Policy*, ed. W. Sichel. New York: Praeger Special Studies, 1978.

Humpage, O. "Should We Intervene in Exchange Markets?" *Economic Commentary* (Federal Reserve Bank of Cleveland) (February 1, 1987).

Johnson, H. "The Monetary Approach to the Balance of Payments: A Nontechnical Guide." *Journal of International Economics* (August 1977): 251–68.

Karamouzis, N. "Lessons from the European Monetary System." *Economic Commentary* (Federal Reserve Bank of Cleveland) (August 15, 1987).

Magee, S. "The Empirical Evidence on the Monetary Approach to the Balance of Payments and Exchange Rates." *American Economic Review* 66 (May 1976): 163–70.

McKinnon, R. "Dollar Stabilization and American Monetary Policy." *American Economic Review* 70 (May 1980): 382–87.

Metzler, L. "The Process of International Adjustment Under Conditions of Full Employment: A Keynesian View." In R. Caves and H. Johnson (eds.), *Readings in International Economics*, Homewood, Ill.: Richard D. Irwin, 1968.

Mundell, R. *International Economics.* New York: Macmillan, 1968.

Mussa, M. "The Exchange Rate, the Balance of Payments and Monetary and Fiscal Policy Under a Regime of Controlled Floating." *Scandinavian Journal of Economics* (May 1976): 229–48.

Rogoff, K. "On the Effects of Sterilized Intervention: An Analysis of Weekly Data." *Journal of Monetary Economics* (September 1984): 133–50.

Sohmen, E. *Flexible Exchange Rates: Theory and Controversy.* Chicago: University of Chicago Press, 1969.

Solomon, R. *The International Monetary System 1945–1981.* New York: Harper and Row, 1982.

Trehan, B. "The September G-5 Meeting and Its Impact." *FRBSF Weekly Letter*, December 13, 1985.

Triffin, R. *Gold and the Dollar Crises*. New Haven, Conn.: Yale University Press, 1960.

Webber, W. "Do Sterilized Interventions Affect Exchange Rates?" *Quarterly Review* (Federal Reserve Bank of Minneapolis) (Summer 1986): 14–23.

Westerfield, J. "An Examination of Foreign Exchange Risk Under Fixed and Floating Regimes." *Journal of International Economics* (May 1977): 181–200.

Williamson, J. "Surveys in Applied Economics: International Liquidity." *Economic Journal* 83 (September 1973): 685–746.

3

AN OVERVIEW OF FOREIGN EXCHANGE BEHAVIOR

The behavior of the foreign currency market is of importance to investors and multinational firms, whether they are interested in making speculative profits or in protecting their investments from changes in the value of currencies. Exchange rates have been observed to follow certain empirical regularities, which have been formalized in economic relations known as the international parity conditions. These relationships can be incorporated into formal models that seek to explain and predict the behavior of exchange rates.

A conventional approach to explaining these observed regularities is to regard the exchange rate as an asset price, that is, as a relative price of two national currencies. From this perspective, the behavior of exchange rates is determined by the framework applicable to other asset prices, particularly by the efficient markets hypothesis. According to this hypothesis, asset prices depend primarily on expectations that are formed concerning the future behavior of the relevant variables. Rapid market adjustment to new information immediately eliminates any unusual profit opportunities for investors.

Various tests have been devised to determine the validity of different theories of exchange rate behavior. Empirical support for the efficient markets hypothesis leads to the conclusion that investors will not be able to consistently make unusual profits in the currency markets. To the extent that the hypothesis is not supported by testing, it may be possible to develop methods such as trading rules or technical analysis that can produce abnormal returns for investors.

Since the profitability of trading on the currency markets depends on the accuracy with which expectations are formed, expectations are usually generated by an optimal forecasting scheme. The information and the procedure to derive optimal forecasts of exchange rates become an important topic in the analysis of the foreign exchange markets.

To provide a broad overview of the recent behavior of exchange rates, in this chapter we first outline the empirical regularities since the adoption of the floating exchange rate regime in March 1973. We then consider the international parity conditions and the application of the efficient markets hypothesis to foreign exchange markets. Various financial-analysis methods, such as fundamental and technical analyses, are also presented and integrated into the currency markets. We conclude with a brief discussion of the predications of exchange rates employing different models.

EMPIRICAL REGULARITIES OF EXCHANGE RATE BEHAVIOR

Since the introduction of a floating system in 1973, exchange rates have tended to exhibit several empirical regularities. An examination of these regularities will help us to understand the fundamental characteristics of exchange rate behavior.

First, levels of exchange rates may display some degree of persistence; that is, there may be a tendency toward continual appreciation or depreciation over a period of time. However, when we look at the rate of change of the spot rate, on a week-to-week or month-to-month basis, it appears to be random, and the process can be best described as a random walk.

Second, the spot rate and the forward rate tend to move together, or covary, over time. The forward rate, F_t, can, under certain selective assumptions, be viewed as the market's expectation of the future spot rate, S_{t+1}^e. The evidence concerning whether the forward rate is an unbiased predictor of the future spot rate is mixed. The forward rate does not, in any event, constitute a good predictor of the future spot rate. This can be explained by the arrival of unanticipated shocks (news), which alter the market's expectation of the future spot rate.

Third, since the introduction of the floating exchange rate regime, exchange rates have tended to be highly volatile, or turbulent. With the exception of interest rate differentials, exchange rates have been more volatile than the fundamental factors on which they depend, including domestic and foreign money supplies, real incomes, price levels, and the balance of international payments (Meese 1990).

Fourth, exchange rate movements essentially display an asset behavior. The spot exchange rate in the short run is sensitive to economic news and political events. However, in the long run it is functionally related to economic fundamentals, which are reflected in a set of relationships known as the international parity conditions. Survey data also show that expectations for short horizons seem to exhibit "bandwagon" effects, which are destabilizing, while expectations for long horizons appear to be regressive, and thus stabilizing.

Fifth, in a short time horizon no model can outperform the random walk hypothesis. In particular, no other variables can predict the future spot rate better than the current spot rate.

These empirical regularities suggest that, in part, exchange rate movements can be explained by economic variables. In this event investors can make use of these variables to predict exchange rate behavior and engage in profitable trading. However, the volatility of exchange rates also implies that they are largely unpredictable by any observable economic reasoning and exhibit random behavior. The consequence is that no particular trading rule can be developed to allow investors to realize excess profits in the currency markets.

We first investigate exchange rate behavior in relation to a set of economic fundamentals organized around the international parity conditions. The departure of exchange rates from these fundamentals is also discussed in the framework of the efficient markets hypothesis.

INTERNATIONAL PARITY CONDITIONS

The components of the balance of payments involve transactions in commodities, services, and assets. These transactions are the results of decisions by traders shipping goods across countries, manipulation of international funds by interest arbitragers, and expectations by speculators, as well as their attitudes and actions toward risk. The central question we are concerned with here is: What are the guiding principles that dictate international trade flows and capital movements? These principles can be summarized by the following international parity conditions:

- Purchasing power parity

$$(\Delta s_t^e = \Delta p_t^e - \Delta p_t^{e^*})$$

- Interest rate parity

$$(f_t - s_t = r_t - r_t^*)$$

- Unbiased forward rate hypothesis

$$(s_{t+1}^e = f_t, \ or \ s_{t+1}^e - s_t = f_t - s_t)$$

- Fisher parity condition

$$(r_t - r_t^* = \Delta p_t^e - \Delta p_t^{e^*})$$

- International Fisher parity

$$(s_{t+1}^e - s_t = r_t - r_t^*)$$

- Real interest rate parity

$$[\Delta s_t^e - (\Delta p_t^e - \Delta p_t^{e^*}) = (r_t - \Delta p_t^e) - (r_t^* - \Delta p_t^{e^*})]$$

where notations, with the exceptions of r_t and r_t^*, expressed in lowercase are natural logarithms. The terms s_t and f_t are, respectively, the spot and forward exchange rates, denominated by units of domestic currency per unit of foreign currency; Δp_t^e denotes the expected inflation rate; and r_t is the nominal rate of interest. An asterisk over the variables refers to the foreign country.

Purchasing Power Parity

Purchasing power parity is a theory that relates the exchange rate to the local currency prices of an individual commodity in the international markets. Commodity arbitrage, in which agents buy the commodity in the cheaper place and sell it in the more expensive place, will exhaust any opportunity for profit. This arbitrage activity leads to the equality of the two commodity prices once the prices are converted into a common currency. If this holds true for all goods at different points of time, the percentage change in nominal exchange rates will equal the differential in inflation rates between countries. This is usually called the *relative* form of purchasing power parity. This parity condition can also be expressed in an ex ante perspective: it states that the expected change in exchange rates is equal to the expected inflation differential. For example, using the data given in Exhibit 3.1, the current consumer price indexes for the United States and the United Kingdom are assumed to be 115 and 124, and the respective values for next year are expected to be 120.9 and 134.29. From these figures we can calculate that the expected inflation rate is 5% for the United States and 8% for the United Kingdom. If *ex ante* relative purchasing power parity holds, we can predict that the expected appreciation rate for the U.S. dollar is 3%. Thus, information about the expected inflation rates can be used to project the expected change in the exchange rate. Further elaboration of purchasing power parity is given in Chapter 6.

Interest Rate Parity

Interest rate parity states that the interest rate differential between two countries will be matched by the forward premium of the exchange rate. This relation holds due to efficient arbitrage in risk-free assets. It can be applied to international investments as well as to international lending. The rationale behind the application of interest rate parity to both international investments and lending is that for investment projects, investors compare the return from the domestic market with the return from the foreign market; the latter is the return from the foreign asset plus the forward premium. For financing projects, borrowers compare the costs from the domestic market with those from the foreign market. Equilibrium will be achieved when the parity condition is established.

Consider, for example, the case in which the 1-year interest rate in New York is 8.75% and that in London is 11.75%. This seems to suggest that investors will earn an excess return of 3% if the funds are invested in the London bond market (or borrowers will acquire funds more cheaply in New York). However, if the prevailing current spot rate is $1.6375/£1 and the 1-year forward rate is $1.5883/£1, then investors who convert their proceeds back to U.S. dollars will have to pay a 3% forward discount on the pound sterling in the forward market.[1] We see that the interest rate advantage is offset by the forward discount on the pound. Clearly, in an investment environment with full information investors cannot earn excess profits through asset market arbitrage; this is the conclusion implied by the interest rate parity condition. The application

---

[1] A forward rate is an exchange rate at which a bank is willing to exchange one currency for another at some specified future date. Forward discount measures the percentage by which the forward rate is less than the spot rate at a specific date. The forward market is described more fully in Chapter 4.

of interest rate parity to the money market and bond market is demonstrated in Chapters 7 and 8.

Unbiased Forward Rate Hypothesis

The *unbiased forward rate hypothesis* emphasizes effective use of information in the forward exchange rate to predict the future spot exchange rate. This hypothesis claims that market expectations of the economic fundamentals that determine exchange rates are reflected in the forward exchange rate. The forward exchange rate sometimes overpredicts or underpredicts the future spot rate, but on average the forward rate is approximately equal to the future spot rate. For instance, if the forward rate $[F_t(\$/£)]$ is \$1.5883/£1 and the market's expectation of the future spot rate $[S_{t+1}^e(\$/£)]$ is \$1.5880/£1, the difference between the two rates is $\$1.5880 - \$1.5883 = -0.0003$, which is quite negligible. On average we can observe that the difference of the two rates is not significantly different from zero. This is why the forward rate is often viewed as an unbiased predictor of the future spot rate. Chapter 5 provides additional discussion of the unbiased forward rate hypothesis.

Fisher Parity Condition

The *Fisher parity condition* in asset markets is derived from the standard Fisher equation, which states that the nominal rate of interest approximately equals the real rate of interest plus the expected rate of inflation. If the Fisher equation holds true for both countries and the real interest rates are equal in the two countries, the nominal interest rate differential will reflect the expected inflation differential between the two countries. The condition is particularly applicable in the case of highly inflationary periods. As shown in Exhibit 3.1, the nominal interest rate differential $(r_t - r_t^*)$ is -3%; the expected inflation differential $(\Delta p_t^e - \Delta p_t^{e*})$ is also -3%.

International Fisher Parity

Fisher parity has an application in the international setting. If the ex ante purchasing power parity condition is incorporated into the Fisher parity condition, we can see that the expected change in exchange rates corresponds to the interest rate differential. This is usually called the international Fisher parity condition. As a continuation of our example, if the interest rate differential between the United States and the United Kingdom $(r_t - r_t^*)$ is -3%, this condition can be used to predict that the U.S. currency will appreciate by 3%. If this figure turns out to be consistent with market predictions, then the data support the international Fisher parity condition. This condition is covered in more detail in Chapter 5.

Real Interest Rate Parity

Sometimes, researchers or investors are concerned not only with the nominal relationship but also with the real relationship between the exchange rate and the interest rate differential. Thus, it is appropriate to

Exhibit 3.1

Numerical Example of
International Parity Conditions

Notations and the observed data: (s_t, f_t, p_t, and p_t^* expressed in lowercase are natural logarithms).

Spot exchange rate:

$$S_t(\$/£) = \$1.6375/£1 \ (s_t = 0.4931)$$

Forward exchange rate:

$$F_t(\$/£) = \$1.5883/£1 \ (f_t = 0.4627)$$

Forecast 1-year-ahead spot rate:

$$S_{t+1}^e \ (\$/£) = \$1.5880/£1 \ (s_{t+1}^e = 0.4624)$$

Current price index (CPI), for the United States:

$$P_t = 115 \ (p_t = 4.745);$$

for the United Kingdom:

$$P_t^* = 124 \ (p_t^* = 4.820).$$

Forecast 1-year-ahead price index, for the United States:

$$P_{t+1}^e = 120.9 \ (p_{t+1}^e = 4.795);$$

for the United Kingdom:

$$P_{t+1}^{e*} = 134.29 \ (p_{t+1}^{e*} = 4.900).$$

Interest rate on 1-year government securities, for the United States:

$$r_t = 8.75\%;$$

for the United Kingdom:

$$r_t^* = 11.75\%.$$

On the basis of the data just given we can calculate:

Forward premium on $ (or discount on £):

$$f_t - s_t = 0.4627 - 0.4931 = -0.0304 \approx -3\%$$

Forecast error using forward rate:

$$s_{t+1}^e - f_t = 0.4624 - 0.4627 = -0.0003 \approx 0$$

Expected change in spot exchange rate:

$$s_{t+1}^e - s_t = 0.4624 - 0.4931 = -0.0307 \approx -3\%$$

Interest rate differential (nominal):

$$r_t - r_t^* = 8.75\% - 11.75\% = -3\%$$

Expected inflation rate differential:

$$\Delta p_t^e - \Delta p_t^{e*} = (4.795 - 4.745) - (4.900 - 4.820)$$
$$= 0.05 - 0.08 = -3\%$$

Expected changes in real exchange rate:

$$\Delta s_t^e - (\Delta p_t^e - \Delta p_t^{e*}) = s_{t+1}^e - s_t - [(p_{t+1}^e - p_t) - (p_{t+1}^{e*} - p_t^*)]$$
$$= (0.4624 - 0.4931) - [(4.795 - 4.745) - (4.900 - 4.820)] \approx 0.$$

Exhibit 3.1

continued

Real interest rate differential:

$$(r_t - \Delta p_t^e) - (r_t^* - \Delta p_t^{e^*}) = [r_t - (p_{t+1}^e - p_t)] - [r_t^* - (p_{t+1}^{e^*} - p_t^*)]$$
$$= [0.0875 - (4.795 - 4.745)] - [0.1175 - (4.900 - 4.820)] = 0.$$

Specifically, we can see:

A. Ex ante purchasing power parity:

$$\Delta s_t^e = \Delta p_t^e - \Delta p_t^{e^*} = -3\%$$

B. Interest rate parity:

$$f_t - s_t = r_t - r_t^* = -3\%$$

C. Unbiased forward rate hypothesis:

$$s_{t+1}^e - s_t = f_t - s_t = -3\%$$

D. Fisher parity:

$$r_t - r_t^* = \Delta p_t^e - \Delta p_t^{e^*} = -3\%$$

E. International Fisher parity:

$$s_{t+1}^e - s_t = r_t - r_t^* = -3\%$$

F. Real interest rate parity:

$$\Delta s_t^e - (\Delta p_t^e - \Delta p_t^{e^*}) = (r_t - \Delta p_t^e) - (r_t^* - \Delta p_t^{e^*}) = 0$$

From A through F, we conclude:

$$s_{t+1}^e - s_t = \Delta p_t^e - \Delta p_t^{e^*} = r_t - r_t^* = f_t - s_t = -3\%$$

express the international Fisher parity condition in real terms. This can be achieved by deflating the relative expected inflation rate (or by subtracting the natural log-difference of price levels) from the international Fisher parity condition. This resulting relation is called the *real interest rate parity*, which states that the expected change in real exchange rates equals the real interest rate differential. As can be seen in our example, both the expected change in real exchange rates and the real interest rate differential are equal to zero, suggesting that the real interest rate parity holds in this case.

To summarize the preceding numerical examples, we see that the expected U.S. dollar depreciation rate, the inflation differential, the interest rate differential, and the forward premium on the dollar are all equal to −3%. We should keep in mind that the validity of these conditions is based on the assumptions that international markets are efficient and that there are no transaction costs or other forms of market imperfections such as tax differentials and government intervention. More precisely, the purchasing power parity theory assumes that the commodity markets are efficient, while the interest rate parities assume that the asset markets are efficient. The unbiased forward rate hypothesis, Fisher parity, and the international Fisher equation require rational expectations and intertemporal efficiency. To gain further insights into the validity of the parity conditions, we now briefly discuss the concepts and characteristics of the efficient market hypothesis.

EFFICIENT MARKET HYPOTHESIS

The term *efficiency* as used in financial markets includes allocational, operational, and pricing efficiency. Allocational efficiency means that resource allocation is in an optimal state, and further rearrangement of resources would not improve the well-being of economic agents. Operational efficiency emphasizes that efficiency is achieved when transactions are carried out with minimum transaction costs. Pricing efficiency concerns whether an asset's price is equal to its intrinsic economic value. Since efficiency depends on the speed of information being processed and on the accuracy of the information to be delivered, pricing efficiency is usually interpreted as informational efficiency. Under this perspective, a market is said to be efficient if investors effectively use information to make their profits. In seeking a profit opportunity, investors are comparing the actual asset prices with the equilibrium prices calculated through use of publicly available information. When the actual asset price deviates from its equilibrium price, investors rapidly process information so as to make an appropriate transaction. As a result of the profit motive, the actual asset price adjusts until the equilibrium price is achieved.

Following Fama's (1970) definition, the market is efficient if market prices fully reflect all relevant information instantly. Under such circumstances, no particular market operation can earn an excess profit. To state the concept more precisely, let us define the excess market return for asset j (a security or currency) at time $t + 1$ as $Z_{j, t+1}$, which is the difference between the realized one-period percentage return, $R_{j, t+1}$, and the market expectation of return at time $t + 1$, $E(R_{j, t+1} \mid I_t)$, based on the information available at time t. In symbols it is given by

3.1
$$Z_{j, t+1} = R_{j, t+1} - E(R_{j, t+1} \mid I_t)$$

where $E(\cdot)$ is an expectation operator and I_t is an information set that is assumed to be fully reflected in the price at time t. If the excess return sequence $\{Z_{j, t+1}\}$ is a "fair game" with respect to the information set I_t, we say that the market is efficient. Thus, the condition for the existence of market efficiency is that the expected value of the excess return sequence equals zero. That is,

$$E(Z_{j, t+1}) = 0.$$

When this condition is met, the actual asset returns vibrate randomly about the expected equilibrium return. Thus, testing this proposition is equivalent to examining whether investors efficiently set the actual return equal to its equilibrium value. To do so, investors need to know the scope of information, and they need to have a model showing the impact of information on prices. Therefore, the study of the efficient market hypothesis involves joint tests of equilibrium price determination and of efficiency.

Weakly Efficient Markets

Varying degrees of informational efficiency have been suggested by researchers. The first is the *weakly efficient markets hypothesis*. It states that past prices and trading information are instantaneously incorporated into the current price. Thus the information contained in past prices and volumes is worthless for improving the predictions of future price changes. Weak-form efficiency in foreign exchange markets implies that the expectation of the one-period-ahead exchange rate is the current spot exchange rate. This means that today's spot exchange rate is the best predictor of the future spot rate. That is,

3.2 $$E(s_{t+1} \mid I_t) = s_t$$

where s_t is the natural logarithm of the spot exchange rate. The implication of eq. 3.2 is that the expected change in the exchange rate is zero. If the realized future spot rate differs from market expectations, it must be because of a disturbance that randomly hits the market. Thus, we observe

3.3 $$s_{t+1} - s_t = \varepsilon_{t+1}$$

where $s_{t+1} - s_t$ is a prediction error associated with a shock (news or innovation) that occurs between time t and time $t + 1$. Since ε_{t+1} behaves randomly and is uncorrelated with the information set I_t, investors cannot find a systematic pattern, nor additional information to improve their predictions of exchange rate movements. The viewpoint that actual values of exchange rates vary randomly around a constant expected equilibrium rate has been called the random-walk hypothesis. This idea is equivalent to saying that exchange rate changes are drawn from a distribution that does not shift over time. However, we can observe that the exchange rate behaves as in eq. 3.2, but that the expected equilibrium exchange rate, which reflects the distribution of the currency price, could vary over time. Thus, the random-walk hypothesis is neither a necessary nor a sufficient condition for the existence of market efficiency (Levich 1985). One thing we should bear in mind is that weak-form efficiency in its very nature is a short-run phenomenon. Its behavior is largely unpredictable, especially for the time horizon involving daily or weekly rates. However, for longer time intervals, such as quarters or years, exchange rate movements may follow a swing or a deterministic trend, representing a return for an investment or a reward for risk-taking through transactions in currency markets. Further discussions of testing weak-form efficiency are available in the appendix to this chapter and in Chapter 5.

Semistrong Market Efficiency

The *semistrong market efficiency hypothesis* argues that the information reflected in the current spot exchange rate is more than just the exchange rate history. In addition, the exchange rate also reflects all publicly available information. In this case no further information can be gained from public sources that will help to explain the movement of exchange rates. It follows that in testing semistrong efficiency, a formal model to determine the market equilibrium must be chosen. Moreover, the anticipated and unanticipated components of the exchange rate determinants must be distinguished in order to examine the nature of semistrong market efficiency.

For example, the equilibrium exchange rate may be related to the relative price indexes of the two countries. Since, according to the quantity theory, the price level in each country is determined by the money supply, real income, and the interest rate, it follows that the equilibrium exchange rate is governed by the relative magnitudes of variables such as money supplies, real incomes, and interest rates. To test the impact of these exchange rate determinants on the exchange rate in the context of the semistrong form of the efficiency hypothesis, we usually divide these determinants into anticipated and unanticipated components. Since the anticipated components have been observed by the market participants and this information, therefore, has been incorporated into the determination of the current exchange rate, surprise deviations of the actual spot rate from the market expectations must be associated with the unanticipated components (innovations or news) of the determinants. Empirical evidence in the literature does not find a strong confirmation of the semistrong efficiency form. The difficulty may come either from a lack of a well-specified model for the determination of exchange rates or from an insufficiently precise procedure to decompose the anticipated and unanticipated parts in testing the model.

Strongly Efficient Markets

In a *strongly efficient market*, all information, not just publicly available information, is reflected in asset prices. In some security markets, evidence shows that insiders have been able to profit from inside information without violating the laws, which is a rejection of the strong form of market efficiency. However, given the complexity of the currency market, it is not easy for financial analysts to find inside information that leads to forecasting returns accurately enough to outweigh the research and transaction costs. From this perspective it is difficult to set up a formal procedure to test the strong form of the efficient markets hypothesis. This is why we have not yet found a consistent piece of research work designed to investigate the strong-form hypothesis in the foreign exchange markets.

FINANCIAL ANALYSIS IN CURRENCY MARKETS

Financial analysts have developed several techniques to analyze the value of a national currency. *Fundamental analysis* emphasizes economic reasoning. *Technical analysis* stresses tracking the historical movements of exchange rates.

Fundamental Analysis

The most popular method of estimating the value of a national currency is *fundamental analysis;* financial analysts who use this method are called fundamental analysts. In projecting the future path of a national currency, fundamental analysts study the basic factors thought to be important in exchange rate determination: the elements that constitute the international parity conditions. Inflation rate differentials, interest rates differentials (nominal and real), and forward premiums are often viewed as the fundamental factors. However, some fundamental analysts even check the causal variables that lie behind these fundamental factors, such as the relative growth rates of money supplies, the state of current accounts, the balance-of-payments positions, and central bank behavior and other institutional factors.

Technical Analysis

Technical analysis involves the use of historical exchange rate series in deriving patterns to predict exchange rate movements. Technical analysts' methodology depends heavily on examination of past price and volume movements, since they believe that the underlying economic theories or nontechnical information are not necessarily relevant. To carry this belief to an extreme, some technicians provide no logic or explanation behind the predicted figures they derive. Other technicians recognize the importance of the fundamental factors used to forecast exchange rates. However, they argue that the underlying economic structure is too complex to understand; the economic model recommended by fundamentalists may not be valid or may be too time-consuming. Thus, instead of relying on economic analysis, technical analysts believe that market behavior can be systematically revealed in the historical data. They contend that shifts in market conditions can be detected in charts of market activity. Since some chart patterns tend to recur, these patterns can be extracted and used for forecasting purposes.

To inspect the actual movements of exchange rates, the chartists usually construct line charts and bar charts based on available data. Line charts connect the successive daily closing prices of foreign exchanges. They provide general information on recent movements of the series; the technician then can analyze the general trend, peaks, valleys, and major turning points. Line or bar charts plot a vertical bar spanning the distance of open-close prices; the distance shows the range of fluctuations of the daily exchange rate.

The horizontal axis in Figure 3.1 records the date of trade, and the vertical axis measures the dollar prices (in scale of 10^{-4}) for the deutsche mark (for instance, 6000 means $\$6000 \times 10^{-4} = $ DM1). The opening price is marked on the left-hand side of the vertical line for a particular trading date, and the closing price is marked on the right-hand side for the same trading date.

In addition, a curve of a moving average for a given time interval is also constructed. A moving-average line is obtained by summing the actual data points, say 20, and then dividing by the number of observa-

Figure 3.1

Daily Exchange Rate and 20-day
Moving Average

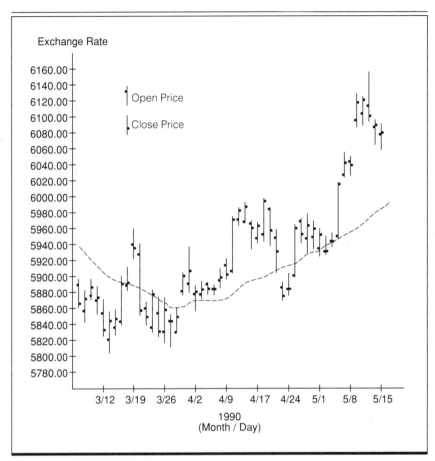

SOURCE: Knight-Ridder Trade Center

tions (20). The process is advanced by continuously adding the most recent observation and discarding the most distant observation. The broken line in Figure 3.1 is constructed by using a 20-day moving average, and the broken line in Figure 3.2 is constructed using a 34-day moving average. This moving-average line can be compared with the actual closing-price line to provide information for technicians to form their strategies. Particularly, whenever the actual-price line passes through the moving-average line, technicians view this penetration as a signal for deciding to buy or to sell. In general, when technicians see the daily exchange rate move downward through the moving-average line, they expect there is a continual tendency to move further down; thus a downward trend penetration through a moving-average line is a signal to sell. On the other hand, an upward penetration through a moving-average line can be interpreted as a signal to buy. For example, when technicians look at the exchange rate behavior around 21 November 1989 or 2 April 1990, the daily exchange rate moves above the moving-average line, suggesting it would be a good opportunity to buy the deutsche mark. Of course, this trading strategy does not necessarily lead

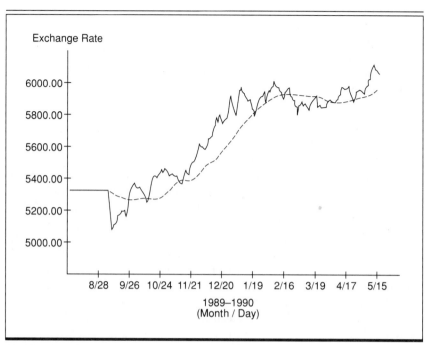

Figure 3.2

Daily Exchange Rate and
34-day Moving Average

SOURCE: Knight-Ridder Trade Center

to a profitable transaction should market conditions move in a contrary direction.[2]

Two points in relation to technical analysis are worth noting. First, the rule used in technical analysis can easily be translated into an extrapolative behavior. Particularly, when the actual closing price passes above the moving-average line, it portends a currency appreciation beyond the expectations implied in the moving-average line. Thus, it is profitable to buy and hold the foreign currency. The reverse transaction should be made when the actual price falls below the moving-average line, indicating the foreign currency has a tendency to depreciate. This behavior is consistent with the survey data conducted by Frankel and Froot (1987), in that expectations data for short horizons exhibit a bandwagon effect.

Second, what the chartists search for is patterns of currency price fluctuations. They often claim that the technical patterns derived from the charts will repeat themselves and can therefore be used for forecasting; the trends and patterns of currency prices can be inefficiently driven away from their fundamental equilibrium. Thus, the success of technical analysis provides an alternative scheme to reject the efficient markets hypothesis.

---

[2] Notice that, in a "whipsaw" position, where actual prices (around 19 March 1990 in Figure 3.1) are fluctuating around the moving-average line, no buy or sell decision will be recommended by the technicians since an uncertainty situation prevails.

ANOMALIES

In addition to the possible existence of trading rules that may be uncovered by technical analysis, there are certain anomalies, such as the January effect and speculative bubbles, that are inconsistent with the efficient markets hypotheses.

January Effect

Although most of the evidence indicates that studying the history of exchange rate changes does not reveal useful patterns, there remain certain anomalies that are not easily reconcilable with an efficient market hypothesis in the foreign exchange markets. For example, as in the stock market, a January effect has been detected for the dollar.[3] Specifically, over the past 10 years the dollar has appreciated against a basket of foreign currencies in every January except 1986 and 1987. Moreover, the dollar's January performance was able to predict its subsequent performance for the year in every year except 1985. The pattern is presented by the bar chart in Figure 3.3. According to Finex, the financial instruments division of the New York Cotton Exchange, traders who bought the dollar index on the last day of the preceding year and sold it on the last day of January would have gained an average of some 3.2% in each of the eight Januarys in which the dollar appreciated. A possible explanation of the phenomenon is that many corporations make their currency plans in January of the year and immediately act on them. If expectations are that the dollar will be strong for the year, corporations start buying dollars; if the expectations are of a weak dollar, they become sellers. Thus, the expectations tend to produce the appreciation or depreciation and become a self-fulfilling prophecy. Given the regularity of this phenomenon, and the fact that under the efficient markets hypothesis, markets are supposed to quickly reflect all available information, the market should have recognized and competed away this effect.

Speculative Bubbles

Although a number of economic models have been used to interpret exchange rate movements, virtually none of the existing models can explain exchange rate behavior well. Some international analysts attempt to interpret the phenomenon of deviation of the actual currency values from their fundamental values as speculative bubbles. Particularly, economic agents form their exchange rate expectations based on a certain kind of extrapolative behavior. Thus, favorable changes in finan-

---

[3] In their empirical study of the nature of price changes for seven foreign currency markets, McFarland, Pettet, and Sung (1982) found trading day effects. In particular, their results indicate that dollar-denominated price changes are high on Mondays and Wednesdays and low on Thursdays and Fridays for the currencies under examination. They argued that the Wednesday-Thursday result is consistent with foreign currency trading settlement procedures, whereas the Friday-Monday effect is consistent with an increase in demand for the dollar before the weekend.

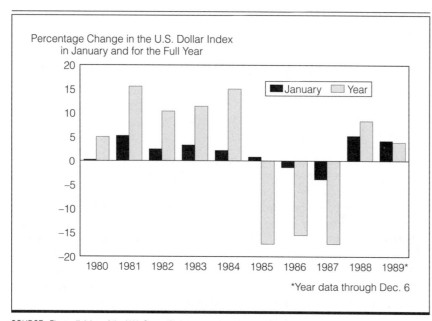

Figure 3.3
The January Effect on the U.S. Dollar

SOURCE: Finex, division of the N.Y. Cotton Exchange, reprinted in the *Wall Street Journal*.
* Year data through Dec. 6

cial variables or in the investment environment may tend to generate an exchange rate appreciation that, in turn, may lead to expectations of a further appreciation. The process continues as long as the market believes the currency price will continue moving in the same direction. Since the actual price moves farther away from the fundamentals as time passes, capital gains would have to be sufficiently large to compensate the risk of a bursting bubble.

Speculative bubbles have gained some empirical support. These were found in the DM/U.S. dollar and French franc/U.S. dollar rates for the period June to October 1978. Evidence indicates that the German mark was overvalued with respect to its fundamental value by 12%, and the French franc was overvalued by 11% (Woo 1987). A speculative bubble was also found in the United States, where the dollar appreciated substantially for the period 1980 through 1985.

ECONOMETRIC MODELS

Econometric models for generating exchange rate forecasts are based on fundamental analysis. They try to measure and quantify the relationships between exchange rates and a set of economic fundamentals, such as relative money supplies $(m_t - m_t^*)$, relative real incomes $(y_t - y_t^*)$, interest rate differentials $(r_t - r_t^*)$, inflation differentials $(\pi_t - \pi_t^*)$, and the two countries' current account balances $(ca_t - ca_t^*)$. This relationship can be represented by the following regression model:

3.4
$$s_t = \beta_0 + \beta_1(m_t - m_t^*) + \beta_2(y_t - y_t^*) + \beta_3(r_t - r_t^*) \\ + \beta_4(\pi_t - \pi_t^*) + \beta_5(ca_t - ca_t^*) + \varepsilon_t,$$

where $\beta_j (j = 0, 1, \ldots, 5)$ is the coefficient for the explanatory variables, and an asterisk denotes a foreign-country variable. Based on past statistical data, exchange rate forecasters estimate the values of the coefficients. Predictions can then be done by assuming that the past relationships will carry into the future. To predict the future exchange rate, eq. 3.4 can be rewritten as:

3.5 $$s_{t+1} = \beta_0 + \beta_1(m^e_{t+1} - m^{e*}_{t+1}) + \beta_2(y^e_{t+1} - y^{e*}_{t+1}) + \beta_3(r^e_{t+1} - r^{e*}_{t+1})$$
$$+ \beta_4(\pi^e_{t+1} - \pi^{e*}_{t+1}) + \beta_5(ca^e_{t+1} - ca^{e*}_{t+1}) + \varepsilon_{t+1}.$$

where the superscript e refers to the expectations of the explanatory variables. These expected values usually need to be generated by using an optimal forecasting scheme or by using the actual values. In practice, there is no easy and accurate way to measure these future values, especially in an economy that is experiencing ongoing structural changes. Empirical studies of eq. 3.5 for the 1980s do not lend much support for the model, especially judging by its performance in the out-of-sample predictions. This should not be surprising, since the components of the fundamentals are not certain and it is by no means clear that the future values of the fundamentals can be precisely predicted.

There is a different way to measure the expected values of the exchange rate determinants. Based on the rational expectations hypothesis and the efficient markets theory, the expectations of the future exchange rate determinants will be reflected in the forward exchange rate, f_t. With this assumption,

3.6 $$s_{t+1} = \beta_0 + \beta_1 f_t + \varepsilon_{t+1},$$

where f_t reflects a linear combination of the expectations of the determinants in eq. 3.5. This specification implies that the forward rate is a good predictor of the future spot rate. Empirical evidence, however, indicates that this hypothesis cannot be strongly supported by the data. Often, the forward rate performs even more poorly than the current spot rate.

Based on the effective use of information or on the weak form of the efficient markets hypothesis, the current spot rate is usually the best alternative to use in predicting the future exchange rate. Accumulated empirical results show that this hypothesis outperforms all the alternative models. The interpretation for these results is, perhaps, that the market participants place too much weight on the current spot rate and not enough weight on fundamentals in predicting the future spot rates. The confirmation of the dominant position of the current spot rate in prediction implies that additional information about the exchange rate history to be included in the forecasting process, such as time series analysis or technical analysis, would not lead to a better performance. That is, no unusual profits result from the use of the advanced econometric or time series models.

SUMMARY

A number of approaches exist to model exchange rates and forecast their future values. If the efficient markets hypothesis can explain the behavior of exchange rates, it should not be possible for investors to obtain abnormal returns. If it is inapplicable, then such methods as trading rules and fundamental analysis may afford investors superior results. The evidence is somewhat mixed, but, consistent with the efficient markets hypothesis, the random-walk model outperforms all other models; thus, the current spot rate is usually the best predictor of the future spot rate. Technical and fundamental analysis, and the quantitative time series and econometric methods that build on these approaches, have not produced impressive results and have yet to yield models that improve on the random walk.

Questions and Problems

1. What is the unbiased forward rate hypothesis? Can you think of some reasons why the forward rate might not be a good predictor of the future spot rate?

2. Discuss the relationship between the Fisher parity condition and the international Fisher parity condition.

3. Explain the rationale behind the international Fisher parity condition.

4. "The rejection of the unbiased forward rate hypothesis is equivalent to the rejection of the international Fisher parity condition." Why or why not?

5. Explain the efficient markets hypothesis. If an individual investor earns an excess return by speculating in the currency market, does this contradict the hypothesis? Why or why not?

6. Discuss the three forms of the market efficiency hypothesis. How are these hypotheses related to the information set?

7. Describe and distinguish fundamental analysis and technical analysis. Are these analyses consistent with the efficient markets hypothesis?

8. What are speculative bubbles? How can they occur? Is the existence of bubbles compatible with the efficient markets hypothesis?

9. Describe a limitation in testing the existence of speculative bubbles.

10. Discuss the tenet of the asset-approach econometric model in forecasting exchange rates. What are the main difficulties that may be encountered by such a model?

11. What is meant by the random-walk hypothesis? How do you test the random-walk hypothesis?

12. Most empirical evidence (Meese and Rogoff 1983; Chiang 1986) shows that the random-walk model outperformed the alternative models. Why?

References

Angrist, S. W. "Looking at Dollar Plays in January: Gain is Common, Signaling Trend." *Wall Street Journal* (27 December 1989): C1, C17.

Box, G., and G. Jenkins. *Time Series Analysis, Forecasting and Control.* San Francisco: Holden Day, 1976.

Chiang, T. "Empirical Analysis on the Predictors of the Future Spot Rates." *Journal of Financial Research* 9, no. 2 (June 1986): 153–62.

————. "The Forward Rate as a Predictor of the Future Spot Rate—A Stochastic Coefficient Approach." *Journal of Money, Credit, and Banking* 20 (May 1988): 212–32.

Cumby, R., and M. Obstfeld. "A Note on Exchange-Rate Expectations and Nominal Interest Differentials: A Test of the Fisher Hypothesis." *Journal of Finance* 36 (June 1981): 697–704.

Dornbusch, R. "Exchange Rate Risk and the Macroeconomics of Exchange Rate Determination." In *Research in International Business and Finance* vol. 3 eds. R. Hawkins et al. Greenwich, Conn.: JAI Press, 1983.

Edwards, S. "Exchange Rates and 'News': A Multi-Currency Approach." *Journal of International Money and Finance* 1 (December 1982): 211–24.

Fama, E. "Efficient Capital Markets: A Review of Theory and Empirical Work." *Journal of Finance* 25 (May 1970): 383–417.

Flood, R., and R. Hodrick. "On Testing for Speculative Bubbles." *Journal of Economic Perspectives* 4, no. 2 (Spring 1990): 85–101.

Frankel, J., and K. Froot. "Using Survey Data to Test Standard Propositions Regarding Exchange Rate Expectations." *American Economic Review* 77, no. 1 (March 1987): 133–53.

Frenkel, J. "Flexible Exchange Rates, Prices, and the Role of 'News': Lessons from the 1970s." *Journal of Political Economy* 89 (August 1981): 665–705.

Levich, R. "Empirical Studies of Exchange Rates: Price Behavior, Rate Determination and Market Efficiency." In *Handbook of International Economics* II, eds. R. Jones and P. Kenen, 979–1040, vol. 2. New York: Elsevier Publisher B.V. 1985.

McFarland, J., R. Pettit, and S. Sung. "The Distribution of Foreign Exchange Price Changes: Trading Day Effects and Risk Measurement." *Journal of Finance* 37 (June 1982): 693–715.

Meese, R. "Currency Fluctuations in the Post-Bretton Woods Era." *Journal of Economic Perspectives* 4, no. 1 (Winter 1990): 117–34.

Meese, R., and K. Rogoff. "Empirical Exchange Rate Models of the Seventies: Do They Fit Out of Sample?" *Journal of International Economics* 14 (February 1983): 3–24.

Mussa, M. "Empirical Regularities in the Behavior of Exchange Rates and Theories of the Foreign Exchange Market." In *Policies for Employment, Prices, and Exchange Rates*, eds. Karl Brunner and Allan J. Meltzer, 9–57. Carnegie-Rochester Conference Series on Public Policy, vol. 1. Amsterdam: North Holland, 1979.

Roll, R., and Bruno Solnik. "On Some Parity Conditions Encountered Frequently in International Economics." *Journal of Macroeconomics* 1, no. 3 (Summer 1979): 267–83.

Woo, W. "Some Evidence of Speculative Bubbles in the Foreign Exchange Markets." *Journal of Money, Credit, and Banking* 19 (November 1987): 499–514.

Appendix 3.A

TESTS FOR THE EFFICIENT MARKETS HYPOTHESIS

A number of tests of market efficiency are used to determine whether asset price changes will fluctuate randomly. These tests include a non-parametric runs test, tests of filter rules, and tests for serial correlation.

Runs Test

A runs test can be used to detect nonrandom patterns of reversals in the sign of exchange rate changes. The runs test simply counts the number of such sign reversals. This number can then be compared to an expected number of runs for a series of random numbers of the same size as the test sample. A significant difference of the test statistic from the expected value indicates nonrandomness.

Filter Rule Tests

Filter rules are mechanical trading rules. A commonly employed filter is the following: if prices rise $x\%$, buy and hold until the price drops at least $x\%$ from a previous high, in which case sell. These rules can be tested for different values of x. If exchange rates fluctuate randomly, then filter rules should not yield abnormal returns. On the other hand, if patterns do exist in exchange rates, then it should be possible to earn substantial profits following such a rule. Empirical tests have indicated that profitable rules can be devised, but they may not yield an abnormal profit if transaction costs are included.

Serial Correlation

Tests to detect serial correlation measure the correlation coefficient between successive values of the exchange rate. This coefficient can capture not only successive changes in the same direction but also patterns of reversals. The standard formula for calculating autocorrelation coefficients is given by:

$$\rho_k = \left[\sum_{t=1}^{n-k} (s_t - \bar{s})(s_{t+k} - \bar{s}) \right] \bigg/ \sum_{t=1}^{n} (s_t - \bar{s})^2$$

where ρ_k is the coefficient of autocorrelation for the exchange rates k periods apart. If the coefficient is positive it means that exchange rate rises in the current period would be followed by an exchange rate rise. A negative coefficient would indicate that the currency prices follow a pattern of reversals, in which currency price changes in one direction will be followed by changes in the opposite direction. The statistical test of serial correlation has important implications for the investor's position. Particularly, the finding of statistical significance of the exchange rate series provides a trading rule, which can be exploited by investors to earn an excess profit. This would violate the efficient markets hypothesis. However, the evidence from the study of various exchange returns has failed to detect any significant correlations.

These tests for patterns in exchange rate changes are ways to evaluate the weak form of the efficient markets hypothesis. To test semistrong efficiency, it is also necessary to examine the speed of adjustment of prices to new information; the faster the adjustment, the greater the degree of efficiency. Some empirical evidence shows that lagged news, such as delayed effects of monetary announcements, appears to be significant in explaining exchange rate movements. Does such delay or persistence reflect irrational information processing by economic agents? We should interpret the results with care. As we mentioned in the text, empirical tests of the news approach require the measurement of the expectational values. The generated news variable may have built-in serial or lagged correlation, especially if overlapping data are used in the tests of the model. Moreover, information or data may be published with a time lag; even if in fact the market participants responded instantly, we still find the lagged news variable to be significant.

FOREIGN EXCHANGE MARKETS: FUNDAMENTALS

In daily economic activities, a considerable amount of goods and services, as well as financial securities, are traded in the international markets. For a monetary system to facilitate these transactions, such trading must be accompanied by the exchange of international monies or claims. Two issues arise: What is the exchange ratio between two national currencies? And what fundamental factors determine the value of national currencies?

In this chapter, we briefly discuss the concept of exchange rates, including spot and forward markets in practice, and then present three different theories that are commonly used to explain exchange rate movements. We also provide empirical evidence in our discussion.

FOREIGN EXCHANGE QUOTATIONS AND TRADING

Foreign exchange trading refers to trading one country's currency for that of another. The exchange ratio for the two countries' currencies is called the bilateral exchange rate. Thus, an exchange rate is the price of one country's currency in terms of another country's currency. Exhibit 4.1 gives foreign exchange rate quotations for 28 June 1990. The caption of the table published by the *Wall Street Journal* on Friday, 29 June 1990, indicates the selling rates that apply to trading among banks in the amount of $1 million or more. The rates are wholesale prices. This means that the retail prices that banks offer to customers on smaller amounts are usually more expensive, implying that customers will have to pay more U.S. dollars to obtain each unit of foreign currency.

The first column in Exhibit 4.1 lists the name of the country and the corresponding currency. The next four columns give exchange rates for the two business days preceding the publication of the newspaper (Thursday, 28 June and Wednesday, 27 June).

Exhibit 4.1   Foreign Exchange Rate Quotations

EXCHANGE RATES

Thursday, June 28, 1990

The New York foreign exchange selling rates below apply to trading among banks in amounts of $1 million and more, as quoted at 3 p.m. Eastern time by Bankers Trust Co. Retail transactions provide fewer units of foreign currency per dollar.

Country	U.S. $ equiv. Thurs.	Wed.	Currency per U.S. $ Thurs.	Wed.
Argentina (Austral)	.0001876	.0001876	5330.21	5330.21
Australia (Dollar)	.7869	.7878	1.2708	1.2694
Austria (Schilling)	.08503	.08543	11.76	11.70
Bahrain (Dinar)	2.6522	2.6522	.3771	.3771
Belgium (Franc)				
Commercial rate	.02910	.02927	34.36	34.17
Brazil (Cruzeiro)	.01676	.01676	59.65	59.65
Britain (Pound)	1.7385	1.7440	.5752	.5734
30-Day Forward	1.7290	1.7342	.5784	.5766
90-Day Forward	1.7112	1.7171	.5844	.5824
180-Day Forward	1.6859	1.6915	.5932	.5912
Canada (Dollar)	.8557	.8554	1.1687	1.1690
30-Day Forward	.8517	.8516	1.1741	1.1743
90-Day Forward	.8446	.8444	1.1840	1.1843
180-Day Forward	.8348	.8349	1.1979	1.1977
Chile (Official rate)	.003507	.003507	285.15	285.15
China (Renmimbi)	.211752	.211752	4.7225	4.7225
Colombia (Peso)	.002062	.002062	485.00	485.00
Denmark (Krone)	.1572	.1579	6.3595	6.3325
Ecuador (Sucre)				
Floating rate	.001163	.001163	860.00	860.00
Finland (Markka)	.25452	.25556	3.9290	3.9130
France (Franc)	.17808	.17921	5.6155	5.5800
30-Day Forward	.17783	.17896	5.6233	5.5878
90-Day Forward	.17730	.17848	5.6400	5.6030
180-Day Forward	.17655	.17771	5.6640	5.6273
Greece (Drachma)	.006116	.006135	163.50	163.00
Hong Kong (Dollar)	.12839	.12840	7.7885	7.7880
India (Rupee)	.05760	.05760	17.36	17.36
Indonesia (Rupiah)	.0005420	.0005420	1845.02	1845.02
Ireland (Punt)	1.6093	1.6120	.6214	.6203
Israel (Shekel)	.4770	.4770	2.0966	2.0966
Italy (Lira)	.0008150	.0008210	1227.01	1218.01
Japan (Yen)	.006536	.006477	153.00	154.40
30-Day Forward	.006541	.006482	152.89	154.28
90-Day Forward	.006548	.006491	152.72	154.05
180-Day Forward	.006559	.006504	152.46	153.75
Jordan (Dinar)	1.5076	1.5076	.6633	.6633
Kuwait (Dinar)	3.4130	3.4130	.2930	.2930
Lebanon (Pound)	.001499	.001499	667.00	667.00
Malaysia (Ringgit)	.3691	.3690	2.7090	2.7100
Malta (Lira)	3.0864	3.0864	.3240	.3240

Country	U.S. $ equiv. Thurs.	Wed.	Currency per U.S. $ Thurs.	Wed.
Mexico (Peso)				
Floating rate	.0003510	.0003510	2849.00	2849.00
Netherland (Guilder)	.5313	.5336	1.8820	1.8740
New Zealand (Dollar)	.5875	.5875	1.7021	1.7021
Norway (Krone)	.1557	.1561	6.4245	6.4050
Pakistan (Rupee)	.0461	.0461	21.70	21.70
Peru (Intl)	.00001372	.00001372	72891.61	72891.61
Philippines (Peso)	.04454	.04454	22.45	22.45
Portugal (Escudo)	.006793	.006793	147.20	147.20
Saudi Arabia (Riyal)	.26681	.26681	3.7480	3.7480
Singapore (Dollar)	.5435	.5423	1.8400	1.8440
South Africa (Rand)				
Commercial rate	.3767	.3762	2.6546	2.6582
Financial rate	.2469	.2463	4.0502	4.0601
South Korea (Won)	.0014145	.0014145	706.96	706.96
Spain (Peseta)	.009737	.009766	102.70	102.40
Sweden (Krona)	.1652	.1657	6.0515	6.0350
Switzerland (Franc)	.7040	.7095	1.4205	1.4095
30-Day Forward	.7035	.7091	1.4214	1.4103
90-Day Forward	.7029	.7085	1.4226	1.4115
180-Day Forward	.7026	.7083	1.4232	1.4118
Taiwan (Dollar)	.037009	.037009	27.02	27.02
Thailand (Baht)	.03887	.03887	25.73	25.73
Turkey (Lira)	.0003824	.0003824	2615.00	2615.00
United Arab (Dirham)	.2723	.2723	3.6725	3.6725
Uruguay (New Peso)				
Financial	.000847	.000847	1180.00	1180.00
Venezuela (Bolivar)				
Floating rate	.02123	.02123	47.10	47.10
W. Germany (Mark)	.5981	.6010	1.6720	1.6640
30-Day Forward	.5982	.6011	1.6717	1.6637
90-Day Forward	.5982	.6011	1.6716	1.6636
180-Day Forward	.5978	.6009	1.6727	1.6643
SDR	1.32231	1.32384	.75625	.75538
ECU	1.23629	1.23982	....	....

Special Drawing Rights (SDR) are based on exchange rates for the U.S., West German, British, French and Japanese currencies. Source: International Monetary Fund.

European Currency Unit (ECU) is based on a basket of community currencies. Source: European Community Commission.

The exchange rates are given by two definitions. The first is labeled as "U.S. $ equivalent," which expresses the units of U.S. dollars for one unit of foreign currency. For example, the dollar price of one unit of British pound sterling on Thursday, 28 June 1990, was $1.7385; the dollar price of Japanese yen on the same day was $0.006536. The second definition of exchange rates is labeled as "Currency per U.S. $," which is the units of foreign currency per U.S. dollar. The price of dollars in terms of the British pound on Thursday, 28 June 1990, was £0.5752; and the price of dollars in terms of the Japanese yen was ¥153.00 on the same day.

In the absence of transaction costs, the preceding two definitions should be in a reciprocal relation. For example, the units of U.S. dollar per pound ($1.7385) should be equal to one divided by the units of pound per U.S. dollar (£0.5752). That is, 1.7385 = 1/0.5752. In practice, the unmatched figures derived from the two definitions may be due to transaction costs, particularly the markup between the buying and selling rates by banks.

Most currencies give only one quotation, the price of currency for immediate delivery. This is called the spot exchange rate. The spot rate in practice means that the funds will be delivered in two business days after the transaction has been agreed. For example, Company A in New York City buys 1 million British pounds from the Banker's Trust Co. at the spot rate of $1.7365 on Thursday, 28 June 1990; a draft can be written against a bank in London for payment due on 2 July 1990. Some currencies are written in forward contracts that are transactions arranged for future delivery. The specific rate is known as the forward exchange rate. In Exhibit 4.1, the British pound lists three different forward exchange rates: 30, 60, and 90 days. If Company A needs 1 million British pounds 3 months from now, the company can enter into a 90-day forward contract with a rate of $1.7112 on Thursday, 28 June 1990, and agree to pay $1,711,200.00 for 1 million pounds delivered.

The forward rates are usually different from the spot rate. This differential is principally attributable to differing interest rates in the two national economies. For example, the 90-day forward rate for British pounds is $1.7112, which is lower than the spot rate, $1.7385. Under this circumstance, we say that pound sterling is traded at a forward discount, or the U.S. dollar is at a forward premium. The annual rate of forward discount on the pound is calculated by

$$\{[(\text{forward rate} - \text{spot rate})/\text{spot rate}] \cdot [360/90]\} \cdot 100$$
$$= \{[(1.7112 - 1.7385)/1.7385] \cdot [360/90]\} \cdot 100$$
$$= -6.28\%.$$

Not all forward rates are lower than the contemporaneous spot rates. For instance, in the case of the Japanese yen, the 90-day forward rate is higher than the spot rate. This means that the traders pay more U.S. dollars in the forward market ($0.006548) than the traders pay in the spot market ($0.006536) to obtain Japanese yen. The Japanese yen is said to trade at a forward premium relative to the dollar, or the U.S. dollar is at a forward discount. The annual rate of forward premium on yen is

$$\{[(0.006548 - 0.006536)/0.006536] \cdot [360/90]\} \cdot 100 = 0.73\%.$$

Figure 4.1

Determination of Exchange Rate in
Balance-of-Payments Approach

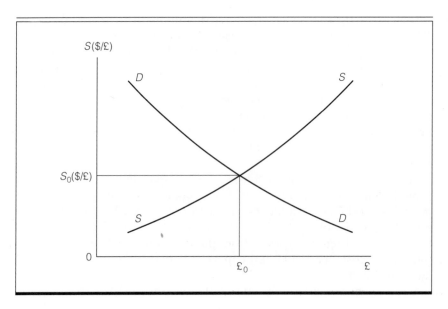

EXCHANGE RATE DETERMINATION

Participants in international markets are vitally concerned with determining rates of exchange, since such rates largely affect the costs and benefits of engaging in the international trade of goods and services as well as financial securities. It is generally agreed that the factors likely to determine the value of a nation's currency are the relative money supplies, real incomes, inflation rates, and interest rates of the home and foreign countries. We describe here three popular approaches to determining rates of exchange that incorporate these and other factors.

Balance-of-Payments Approach

Under the freely fluctuating exchange rate system, the exchange rate of two national currencies, like any commodity price, is determined by the interplay of demand and supply. The demand for foreign exchange comes from individuals or traders who make payments to foreigners in foreign currencies. The transactions may involve the import of goods and services or the purchase of foreign securities. These are the items listed on the debit side of the U.S. balance of payments. The supply of foreign exchange derives from the receipts of foreign currencies obtained from exporting goods and services or selling financial securities to foreigners. These items are entered in the credit column of the U.S. balance of payments.

In Figure 4.1, the exchange rate, designated by the price of the British pound in terms of the U.S. dollar, is measured on the vertical axis, and the volume of the foreign currency (the pound sterling) demanded and supplied is measured on the horizontal axis. The demand relationship of foreign exchange, labeled by *DD*, is downward-sloping. This is because a higher exchange rate makes imported goods and services, as well as

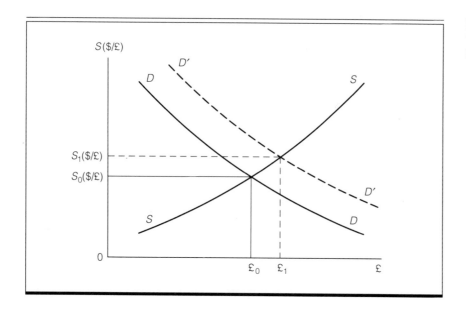

Figure 4.2

The Effect of an Increase in the Demand for Foreign Currency

financial securities, more expensive to the domestic buyers since they have to pay more domestic money to obtain a unit of foreign money. As a result, the demand for the volume of the imports and, in turn, the demand for the amount of foreign exchange by the domestic residents, is reduced.

The supply relationship, depicted by SS in Figure 4.1, is upward-sloping. A higher exchange rate makes our exports relatively cheaper in the eyes of foreign buyers since every unit of domestic currency costs less in the foreign currency. The result of a higher exchange rate stimulates the demand for the volume of our exports and hence increases the supply of foreign currency.

The equilibrium exchange rate, $S_0(\$/£)$, is determined by the intersection of the demand and the supply schedules. Changes in domestic prices, real income, tastes, and other factors cause shifts of the entire demand schedule. For instance, a rapid growth of domestic real income causes an increase in the demand for imports, shifting the entire demand schedule rightward, as labeled by $D'D'$ in Figure 4.2. The new equilibrium exchange rate, at point $S_1(\$/£)$, indicates a depreciation of the U.S. dollar.

Similarly, changes in prices, real income, and tastes in the foreign country cause shifts of the supply schedule. For example, if a higher inflation occurs in the United Kingdom, this inflation encourages the residents of Britain to purchase more of our exports and brings about an increase in the supply of pounds sterling. This change shifts the supply schedule to the right, as depicted by $S'S'$ in Figure 4.3. As a consequence, the U.S. dollar appreciates and the equilibrium exchange rate settles at $S_2(\$/£)$.

Clearly, the continuing shifts in demand and supply conditions force the exchange rate to adjust continuously to a new equilibrium. It is natural to ask: What are the factors behind the demand and supply

Figure 4.3

The Effect of an Increase in the
Supply of Foreign Currency

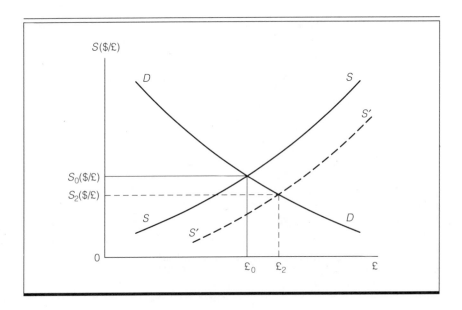

schedules that cause the exchange rate to fluctuate? To answer this
question, it is convenient to write the balance-of-payments (BOP) equation as follows:

4.1 $$BOP_t = C(P_t/S_t P_t^*, \ Y_t/Y_t^*, \ Z_t) + K(r_t - r_t^*).$$

Equation 4.1 states that the balance of payments is the sum of the current account, C, and the capital account, K. The current account balance
is dictated by relative prices, $P_t/S_t P_t^*$, relative real incomes, Y_t/Y_t^*, and a
shift variable, Z_t, which captures the factors such as tariffs, export subsidies, and other interventions. The capital account balance is governed
by the interest rate differential, $r_t - r_t^*$. An asterisk denotes a foreign
variable.

As argued in Chapter 2, under a truly floating exchange rate system,
balance of payments equilibrium is maintained by a continual adjustment of the exchange rate. Thus, the exchange rate equation expressed
in natural logarithm is given by

4.2 $$s_t = \eta(p_t - p_t^*) + \phi(y_t - y_t^*) - \lambda(r_t - r_t^*),$$

where lowercase denotes the natural logarithm, and η, ϕ, and λ are
constant coefficients (the shift variable has been ignored). Equation 4.2
summarizes the determinants of exchange rates into three groups,
namely relative prices, relative real incomes, and nominal interest rate
differentials.

The balance-of-payments approach predicts η is positive in that an
increase in domestic prices relative to foreign prices will lead to deterioration of the domestic country's competitive position and has a negative
effect on the current account. This in turn causes a depreciation of the
domestic currency. Next, the approach predicts that the sign of ϕ is
positive. It predicts that a rapid growth in real output tends to increase
imports, leading to a domestic currency depreciation. Third, an increase

in the domestic interest rate, with no comparable change in foreign interest, will attract capital inflows that bring about an appreciation of the domestic currency. Thus, the coefficient of $(r_t - r_t^*)$ is negative.[1]

Monetary Approach: Flexible Price Version

Instead of emphasizing trade flows and capital movements as the key factors determining exchange rates, the monetary approach focuses on the stock equilibrium condition in each country's money markets. The approach posits that the equilibrium exchange rate is critically dependent on the money supply and money demand. The exchange rate under this perspective is further determined by the factors governing a nation's money demand and supply functions.

To set a benchmark for discussing the alternative theories, let us first consider the flexible price version of the monetary approach. In this version, the exchange rate is derived by combining the quantity theory of money and purchasing power parity. It is assumed that each country's money demand and money supply determines its own prices; the prices in these two countries are linked by the exchange rate. To illustrate this, let two countries' money market equilibrium conditions be represented by

4.3
$$m_t = p_t + \phi y_t - \lambda r_t,$$

4.4
$$m_t^* = p_t^* + \phi y_t^* - \lambda r_t^*,$$

where the left-hand side variables of eqs. 4.3 and 4.4, m_t and m_t^*, are the logs of the domestic and foreign money supplies, respectively, and the right-hand side variables are the elements of the money demand functions. The money demand functions are assumed to be positively related to the prices, p_t(or p_t^*), and real output, y_t(or y_t^*), and negatively related to the rates of interest, r_t(or r_t^*). The parameters ϕ and λ are assumed to be constant and equal across countries.

Assuming that goods prices are perfectly flexible and that international goods arbitrage is efficient, purchasing power parity holds in the short run. That is,

4.5
$$s_t = p_t - p_t^*.$$

By combining eqs. 4.3 through 4.5, we have a naive version of the monetary equation:[2]

---

[1] The model implicitly assumes that domestic and foreign bonds are imperfect substitutes in a portfolio.

[2] Equation 4.6 can be derived as follows:

First, it is assumed that the money market equilibrium determines the commodity prices. Thus, eqs. 4.3 and 4.4 can be expressed as

4.3'
$$p_t = m_t - (\phi y_t - \lambda r_t),$$

4.4'
$$p_t^* = m_t^* - (\phi y_t^* - \lambda r_t^*).$$

Further, assuming purchasing power parity (*PPP*) holds, the relationship between the two nations' prices is linked by the spot exchange rate. Substituting eqs. 4.3' and 4.4' into 4.5 in the text, we derive 4.6.

4.6 $$s_t = (m_t - m_t^*) - \phi(y_t - y_t^*) + \lambda(r_t - r_t^*).$$

Equation 4.6 contends that the equilibrium exchange rate is explained by the differences between the two countries' money supplies, interest rates, and real incomes.

Under the monetary approach, the effect of parametric changes of these explanatory variables on exchange rates is given as follows. First, the model predicts that an increase in the domestic money supply causes an increase in domestic prices proportionately and hence, through purchasing power parity, leads to a depreciation of the domestic currency. The coefficient of $(m_t - m_t^*)$ is expected to be 1.

Second, the relationship between exchange rates and the relative real incomes, in contrast to the balance-of-payments approach, is negative; that is, $-\phi < 0$. The reason is that an increase in domestic real income causes excess demand for money balances that, without changes in money supply, can be fulfilled only by a decrease in domestic prices. Again, through purchasing power parity the reduction in prices results in an appreciation of the domestic currency.

Third, the model predicts that a higher interest rate differential causes a decrease in the demand for domestic money, leading to a domestic currency depreciation. Thus, the coefficient of the interest rate differential should be positive.

The validity of the monetary model hangs on the realism of four underlying assumptions. First, researchers in international finance have often criticized the flexible price approach, since purchasing power parity does not hold in the short run. Second, eq. 4.6 does not explicitly incorporate expectations and, hence, the model fails to capture the dynamic characteristics of exchange rate behavior. Such dynamic characteristics are the subject of Chapter 5. Third, to some extent the money supplies and the interest rates are endogenous, depending on the monetary operating regimes and banking behavior. The monetary approach does not explicitly make this distinction. Fourth, domestic and foreign bonds are assumed to be perfect substitutes. Thus, the interest rate differential is offset by the expected change in exchange rates as implied by the international Fisher condition (see Chapter 3); that is,

4.7 $$s_{t+1}^e - s_t = r_t - r_t^*,$$

where s_{t+1}^e is the expected exchange rate at time $t + 1$ based on the information available at time t. This view ignores the possibilities of market segmentation and international diversification of portfolios.

Monetary Approach: Sticky Price Version

Two assumptions are revised in the sticky price version (Keynesian) of the monetary approach. First, each nation's money supply is endogenous in the sense that it is positively related to the market rate of interest. This alters the money market equilibrium conditions:

4.8 $$m_t + \delta r_t = p_t + \phi y_t - \lambda r_t,$$

4.9 $$m_t^* + \delta r_t^* = p_t^* + \phi y_t^* - \lambda r_t^*,$$

where m_t and m_t^* are exogenous components of money supply. The second term on the left-hand side of eqs. 4.8 and 4.9 captures the endogenous argument that the money supplies are sensitive to interest rates. The right-hand sides of the equations are the money demand components, as we specified earlier.

Second, the assumption of flexible prices is replaced by the one with sticky prices. Thus, purchasing power parity can hold only in the long run,

4.10
$$s_t' = p_t - p_t^*,$$

where a prime symbol denotes long-run equilibrium.

In the short run, it is assumed that the uncovered interest rate parity theorem, as represented by eq. 4.7, holds. However, under the sticky version of the monetary approach, the expectation of the exchange rate change is assumed to obey the following scheme:

4.11
$$s_{t+1}^e - s_t = \theta(s_t' - s_t) + (\pi_t^e - \pi_t^{e*}).$$

Equation 4.11 says that if the spot rate is below (above) the long-run equilibrium level, the exchange rate is expected to depreciate (appreciate). In addition, the expected inflation differential $(\pi_t - \pi_t^*)$ leads to expected currency depreciation. Thus, the sticky version attempts to account for market expectations by incorporating the information from market equilibrium as well as the effect from the inflation expectations. Combining eqs. 4.11 and 4.7 implies that the deviation of the current spot rate from the equilibrium rate is due to the real interest rate differential (Frankel 1979). Thus,

4.12
$$s_t - s_t' = -1/\theta[(r_t - \pi_t^e) - (r_t^* - \pi_t^{e*})].$$

The effect of monetary policy on exchange rate movements can be seen in eq. 4.12. For instance, a tight monetary policy increases the real interest rate differential, attracts an incipient capital inflow, and appreciates the domestic currency above its equilibrium level.

Putting eqs. 4.8 through 4.10 and 4.12 together, we obtain:[3]

4.13
$$s_t = (m_t - m_t^*) - \phi(y_t - y_t^*) + (\delta + \lambda - 1/\theta)(r_t - r_t^*) + (1/\theta)(\pi_t^e - \pi_t^{e*}).$$

Under the sticky version, the coefficients of the money supply and the inflation expectations are positive, and that of the real income continues to be negative. However, the coefficient of the interest rate bears an ambiguous sign. Specifically, the coefficient on $(r_t - r_t^*)$ comprises three different components representing various channels through which the interest rate differential affects the exchange rate movements. To this extent, the sticky price version of the monetary approach is richer descriptively.

The δ and λ represent the two channels associated with adjustments in money supply and money demand in response to changes in interest

---

[3] As with the flexible price version, for the sticky price version eqs. 4.8 through 4.10 determine s_t'. The resulting s_t' together with eqs. 4.7 and 4.11 leads to eq. 4.13.

rates. In particular, a rise in the domestic interest rate encourages financial institutions to increase funds supplied to the money market. At the same time, a higher interest rate discourages the public from holding money balances. As a result, excess money balances emerge on the domestic market that lead to a currency depreciation. The third component, $-1/\theta$, captures the effect of capital movements on the exchange rate. A rise in the domestic interest rate means that it is more profitable for the investor to move funds into the country. This attracts capital inflow and brings about a domestic currency appreciation.

Ultimately, the coefficient of the interest rate differential under the sticky price version depends on a complicated interaction between the previously mentioned components. If the country is experiencing a highly inflationary process, the sign is expected to be positive. However, if the country has relatively low or comparable inflation rates and the capital markets are very sensitive to interest rate changes, the sign is expected to be negative since the real interest rate effect is predominant (Chiang 1984).

Equation 4.13 is slightly different from the specification of Frankel (1979 and 1984), in which he assumes money is exogenous and the interest rate differential in eq. 4.6 is equal to the expected inflation differential. In Frankel's treatment, the reduced form equation can be expressed as

4.14 $s_t = (m_t - m_t^*) - \phi(y_t - y_t^*) - (1/\theta)(r_t - r_t^*) + (\lambda + 1/\theta)(\pi_t^e - \pi_t^{e*}).$

Obviously, the coefficient of $(r_t - r_t^*)$ is unambiguously negative; the inflation expectations effect, λ, has been extracted and is collapsed into the coefficient of $(\pi_t^e - \pi_t^{e*})$. The difficulty is that in the empirical estimation the inflation expectations effect can never be extracted from $(r_t - r_t^*)$, unless the real interest rate differential can be precisely measured, which is very unlikely. The remaining question associated with this model is whether the domestic and foreign bonds are perfect substitutes, as they are in the flexible price version. The violation of this assumption means that the interest differential will differ from the expected rate of currency depreciation; the difference may be a term such as transaction costs, expectation errors, or a risk premium. But most financial analysts consider that the risk premium is a more reasonable explanation. Given the argument that internationally traded assets are imperfectly substitutable, we turn next to a discussion of the portfolio approach.

Portfolio Balance Approach

Since the monetary approach emphasizes the monetary phenomenon, other types of financial assets have been excluded from consideration. The portfolio balance approach highlights the role of wealth and views assets as imperfect substitutes. It is argued that any shock, in the form of a change in wealth, produces a wealth effect, which is an increase in the demand for each financial asset, and a substitution effect, substituting a high-yield financial asset for the alternatives. As a result, the exchange rate and interest rates have to adjust to ensure portfolio equilibrium. As

the approach stands, the exchange rate and interest rates are determined simultaneously by the portfolio equilibrium conditions for asset
holders in each country.

The following four equations represent a simple version of the portfolio balance model proposed by Branson et al. (1977):

4.15
$$M_t = m(r_t, r_t^*)W_t,$$

4.16
$$B_t = b(r_t, r_t^*)W_t,$$

4.17
$$S_t F_t = f(r_t, r_t^*)W_t,$$

4.18
$$W_t = M_t + B_t + S_t B_t^*,$$

where an asterisk denotes the corresponding variable for the foreign
country. The model consists of three financial assets, which determine
two relative prices, an interest rate and the exchange rate. The demand
for each asset is assumed to be a fraction of wealth, W_t, that people wish
to hold in the form of domestic money, $m(r_t, r_t^*)$, domestic bonds,
$b(r_t, r_t^*)$, and foreign bonds, $f(r_t, r_t^*)$.[4] The desired proportions of these
financial assets are assumed to be positively related to their own rates of
returns and negatively to the cross-rates of returns. Equilibrium in these
markets requires that the existing supply of money, M_t, domestic
bonds, B_t, and foreign bonds evaluated in the domestic currency, $S_t F_t$,
equals the corresponding demand.

The financial portfolio makes up the total wealth, W_t, which is the
sum of the three assets as represented by eq. 4.18.[5] At each moment of
time, the existing stocks of these assets are fixed and the domestic interest rate and exchange rate must adjust so that the assets are willingly
held by investors. However, the stocks of financial assets may change
over time. Bond-financed government deficits increase the supply of
domestic government bonds. Autonomous growth of money supply or
monetization of the government debts increases the stock of money
balances. Current account surpluses increase the net domestic holdings
of foreign bonds.

The exchange rate equation of the portfolio balance model is given by

4.19
$$S_t = S(M_t, B_t, F_t, r_t^*).$$

Suppose that the r_t^* is determined by the foreign asset markets; we can
write

4.20
$$r_t^* = g(M_t^*, B_t^*, F_t^*).$$

Substituting eq. 4.20 into 4.19 yields

4.21
$$S_t = S(M_t, B_t, F_t, M_t^*, B_t^*, F_t^*).$$

Equations 4.19 and 4.21 specify the relationship between exchange
rates and assets supplies. The effects of changes in assets' stocks on
exchange rates are considered in order.

---

[4] In this model, the domestic money does not explicitly earn positive financial yields.
[5] With this constraint, if two of the markets are in equilibrium, by Walras' law, the third
market must also be in equilibrium.

First, consider an expansionary monetary policy in the form of an exogenous increase in money supply. This means an equal increase in wealth. The wealth effect leads to excess demand for both domestic and foreign bonds. With given foreign interest rates, excess demand for domestic bonds would raise their price and lower the domestic interest rate. The excess demand for foreign bonds results in increases in the demand for foreign currency, leading to a depreciation of the domestic currency.

Second, the effect of changes in domestic bonds on the exchange rate is ambiguous. Particularly, an increase in domestic government bonds, through the wealth effect, would increase the excess demand for foreign bonds and, in turn, the foreign currency, leading to a depreciation of the domestic currency. On the other hand, a higher interest rate due to an increase in government debt would make foreign bonds less attractive. If this substitution effect dominates the wealth effect, the domestic currency appreciates.

Third, an increase in net holdings of foreign bonds induced by a current account surplus would increase the demand for domestic assets via the wealth effect. The results would be lower domestic interest rates and an exchange rate depreciation.

The contribution of the portfolio balance approach is to direct the focal point from a single-asset approach (money) to the multi-asset dimension. Thus, the analysis of exchange rate behavior can be integrated with other financial assets, such as bonds and stocks. Moreover, since the net holdings of foreign assets are explicitly included in the approach, it allows current account imbalances to affect the exchange rate. Therefore, it can be argued that the portfolio balance model contains the special features provided by the monetary approach and the balance-of-payments approach.

EMPIRICAL EVIDENCE

We provide here a summary and analysis of empirical evidence regarding the three approaches to determining exchange rates described earlier. In some cases the evidence is, unfortunately, a bit dated. Overall, the evidence for each approach is somewhat mixed, due to either ambiguous coefficients or data limitations.

Balance-of-Payments Model: Evidence

To estimate the behavior of the balance-of-payments approach, eq. 4.2 is rewritten in regression form as

4.22 $s_t = \beta_0 + \beta_1(p_t - p_t^*) + \beta_2(y_t - y_t^*) + \beta_3(r_t - r_t^*) + \varepsilon_t,$

where the estimated coefficients are expected to be $\beta_1 > 0$, $\beta_2 > 0$, and $\beta_3 < 0$. The model has been estimated by using Canadian dollar/U.S.

dollar exchange rates for the period 1971.Q1–1982.Q1. The estimated result by Pearce (1983) is

$$s_t = 0.143 + 0.347(p_t - p_t^*) - 1.155(y_t - y_t^*) - 0.004(r_t - r_t^*)$$
$$\quad (0.32) \quad (1.24) \qquad\qquad (-1.16) \qquad\qquad (-1.82)$$

$$R^2 = 0.14 \qquad SEE = 0.015 \qquad D.W. = 1.41 \qquad \rho = 0.99$$

where the starred variable refers to the United States, the exchange rate is defined as the number of Canadian dollars per U.S. dollar, and the t-statistics are given in parentheses.

Subject to certain econometric issues, the estimated result is not very encouraging. Both the price variable and the interest rate have the anticipated sign. However, the real output variable bears the wrong sign. Looking at the t-statistics, none of the explanatory variables are significant at the 5% level. This, along with the low explanatory power associated with the R^2, indicates that the balance-of-payments theory cannot be supported by the data. The result suggests that an alternative theory may be called for to interpret the data.

Monetary Approach: Evidence

The estimated form of the monetary approach can be written as

4.23
$$s_t = \beta_0 + \beta_1(m_t - m_t^*) + \beta_2(y_t - y_t^*) + \beta_3(r_t - r_t^*) + \beta_4(\pi_t^e - \pi_t^{e*}) + \varepsilon_t$$

where the coefficients follow the restriction $\beta_1 > 0$, $\beta_2 < 0$, $\beta_3 = ?$, $\beta_4 > 0$. The ambiguous sign of β_3 reflects the different information content of the interest rate differential in the monetary approach; recall that β_3 is positive in eq. 4.6, negative in 4.14, and bears an ambiguous sign in 4.13.

Exhibit 4.2 summarizes the empirical results of estimating eq. 4.23 for the period January 1975 to December 1979 (Chiang 1981). The data apply to the United Kingdom, Canada, France, West Germany, Italy, and the Netherlands. The exchange rate is defined as the national currency per U.S. dollar, and the United States is treated as the foreign country (starred variable) in the estimation.

The results given in Exhibit 4.2 indicate that the money supply differential coefficients for the six countries all have the correct signs and are statistically significant for Canada, France, and Italy. The coefficients are not significant for the United Kingdom, the Netherlands and West Germany. These findings provide some support for the hypothesis that a relative rise in the money supply results in a depreciation of the exchange rate.

With the exception of the Netherlands, the test also produces evidence to support the second hypothesis of the monetary model, namely that a relative rise in real output would bring about an appreciation of domestic currency, although only the coefficients for the United Kingdom and Italy are statistically significant.

Exhibit 4.2

Estimation of Exchange Rate
Equation (with m_2): Monthly,
1975/1–1979/12[a]

Constant	Money Supply (m_2)[b] $m_t - m_t^*$	Real Income $y_t - y_t^*$	Short-term Interest Rate $r_t - r_t^*$	Inflation Rate $\pi_t^e - \pi_t^{e^*}$	Country	R^2	$F(1.55)$	D.W.
−7.0336 (−5.4872)[c]	0.3153 (0.9881)	−1.5327 (−10.8915)	−0.0018 (−0.5051)	0.0406 (11.5632)	U.K.	0.8000	54.9866	1.0146
−3.5203 (−14.8682)	0.4295 (3.6978)	−0.033 (−0.1648)	−0.0206 (−5.5860)	−0.0062 (−1.3287)	Canada	0.9010	125.1950	0.5802
−3.2808 (−135.9750)	0.5777 (4.4391)	−0.0723 (−0.3882)	−0.0321 (−1.4000)	0.0671 (2.8956)	France	0.7471	40.6211	1.0443
0.7394 (11.0747)	0.1914 (0.5362)	−0.2414 (−0.8295)	−0.0097 (−1.5335)	0.0639 (9.6511)	Germany	0.8729	94.4578	0.7719
−1.1453 (−6.7395)	0.5821 (18.1916)	−0.2877 (−2.7730)	0.1075 (6.7074)	0.0027 (0.6628)	Italy	0.9277	176.4950	1.0694
−1.3717 (3.8973)	0.3027 (1.5394)	0.6295 (2.2356)	−0.0137 (−4.5270)	0.0734 (5.8980)	Netherlands	0.7508	41.4196	0.4295

SOURCE: Chiang (1981)

[a] The data for the United Kingdom, Canada, France, and Italy are taken from *Main Economic Indicators* (OECD), 1975–1979. The data for the United States, West Germany, and the Netherlands are taken from *International Financial Statistics* (IFS), 1975–1979.
[b] The term m_2 is a broad definition of money supply.
[c] The t-statistics are in parentheses beneath the estimated coefficients.

Turning to the coefficient on the short-term interest rate differential, we find the signs are diverse. Specifically, Italy has a positive sign, but the rest of the countries have a negative sign. This indicates that neither the balance-of-payments view nor the monetarist view can be fully justified by the data. As we discussed earlier, the positive sign for Italy may be interpreted by the dominance of an inflation expectation effect. This is consistent with an economy like that of Italy, which has experienced relatively greater inflationary pressure. The negative sign for the rest of countries can be explained by the dominance of the portfolio balance effect; a higher interest rate differential attracts capital inflow and brings about the appreciation of the domestic currency.

The estimation presented in Exhibit 4.2 also includes the inflation rate differential; the long-term interest rate differential is used as a proxy for measuring the inflation rate differential. The test results show that the estimated coefficient is positive, which is consistent with the theoretical expectation. The exception is Canada, for which the sign is negative. This may be because the United States and Canada have parallel inflation rates and a high degree of capital mobility.

Extending the data to July 1981, a similar set of countries were also examined by Frankel (1984). In his sample, Japan was added and the Netherlands and Italy were removed. As shown in Exhibit 4.3, the results reported by Frankel lend very little support to the monetary model. Among all the countries, only France continually produces all coefficients consistent with the hypothesized signs. The short-term interest rate differentials now all have negative signs consistent with the

Country	Constant	$m_t - m_t^*$	$y_t - y_t^*$	$\pi_t^e - \pi_t^{e^*}$	$r_t - r_t^*$	Sample	ρ	s.e.r.
Germany	0.80	−0.05	0.07	1.34	−0.61[a]	90	0.95	0.033
	(0.21)	(0.33)	(0.22)	(0.82)	(0.27)			
	1.37	1.00	0.12	1.59	−0.62[a]		0.96	0.034
	(0.12)	(Constrained)	(0.23)	(0.86)	(0.28)			
France	1.34	0.17	−0.23	2.41[a]	−0.24	87	0.81	0.029
	(0.07)	(0.17)	(0.13)	(0.69)	(0.24)			
	1.07	1.00	−0.16	1.53	−0.28		0.90	0.032
	(0.06)	(Constrained)	(0.14)	(0.83)	(0.27)			
United Kingdom	−0.20	0.12	−0.13	−0.06	−0.28	89	0.97	0.029
	(0.61)	(0.22)	(0.17)	(0.05)	(0.21)			
	2.10	1.00	−0.09	−0.07	−0.24		0.98	0.032
	(0.23)	(Constrained)	(0.18)	(0.05)	(0.22)			
Japan	4.39	0.21	0.27	0.53	−0.40	89	0.98	0.031
	(1.00)	(0.20)	(0.23)	(0.33)	(0.27)			
	0.44	1.00	0.60[b]	0.73[a]	−0.61[a]		0.98	0.034
	(0.17)	(Constrained)	(0.23)	(0.36)	(0.29)			
Canada	0.44	0.08	0.18	−0.48	−0.27	89	0.98	0.014
	(0.32)	(0.12)	(0.12)	(0.32)	(0.17)			
	2.85	1.00	0.18	−0.31	−0.29		0.99	0.018
	(0.15)	(Constrained)	(0.15)	(0.41)	(0.22)			

SOURCE: Frankel (1984). Used with permission.

[a] Significant at the 95% level and of the correct sign

[b] Significant at the 95% level and of the incorrect sign (standard errors in parentheses)

Technique: Cochrane-Orcutt

Samples: 90 = 2/74–7/81, 87 = 2/74–4/81, 89 = 2/74–6/81

Exhibit 4.3

Monetary Equation (Dependent Variable: Log of Exchange Rate per United States Dollar)

sticky price version. But the other three variables do not have consistent signs. Furthermore, most of the estimated coefficients do not have a high degree of significance. The evidence, somewhat contrary to Frenkel and Johnson (1978) and Chiang (1981), indicates that the monetary approach cannot perform well for the data extending to the early 1980s.[6]

---

[6] On the basis of this disturbing evidence, we would question how much and to what extent the monetary model can be reliably used. It appears that we must reevaluate the monetary model by considering theoretical modifications, institutional changes, and financial market developments. First, we consider changes in the terms of trade due to the shocks of the oil embargo and rapid growth in the newly industrialized countries. The persistent deviations of the purchasing power parity in the long run lead to persistent disparity in the current accounts. Thus, some research suggests that the current accounts for two trading nations (Dornbusch 1978) or the real exchange rate (Hooper and Morton 1982) should be an additional argument to be included in the monetary equation. The second consideration is to look into aspects of institutional changes and financial markets developments. We have witnessed the change of federal operating procedures from the interest rate target to the monetary target (October 1979). Similarly, the implementation of the Monetary Control Act of 1980 caused the unpredictable movement of interest rates, shifting the velocity. To take this factor into account, it is natural to add the shift terms of the velocity into the equation. However, as Frankel (1984) observes, "shifts in money demand are more a manifestation that an explanation for the failure of the monetary models."

Exhibit 4.4

Empirical Evidence on Portfolio
Balance Model

$$S_t(\text{US\$/DM}) = -4.85 - 0.618M_t^{WG} + 0.09M_t^{US} + 0.676F_t^{WG} - 0.398F_t^{US}$$
$$\phantom{S_t(\text{US\$/DM}) = } (-1.0)\ (-1.7) \quad\quad (2.8)^* \quad\quad (1.7) \quad\quad (-1.9)$$
$$\rho = 0.87 \quad R^2 = 0.94 \quad \text{D.W.} = 1.35$$

$$S_t(\text{US\$/CA\$}) = 1.205 - 0.140M_t^{CA} + 0.006B_t^{CA} - 0.435(10^{-5})F_t^{CA} - 0.0018r_t^{US}$$
$$\phantom{S_t(\text{US\$/CA\$}) = } (14.36)^*\ (1.11) \quad\quad (2.55)^* \quad\quad (-1.38) \quad\quad\quad (-0.93)$$
$$\rho = 0.90 \quad R^2 = 0.96 \quad \text{D.W.} = 1.35$$

$$S_t(\text{US\$/CA\$}) = 1.193 + 0.644(10^{-3})M_t^{US} - 0.0317M_t^{CA} - 0.456(10^{-3})B_t^{US}$$
$$\phantom{S_t(\text{US\$/CA\$}) = } (13.88)^*\ (0.86) \quad\quad\quad (-2.12)^* \quad\quad (-0.16)$$
$$ -0.224(10^{-3})^\dagger B_t^{CA} + 0.395(10^{-5})^\dagger F_t^{US,P} - 0.360(10^{-4})F_t^{US,G}$$
$$ (-0.61) \quad\quad\quad (2.35)^* \quad\quad\quad (-1.54)$$
$$ + 0.916(10^{-6})F_t^{CA,P} + 0.616(10^{-5})F_t^{CA,G}$$
$$ (0.51) \quad\quad\quad\quad (0.02)$$
$$\rho = 0.86 \quad R^2 = 0.96 \quad \text{D.W.} = 2.24$$

SOURCE: Branson et al. (1977) and Bisignano and Hoover (1982). Used with permission.

Notes: a. The t-statistics are in parentheses.
         b. F_t in the first two equations is the net private international investment positions against the rest of the world; $F_t^{j,P}(F_t^{j,G})$ is country j's private holdings of foreign private (government) debt; US = United States, CA = Canada; WG = West Germany.
         c. An asterisk (*) indicates significant at the 5% level; a dagger (†) indicates the estimator bears a wrong sign.

Portfolio Balance Approach: Evidence

Empirical estimations of the portfolio balance model are based on the following regression forms:

4.24 $$S_t = \beta_0 + \beta_1 M_t + \beta_2 B_t + \beta_3 F_t + \beta_4 r_t^* + \varepsilon_t,$$

where $$\beta_1 > 0, \beta_2 = ?, \beta_3 < 0, \beta_4 > 0;$$

4.25 $$S_t = \beta_0 + \beta_1 M_t + \beta_2 M_t^* + \beta_3 B_t + \beta_4 B_t^* + \beta_5 F_t + \beta_6 F_t^* + \varepsilon_t,$$

where S_t is defined as units of domestic currency per unit of foreign currency. The coefficients of eq. 4.25 have the anticipated signs: $\beta_1 > 0$, $\beta_2 < 0, \beta_3 = ?, \beta_4 = ?, \beta_5 < 0, \beta_6 > 0$. If we assume that the substitutability of domestic and foreign bonds is greater than the substitutability of domestic bonds and money, we will have the signs $\beta_3 < 0$ and $\beta_4 > 0$.

The empirical results are summarized in Exhibit 4.4. Unlike the previous treatments in estimating the balance-of-payments and monetary approaches, in Exhibit 4.4 the United States is the domestic country. The evidence (Branson et al. 1977) shows that only the coefficient for the United States money supply is significant, although the coefficients have the anticipated signs. Notice that the variables B_t and B_t^* were excluded from the estimated equation.

Similar equations were estimated for the US\$/CA\$ rate by Bisignano and Hoover (1982). The results are less satisfactory; some coefficients even bear the wrong sign. Thus, the model cannot be supported by the data.

There could be several reasons for the lack of success of the portfolio balance approach. First, an accurate measure of data is a main problem, especially the lack of consistency in constructing the bilateral financial asset variables. Second, because of the emphasis on the financial asset aspect in the exchange rate determination, key factors such as relative prices and the real sector are excluded from the model. Further, the expectations have not explicitly been incorporated into the model. If there are any, expectations must be static. Clearly, the static expectations hypothesis is incapable of explaining dynamic exchange rate behavior, as discussed further in Chapter 5.

SUMMARY

The exchange rate is the relative price of two countries' currencies. The fundamental factors most likely to determine the value of a country's currency are significantly related to the relative money supplies, relative real incomes, relative prices, differences in inflation, the interest rate differentials, and the relative asset supplies and demands in the two national economies. We organized these arguments as three exchange rate theories: the balance-of-payments approach, the monetary approach, and the portfolio balance approach.

The balance-of-payments approach emphasizes the flow concept. The exchange rate is determined by the flow supply and demand conditions in the foreign exchange market. The equilibrium exchange rate is determined by the overall balance, defined as the sum of current account and capital account balances. Since (a) the current account is dependent on relative prices and relative real incomes, and (b) capital flows are governed by relative interest rates and exchange rate expectations, we can say that the exchange rate, given expectations, is determined by relative prices, relative real incomes, and interest rate differentials. Exchange rate movements may result from a parametric change in these determinants, or from an artificial intervention by governments. Overall, the empirical evidence regarding this approach is less satisfactory.

The monetary approach stresses the monetary factors underlying the money demand and money supply functions as main determinants of exchange rate movements. According to this approach, the exchange rate is determined by the relative money supplies, relative real incomes, interest rate differentials, and differences in inflation rates in the two national economies. The empirical evidence from the 1970s confirms the monetary theory. However, the experience from the early 1980s cannot support the theory. The poor performance during this period may be caused by the instability of the money demand equation or the misspecification of the model.

We also discussed the portfolio balance approach, which highlights the role of the stock demand and supply of financial assets traded in international markets. By this perspective, the exchange rate is determined through the relative supply and demand of financial assets to be included in the portfolio. Owing to the limitations of reliable data available to researchers, no strong evidence has been presented to support this approach.

Questions and Problems

1. Define the forward premium and forward discount. Explain why the forward prices are not generally equal to the spot prices.

2. Look at Exhibit 4.1. Calculate the 180-forward premium (or discount) for Japanese yen and pound sterling on Thursday, 28 June 1990.

3. Given the information derived from the previous problem, what would you expect the 180-day forward rate between the Japanese yen and the pound sterling to be?

4. Indicate the most likely effects of the following independent events on the exchange rates. Be prepared to justify your opinions.
   (a) An increase of tariffs on the imported goods.
   (b) An expected decline in value of the U.S. dollar.
   (c) An expected change in the money target growth rate from 2.5–5.5% to 4.8–8.0%.
   (d) Government removal of all legal restrictions on banks and nonbank financial intermediaries.

5. Discuss the relationship between the exchange rate and the nominal interest rate differential for the two trading nations. Will a higher interest rate in the United States cause a depreciation of the U.S. dollar? Explain.

6. It has been argued that higher inflation expectations will lead to a depreciation of the domestic currency. Will currency depreciation cause higher inflation expectations? Explain.

7. How do you detect the bilateral causality for the relationship between inflation and the exchange rate in an empirical context?

8. Milton Friedman has long advocated a constant money growth rule. What is the implication of Friedman's monetary rule on exchange rate movements?

9. Assume the exchange rate equation is represented by the following expression:

   4.26 $$s_t = \psi\,(m_t - m_t^*) + \phi(y_t - y_t^*) + \lambda(r_t - r_t^*) + \xi(x_t - x_t^*)$$

   where ψ, ϕ, λ, and ξ are constant coefficients, and x_t represents other potential exogenous variables.
   (a) What is the sign of ψ, ϕ, λ, and ξ (positive or negative)?
   (b) What variables could x_t (and x_t^*) represent? Explain.

10. Given the information provided in the previous question, how would eq. 4.26 be tested under alternative operating procedures conducted by the Fed?

11. What are the limitations of the monetary approach to the determination of exchange rates?

12. Use the monthly data spanning the period from July 1982 through June 1990 to replicate the monetary model designated by eq. 4.23. Compare and discuss your results with those in Exhibits 4.2 and 4.3.

References

Bilson, J. "Rational Expectations and the Exchange Rate." In *The Economics of Exchange Rates*, eds. Jacob A. Frenkel and Harry G. Johnson, 75–96. Reading, Mass.: Addison-Wesley, 1978.

Bilson, J., and R. Marston (eds.). *Exchange Rate Theory and Practice*. Chicago: The University of Chicago Press, 1984, 239–59.

Bisignano, J., and K. Hoover. "Some Suggested Improvements to a Simple Portfolio Balance Model of Exchange Rate Determination with Special Reference to the U.S. Dollar/Canadian Dollar Rate." *Weltwirschaftliches Archiv,* heft 1 (1982): 19–37.

Branson, W., H. Halttunen, and P. Masson. "Exchange Rates in the Short Run." *European Economic Review* 10 (December 1977): 303–24.

Chiang, T. *Interest Rates, Price Expectations, and Exchange Rate Movements—A Monetary Analysis.* Unpublished Ph.D. dissertation, Pennsylvania State University (May 1981).

————. "On the Relationship between the Exchange Rate and the Interest Rate Differential in Monetary Models." *Quarterly Review of Economic and Business* 24, no. 3 (Autumn 1984): 49–57.

Dornbusch, R. "Expectations and Exchange Rate Dynamics." *Journal of Political Economy* 84 (December 1976): 1161–76.

Dornbusch, R. "Monetary Policy under Exchange-Rate Flexibility." *Federal Reserve Bank of Boston Conference Series,* no. 20, 90–122. Boston: Federal Reserve Bank of Boston, October 1978.

Frankel, J. "On the Mark: A Theory of Floating Exchange Rates Based on Real Interest Differentials." *American Economic Review* 69 (September 1979): 610–22.

Frankel, J. "Tests of Monetary and Portfolio Balance Models of Exchange Rate Determination." In *Exchange Rate Theory and Practice,* eds. John F. O. Bilson and Richard C. Marston, Chicago: The University of Chicago Press, (1984), 239–59.

Frenkel, J., and H. Johnson, eds. *The Economics of Exchange Rates.* Reading, Mass.: Addison-Wesley, 1978.

Frenkel, J., and A. Razin. "The Mundell-Fleming Model a Quarter Century Later: A Unified Exposition." *IMF Staff Papers* vol. 34, no. 4 (December 1987): 567–620.

Hooper, P., and J. Morton. "Fluctuations in the Dollars: A Model of Nominal and Real Exchange Rate Determination." *Journal of International Money and Finance* vol. 1, no. 1 (April 1982): 39–56.

Mundell, R. "The Monetary Dynamics of International Adjustment Under Fixed and Flexible Exchange Rates." *Quarterly Journal of Economics* vol. 74 (May 1960): 227–57.

Mussa, M. "The Exchange Rate, the Balance of Payments, and Monetary Policy Under a Regime of Controlled Floating." *Scandinavian Journal of Economics* vol. 78, no. 78 (May 1976): 229–48.

Pearce, D. "Alternative Views of Exchange-Rate Determination." *Economic Review,* (Federal Reserve Bank of Kansas City) (February 1983): 16–30.

FOREIGN EXCHANGE MARKETS: EFFICIENCY, EXPECTATIONS, AND RISK

In this chapter we discuss the important aspects of efficiency, expectations, and risk in the foreign exchange market. An understanding of these issues is important to government policymakers, multinational financial managers, and international investors. The importance to government policymakers stems from their need to design an appropriate macro policy for achieving the goal of efficient resource allocation. This topic is also important to international investors and multinational financial managers because of their need to assess foreign asset returns and risks in order to make optimal portfolio decisions.

We first discuss the efficient market hypothesis as applied to both the spot and forward markets. Second, we present several expectations hypotheses and discuss their implications for the foreign exchange market. Finally, we describe the issue of the risk premium and explain the sources of risk in the forward foreign exchange market.

EFFICIENT MARKETS HYPOTHESIS

"An *efficient market* is one where all new information is quickly understood by market participants and becomes immediately incorporated into market prices" (Samuelson and Nordhaus 1985). The *efficient markets hypothesis* has been extensively developed in the domestic finance literature (Fama 1970). Its importance is due to the fact that if the market is efficient, the current price of an asset will fully reflect available information with regard to its valuation. The prices of financial assets thus provide signals for portfolio allocation.

The notion of market efficiency is usually associated with the rationality of market expectations. One way to examine this issue is to determine whether market participants could systematically earn an excess profit. Following Fama (1970), Levich (1985), and Mishkin (1983), we write

5.1 $$E[x_{t+1} - x^e_{t+1} \mid \Omega_t] = 0,$$

where x^e_{t+1} is the expectation derived from the one-period-ahead forecast of the actual value x_{t+1}, and E is the expectations operator conditioned on the information set Ω_t available at the end of period t. If we designate x_{t+1} as series of asset returns, and x^e_{t+1} as market expectations of these returns, eq. 5.1 implies that there are no systematic unexploited profits over time.

If there are systematic forecast errors that may be detected or observed by investors, the information presumably would be incorporated into the forecast process. The investor inspects the forecast errors, $x_{t+1} - x^e_{t+1}$, to see whether there are unexploited patterns in the form of serial correlations or empirical regularities that may be used to improve his or her investment strategy. As a result, the systematic information will be exploited and the resulting error becomes "white noise." Thus, to satisfy the efficiency condition (5.1), we can argue that an optimal forecast of asset prices is consistent with rational expectations behavior.

In the foreign exchange markets, the efficient markets hypothesis has been applied to both the spot and forward markets. Equation 5.1 can be used to express

5.2 $$E[s_{t+1} - s^e_{t+1} \mid \Omega_t] = 0,$$

where s_{t+1} and s^e_{t+1} are, respectively, the spot rate and the expected spot rate based on the information available at time t. Equation 5.2 states that the expectations errors will be zero on average, and that no excess profits can be exploited by observing serial correlation in the foreign exchange markets. Now the point is how to form the optimal forecast value that results in residuals displaying no informational content. Let us consider the following three efficient markets hypotheses.

Random-Walk Hypothesis

In practice, the investor may not use all the information in Ω_t. On the basis of experience, empirical regularities, market conditions, and information costs, a rational investor may use a smaller set of information, say I_t, to form exchange rate expectations. One simple approach to forming expectations is to use the information revealed in the spot market. Economists (Mussa 1979; Meese and Rogoff 1983; Huang 1984; Chiang 1986) have long observed that the exchange rate follows a *random-walk* process, meaning that the expected one-period-ahead exchange rate, s^e_{t+1}, is also s_t.[1] It follows that

5.3 $$s^e_{t+1} = s_t.$$

Substituting this relationship into eq. 5.2, we obtain

5.4 $$E[s_{t+1} - s_t \mid I_t] = 0.$$

This equation suggests that if the market is efficient, the current price of a currency will reflect all the available information. The unexpected

---

[1] The random walk process also implies that $s^e_{t+j} = s_t$ for $j = 1, 2, \ldots, J$.

change in the spot rate, $s_{t+1} - s_t$, is essentially caused by the random shock, ε_{t+1}, which hits the market between time t and time $t + 1$. Market rationality suggests that the investor finds no particular pattern from the history of ε_{t+1}.

The random-walk hypothesis provides a good economic reason to explain the erratic behavior of exchange rate movements. Specifically, exchange rates respond to surprises, to news. But surprises are unpredictable. Because exchange rates respond sensitively to the unexpected events that randomly hit markets, exchange rates themselves also move randomly. This is the nature of market efficiency.

Unbiased Forward Rate Hypothesis

An alternative scheme to measure the expected exchange rate is to use the information reflected in the forward exchange rate. The forward rate has been widely viewed as an unbiased predictor of the future spot rate (the unbiased forward rate hypothesis). This proposition is derived from an efficient arbitrage activity by investors. For arbitrage to occur, investors must merely prefer more wealth to less and are in a position of risk neutral.

The hypothesis can be illustrated by the following scenarios. Assume that the 30-day forward rate for the British pound is currently set at $1.735; then the natural logarithm is $f_t = 0.551$. If market participants form an expectation that the future spot rate is 30 days will be $1.800 per pound—that is, $s^e_{t+1} = 0.588$ (in the natural logarithm)—no one would sell the pound in a 30-day forward contract. On the other hand, if the expectation of the future spot rate in 30 days is $1.700—that is, $s^e_{t+1} = 0.531$—then no one would enter a 30-day forward contract to buy pounds sterling, since it would be cheaper to make the transaction in the future spot market. Thus, this rationality leads to the transaction being settled at the point where the forward rate is equal to the expectation of the future spot rate. In symbols, we express this idea as

5.5
$$s^e_{t+1} = f_t$$

Substituting eq. 5.5 into 5.2 yields

5.6
$$E[s_{t+1} - f_t \mid I_t] = 0.$$

Equation 5.6 states that the forecast errors resulting from using forward rates will equal zero on average. A nonzero value of $E[s_{t+1} - f_t \mid I_t]$ suggests the rejection of the unbiased forward rate hypothesis. The sources of rejection may be attributable to nonnegligible transaction costs associated with arbitrage, a risk premium if investors are not risk-neutral, or a specification error if the model is not well specified. In other words, the validity of the unbiased forward rate hypothesis implies that the investor is risk-neutral, transaction costs are insignificant, and the arrival of important informational events is random.

Composite Efficiency Hypothesis

The composite efficiency hypothesis combines the merits of the previous two hypotheses. It posits that the expectation of the future spot rate is a weighted average of the current spot rate and the forward rate. It can be specified as

5.7 $s^e_{t+1} = \omega s_t + (1 - \omega) f_t.$

This formulation is based on the following reasoning. First, the information contained in s_t reflects current market conditions. From the weak-form viewpoint of market efficiency (Fama 1970), s_t summarizes all historical information that affects exchange rates. Second, from the rational expectations perspective, the forward rate, f_t, reflects the information concerning factors that are expected to determine future exchange rates. Thus, the composite efficiency hypothesis contains two sets of information involving the future and past elements governing exchange rate movements.

Empirical Evidence on Market Efficiency

To provide some evidence concerning the market efficiency hypothesis, we employ exchange rates for the Canadian dollar, French franc, German mark, and British (U.K.) pound. The data are nonoverlapping monthly observations of the spot and 1-month-forward exchange rates. The sample spans the period January 1974 through August 1983.[2] Both spot and forward exchange rates are defined as the U.S. dollar price of a unit of foreign exchange and are expressed as natural logarithms.

To test the nature of market efficiency, we begin with an examination of the time series characteristics of the various exchange rates. The first step is to investigate their serial dependency. To this end we calculate the autocorrelation functions (ACF) for spot rate changes (in logarithms) from 1- through 12-month lags for the following three periods: the full-sample period (January 1974–August 1983) and two subsample periods (January 1974–September 1979 and October 1979–August 1983). The standard formula for calculating coefficients is

5.8 $\rho_k = \left[\sum_{t}^{n-k} (y_t y_{t+k})\right] \bigg/ \left[\sum_{t}^{n} (y_t)^2\right],$

where ρ_k is the estimated autocorrelation coefficient with kth lag of y_t, and y_t is defined as the deviation of the change of the natural logarithm of spot rates from its mean value. Empirically, detection of serial correlations is accomplished by examining the significance of each ρ_k using a t-statistic, or by investigating the joint randomness of the residuals using a Q-statistic, or both.[3]

These serial correlation tests for the three sample periods are reported in Exhibit 5.1. With the exception of the higher-order lags for the Canadian dollar, the estimated autocorrelation coefficients in most cases are quite small in absolute magnitude and are statistically insignificant at the 5% level.

---

[2] All the data, taken from the data bank of Data Resources, Inc., are measured at the end of the month.
[3] An early version of Q is called the Box-Pierce statistic, and the later version is called the Ljung-Box statistic.

Exhibit 5.1 Autocorrelations, Means, and Standard Deviations of Exchange Rates

ACF	1974.01–1983.08				1974.01–1979.09				1979.10–1983.08			
	Can. Dollar	French Franc	Deutsche Mark	U.K. Pound	Can. Dollar	French Franc	Deutsche Mark	U.K. Pound	Can. Dollar	French Franc	Deutsche Mark	U.K. Pound
ρ_1	−0.125	−0.069	−0.018	0.070	−0.055	−0.273	−0.158	0.101	−0.168	0.002	0.076	0.046
ρ_2	−0.175	0.139	0.103	0.101	−0.156	0.173	0.190	0.121	−0.227	−0.046	−0.096	0.104
ρ_3	0.104	0.082	−0.022	−0.025	0.167	0.023	−0.099	−0.028	0.052	−0.022	−0.077	0.038
ρ_4	0.011	0.087	−0.001	−0.076	0.069	0.134	−0.052	−0.049	−0.063	−0.082	−0.034	−0.130
ρ_5	0.111	0.041	−0.082	0.179	0.043	−0.044	−0.178	0.077	0.060	−0.048	−0.113	0.166
ρ_6	−0.101	0.008	−0.068	0.054	0.007	0.013	−0.131	0.110	−0.131	−0.049	−0.004	−0.060
ρ_7	−0.117	0.085	0.093	0.017	−0.094	−0.050	−0.067	0.007	−0.055	0.069	0.147	0.054
ρ_8	0.085	0.038	0.078	0.056	0.069	0.016	0.121	0.068	0.091	−0.070	−0.064	0.077
ρ_9	−0.022	−0.013	0.055	0.036	−0.113	−0.006	−0.011	0.135	0.009	−0.170	−0.235	−0.148
ρ_{10}	−0.024	0.077	0.119	0.107	−0.087	0.017	0.122	0.235	−0.059	−0.030	−0.022	−0.054
ρ_{11}	0.188	0.115	0.099	0.193	0.274*	0.070	0.054	0.105	0.100	−0.090	−0.066	0.086
ρ_{12}	−0.278*	0.004	−0.004	−0.010	−0.229	0.108	0.075	0.164	−0.151	−0.147	−0.209	−0.155
Mean ($\times 10^{-3}$)	−1.92	−4.07	0.26	−3.65	−2.30	3.17	6.87	−0.50	−0.89	−14.26	−8.79	−7.22
S.E. ($\times 10^{-3}$)	13.82	30.93	32.36	29.53	13.32	27.25	30.92	27.62	14.27	33.18	32.17	31.18
Q(12)	26.99	3.38	8.06	14.03	17.93	10.63	12.45	12.96	8.46	4.99	9.69	·7.32

Notes: a. One asterisk (*) denotes significance at the 0.05 level, and two asterisks (**) denote significance at the 0.10 level.
   b. ρ_k is the estimated autocorrelation function (ACF) at the kth lag for the first difference of spot rates ($s_{t+1} - s_t$).
   c. Q(12) is the Box-Pierce statistic, which is distributed as χ^2 with twelve degrees of freedom.
   d. All exchange rates are U.S. dollars per unit of foreign currency. All numbers are based on the logarithmic transformation of the original values.

The Box-Pierce Q-statistics for testing the randomness of the residuals indicate the same conclusion as that derived from the individual significance tests. Only for the case of the Canadian dollar can the hypothesis of the randomness of the residual autocorrelation be rejected at the 5% level. In that case the calculated Q-statistic (26.99) for the full-sample estimation is greater than the corresponding critical value. In general, there is no substantial difference between sample periods.

Next, we conduct significance tests for the efficient markets hypotheses. To do so, eqs. 5.3, 5.5, and 5.7 are rewritten in test form as

5.9
$$s_{t+1} = \beta_0 + \beta_1 s_t + \varepsilon_{t+1},$$

5.10
$$s_{t+1} = \beta_0 + \beta_2 f_t + \varepsilon_{t+1},$$

5.11
$$s_{t+1} = \beta_0 + \beta_1 s_t + \beta_2 f_t + \varepsilon_{t+1}.$$

Testing spot market efficiency involves a test of the joint hypothesis that $\beta_0 = 0$ and $\beta_1 = 1$ for eq. 5.9; for forward market efficiency the test is that $\beta_0 = 0$ and $\beta_2 = 1$ for eq. 5.10; and for composite market efficiency the test is that $\beta_0 = 0$ and $\beta_1 + \beta_2 = 1$ for eq. 5.11. In addition, the error terms in each case should not exhibit serial correlation. The regression estimations for eqs. 5.9 to 5.11 are presented in Exhibit 5.2; the corre-

Exhibit 5.2

Regression Estimates of the
Efficient Markets Hypothesis in the
Foreign Exchange Market

Country	β_0	β_1	β_2	R^2	D.W.	SEE
Canada	−0.0035	0.985*		0.975	2.212	0.0139
	(0.002)	(0.015)				
	[1.696]	[65.760]				
	−0.002		0.988*	0.973	2.132	0.0142
	(0.002)		(0.015)			
	[1.044]		[64.383]			
	−0.005*	2.108*	−1.127	0.975	2.148	0.0138
	(−0.002)	(0.815)	(0.818)			
	[2.15]	[2.585]	[1.377]			
France	0.028	1.019*		0.970	2.173	0.0310
	(0.027)	(0.017)				
	[1.031]	[60.684]				
	0.008		1.006*	0.968	1.987	0.0319
	(0.027)		(0.017)			
	[0.315]		[58.901]			
	−0.047	2.163*	−1.127	0.971	2.348	0.03078
	(−0.029)	(0.703)	(0.694)			
	[1.608]	[3.077]	[1.627]			
W. Germany	−0.026	0.967*		0.941	1.987	0.0324
	(0.018)	(0.023)				
	[1.408]	[42.485]				
	−0.038*		0.955*	0.941	1.946	0.0324
	(0.018)		(0.023)			
	[2.113]		[42.457]			
	−0.032	0.533	0.429	0.941	1.970	0.0325
	(0.021)	(0.835)	(0.825)			
	[1.478]	[0.638]	[0.520]			
U.K.	0.0027	0.991*		0.954	1.840	0.0298
	(0.014)	(0.020)				
	[0.192]	[48.651]				
	0.005		0.991*	0.952	1.746	0.0305
	(0.014)		(0.021)			
	[0.330]		[47.356]			
	0.0013	2.4138*	−1.424**	0.956	1.907	0.0295
	(0.014)	(0.790)	(0.792)			
	[0.092]	[3.053]	[1.800]			

Notes: a. One asterisk (*) denotes significance at the 0.05 level, and two asterisks (**) denote significance at the 0.10
         level.
       b. The numbers in parentheses are standard errors, and the numbers in brackets are absolute values of
           t-statistics for testing the null hypothesis ($\beta = 0$).
       c. D.W. denotes Durbin-Waston statistics; SEE denotes standard error estimates.

sponding F-statistics for testing joint hypotheses are reported in Exhibit
5.3.

In explanatory power, all equations perform reasonably well, as witnessed by the high R^2 for each estimating equation. The evidence from
Exhibits 5.2 and 5.3 indicates that the hypothesis $\beta_0 = 0$ and $\beta_1 = 1$ for
eq. 5.9 cannot be rejected at the 5% level for the four countries. This
holds true for both the individual and the joint tests. This finding, together with the evidence presented in Exhibit 5.1, indicates that the spot
markets are efficient and consistent with the random-walk hypothesis.

Country	Hypothesis		
	$\beta_0 = 0$ and $\beta_1 = 1$	$\beta_0 = 0$ and $\beta_2 = 1$	$\beta_0 = 0$ and $\beta_1 + \beta_2 = 1$
Canada	1.580 (0.211)	0.546 (0.581)	0.386 (0.5360)
France	1.697 (0.188)	0.104 (0.901)	3.448 (0.0660)
W. Germany	1.041 (0.356)	2.435 (0.092)	0.155 (0.6950)
U.K.	0.969 (0.383)	0.195 (0.823)	4.738 (0.0315)

Exhibit 5.3

Tests of the Joint Hypothesis of Market Efficiency

Notes: a. The joint hypothesis is associated with the tests of restrictions of the following equations:

$$s_{t+1} = \beta_0 + \beta_1 s_t + \varepsilon_{t+1},$$

$$s_{t+1} = \beta_0 + \beta_2 f_t + \varepsilon_{t+1},$$

$$s_{t+1} = \beta_0 + \beta_1 s_t + \beta_2 f_t + \varepsilon_{t+1}.$$

b. The tests were based on the following F-statistics (Kmenta 1986):

$$[(SSE_r - SSE_u)/r]/[(SSE_u)/(n - k)] \sim F_{r,n-k}.$$

Critical value for F (2, 113) is 3.09 for 5% significance level.

c. The numbers in column 2 are slightly different (at the second decimal place) from those that appeared in Chiang (1988). The reason is that Statistical Analysis System (SAS) was used in Chiang's paper, while the current figures were recomputed by using Regression Analysis of Time Series (RATS). However, the qualitative results are the same.

Next, let us inspect the results from the forward parity condition of eq. 5.10. Interestingly, the data also support the hypothesis that $\beta_0 = 0$ and $\beta_2 = 1$. The only exception is the German mark, for which the constant term is statistically significant. Overall, the significance test and the Durbin-Waston (D.W.) statistics lead to the conclusion that we are unable to reject the hypothesis of forward exchange market efficiency.

Finally, we test the composite efficiency hypothesis. This test allows us to examine whether the current spot rate is a better predictor of the future spot rate than is the current forward rate. Our evidence indicates that the current spot rate dominates the current forward rate in explaining movements of the future spot rate. This finding is consistent with the results achieved by Meese and Rogoff (1983), Huang (1984), and Chiang (1986).

The general conclusion from this analysis is that no evidence is offered against the efficient market hypothesis, whether it is applied to the spot market or the forward market.[4] In the following sections we first con-

---

[4] However, we should interpret this conclusion with care. Some evidence in the literature (Chiang 1988) has shown that the efficient markets hypotheses underlying eqs. 5.9 and 5.10 are rejected in shorter sample periods, indicating that the results derived from the long sample period tend to average out the exchange rate fluctuations, and thus favor the maintained hypothesis that $\beta_0 = 0$ and $\beta_1 = 1$ or $\beta_0 = 0$ and $\beta_2 = 1$. Moreover, it is likely that the true value of the coefficient β_1 or β_2 may transitorily deviate from unity due to unexpected shocks. The standard constant-coefficient procedure, such as the one we used to estimate the exchange rate equations, is unable to identify whether or not there were periods of transient deviations from market efficiency, that is, periods when β_1 or β_2 differed significantly from unity (Garbade and Wachtel 1978). The transient deviations from unity in the test equations imply that exchange rate expectations may be biased or imply the existence of a risk premium.

sider a variety of expectations formations that deviate from spot market efficiency. Then we consider alternative hypotheses associated with orthogonality tests, which can be viewed as derivatives of the unbiased forward rate hypothesis.

EXCHANGE RATE EXPECTATIONS

Static Expectations

Several schemes have been proposed to model exchange rate expectations. The simplest form is *static expectations,* meaning that expectations of the future spot rate are nothing but the current spot rate. This process can be rationalized by the fact that the observed exchange rates appear to be stationary and investors see no particular reason why the next-period exchange rates would deviate from the current spot rate.[5] An implication of this formulation is that the expected currency depreciation (appreciation) is zero. That is,

5.12 $\Delta s_{t+1}^{e} = 0.$

Empirically, we may find that the expected changes in exchange rates are positive in some periods and negative in others; but on average the expected currency depreciation should be zero. This phenomenon is similar to that of the random-walk hypothesis, although the motive is quite different. According to the random-walk hypothesis, investors know very little about the future movements of the exchange rate, since the probability of moving up or down is about 50%. Thus, the best predictor is the current spot rate. Static expectations, on the other hand, contend that the exchange rate is stable. Thus, the current spot rate is *equal* to the future spot rate.

Extrapolative Expectations

Some investors expect that movements in exchange rates will be dictated by a recent trend. This is known as extrapolative expectations. The static model can be modified to

5.13 $s_{t+1}^{e} = s_t + \alpha(s_t - s_{t-1}),$

where α is a constant coefficient and $(s_t - s_{t-1})$ represents the recent changes in exchange rates. The rationale of eq. 5.13 is that recent movements of exchange rates are nonstationary. In particular, we can hypothesize the market behavior by saying that currency depreciation in the current period will generate an expectation of further depreciation. In symbols, we can write

5.14 $\Delta s_{t+1}^{e} = \alpha \Delta s_t.$

---

[5] This notion is consistent with either a perfect-foresight or a fixed-price approach.

Hypothesizing that the expectations of market behavior continually move in the same direction implies that $\alpha > 0$. Such bandwagon expectations are thought to be highly unstable since investors sell a currency that they expect to depreciate and vice versa.

However, speculative activities can be stabilizing if the opposite direction is expected (a depreciation of the currency is expected to be followed by an appreciation of the currency, and vice versa.) Thus, the stabilizing expectations must imply that the coefficient in eqs. 5.13 and 5.14 is negative. Expressing this notion in terms of eq. 5.14, we specify

5.15
$$\Delta s_{t+1}^e = -\alpha \Delta s_t,$$

or equivalently,

5.16
$$s_{t+1}^e = (1 - \alpha)s_t + \alpha s_{t-1}.$$

Equation 5.16 is labeled the distributed lag expectations model. It states that the expectations of exchange rates are formed on the basis of current and lagged spot rates. In this specification, longer lags (beyond period $t - 1$) are assumed to have no informational content.[6]

Adaptive Expectations

Aside from extrapolative expectations, the adaptive expectations approach has been commonly used to model price behavior. In adaptive expectations, the expectations of the future spot rate are formed by the weighted average of the current spot rate and the lagged expected rate:

5.17
$$s_{t+1}^e = (1 - \theta)s_t + \theta s_t^e,$$

where $1 > \theta > 0$, and s_t^e is the expected rate at time t given the information at time $t - 1$. Equation 5.17 can be rewritten as

5.18
$$\Delta s_{t+1}^e = \theta(s_t^e - s_t).$$

Equation 5.18 states that expectations are revised on the basis of the expectations error, $(s_t^e - s_t)$. The magnitude of the revision depends on the coefficient θ. For instance, if the expected rate between the Japanese yen and the U.S. dollar was set at \$0.00784/¥, and the current spot rate is \$0.00744/¥, then the expected rate will be revised by some fraction of the difference between \$0.00784 and \$0.00744. If we set $\theta = 0.7$, then

$$\Delta s_{t+1}^e = 0.7[ln(0.00784) - ln(0.00744)]$$
$$= 0.0367.$$

The expected exchange rate can be computed by using

$$s_{t+1}^e = s_t + \Delta s_{t+1}^e$$
$$= ln(0.00744) + 0.0367$$
$$= -4.8642.$$

---

[6] We will consider the rational expectations hypothesis in the section on orthogonality tests, later in this chapter.

Equivalently, this figure can be derived by using eq. 5.17. That is,

$$s_{t+1}^e = (1 - 0.7)ln(0.00744) + (0.7)ln(0.00784)$$
$$= -4.8642.$$

Taking the anti-natural log of (-4.8642) gives us the value of 0.00772 dollars per yen. From this exercise, we can see that adaptive expectations represent an error learning process. Market participants adjust their expectations partially based on their experience.[7]

Regressive Expectations

In regressive expectations economic agents assume that the expected future spot rate is a weighted average of the current and the equilibrium exchange rates:

5.19 $$s_{t+1}^e = (1 - \gamma)s_t + \gamma s_t',$$

where γ is a constant that lies between one and zero and s_t' is the long-run equilibrium exchange rate. The expectations are assumed to be formed regressively since exchanges rates in the long run regress toward the long-run equilibrium exchange rate s_t'. Giving eq. 5.19 in a slightly different representation, we obtain:

5.20 $$\Delta s_{t+1}^e = \gamma(s_t' - s_t).$$

Equation 5.20 states that if the spot rate is below the long-run equilibrium rate, it is expected to climb. On the other hand, if the current spot rate is higher than the long-run equilibrium level, it is expected to fall. In this manner the spot rate tends to converge to the long-run equilibrium rate. The long-run equilibrium rate does not have to be stationary, and it is often tied to purchasing power parity.[8]

It is possible to integrate extrapolative expectations and regressive expectations into one equation, as specified by

5.21 $$\Delta s_{t+1}^e = \alpha(s_t - s_{t-1}) + \gamma(s_t' - s_t).$$

Equation 5.21 is a combination of eqs. 5.13 and 5.20. The first term on the right-hand side of eq. 5.21 is the extrapolative component, and the second term is the regressive component. The extrapolative component indicates a tendency for current spot rate depreciation (appreciation) to lead to a further depreciation (appreciation) in the near future. This component contributes to exchange rate overshooting and destabilization. The regressive component suggests that the current spot rate will move toward the long-run equilibrium level, so it is converging and stabilizing. The extrapolative behavior captures the immediate market trend, which reflects a short-run phenomenon, and the regressive expectations element concerns fundamentals, involving a longer time to make the adjustments.

---

[7] The adaptive expectations model is equivalent to the ARIMA(0,1,1) model. See the appendix to this chapter for details.
[8] As we discussed in Chapter 4 this long-term equilibrium rate can also be determined by other structural models.

General Specifications of Expectations

To summarize the discussion so far, we can see the formation of expectations depends on the available information and the knowledge of exchange rate determination. Using spot market efficiency as a starting point, the three expectation formations just described can be viewed as a particular form of deviation from the random-walk hypothesis. In an empirical context this is equivalent to testing the incremental efficiency of market information. We can generally write the expectations equation in the following form:

5.22
$$s^e_{t+1} - s_t = x_t \delta,$$

where x_t can be treated as an additional information set to eq. 5.3. Using the realized value of the expected spot rate to estimate eq. 5.22, the specification is given by

5.23
$$s_{t+1} - s_t = x_t \delta + \varepsilon_{t+1},$$

where δ is a $(k \times 1)$ vector of unknown parameters, x_t the $(1 \times k)$ row vector, and ε_{t+1} an error term.[9] Alternative expectation models can be tested in light of eq. 5.23. In extrapolative expectations we set $x_t = (s_t - s_{t-1})$, in adaptive expectations, $x_t = (s^e_t - s_t)$, and in regressive expectations, $x_t = (s'_t - s_t)$. Clearly, for the random-walk hypothesis, we test $x_t = 0$.[10] The empirical examination involves the test of the restriction that $\delta = 0$. The relevancy of the information for x_t or the accuracy of the expectations formation depends on the observed exchange rate behavior, which is more or less an empirical question rather than an theoretical argument.

Empirical Evidence on Exchange Rate Expectations

The extrapolative expectations, adaptive expectations, and regressive expectations models are tested by Frankel and Froot (1987), using survey data to measure market expectations. Their original estimations involve three independent surveys, including the Economist Financial Report (Economist), Money Market Services, Inc. (MMS), and Amex Bank Review (Amex). Since the results from these surveys are quite compatible with each other, only the results from the Economist are given in Exhibit 5.4.

---

[9] If market adjustment is sluggish, the expectations can be generated in dynamic fashion as follows:

$$s_{t+1} = \alpha(L)s_t + \beta(L)x_t + \varepsilon_{t+1}$$

where $\alpha(L) = \alpha(L) + \alpha_1(L^2) + \ldots + \alpha_p(L^p)$, $\beta(L) = \beta_0 + \beta_1(L) + \ldots + \beta_r(L^r)$, $\alpha(L)$ and $\beta(L)$ are lag coefficients, and L is a lag operator. Now the sum of $\alpha(L)$ and $\beta(L)$ does not have to be unity. Once again, the lag lengths of s_t and x_t are determined by empirical regularities. For a nonstationary series, the equation should be taken in first difference.

[10] One can test the nonstationary version of the unbiased forward rate hypothesis by setting $x_t = (f_t - s_t)$. Further, eq. 5.23 can be used to examine the validity of the random-walk model by conducting an orthogonality test.

Exhibit 5.4

Estimates of Survey Expected Depreciation (*Economist*, 6/81–12/85)

Extrapolative expectations: $s_{t+1}^e - s_t = \alpha_0 + \alpha(s_t - s_{t-1})$

Period	α	t: $\alpha = 0$	D.W.	R^2
3-month	−0.0416	−1.98**	1.81	0.30
6-month	−0.0730	−3.25*	1.36	0.54
12-month	−0.2018	−6.82*	1.47	0.84

Adaptive expectations: $s_{t+1}^e - s_t = \theta_0 + \theta(s_t^e - s_t)$

Period	θ	t: $\theta = 0$	D.W.	R^2
3-month	0.0798	3.93*	2.01	0.63
6-month	0.0516	3.20*	1.12	0.53
12-month	−0.0093	−0.38	1.10	0.02

Regressive expectations: $s_{t+1}^e - s_t = \gamma_0 + \gamma(s_t' - s_t)$

Period	γ	t: $\gamma = 0$	D.W.	R^2
3-month	0.0232	1.78**	1.66	0.26
6-month	0.0600	3.77*	1.32	0.61
12-month	0.1750	8.10*	1.25	0.88

SOURCE: Frankel and Froot (*AER*, 1987)

Notes: a. The constant terms were not reported by the original source.

b. Since $(s_t - s_{t-1})$, rather than $(s_{t-1} - s_t)$, is used as an independent variable in the extrapolative expectations equation, a negative sign is added to the coefficients in the reported results. However, the qualitative results remain unchanged.

c. One asterisk (*) denotes significance at the 5% or 1% level, and two asterisks (**) denote significance at the 10% level.

d. In their original article, Frankel and Froot used γ as the parameter in adaptive expectations, and θ in regressive expectations. Since the adaptive expectations model is equivalent to the ARIMA(0,1,1) model, we used θ in the specification of adaptive expectations to maintain a consistency in the time series analysis.

As discussed earlier under the general title of extrapolative expectations, the coefficient α (slope) on the estimated equation is expected to be positive if we hypothesize bandwagon expectations, and negative in the case of a distributed lag. The estimated coefficients turn out to have negative signs and are statistically significant. The evidence thus confirms the distributed lag expectations hypothesis. Since the estimated coefficients are less than unity, in absolute value, we can say the expectations are stabilizing. In particular, the point estimate of 0.0416 in the 3-month data means that a depreciation of 10% today generates an expectation of a 0.416% appreciation over the next three months, or about 1.66% per year.

Next, we examine the adaptive expectations hypothesis. This has been done by regressing expected currency depreciation on the lagged survey prediction error. The estimated coefficients are positive for both the 3-month and the 6-month horizons and are statistically significant. This finding indicates that the expectations are positively related to the past expectations. The evidence thus suggests that the expectations are inelastic, which supports the view that speculation is stabilizing.

In testing regressive expectations, the long-run equilibrium rate, s_t', is assumed to move with the relative inflation differentials, measured by changes in the U.S. and foreign consumer price indexes (CPIs). The results from Exhibit 5.4 show that expected currency depreciation is significantly explained by the long-run equilibrium rate. This means that investors expect the exchange rate to regress toward its long-run equilibrium.

The general conclusion derived from the tests in Exhibit 5.4 is that the expected future spot rate is positively correlated to the current spot rate, and the estimated coefficients are less than unity. In addition, the investor also gives weight to factors such as the lagged spot rate, lagged expectations, and the long-run equilibrium rate. The evidence suggests that expectations are essentially inelastic and that speculation is stabilizing. This finding is important since it tempers fears of destabilization caused by speculative activities. This empirical evidence supports Friedman's argument that speculation is stabilizing.

FORWARD RATE FORECAST ERRORS AND INFORMATION

Although the evidence presented earlier confirms the hypothesis of forward exchange market efficiency, some recent studies show that the evidence supporting the unbiased forward rate hypothesis is quite weak (Levich 1985; Boothe and Longworth 1986; Frankel 1988). Various studies suggest that the forecast errors (foreign exchange excess returns) generated by using forward rates are not independent of variables such as "news," latent variables, other asset prices, and risk factors. We shall briefly discuss these variables in the following sections.

Orthogonality Tests

To examine whether additional information can be used to interpret the forecast errors, researchers usually set up a different "alternative hypothesis" and conduct a so-called orthogonality test. The orthogonality test is often specified as

5.24
$$s_{t+1} - f_t = x_t \phi + v_{t+1},$$

where ϕ is a $(k \times 1)$ vector of unknown parameters and v_{t+1} is an error term. The orthogonality test of f_t as an optimal predictor of s_{t+1} is designed to determine whether the forecast error is correlated to some subset of the current information set I_t, for example, the $(1 \times k)$ row vector x_t. Thus, testing the null hypothesis that $\phi = 0$ involves testing whether any elements of x_t are statistically significant.

The rejection of the null hypothesis leads to several economic interpretations, depending on the elements to be included in x_t. Although any element of the information set, I_t, could be used as a candidate to test the hypothesis that $s_{t+1} - f_t$ is orthogonal to I_t, we would want to consider the elements that are likely to have economic meaning in order to construct a powerful test.

News and Market Forecast Error

To provide a plausible explanation for the forecast error, various alternative hypotheses have been advanced on the basis of eq. 5.24. One popular approach is to relate the forecast errors (excess returns) to the news variables, $u_{t+1} = \{z_{t+1} - z_{t+1}^e\}$, $u_{t+1}^* = \{z_{t+1}^* - z_{t+1}^{e*}\}$, where $z_{t+1}(z_{t+1}^*)$ is an appropriate exogenous variable to explain the exchange rates. In this case we set $x_t = \{u_{t+1}, u_{t+1}^*\}$ and write eq. 5.24 as

5.25 $$s_{t+1} - f_t = \phi u_{t+1} + \phi^* u_{t+1}^* + v_{t+1}.$$

The choice of z_{t+1} depends on the model at hand. For instance, the monetary model (see Chapter 4) implies that the excess returns in the foreign exchange market must correlate with news from changes in relative money supplies, relative real incomes, and interest rate differentials. The rationale of this specification is that since the forward rate, by the rational/efficient assumption, reflects the market expectations of the exogenous variables $\{z_{t+1}^e\}$ in determining the exchange rate, the errors must be associated with the unexpected changes in these exogenous variables.

The model tested by Frenkel (1981) using unexpected changes in interest rate differentials as a news variable for three currencies over the period June 1973 to June 1979 finds that only the coefficient of news for the British pound is statistically significant. Further studies by Hoffman and Schlagenhauf (1985) using a variety of exchange rate determination models to evaluate the news framework find that all test models are characterized by low R^2 or frequent counterintuitive signs. Thus, the data do not provide strong support for the news approach. The poor performance of the news approach may account for the misspecification of the structural model or the correctness of generating expectation variables and, in turn, the news variables.

Latent Variables and Market Forecast Error

An alternative approach to examining the issue of a risk premium is the inspection of serial correlation. The study proposed by Hansen and Hodrick (1980) relates the forecast errors to the lagged dependent variables in light of the efficient market approach. For the weak form of market efficiency they test the significance of lagged dependent variables, which involves a test of the hypothesis that $\phi = 0$ for $x_t = \{s_{t+1-j} - f_{t-j}\}$, where $j = 1, \ldots, J$.[11]

Moreover, if the interest is in testing the semistrong form of market efficiency, the elements to be included in the information set should be extended to the lagged forecast errors from the other country's exchange rates or other observable variables. That is, the information set can be specified as $x_t = \{(s_{t+1-j} - f_{t-j}), (s_{t+1-j}^* - f_{t-j}^*)\}$ for $j = 1, \ldots, J$. Since the simple efficient hypothesis (unbiased forward rate hypothesis) implies that $s_{t+1} - f_t$ is uncorrelated to x_t, the rejection of the null hypothesis that $\phi = 0$ implies the rejection of the efficient markets hypothesis. The tests

---

[11] Notice that when $j = 1$, we have $x_t = (s_t - f_{t-1})$.

conducted by Hansen and Hodrick (1980) found that for the German mark, the Swiss franc, and the Italian lira, the forecast errors are autocorrelated with their own lags, indicating the rejection of weak-form efficiency for these currencies. They also found that lagged forecast errors for some currencies have explanatory power in predicting the current forecast errors for the Canadian dollar, the German mark, and the Swiss franc. The evidence implies the rejection of the semistrong form of the efficient markets hypothesis.

Asset Prices, Risk, and Market Forecast Error

As recognized by many researchers, fluctuations in the risk premia may account for the existence of serial correlation (Cumby and Obstfeld 1981; Hakkio 1981). The problem is how to establish a relationship between exchange risk premia and the measure of risk. To search for a meaningful interpretation of the existence of risk premia, we need to construct a coherent theory from which valid empirical evidence can be derived. One popular approach is the consumption-based international asset pricing model, which is built on the premise that the economic agent chooses an optimal time path of consumption and assets that yield uncertain returns. It posits that the risk premium is dependent on the conditional covariance of the intertemporal marginal rates of substitution and returns on foreign exchange speculation. The excess exchange returns in the empirical studies are often linked to the variability of the conditional variance.

Among various empirical studies, Roll and Solnik (1977) have estimated a pure foreign exchange asset pricing model by investigating the correlation between the forecast error of each currency and a weighted average of the forecast errors of all currencies; Domowitz and Hakkio (1985) have directly linked the risk premium to the conditional variances of the forecast errors of the domestic and the foreign money supplies; Lyons (1988) has generated the conditional variance extracted from option prices. Since the conditional covariance from these models depends on elements to be selected from the information set, no general agreement can be derived from these studies.

Because some recent empirical regularities have convincingly shown that movements in the conditional risk premia of returns on the U.S. stock market are similar to those of the conditional risk premia in the forward foreign exchange markets, an attempt has been made to establish an empirical link between the exchange risk premium and these financial variables. In their empirical specifications, Giovannini and Jorion (1987) relate the realized returns in the foreign exchange markets to the nominal interest rates. A reduced-form equation is

5.26 $$s_{t+1} - s_t - (r_t - r_t^*) = c_0 + c_1 r_t + c_2 r_t^* + \varepsilon_{t+1},$$

where $c_1 < 0$, $c_2 > 0$, and $f_t = s_t - (r_t - r_t^*)$ is the covered interest rate parity condition. As shown in Exhibit 5.5, the authors find that nearly all coefficients on the U.S. interest rate are negative, all the coefficients on the foreign interest rate are positive, and the coefficients are statistically significant. The only exception is the French franc. The joint test of zero

Exhibit 5.5

Foreign Exchange Return and
Interest Rates

Country	Constant	r_t	r_t^*	R^2	P-Value	Period
The Netherlands	0.07	−4.19**	4.35**	0.0450	2.E-7**	1973–84
Switzerland	0.34	−2.74*	0.98	0.0143	0.039*	1973–84
W. Germany	0.25	−3.49**	2.40	0.0189	0.019	1973–84
U.K.	−0.43	−2.20*	3.32**	0.0238	0.001**	1973–84
France	0.08	−2.08	0.56	0.0366	0.067	1979–84
Italy	−0.27	−2.48	1.89**	0.0287	0.025*	1979–84
Japan	−0.50	−2.07	6.06**	0.0489	0.004**	1979–84

SOURCE: Table 3 in Giovannini and Jorion (*JIMF*, 1987).

Notes: a. Estimations were made by using the generalized method of moments (GMM).
       b. P-value denotes the significance level for testing that the coefficients of r_t and r_t^* equal zero.
       c. One asterisk (*) denotes significance at the 5% level, and two asterisks (**) denote significance at the 1%
           level.

slope coefficients is rejected in the majority of cases. Thus increases in foreign exchange risk premia, that is, higher values of $(s_{t+1} − f_t)$, are reliably associated with decreases in U.S. interest rates and increases in foreign interest rates.

Built on the empirical regularity (Giovannini and Jorion 1987) that returns in the foreign exchange market and the stock market move together over time, Chiang (1991) has developed a model to link the risk premia in foreign exchange markets to the equity risk premia in stock markets. Specifically, the estimated equation is

5.27 $$s_{t+1} − s_t − (r_t − r_t^*) = b_0 + b_1(R_{m,t+1}^e − r_t) + b_1(R_{m,t+1}^{e^*} − r_t^*)$$
$$+ \varepsilon_{t+1}, \, b_1 > 0, \, b_2 < 0,$$

where $R_{m,t+1}^e − r_t$ and $R_{m,t+1}^{e^*} − r_t^*$ are, respectively, the expected equity risk premium in the domestic and the foreign markets. As shown by Chiang, the results indicate that the coefficient of $(R_{m,t+1}^e − r_t)$ is positive and that of $(R_{m,t+1}^{e^*} − r_t^*)$ is negative; t-statistics for four major currencies are found to be significant at the 5% level. The evidence thus supports the hypothesis that the exchange risk premia are empirically associated with the relative expected equity risks in stock markets. The confirmation of the hypothesis validates the argument for the existence of a risk premium in the foreign exchange markets.

SUMMARY

For the spot market efficiency hypothesis, we assume that the current spot rate fully reflects available information, providing an accurate signal for asset and resource allocations. The random nature of the spot market suggests that the current spot rate is the best predictor of the future spot rate. In the case of the forward foreign exchange market, the forward rate is assumed to summarize all current information that is relevant for predicting the future spot rate. Thus, the forward rate has been viewed as an unbiased predictor of the future spot rate. To combine the information from both markets, the composite efficiency hypothesis assumes that prediction of the future spot rate should be based on a weighted average of current spot and forward rates. In the long sample horizon, we cannot find evidence to reject the efficient market hypotheses, either in the spot market or in the forward market. However, most evidence appears to support the hypothesis that the current spot rate outperforms the current forward rate in predicting the future spot rate.

There are at least three different hypotheses of exchange rate expectations: extrapolative expectations, adaptive expectations, and regressive expectations. These expectation formations can be viewed as variations of the spot market efficiency hypothesis. The difference is that in addition to the current spot rate, the recent trend is added to extrapolative expectations, the past forecast error to adaptive expectations, and the deviation from the equilibrium rate to the regressive model. Using survey data in testing the expectation hypothesis, Frankel and Froot (1987) report that the expected future spot rate is positively correlated to the current spot rate and other information, such as the lagged change in the spot rate, lagged expectations, and the long-run equilibrium exchange rate. The evidence concludes that expectations are essentially inelastic and speculation is stabilizing. The evidence somewhat negates the spot market efficiency hypothesis.

Recent studies also provide evidence rejecting the forward foreign exchange market efficiency hypothesis. Orthogonality tests suggest that rejection of the unbiased forward rate hypothesis is caused by variables such as news, latent variables, forecast errors in money supplies, interest rate differentials, stock market premia, or various forms of conditional variance. By and large, the evidence is consistent with the existence of a risk premium in the forward foreign exchange market.

Questions and Problems

1. Discuss the significance of the efficient markets hypothesis in the foreign exchange market. Explain how you test the spot market efficiency. Does the random-walk process mean market efficiency?

2. In addition to examining the serial correlation of the changes in exchange rate, what other procedures can you use to test the market efficiency?

3. Develop an empirical model that could be used to examine the hypothesis that the current spot exchange rate contains all the historical information.

4. Based on the model you developed in the previous question, how do you revise the model if the current spot rate is believed to reflect both the historical and the publicly available information?

5. Provide reasons why the efficiency hypothesis does not hold. Could you offer some empirical evidence to justify your arguments?

6. Many techniques used to test efficiency in equity markets have been applied to test the foreign exchange market. Do you see any difference between these two markets in their model specification?

7. Discuss the role of expectations with respect to the effect of unexpected change in money supply on exchange rate.

8. Use daily data from the *WSJ* or the *Financial Times* with, say, 60 continuous observations to plot the 30-day forward exchange rate at time t and spot rate at $t + 30$ days. See whether you can identify any systematic patterns or correlations, and then provide your explanation.

9. Using the set of data from question 5, calculate the differences (in natural logarithm) between s_{t+30} and f_t. Are the differences related to any variable you can think of?

10. Develop a regression model that consists of both "news" and "risk" variables to explain the exchange rate movements.

References

Abraham, B., and J. Ledolter. *Statistical Methods for Forecasting*. New York: Wiley, 1983.

Bilson, J. "The Speculative Efficiency Hypothesis." *Journal of Business* vol. 54, no. 3 (July 1981): 435–559.

Boothe, P., and D. Longworth. "Foreign Exchange Market Efficiency Tests: Implications of Recent Empirical Findings." *Journal of International Money and Finance* 5 (1986): 135–52.

Borensztein, E. "Alternative Hypotheses About the Excess Return of Dollar Assets." *Staff Papers* (International Monetary Fund) 34 (March 1987): 29–59.

Box, G., and G. Jenkins. *Time Series Analysis, Forecasting and Control*. San Francisco: Holden Day, 1976.

Chiang, T. "Empirical Analysis on the Predictors of the Future Spot Rates." *Journal of Financial Research* vol. 9, no. 2 (June 1986): 153–62.

———. "The Forward Rate as a Predictor of the Future Spot Rate—A Stochastic Coefficient Approach." *Journal of Money, Credit, and Banking* 20 (May 1988): 212–32.

———. "International Asset Pricing and Equity Market Risks." *Journal of International Money and Finance* (forthcoming, September 1991).

Cumby, R., and M. Obstfeld. "A Note on Exchange-Rate Expectations and Nominal Interest Differentials: A Test of the Fisher Hypothesis." *Journal of Finance* 36 (June 1981): 697–704.

Domowitz, I., and C. Hakkio. "Conditional Variance and the Risk Premium in the Foreign Exchange Market." *Journal of International Economics* 19 (August 1985): 47–66.

Dornbusch, R. "Exchange Rate Risk and the Macroeconomics of Exchange Rate Determination." In *Research in International Business and Finance* 3, ed. R. Hawkins et al. Greenwich, Conn.: JAI Press, 1983.

Edwards, S. "Exchange Rates and 'News': A Multi-Currency Approach." *Journal of International Money and Finance* 1 (December 1982): 211–24.

Fama, E. "Efficient Capital Markets: A Review of Theory and Empirical Work." *Journal of Finance* 25 (May (1970): 383–417.

———. "Forward and Spot Exchange Rates." *Journal of Monetary Economics* 4 (November 1984): 319–38.

Frankel, Jeffrey A. "The Implications of Mean-Variance Optimization for Four Questions in International Macroeconomics." *Journal of International Money and Finance* 5 (March 1986): Supplement S53–75.

———. "Recent Estimates of Time-Variation in the Conditional Variance and in the Exchange Risk Premium." *Journal of International Money and Finance* 7 (March 1988): 115–25.

Frankel, J., and K. Froot. "Using Survey Data to Test Standard Propositions Regarding Exchange Rate Expectations." *American Economic Review* 77, no. 1 (March 1987): 133–53.

Fratianni, M., and L. M. Wakeman. "The Law of One Price in the Eurocurrency Market." *Journal of International Money and Finance* 1 (1982): 307–23.

Frenkel, J., and R. Levich. "Covered Interest Arbitrage: Unexploited Profits?" *Journal of Political Economy* 83 (April 1975): 325–38.

Frenkel, J. "Flexible Exchange Rates, Prices, and the Role of 'News': Lessons from the 1970s." *Journal of Political Economy* 89 (August 1981): 665–705.

Garbade, K. and P. Wachtel. "Time Vacation in the Relationship Between Inflation and Interest Rates." *Journal of Monetary Economics* 4 (1978): 755–65.

Giovannini, A., and Philippe Jorion. "Interest Rates and Risk Premia in the Stock Market and in the Foreign Exchange Market." *Journal of International Money and Finance* 6, no. 1, (March 1987): 107–24.

Hakkio, C. S. "Expectations and the Forward Exchange Rate." *International Economic Review* vol. 22, no. 3 (October 1981): 663–78.

Hansen, L. and R. Hodrick. "Forward Exchange Rates as Optimal Predictors of Future Spot Rates: An Econometric Analysis." *Journal of Political Economy* 88 (October 1980): 829–53.

Hodrick, R. *The Empirical Evidence on the Efficiency of Forward and Futures Foreign Exchange Markets.* New York: Harwood Academic, 1987.

Hodrick, R. and Sanjay Srivastava. "An Investigation of Risk and Return in Forward Foreign Exchange." *Journal of International Money and Finance* 3, no. 1 (April 1985): 5–29.

Hoffman, D., and Don E. Schlagenhauf. "The Impact of News and Alternative Theories of Exchange Rate Determination." *Journal of Money, Credit, and Banking* 17 (August 1985): 328–46.

Huang, R. "Some Alternative Tests of Forward Exchange Rates as Predictors of Future Spot Rates." *Journal of International Money and Finance* 3, no. 2 (August 1984): 153–78.

Kmenta, J. *Elements of Econometrics.* New York: Macmillan Publishing, 1986.

Levich, R. "Empirical Studies of Exchange Rates: Price Behavior, Rate Determination and Market Efficiency." In *Handbook of International Economics II*, eds. R. W. Jones and P. B. Kenen, 979–1040. New York: Elsevier Publisher B.V., 1985.

Lyons, R. "Tests of the Foreign Exchange Risk Premium Using the Expected Second Moments Implied by Options Pricing." *Journal of International Money and Finance* 7 (March 1988): 91–108.

Meese, R. and K. Rogoff. "Empirical Exchange Rate Models of the Seventies: Do They Fit Out of Sample?" *Journal of International Economics* 14 (February 1983): 3–24.

Mishkin, F. *A Rational Expectation Approach to Macroeconomics.* Chicago: University of Chicago Press, 1983.

Mussa, Michael. "Empirical Regularities in the Behavior of Exchange Rates and Theories of the Foreign Exchange Market." In *Policies for Employment, Prices, and Exchange Rates*, eds. K. Brunner and A. Meltzer, Carnegie-Rochester Conference Series on Public Policy, vol. 1, 9–57. Amsterdam: North Holland, 1979.

Robichek, A., and M. Eaker. "Foreign Exchange Hedging and the Capital Asset Pricing Model." *Journal of Finance* 33 (June 1978): 1011–18.

Roll, R., and B. Solnik. "A Pure Foreign Exchange Asset Pricing Model." *Journal of International Economics* 7 (May 1977): 161–79.

Samuelson, P. A. and W. D. Nordhaus. *Economics*, 12th ed. New York: McGraw-Hill, 1985.

Appendix 5.A

EXPECTATIONS AND TIME SERIES ANALYSIS

Emphasizing the extraction of information from time series data, the Box and Jenkins (1976) methodology has become a popular procedure to generate expectations and to conduct diagnostic checks to see whether residuals appear to be random. Applying the Box-Jenkins methodology to form exchange rate expectations, we assume that the exchange rate is correlated either to its past values, the autoregressive components, or to its past shocks (disturbances), the moving-average components, or to both. In particular, a stationary exchange rate series can be generally represented by

$$s_{t+1} = \phi_p^{-1}(L)\theta_q(L)\varepsilon_{t+1},$$

where $\phi_p(L) = 1 - \phi_1 - \ldots - \phi_p$, $\theta_q(L) = 1 - \theta_1 - \ldots - \theta_q$, and $\phi_p(L)$ and $\theta_q(L)$ are lag coefficients with order p for autoregressive components and order q for moving-average components, L is a lag operator, and ε_t is a vector of shocks. A specific pattern that is used to generate the expectations can be obtained by examining the statistical significance of the coefficients for the autocorrelation function (ACF) and the partial autocorrelation function (PACF). Assuming the empirical patterns are stable over time, the identified pattern then is used to forecast the exchange rate.

The time series model is useful for at least two reasons. First, if one can precisely observe a time series pattern for a particular exchange rate series, our experience is that the predicted values derived from the Box-Jenkins model usually outperform alternative specifications. Second, if the exchange rate series appears to have a particular pattern, this suggests that a *trading rule* can be extracted to formulate a speculative strategy. As a result, a speculator could profit from using this trading strategy, which is evidence against the efficient markets hypothesis.

It is interesting to note that the adaptive expectations model is equivalent to the ARIMA(0,1,1) model in the time series analysis. Recall that $\Delta s^e_{t+1} = \theta(s^e_t - s_t)$, which can be rewritten as

$$(1 - L)s_{t+1} = -(1 - \theta L)\varepsilon_{t+1}.$$

6

PURCHASING POWER PARITY

As we discussed in Chapter 5, the short-term variations of exchange rates are complex and unpredictable. The asset approach suggests that the forces governing short-run exchange rate variations are essentially due to changes of market expectations in response to "news," such as economic shocks and unexpected political and social events. However, for a longer time horizon, it is possible to use economic fundamentals to project the movements of exchange rates. The economic variables may include the relative rates of inflation, interest rate differentials (both nominal and real), relative productivities, and the variables that explain differences in economic structure.

This chapter concerns one of these factors, focusing on the long-run relationship between exchange rate changes and relative inflation rates. We first discuss the law of one price and different versions of purchasing power parity. Second, we present empirical evidence and provide some explanations for departures from the purchasing power parity condition. Violations of this parity suggest that goods prices do not keep pace with exchange rate movements, leading us to a discussion of the real exchange rate and its application at both the micro and the macro levels. In the final section, we present a time series analysis of real exchange rate behavior.

THEORY OF PURCHASING POWER PARITY

Fundamental economics tells us that the profit motive is an essential driving force that encourages a trader to engage in various economic activities. A trader may spend a great deal of time searching out prices quoted in different locations or at different times. With this information in hand, the profit-maximizing trader may engage in one of the following activities: (a) buy a commodity in one market and resell it in another market; or (b) buy a commodity today and sell it in the future by signing a contract or just holding it. The former activity involves commodity arbitrage; the latter is speculation.

Arbitrage and the Law of One Price

To illustrate the concept of the law of one price, let us consider the following scenario. An arbitrager observes that the price of wheat in the United States is $5.00 per bushel and the price in the United Kingdom is £2.50. He may decide to spend $1,000,000 to buy 200,000 bushels of wheat in the United States and ship them to the United Kingdom for sale for £500,000. Will this decision be profitable? The answer depends on the going exchange rate and the shipping costs.

Assuming for the moment that there are no shipping costs, it is obvious that the break-even spot exchange rate at the time the wheat is sold in the United Kingdom is $S_t = \$2.00/\pounds1.00$, since at this rate the proceeds of £500,000 are equal to $1,000,000. Thus, for profitable trading the spot exchange rate must be higher than $2.00/£1.00. Assume the going exchange rate is set at $S_t = \$2.10/\pounds1.00$. The proceeds of £500,000 then can be converted to $1,050,000. As long as the shipping costs are lower than $50,000, the arbitrager exhibits a net profit. Similarly, the reverse transaction, buying wheat in the United Kingdom and selling in the United States, will take place if the spot exchange rate is low enough to offset the shipping costs. For example, at a rate of $1.90/£1.00, $1,000,000 would be converted to £526,315.79, covering shipping costs up to £26,315.79.

These examples make two points clear. First, efficient commodity arbitrage eliminates any opportunity for excess profit that may exist. Second, if it is assumed that transaction costs, tariffs, quotas, and other forms of trade impediments are zero, the commodity prices, once they are converted into a common currency unit, are everywhere equal. This is called the law of one price.

To state the law formally, let us define the exchange rate S_t to be the number of units of domestic currency ($) per unit of foreign money (£). That is, $S_t = \$/\pounds$. Further, let $P_{j,t}$ and $P_{j,t}^*$ be the price of commodity j at home and abroad, quoted in the respective currencies. The law of one price implies that

6.1 $$P_{j,t} = S_t P_{j,t}^*.$$

That is, the domestic price of good j is equal to the domestic currency price of foreign currency times the foreign price of good j. For instance, if the price of gold in New York ($P_{j,t}$) is $380.00 per ounce, while the price in London ($P_{j,t}^*$) is £240.00 per ounce, eq. 6.1 suggests that the exchange rate, S_t, is equal to $1.5833/£1: $P_{j,t} = S_t P_{j,t}^* = (\$1.5833 \times 240.00) \approx \$380.00$. Once we convert pounds sterling into dollars at the prevailing exchange rate, the price of one ounce of gold in London is the same as the one quoted in New York. Thus, spatial arbitrage leads to the law of one price, in which the domestic price of any good must equal its foreign price quoted in the same currency.

Forms of Purchasing Power Parity

The commodities and services traded in the international markets are essentially determined by the relative prices between the domestic and the foreign countries. Purchasing power parity (PPP) focuses on the long-term relationship between the exchange rate and relative commodity prices. The theory, which is usually credited to the Swedish economist Gustav Cassel (1916, 1921), has two versions: absolute and relative.

Absolute Purchasing Power Parity   An important message emerging from the law of one price is that the exchange rate has to be adjusted to bring about the equality of the two prices. It follows that eq. 6.1 can be rewritten as

6.2 $$S_t = P_{j,t}/P_{j,t}^*.$$

In this formulation the exchange rate is directly related to the relative prices of good j. This relationship holds not only for one good but also for all goods. Consequently, we could write the relationship in terms of prices in general, that is, the prices of a standard basket of commodities for the two trading countries. Equation 6.2 becomes

6.3 $$S_t = P_t/P_t^*,$$

where P_t and P_t^* are, respectively, the weighted average of individual commodity prices in the two countries. That is, $P_t = \Sigma_j w_j P_{j,t}$ and $P_t^* = \Sigma_j w_j^* P_{j,t}^*$ for $j = 1, 2, \ldots, J$; w_j and w_j^* are, respectively, weights for commodity j in the two countries. Equation 6.3 is an absolute version of PPP. It postulates that the exchange rate is expressed in terms of the two nations' price levels. It is important to keep in mind that, to establish the relationship in eq. 6.3, we need to assume that in the calculation of price indexes the baskets of goods are identical, all goods are traded, the relative prices are stable, and the weights of each jth good in the two countries are the same (i.e., $w_j = w_j^*$ for all j).

Relative Purchasing Power Parity   The concept of absolute PPP in its theoretical treatment is quite clear. However, in practice, absolute PPP is not very useful, because most of the price data are available in the form of indexes rather than price levels. A pragmatic way to handle this is to write eq. 6.3 in a relative form. Let us assume two time periods, time t and some later time $t + T$. Absolute PPP in period t is given by eq. 6.3, and the equation for time $t + T$ is

6.4 $$S_{t+T} = P_{t+T}/P_{t+T}^*.$$

Dividing the condition in eq. 6.4 by the condition in eq. 6.3, we obtain the relative version of PPP.

6.5 $$S_{t+T}/S_t = (P_{t+T}/P_{t+T}^*)/(P_t/P_t^*) = (P_{t+T}/P_t)/(P_{t+T}^*/P_t^*).$$

Time t is set as a basis period, and (P_{t+T}/P_t) and (P_{t+T}^*/P_t^*) are, accordingly, the domestic and the foreign price indexes. To be consistent with the theory, the two price indexes must have the same base period, the same bundle of traded goods, and use the same weights.

The relative version of PPP appears to have different characteristics from the absolute version. It states that the change in the exchange rate over time t to time $t + T$ equals the change in the relative purchasing power of the two monies. Since the change in prices from time t to time $t + T$ is the measure of the inflation rate, the relative version of PPP can be used to express the two nations' inflation differential. To illustrate, let us define

6.6 $$P_{t+T}/P_t = 1 + \pi_t$$

6.7 $$P^*_{t+T}/P^*_t = 1 + \pi^*_t$$

where π_t and π^*_t are the inflation rates for the domestic and foreign country, respectively. Substituting eqs. 6.6 and 6.7 into 6.5, we obtain

6.8 $$S_{t+T}/S_t = (1 + \pi_t)/(1 + \pi^*_t).$$

Subtracting unity from both sides of eq. 6.8 yields

6.9 $$(S_{t+T} - S_t)/S_t = (\pi_t - \pi^*_t)/(1 + \pi^*_t).$$

This expression says that the depreciation (appreciation) of the U.S. dollar corresponds to the fact that the United States has a higher (lower) inflation rate than the relevant foreign country. For instance, if the United States had an inflation rate of 9% for the last year and Japan a 4% rate, the theory suggests that the U.S. dollar would have depreciated by approximately 5%.

With a simple manipulation, eq. 6.9 can also be converted into an ex ante framework. Let us assume that at time t, economic agents form their expectations about exchange rates and the two countries' inflation rates to prevail over time $t + T$. It follows that the expected changes in the exchange rate are associated with the expected inflation differentials. That is,

6.10 $$(S^e_{t+T} - S_t)/S_t = (\pi^e_t - \pi^{e*}_t)/(1 + \pi^{e*}_t).$$

In practice, if the inflation rate in the United States is expected to be 7%, and that in Japan is expected to be 3%, the U.S. dollar is expected to depreciate by 4%.

We should bear in mind that the accuracy of using PPP in predicting exchange rate movements may depend, among other things, on the flexibility of prices. Downward rigidity of prices may not sufficiently capture the short-run variations of exchange rate behavior. However, most people believe that the predictions of exchange rate changes based on relative inflation rates are more relevant for a longer time horizon.

Extensions of Purchasing Power Parity

Using inflation rates in predicting changes in exchange rates is based on the assumption that the inflation rates are exogenously determined; that is, inflation rates are not influenced by other economic variables. But standard economic theory suggests that inflation can result from factors of either a demand-pull or cost-push type. A demand-pull inflation may be caused by an excess growth of money supply. According to the quantity theory, the inflation rate is proportionate to the excess growth of the money supply. Incorporating this quantity theory proposition into PPP, as implied in the monetary approach to exchange rate determination, we see that expected currency depreciation is essentially driven by the expected excess growth of the relative money supply and other determinants of money demand. Further, by combining the theory with rational expectations, we can readily argue that an unexpected currency depreciation must be associated with an unexpected excess growth of the domestic money supply, or perhaps with other random disturbances.

Rather than considering inflation as a monetary phenomenon, the cost-push view relates the inflation rate to factors such as changes in wage rates and productivity gains. Combining this approach with PPP, we can argue that expected currency depreciation is positively related to expected higher growth in wage rates and negatively to expected relative productivity gains. In practice, we see that a relatively stable wage rate and a relatively higher productivity growth in Japan, in Germany, and recently in other newly industrialized countries vs. the United States have brought about a persistent currency appreciation in these countries.[1]

EMPIRICAL EVIDENCE ON PURCHASING POWER PARITY

In this section, we begin with a presentation of a model pertinent to the empirical tests for purchasing power parity. Also, we provide evidence to verify the theory. Finally, we explain why purchasing power parity does not hold.

Evidence

The empirical investigation of purchasing power parity usually involves a regression analysis of eqs. 6.3 and 6.5. To conduct the empirical tests it is convenient to write the equations in natural logarithm form. Expressing these equations in a regression form, we simply add a constant and an error term to the model:

6.11
$$s_t = \beta_0 + \beta_1(p_t - p_t^*) + \varepsilon_t,$$

6.12
$$\Delta s_t = \beta_1(\Delta p_t - \Delta p_t^*) + \varepsilon_t,$$

where β_0 and β_1 are constant parameters, and ε_t is an error term. Equation 6.11 is designed for testing absolute PPP, and eq. 6.12 is for testing relative PPP. The empirical verification of PPP involves a test of the null hypothesis that $\beta_0 = 0$ and $\beta_1 = 1$. The significance tests usually consist of individual tests using the t-statistic and a joint test using the F-statistic.

---

[1] Further investigation into the structural relationships may be necessary. This requires a complete macro-asset model for exchange rate determination, which is beyond the scope of this chapter.

Exhibit 6.1

Regression Estimates of
Purchasing Power Parity:
1921.2–1925.5

Spot Rate	β_0	β_1	R^2	D.W.	SEE	ρ	F	Method
A. *Absolute PPP*								
Dollar/Pound	0.525 (0.291)	0.541* (0.160)	0.94	1.94	0.019	0.89	4.67*	CORC
Franc/Dollar	1.219* (0.165)	1.070 (0.114)	0.90	2.02	0.065	0.57	1.46	CORC
Franc/Pound	0.790* (0.261)	1.073 (0.081)	0.94	2.15	0.061	0.53	3.00	CORC
B. *Relative PPP*								
Dollar/Pound	0.002 (0.003)	0.404* (0.164)	0.11	1.97	0.019		6.73*	OLS
Franc/Dollar	0.001 (0.010)	0.828 (0.246)	0.18	2.38	0.073		0.24	OLS
Franc/Pound	0.001 (0.010)	0.796 (0.233)	0.19	2.47	0.069		0.43	OLS

SOURCE: Tables 2 and 3 in Frenkel (*JIE*, 1978). Used with permission.

Notes:
a. The estimates of absolute PPP use $s_t = \beta_0 + \beta_1(p_t - p_t^*) + \varepsilon_t$; those for relative PPP use $\Delta s_t = \beta_0 + \beta_1(\Delta p_t - \Delta p_t^*) + \varepsilon_t$.
b. Standard errors of estimates are in parentheses below each coefficient.
c. An asterisk (*) denotes significance at the 5% level. It applies to the significance test for the null hypothesis that $\beta_0 = 0$ and that $\beta_1 = 1$, respectively.
d. R^2 is the coefficient of determination; D.W. is the Durbin-Watson statistic; SEE is the standard error of estimate.
e. OLS denotes ordinary least-squares estimation, CORC denotes Cochrane-Orcutt estimation, and ρ is the first-order autocorrelation coefficient.

One common problem encountered in testing concerns the choice of an appropriate price index. A price index is a weighted average of the prices of individual commodities for a specific bundle of goods. Such indexes include the consumer price index (CPI), the GNP deflator, the wholesale price index (WPI), and the production price index (PPI). Various indexes have been used by different researchers; our presentation concentrates on the use of the WPI.

The results presented in Exhibit 6.1 were taken from Frenkel (1978), who estimated the PPP equations using the wholesale price indices for the period February 1921 through May 1925. The exchange rates include dollar/pound, franc/pound, and franc/dollar. The results in the upper part of Exhibit 6.1 apply to absolute PPP, and those in the lower part are for relative PPP. The statistics indicate that, except for the case of the dollar/pound rate, one cannot reject the hypothesis that $\beta_1 = 1$. The evidence thus provides some support for PPP in franc/dollar and franc/pound rates.

When the models were reestimated using data in the recent floating period from June 1973 through January 1987, several other currencies were also included. The estimations were conducted using both ordinary least-squares and Cochrane-Orcutt methods. As can be seen from Exhibit 6.2, the coefficients of relative price variables, in most cases, are significantly different from zero; this indicates that exchange rates can be explained, in part, by relative prices. However, the hypothesis that

Spot Rate	β_0	β_1	R^2	D.W.	$Q(M)$	SEE	ρ	F	Method
A. Absolute PPP									
Ca. Dollar/Dollar	0.114*	1.632*	0.891	0.160	1014.82*	0.038			OLS
	(0.003)	(0.045)							
	0.498*	−0.014*	0.990	1.842	64.93*	0.012	0.995*	23.48*	CORC
	(0.180)	(0.150)					(0.008)		
Franc/Dollar	1.542*	2.063*	0.655	0.055	1516.94*	0.162			OLS
	(0.020)	(0.123)							
	1.865*	0.645*	0.985	2.229	19.377	0.033	0.987*	35.59*	CORC
	(0.221)	(0.209)					(0.013)		
Lira/Dollar	6.909*	1.289*	0.948	0.092	885.91*	0.107			OLS
	(0.008)	(0.031)							
	7.090*	0.485*	0.993	2.153	35.87	0.031	0.987*	679.00*	CORC
	(0.215)	(0.226)					(0.010)		
Mark/Dollar	0.813*	0.325*	0.050	0.057	1531.97*		0.148		OLS
	(0.017)	(0.111)							
	0.714*	−0.608*	0.948	1.994	32.40	0.035	0.986*	16.68	CORC
	(0.200)	(0.361)					(0.016)		
Pound/Dollar	−0.593*	0.940	0.607	0.066	1457.55*		0.131		OLS
	(0.010)	(0.059)							
	−0.382*	−0.107*	0.976	1.946	29.60	0.032	0.983*	16.88	CORC
	(0.163)	(0.285)					(0.012)		
Yen/Dollar	5.488*	0.977	0.603	0.097	850.72*		0.105		OLS
	(0.008)	(0.062)							
	5.398*	0.639	0.962	1.973	44.24	0.033	0.978*	1102.64*	CORC
	(0.118)	(0.233)					(0.024)		
B. Relative PPP									
Ca. Dollar/Dollar	0.002	−0.014*	0.001	1.846	66.06*	0.012		24.235*	OLS
	(0.001)	(0.146)							
Franc/Dollar	0.003	0.630*	0.051	2.186	19.117	0.034		1.687	OLS
	(0.003)	(0.213)							
Lira/Dollar	0.002	0.516*	0.030	2.156	35.34	0.0310		2.385	OLS
	(0.003)	(0.227)							
Mark/Dollar	−0.003	−0.446*	0.009	1.897	27.154	0.036		7.780*	OLS
	(0.003)	(0.367)							
Pound/Dollar	−0.003	0.075*	0.0004	1.958	29.99	0.033		9.417*	OLS
	(0.003)	(0.283)							
Yen/Dollar	−0.002	0.523*	0.027	1.986	45.37	0.033		1.988	OLS
	(0.003)	(0.237)							

Exhibit 6.2

Regression Estimates of Purchasing Power Parity: 1973.6–1987.1

Notes: a. The estimates of absolute PPP use $s_t = \beta_0 + \beta_1(p_t - p_t^*) + \varepsilon_t$; those for relative PPP use $\Delta s_t = \beta_0 + \beta_1(\Delta p_t - \Delta p_t^*) + \varepsilon_t$.
   b. Standard errors of estimates are in parentheses below each coefficient.
   c. An asterisk (*) denotes significance at the 5% level. It applies to the significance test for the null hypothesis that $\beta_0 = 0$ and that $\beta_1 = 1$, respectively.
   d. R^2 is the coefficient of determination; D.W. is the Durbin-Watson statistic; $Q(M)$ is the Ljung-Box Q-statistic, which is distributed as chi-square with M ($= 36$) degrees of freedom; SEE is the standard error of estimate.
   e. OLS denotes ordinary least-squares estimation, CORC denotes Cochrane-Orcutt estimation, and ρ is the first-order autocorrelation coefficient.

$\beta_1 = 1$ is generally rejected by the data. The evidence indicates that PPP does not hold in the 1970s and 1980s. This finding is similar to the results reported by Frenkel (1978) and Krugman (1978) in their earlier studies.

Deviations from Purchasing Power Parity

The departure from PPP in the 1970s and 1980s leads us to inquire about the factors that contribute to the rejection of PPP. In the following paragraphs we outline three factors that may account for the failure of PPP: the existence of transaction costs and impediments to trade, changes of relative prices, and the multivariate and simultaneity problems.

Transaction Costs and Impediments to Trade   A popular argument for rejecting PPP is the existence of transaction costs and barriers to trade, such as tariffs and quotas. Nontrivial transaction costs and impediments to trade should distort the relative prices of traded goods and, in turn, frustrate spatial arbitrage between countries and goods that are close substitutes. A standard trade theory would argue that if, for example, the costs of transportation constitute 5% of the commodity price, the difference in prices between two markets (in different countries) ought to reflect the transportation costs. Thus, we can observe that the difference in market prices may not closely correspond to the exchange rate.

Similar effects may be caused by an imposition of tariffs on importable goods. For example, a 10% import duty would create a price wedge of similar magnitude between domestic and foreign goods, leading to a purchasing power disparity. An empirical study by Frenkel (1978) finds stronger evidence of PPP between European countries than between each of these countries and the United States. This condition is caused by lower transportation costs due to geographic integration and a more uniform commercial policy that has been adopted by the European countries.

Changes in Relative Prices   The formulation of PPP is based on the premise that the relative price structure is stable. Suppose that the aggregate price level for each country is constructed from a weighted average of nontraded goods and traded goods. If the prices of the traded goods, say prices of cloth, rise by 10% in both countries and the weights of the traded goods for the two countries are identical, then the relative aggregate prices for the two countries would not change. However, if the exchange rate adjusts only to the relative prices of the traded goods, an empirical estimate based on regressing the exchange rate on the relative aggregate price levels would indicate that the coefficient of the relative price was significantly different from unity. The bias is due to ignoring the change in relative prices between the traded and the nontraded goods. Thus, the presence of time-varying internal relative prices between traded and nontraded goods could be an important source of the failure of PPP. The problem can be more serious if the construction of the price indexes involves different bundles of commodities. Consequently, it is not surprising that one can easily find evidence to reject PPP in practice even when the theory might hold exactly.

Multivariate and Simultaneity Factors   The PPP theory represented by eq. 6.11 or 6.12 highlights the role of commodity flows in determining exchange rates. In this specification the role of capital flows and of other factors is not incorporated into the model. A comparison of eq. 6.11 with eq. 4.22 in Chapter 4 implies that both the relative real incomes and the interest rate differential are ignored in the PPP model.[2] If the specification of eq. 4.22 is supported by empirical results, the exclusion of these variables would generate biased estimates. Thus, omitted explanatory variables may account for violations of PPP.

A more likely scenario explaining PPP violations is that both the changes in exchange rates and the inflation differential are endogenous. This could be the case if an unexpected change in the money supply caused both the exchange rate and the inflation rate to change. Since the exchange rate behaves as an asset price, its speed of adjustment should be faster than that for the goods price.[3] Thus, through investigating the lead and lag relationships between these two series one might find that the exchange rate leads the relative price. Implementing Sims's (1972) two-sided regression to test "causality" between the two series, Frenkel finds that the exchange rates cause prices, and that prices do not cause exchange rates. The causal pattern in Frenkel's study is consistent with the hypothesis that the speeds of adjustment in the asset markets exceed those in the goods markets, which is likely. The evidence also suggests that a simultaneous equation bias problem needs to be addressed. In other words, accounting for such nonsimultaneity may "correct" for the potential violations of PPP.

REAL EXCHANGE RATES

In this section, we first discuss the concept of real exchange rates. Then, we consider the effect of real exchange rates on trade flows, at the micro and macro levels. Finally, we analyze the effect of real exchange rates on asset returns and, hence, on international capital flows.

Definition of Real Exchange Rates

Experience with floating rates since the early 1970s reveals that the behavior of the exchange rate differs significantly from that of aggregate price levels. The asset approach argues that the behavior of exchange rates is very similar to that of asset prices in general. Due to the uncertainty of the future outcome, expectations of exchange rate movements are quite sensitive to the development of new information. Thus any new information that hits the market alters market perceptions, causing asset price fluctuations. Since news is unpredictable, an unexpected shock may even be aggravated by unstable speculative activity, resulting in a high degree of volatility of exchange rates.

---

[2] In the statistical sense this means that, in the restricted equation (6.11), the coefficient of the relative prices equals unity, and that the coefficients on relative income and the interest rate differential equal zero.

[3] Two-stage least squares (2SLS) or the instrumental variables approach are the standard procedures for handling this problem. The first stage is to generate a proxy that is highly correlated with the prices and at the same time independent of the error term; then this proxy is substituted for the explanatory variable in the second-stage regression estimation.

In contrast to the behavior of exchange rates, the characteristics of aggregate price indices such as the CPI appear to be much smoother. Commodity pricing depends on production efficiency, input costs, finite nominal wage contracts, and market structure. All these factors are not as sensitive to market expectations and "news" as are those affecting asset prices. With this understanding, it becomes clear why exchange rates and prices do not intimately covary.

When a shock, monetary or real, alters exchange rates and relative prices simultaneously but to different degrees, it is of interest to look at the nominal exchange rate adjusted by the relative prices, which is the real exchange rate. The real exchange rate, E_{t+T}, can be defined as

6.13 $$E_{t+T} = (S_{t+T}/S_t)/[(P_{t+T}/P_t)/(P^*_{t+T}/P^*_t)].$$

Alternatively, the real exchange rate can be expressed in logarithmic form as

6.14 $$e_t = s_t - (p_t - p^*_t),$$

where e_t denotes the natural logarithm of the real exchange rate. Applying the difference operator on eq. 6.14 yields

6.15 $$\Delta e_t = \Delta s_t - (\Delta p_t - \Delta p^*_t).$$

Equation 6.15 states that the change in the real exchange rate is due to the change in the nominal exchange rate relative to the change in relative prices. This is equivalent to saying that if the changes in the nominal exchange rate are matched by the changes in the relative prices between the two trading countries, the real exchange rate does not vary. Thus, if PPP holds, which is the case in which $\Delta s_t = (\Delta p_t - \Delta p^*_t)$, Δe_t equals zero. Put another way, the changes in the real exchange rate over time must correspond to the deviations from PPP.

The concept of the real exchange rate has an important implication for the assessment of competitive positions in the international commodity markets and the effectiveness of exchange rate policy. If $\Delta e_t > 0$, the domestic currency depreciation is greater than the relative price rise, suggesting that there is an improvement in competitive position, which in turn stimulates exports. If $\Delta e_t < 0$, the domestic currency depreciation is smaller than the relative price rise, leading to a deterioration in the competitive position and hence discouraging exports. If $\Delta e_t = 0$, the rise in the domestic inflation offsets the rate of depreciation, leaving no change in the real exchange rate. Therefore, there is no effect on the country's competitive position.

Real Exchange Rates and Trade Flows: Micro Analysis

Although changes in the real exchange rate, Δe_t, can be used as an indicator for projecting a country's competitive position in international commodity markets, the tactics and the decision-making processes are quite different between the macro and the micro levels.

From the micro point of view, an individual firm has no control over the exchange rate. Therefore, it continuously revises commodity prices to meet the challenges in the international commodity market. At the micro level, each firm has its own real exchange rate, depending on the commodity prices $p_{j,t}$ and $p^*_{j,t}$ that the firm faces. The real exchange rate for the individual firm can be written as

6.16
$$\Delta e_{j,t} = \Delta s_t - (\Delta p_{j,t} - \Delta p^*_{j,t}),$$

where $e_{j,t}$, $p_{j,t}$, and $p^*_{j,t}$ are, respectively, the real exchange rate and the prices applied to the comparable commodity j. As we discussed in Chapter 4, the component Δs_t in $\Delta e_{j,t}$ is determined by market forces, expectations, and central bank policy; the components $\Delta p_{j,t}$ and $\Delta p^*_{j,t}$ in $\Delta e_{j,t}$ depend on the individual firm's pricing mechanism and market strategy.

Note that changes in either component directly affect the value of a multinational firm. Finance theory tells us that the value of a firm can be measured by its present value, which is the sum of future after-tax cash flows capitalized at an appropriate discount rate. The revenues, and in turn the cash flows, are generated from the goods sold in the international markets, which are determined by the multinational firm's competitive position. As we discussed earlier, the competitive position is dependent on the real exchange rate faced by the firm. Thus, a careful monitoring of the variable $\Delta e_{j,t}$ appears to be one of the most important strategies of a multinational firm, since its movements reflect a firm's dynamic competitive position and its variations reflect information about the uncertainty of the cash flows for the firm.

Real Exchange Rates and Trade Flows: Macro Analysis

From the macro point of view, governments may frequently manipulate the nominal exchange rate in the foreign exchange markets, but they seldom intervene to affect aggregate prices. Occasionally, we hear that a government adopts an exchange rate policy to improve the balance-of-payment position. The idea behind this policy is the application of the elasticities approach to the balance of trade. The elasticities model has long been used as a framework to analyze how currency depreciations (or devaluations) will help to lessen a deficit in the balance of trade, depending on the supply and demand elasticities for the foreign goods and the foreign currency.

The rationale of the elasticities approach is that following a depreciation of the domestic currency (in the dollar/pound rate, for example), the dollar price of pounds increases. As a result, goods imported from the United Kingdom become more expensive to the United States, whereas U.S. goods exported to the United Kingdom become cheaper. Given that the demand and supply curves are elastic, imports are discouraged and exports are stimulated. Both forces work together to help improve the balance of trade, ΔB_t. The trade balance continuously improves until the relative prices rise to offset the rate of depreciation. That is, the $\Delta B_t = 0$ when $\Delta e_t = 0$. From this perspective the depreciation of the domestic currency in the long run brings about an equal proportion of domestic inflation. The effect of depreciation is the sum of the cash flows derived from net exports for the periods when Δe_t is greater than zero.[4]

Real Exchange Rates and Asset Returns

From the preceding analysis, we understand that changes in the real exchange rate directly affect competitive positions in international markets. The question is whether the real exchange rate can be affected by economic forces. Since the real exchange rate consists of the nominal exchange rate and inflation rates, both of which are essentially monetary phenomena, it is logical to relate the real exchange rate to monetary policy. To illustrate this idea, let us assume that international capital markets are efficient and investors are risk-neutral; then changes in exchange rate expectations are related to the interest differential by the open Fisher equation:

6.17 $$\Delta s_t^e = r_t - r_t^*.$$

Subtracting the expected inflation differential $(\Delta p_t^e - \Delta p_t^{e*})$ from both sides of eq. 6.17, we derive a real interest rate parity as

6.18 $$\Delta e_t^e = (r_t - \Delta p_t^e) - (r_t^* - \Delta p_t^{e*}),$$

where $\Delta e_t^e = \Delta s_t^e - (\Delta p_t^e - \Delta p_t^{e*})$ is the expected real exchange rate, which, according to eq. 6.18, is related to the relative real interest rates. It is apparent that if, ex-ante, PPP holds (i.e., $\Delta s_t^e = \Delta p_t^e - \Delta p_t^{e*}$), then $\Delta e_t^e = 0$. Moreover, if there are no impediments to capital flows, the real interest rates must be equalized across countries.

The real interest rate parity expression in eq. 6.18 has several implications. First, in view of the efficient market framework, changes in the real exchange rate must correspond to deviations from PPP, which will offer a profitable opportunity for market speculation. For instance, a positive value of Δe_t^e suggests that excess profits may be realized by buying spot exchange and holding a commodity basket quoted in the foreign country's price. If the rate of real depreciation predictably exceeds the real interest rate in the domestic country, the profits from engaging in commodity speculation must be higher than the cost of borrowing or the option of investing in the financial markets. Of course, part of the excess profits can be viewed as a risk premium associated with the variability of the real exchange rate.

Second, real interest rate parity also links real economic activity to monetary policy. To see the relationship between the real exchange rate and the monetary influence, we need to specify the expectation formation process, which is similar to the specifications of exchange rate ex-

---

[4] To determine whether the exchange depreciation will be successful, the Marshall-Lerner condition should be checked. That is, given perfect elasticities of export and import supply, depreciation improves the balance of trade if the sum of the export and import demand elasticities is greater than unity. The discussion is also related to the so-called J-curve effect, which refers to the time pattern of the balance of trade following a depreciation (see Chapter 2). It has been argued that when the elasticities are small, the trade balances in the beginning period may fall for a while and then begin to grow in the later periods.

pectations discussed in Chapter 5. Here we consider only a regressive expectation, which postulates that the actual real exchange rate adjusts only gradually to the trend level, e'_t, according to the process:

6.19
$$\Delta e^e_t = \gamma(e'_t - e_t),$$

where γ is the speed of adjustment. Substituting eq. 6.19 into 6.18 and rearranging yields

6.20
$$e_t = e'_t - [(r_t - \Delta p^e_t) - (r^*_t - \Delta p^{e*}_t)]/\gamma.$$

Equation 6.20 indicates that if the real interest rate is higher in the domestic market than in the foreign market, the real exchange rate will appreciate relative to its trend level. Since the interest rates can be manipulated by monetary policy, the behavioral relationship represented by eq. 6.20 provides us a channel through which the central bank can use its monetary policy to influence the real exchange rate. For instance, a contractionary monetary policy raises the interest rate, and thereby the real interest rate, leading to a real appreciation. However, policymakers should recognize that the economic consequences do not stop at this point, because a real appreciation brings about a deterioration of trade balances. This was the case, for example, in the early 1980s in the United States when relatively higher real interest rates led to real appreciation of the U.S. dollar, which in turn caused consecutive trade deficits in the late 1980s.

EMPIRICAL EVIDENCE ON THE REAL EXCHANGE RATE

Empirical investigation of the real exchange rate is closely tied to verification of PPP. If PPP holds, the errors of the estimated equation must be distributed randomly and will be orthogonal to any particular explanatory variable. The validity of purchasing power parity thus translates into an investigation of the time-series behavior or into an orthogonality test of the related information set for the real exchange rate.

The randomness of the real exchange rate can be investigated by checking the persistence of the series. This can be done by conducting a runs test or by examining the significance of the time-series pattern of the real exchange rates.

Runs Test

The runs test is a nonparametric test used for detecting the frequency of the changes in the direction of the series. The test is designed to determine whether the total number of runs occurring in the sample is consistent with the hypothesis that the changes are independent. The Z-test statistic is a standard normal variable used to conduct a runs test, and is given by

6.21
$$Z = [M - E(M)]/[\sigma^2(M)]^{1/2},$$

where M denotes the number of runs, $E(M) = (2N - 1)/3$, the expected value of M, $\sigma^2(M) = (16N - 29)/90$, the variance of M (runs), and N the

Exhibit 6.3

Runs Test for Real Exchange
Rates: 1973.6–1987.1

	e_t				Δe_t			
	M	E(M)	σ(M)	Z	M	E(M)	σ(M)	Z
Can. dollar	76	109.0	5.370	−6.145*	98	108.33	5.353	−1.930**
French franc	68	100.3	5.150	−6.278*	100	99.67	5.133	0.064
Deutsche mark	58	109.0	5.370	−9.497*	101	108.33	5.353	−1.369
Italian lira	70	109.0	5.370	−7.263*	111	108.33	5.353	0.499
Japanese yen	78	109.0	5.370	−5.773*	102	108.33	5.353	−1.183
U.K. pound	64	109.0	5.370	−8.380*	106	108.33	5.353	−0.435

Notes: a. M is the number of actual runs, $E(M)$ is the expected runs, and $\sigma(M)$ is the standard error of the runs.
   b. One asterisk (*) denotes significance at the 5% level, and two asterisks (**) denote significance at the 10% level.
   c. The real exchange rate is defined as either $e_t = s_t - (p_t - p_t^*)$ or $\Delta e_t = \Delta s_t - (\Delta p_t - \Delta p_t^*)$.
   d. All exchange rates are defined as units of foreign currency per U.S. dollar.

number of observations. When a trend or certain form of persistence is present, the number of runs (M) is relatively small; if the process involves frequent changes in direction, M is large. Thus, a positive value of Z indicates that the number of runs in the sample exceeds the expected number for a random ordering; a negative value for Z suggests fewer than the expected number of runs. Exhibit 6.3 summarizes the statistics concerning the actual runs, the expected runs, and the standard errors of runs; and presents Z-statistics for the series real exchange rate, e_t, and its first difference, Δe_t. Note that the series e_t represents deviation from absolute PPP, and Δe_t is the measure of the deviation from relative PPP.

Looking at the Z-statistics for e_t, the evidence indicates that the hypothesis of a random walk is rejected for all the cases. However, for the first-difference form, none of the Z-statistics are significant at the 5% level. Overall, the evidence indicates that the level of real exchange rates displays some degree of persistence, but that the change in the real exchange rates appears to follow a random-walk process, which is consistent with the efficient markets hypothesis.

Autocorrelation Function

Now we turn to a parametric method to study the time dependency of the series. When we inspected the original real exchange rate series, defined as eq. 6.14, the coefficients of the autocorrelation functions declined slowly and those series were nonstationary. Thus the series were differenced once, with the result that the differenced series are consistent with the notion defined by eq. 6.15. The standard formula for calculating autocorrelation coefficients is given by

6.22
$$\rho_k = \left[\sum_1^{n-k} (\Delta e_t)(\Delta e_{t+k}) \right] \Big/ \sum_1^n (\Delta e_t)^2,$$

where ρ_k is the coefficient of autocorrelation for the log-difference of various real exchange rates (Δe_t). The results are reported in Exhibit 6.4.

ACF	Can. Dollar	French Franc	Deutsche Mark	Italian Lira	Japanese Yen	U.K. Pound
ρ_1	0.003	−0.142	−0.071	−0.123	−0.028	0.051
ρ_2	−0.219*	0.016	0.137	0.127	−0.015	0.024
ρ_3	0.049	0.036	−0.029	0.028	0.116	−0.038
ρ_4	−0.009	0.002	−0.043	−0.036	0.041	0.030
ρ_5	0.132	0.111	0.111	0.204*	0.126	0.059
ρ_6	−0.100	−0.140	−0.104	−0.052	−0.147*	−0.070
ρ_7	−0.086	0.003	0.110	0.074	0.035	−0.028
ρ_8	0.082	−0.003	0.006	−0.026	−0.010	0.008
ρ_9	0.005	−0.006	0.075	0.046	−0.006	0.071
ρ_{10}	0.049	−0.000	0.020	0.046	−0.062	0.018
ρ_{11}	0.152	0.052	0.107	0.050	0.076	0.140*
ρ_{12}	−0.115	0.014	−0.045	−0.031	0.077	−0.031
Mean ($\times 10^{-3}$)	0.320	2.575	−0.032	−0.966	−1.246	−0.9006
S.E. ($\times 10^{-3}$)	13.054	33.505	36.729	31.560	32.805	33.874

Exhibit 6.4

Autocorrelation Coefficients for Real Exchange Rates (Δe_t): 1973.6–1987.1

Notes: a. An asterisk (*) denotes significance at the 5% level.
b. ρ_k is the estimated autocorrelation function (ACF) at the kth lag for the first difference of real exchange rates (Δe_t). The real exchange rate is defined as $e_t = s_t - (p_t - p_t^*)$.
c. All exchange rates are defined as units of foreign currency per U.S. dollar.

As can be seen in the exhibit, only a few cases are statistically significant. In particular, the coefficient is found to be significant at lag 2 for the Canadian dollar, lag 5 for the Italian lira, lag 6 for the Japanese yen, and lag 11 for the British pound.[5] Thus, the results generally affirm those presented in Exhibit 6.3.

Time-Series Pattern

To further study the underlying pattern of the real exchange rate series, we use the methodology proposed by Box and Jenkins (1976). A univariate representation of the model is given by

6.23
$$\phi_p(L)(1 - L)^d e_t = \theta_q(L)\varepsilon_t,$$

where $\phi_p(L)$ and $\theta_q(L)$ are autoregressive and moving-average parameters in the lag (or backshift) operator (L); the superscript d denotes the number of the differencing on the real exchange rate, e_t, to generate a stationary series; and ε_t is white noise.

An empirical estimation of the model involves the following procedures: first, the autocorrelation function (ACF) and the partial autocorrelation function (PACF) are calculated and a tentative model is identified;

---

[5] An overall test of a flat autocorrelation function can be carried out using the Q^*-statistic. Under the hypothesis that all autocorrelations are zero, $Q^* = n(n + 2)\sum_{k=1}^{12}(n - k)^{-1}\rho_k^2(e)$, where n is the number of observations, and ρ_k is the estimated autocorrelation of lag k. The Q^*-statistic is distributed as χ^2 with twelve degrees of freedom.

Exhibit 6.5

Time-Series Models of Real
Exchange Rates

Exchange Rate	Model
Can. dollar	$(1 + 0.237L^2 - 0.181L^5 - 0.183L^{11})(1 - L)e_t = \varepsilon_t$ $\quad(-3.08)^* \quad\quad (2.34)^* \quad\quad (2.44)^*$ $R^2 = 0.95 \quad MSE = 0.0119 \quad Q(8) = 12$
French franc	$(1 - L)e_t = \varepsilon_t + 0.003$ $\quad\quad\quad\quad\quad\quad\quad (0.94)$ $R^2 = 0.97 \quad MSE = 0.034 \quad Q(11) = 11$
Deutsche mark	$(1 - L)e_t = \varepsilon_t - 0.0004$ $\quad\quad\quad\quad\quad\quad\quad (-0.01)$ $R^2 = 0.95 \quad MSE = 0.014 \quad Q(11) = 14$
Italian lira	$(1 - L)e_t = (1 + 0.218L^5)\varepsilon_t - 0.001$ $\quad\quad\quad\quad\quad\quad (-2.71)^* \quad\quad (-0.34)$ $R^2 = 0.94 \quad MSE = 0.001 \quad Q(10) = 8$
Japanese yen	$(1 - L)e_t = \varepsilon_t - 0.001$ $\quad\quad\quad\quad\quad\quad\quad (-0.52)$ $R^2 = 0.90 \quad MSE = 0.001 \quad Q(11) = 10$
U.K. pound	$(1 - L)e_t = \varepsilon_t - 0.001$ $\quad\quad\quad\quad\quad\quad\quad (-0.34)$ $R^2 = 0.93 \quad MSE = 0.001 \quad Q(11) = 12$

Notes: a. One asterisk (*) and two asterisks (**) denote significance at the 5% and 10% levels, respectively.
   b. $(1 - L)$ is a differenced operator. We define $(1 - L)e_t = e_t - e_{t-1} = \Delta s_t - (\Delta p_t - \Delta p_t^*)$.
   c. All exchange rates are defined as units of foreign currency per U.S. dollar.
   d. R^2 is the coefficient of determination; MSE is the mean squared error; $Q(M)$ is the Ljung-Box Q-statistic, which
       is distributed as chi-square with M degrees of freedom.

second, the identified model is estimated using iterative maximum likelihood methods; third, a diagnostic checking on the randomness of the
residual errors is done to ensure "adequacy" of the estimated model.

The estimated model for e_t or Δe_t can provide insights concerning
deviations from PPP. On the basis of the finding in eq. 6.23, if the
estimating returns show that the coefficients in $\phi_p(L)$ and $\theta_q(L)$ are zero,
the series of real exchange rates is not distinguishable from a random
process. Such a finding is consistent with the efficient markets hypothesis as suggested by Roll (1979). However, if the estimated coefficients of
$\phi_p(L)$ and $\theta_q(L)$ are statistically significant, then some degree of persistence is present in the real exchange rate series. This persistence might
lead to profitable trading by exploiting an appropriate systematic pattern
underlying the series.

The estimates of the time-series model for various real exchange rates
are presented in Exhibit 6.5. The evidence shows that both the Canadian
dollar and the Italian lira display a particular pattern. The coefficients at
lags 2, 5, and 11 for Canada and at lag 5 for Italy are statistically significant. For the other currencies, the hypothesis that the real exchange rate
behaves as a random-walk process cannot be rejected. To conclude our
findings, with the exception of the cases of the Canadian dollar and
Italian lira, the evidence is in favor of the hypothesis that the real exchange rate follows a random-walk process. Our results imply that, in

the majority of cases, real exchange rate changes are unpredictable, suggesting that it is difficult to make systematic profits by engaging in commodity speculation.[6]

SUMMARY

The relationship between exchange rates and prices is built on the law of one price. For any particular commodity the law of one price states that through spatial arbitrage, commodity prices, once they are quoted in the same currency, are equal everywhere. When the law of one price holds true for all commodities, we establish purchasing power parity (PPP).

Purchasing power parity has two versions. Absolute PPP states that the exchange rate is equal to the ratio of two nation's prices. Relative PPP states that the percentage change in the exchange rate equals the percentage change in the relative prices for the two countries. If relative PPP holds, the expected inflation differentials can be used to predict the exchange rate changes, at least in the long run.

The empirical evidence does not support PPP. The departure from PPP can be attributed to many factors. We observe the existence of shipping costs and trade restrictions, the lack of substitutes of traded goods, and the presence of structural changes in relative prices and productivities.

Empirical violation of PPP may also imply that goods prices do not keep pace with exchange rate movements. The real exchange rate is the nominal exchange rate adjusted by the two countries' relative prices. The movements of the real exchange rate can be viewed as an indicator for measuring competitive positions in the international commodity markets. Generally speaking, if the domestic currency depreciates more than the rise in the difference of the inflation rates, the real exchange rate rises. At the micro level, the rise in the real exchange rate may improve the cash flows and hence the value of a multinational firm. At the macro level, the rise of the real exchange rate tends to improve a nation's balance of trade.

Consistent with earlier studies, we find the level of the real exchange rate possesses some degree of persistence. However, study of the differenced form of the real exchange rate indicates that it generally follows a random-walk process, implying that no excess profits can be realized by engaging in commodity speculation.

---

[6] As we discussed earlier, the real exchange rate movements may also be associated with changes in central bank policy. For this reason, we regress the real exchange rate on the real interest rate differential. However, the testing results do not support the theoretical prediction. This finding indicates that further research needs to be done to explain real exchange rate movements.

Questions and Problems

1. Explain the rationale behind the law of one price. How do you derive purchasing power parity from the law of one price?

2. Describe two different versions of purchasing power parity. How do you relate them to the real exchange rate?

3. What is the limitation of the absolute version of purchasing power parity?

4. Discuss the procedure for testing purchasing power parity. Why does the relative version of PPP seem to perform more poorly than the absolute version?

5. Can you use expected inflation rates to predict exchange rates? How do you generate the expected inflation rates?

6. Provide economic reasons for why purchasing power parity does not hold.

7. Discuss the difficulties and potential problems in conducting the empirical tests on purchasing power parity.

8. Discuss the significance of the real exchange rate. How does monetary policy affect the real exchange rate, and how does the real exchange rate affect the trade balance?

9. Several studies have shown that the real exchange rate follows a martingale process. How do you conduct the test? How important is the testing result? Discuss.

10. Would you expect the time-series behavior of the real exchange rate to be similar to the nominal exchange rate? Why or why not? How do you determine your answer?

11. We often hear and write the following two statements:
    (a) The exchange rate is more volatile than the commodity price;
    (b) The speed of adjustment of the exchange rate is faster than the commodity price.
    How can you verify these two statements?

12. Develop a model that could be used to explain the movements of the real exchange rates.

References

Aizenman, J. "Modeling Deviations from Purchasing Power Parity." *International Economic Review* 25 (February 1984): 1471–87.

Balassa, B. "The Purchasing Power Parity Doctrine: A Reappraisal." *Journal of Political Economy* 72 (1964): 584–96.

Box, G., and G. Jenkins. *Time Series Analysis, Forecasting and Control.* San Francisco: Holden-Day, 1976.

Cassel, G. "The Present Situation of the Foreign Exchanges." *Economic Journal* 26 (March 1916): 62–65.

———. *The World's Monetary Problems.* London: Constable, 1921.

Dornbusch, R. "Expectations and Exchange Rate Dynamics." *Journal of Political Economy* 84 (1976): 1161–76.

———. "Purchasing Power Parity." *The New Palgrave Dictionary of Economics* (1987): 1075–85.

Frenkel, J. "Purchasing Power Parity: Doctrinal Perspective and Evidence from the 1920s." *Journal of International Economics* 8 (May 1978): 169–91.

————. "The Collapse of Purchasing Power Parities during the 1970s." *European Economic Review* 16 (1981): 145–65.

Krugman, P. "Purchasing Power and Exchange Rates: Another Look at the Evidence." *Journal of International Economics* 8 (1978): 397–407.

Neter, J., W. Wasserman, and G. Whitmore. *Applied Statistics.* Boston: Allyn and Bacon, 1982.

Officer, L. "The Purchasing-Power-Parity Theory of Exchange Rates: A Review Article." *IMF Staff Papers* 18 (March 1976): 1–60.

Roll, R. "Violations of Purchasing Power Parity and Their Implications for Efficient International Commodity Markets." In *International Finance and Trade,* eds. Marshall Sarnat and Giorgio Szego, vol. 1, 133–76. Cambridge, Mass: Ballinger, 1979.

Sims, C. A. "Money, Income and Causality." *American Economic Review* 62, no. 4 (September 1972): 540–52.

Part Two

SECURITY AND INTERNATIONAL LOAN MARKETS

Part II is devoted to primary international security markets and issues in international banking. In Chapter 7 we provide background on international money markets and describe the risk-return characteristics of international money market instruments. In Chapter 8 we discuss international bond markets, their development and use, and the valuation of bonds by investors across international markets. In Chapter 9 we describe international equity markets, identify the associated benefits and risk of international equity portfolios, and discuss methods commonly used to achieve international equity diversification. In Chapter 10 we identify techniques that can be used to value foreign stocks and describe differences in stock market efficiency across countries. We conclude Part II with Chapter 11, in which we provide background on the international loan markets, including issues in international banking.

7

INTERNATIONAL MONEY MARKETS

Opportunities in foreign money markets can improve risk-return trade-offs confronted by some investors and borrowers. International money markets facilitate the transfer of short-term funds across countries. In this chapter, we first provide a background of international money markets, and then describe the return and risk characteristics of international money market securities.

INTERNATIONAL MONEY MARKET SECURITIES

Market interest rates vary among countries, as shown in Figure 7.1. The interest rate differentials result from the segmentation of geographical markets. However, because these markets are accessible to foreign investors and borrowers, interest rate differentials have encouraged international money market transactions. These transactions are also motivated by tax differences among countries, speculation on exchange rate movements, and a reduction in government barriers that were previously imposed on investment in foreign securities. Two of the more commonly traded securities in international money markets are Eurodollar deposits and Eurocommercial paper (Euro-CP), as described in the following text.

Eurodollar Deposits

Eurodollars represent U.S. dollar deposits in non-U.S. banks. When interest rate ceilings were imposed on dollar deposits in U.S. banks, corporations with large dollar balances often deposited their funds overseas to receive a higher yield. These deposits were used by banks to provide loans to other corporations that needed U.S. dollars. Eurodollar deposit growth can be attributed to growth in international trade and investment, much of which involves the U.S. dollar as a medium of exchange.

Figure 7.1

International Money Market Rates
Over Time

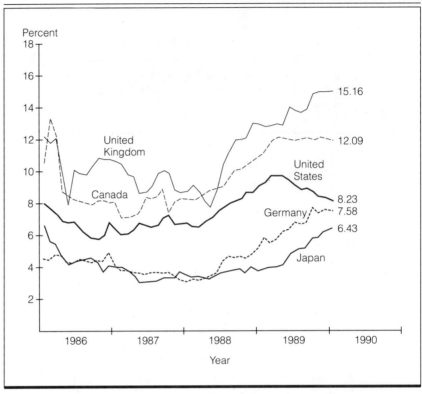

SOURCE: Federal Reserve Bank of St. Louis and International Monetary Fund.

Some non-U.S. firms receive U.S. dollars as payment for exports and invest in Eurodollars. Firms that expect to need dollars for imports retain dollar-denominated deposits rather than converting dollars to their home currency.

Deposits and loan transactions in Eurodollars are typically $1 million or more per transaction. Because transaction amounts are large, investors in the market avoid some costs associated with the continuous small transactions that occur in retail-oriented markets. In addition, Eurodollar deposits are not subject to reserve requirements, so that banks can lend out 100% of the deposits. For these reasons, the spread between the interest rate paid on large Eurodollar deposits and charged on Eurodollar loans is relatively small.

One of the more popular Eurodollar deposits is the fixed-rate Eurodollar CD. Investors in fixed-rate Eurodollar CDs are adversely affected by rising market interest rates, and issuers of these CDs are adversely affected by decreasing rates. To reduce this interest rate risk, Eurodollar floating-rate CDs (called FRCDs) have been used in recent years. The rate adjusts periodically to the London Interbank Offer Rate (LIBOR), which is the interest rate charged on interbank dollar loans. As with other floating-rate instruments, the rate on FRCDs allows the borrower's cost and investor's return to reflect prevailing market interest rates.

Over time, the volume of deposits and loans denominated in other foreign currencies also grew, owing to increased international trade,

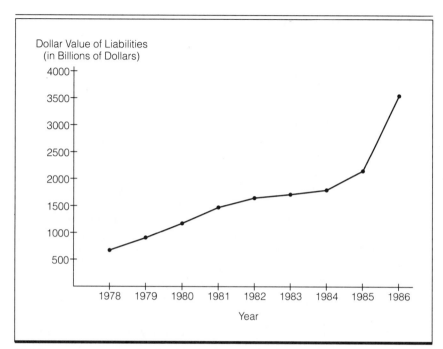

Figure 7.2

Estimated Dollar Value of Commercial Bank Liabilities in the Eurocurrency Market

SOURCE: *International Economic Conditions*, Federal Reserve Bank of St. Louis, various issues.

increased flows of funds among subsidiaries of multinational corporations, and existing differences among country regulations on bank deposit rates. This led to the establishment of the *Eurocurrency market*, composed of several banks (called Eurobanks) that accept large deposits and provide large loans in foreign currencies. These same banks also make up the so-called *Eurocredit market*, which is distinguished from the Eurocurrency market by the longer maturities on loans. Figure 7.2 provides the estimated dollar value of commercial bank liabilities in the Eurocurrency market. This figure shows that since 1978, liabilities have almost quadrupled. Over this time period, the value of dollar liabilities has represented between 70% and 80% of the market value of all Eurocurrency liabilities. In recent years, the percentage has declined slightly, because of the growth in nondollar Eurocurrency deposits.

The lack of regulation led to the initial growth of the Eurocurrency market, yet it could also cause a financial crisis. If some of the large Eurobanks experienced financial problems, this could have a devastating impact on the Eurocurrency market and all of its participants. A greater degree of regulation may enhance the safety of Eurobanks, and the confidence of corporations and governments that use the market. However, country governments would have to agree on a standard set of regulations to be imposed. If governments differed either in the standards imposed or in their enforcement, the future growth of the Eurocurrency market would be concentrated in those areas exhibiting relatively less regulation.

Eurocommercial Paper

Eurocommercial paper (Euro-CP) is a popular instrument for borrowing in international money markets. Dealers that place commercial paper have created a secondary market by being willing to purchase existing Euro-CP before maturity. The Euro-CP market is commonly used by large corporations that wish to hedge future cash inflows in a particular foreign currency. For example, a U.S. firm expecting to receive Swiss francs as payment for goods in three months may borrow francs today and convert them to dollars to support U.S. operations. Then, the francs to be received in three months can be used to repay the loan. Since Swiss interest rates are usually lower than U.S. interest rates, this strategy allows the U.S. corporation to reduce its financing cost without being exposed to exchange rate risk. Some corporations that do not have future cash inflows in a foreign currency may still consider borrowing from a foreign market, if they expect that the value of the foreign currency will depreciate against the dollar.

The Euro-CP rate is typically between 50 and 100 basis points above LIBOR. Euro-CP is sold by dealers at a transaction cost ranging between 5 and 10 basis points of the face value. A review of Figure 7.1 suggests that the interest rates of British and Canadian money market securities may be attractive to U.S. investors. Conversely, German and Japanese money market instruments offer relatively low interest rates.

Whether focusing on Euro-CP or Eurodollar deposits, the globalization of international money markets can have an impact on central bank control of interest rates. The infusion of foreign investment into money markets represents an additional source of funds. However, if an event causes foreign investors to withdraw funds, money market rates could be significantly affected. Furthermore, the increasing influence of foreign factors may complicate interest rate forecasts. For these reasons, central bank control of money market rates is becoming more complex.

INVESTING IN INTERNATIONAL MONEY MARKETS

An investor in foreign money market securities who holds the securities to maturity earns a yield that is dependent on the security's interest rate and the exchange rate movement, as described in eq. 7.1:

7.1
$$Y = (1 + i_f)\left(\frac{S^*}{S}\right) - 1,$$

where i_f is the interest rate on the foreign money market security, S is the spot rate of the foreign currency denominating the investment (with respect to the investor's currency), and S^* is the spot rate of the foreign currency at the end of the investment horizon.

Equation 7.1 can be restructured to specify the impact of the exchange rate movement on the investor's yield, as shown in eq. 7.2:

7.2
$$Y = (1 + i_f)\left(\frac{S^*}{S}\right) - 1$$
$$= (1 + i_f)(1 + E_f) - 1,$$

Exhibit 7.1

Deriving the Probability
Distribution of Effective Yields

Possible Outcome of E	Probability	Possible Outcome of Y
+2%	20%	$(1 + 13\%)(1 + 2\%) - 1 = 15.26\%$
−1%	40%	$(1 + 13\%)[1 + (-1\%)] - 1 = 11.87\%$
−4%	30%	$(1 + 13\%)[1 + (-4\%)] - 1 = 8.48\%$
−9%	10%	$(1 + 13\%)[1 + (-9\%)] - 1 = 2.83\%$

where E represents the percentage change in the exchange rate of the foreign currency over the investment horizon. For a single period, i_f is known and the only uncertainty about Y revolves around S^* (and therefore E).

To illustrate the exchange rate risk involved, consider a U.S. investor who could either invest funds for one year in the U.S. at 9% or in France at 13%. Assume the investor develops a probability distribution of the percentage change in the spot rate (E) of the French franc over the investment horizon as specified in the first two columns of Exhibit 7.1. The *effective yield* (adjusted for exchange rate) is shown in the third column, based on each expected outcome of E. This column suggests a 60% chance that the French investment will generate a yield that exceeds the yield on an alternative U.S. investment. Any degree of appreciation in the franc would only enhance the French investment's yield. A depreciation in the franc by 1% would reduce the French investment's yield to the U.S. investor, but the yield still exceeds that of the U.S. investment. A depreciation of either 4% or 9% in the franc reduces the French investment's yield below that of the U.S. investment's yield.

The exchange rate risk can be hedged by negotiating (at the beginning of the investment horizon) a forward sale of the foreign currency as of the end of the investment horizon. The yield to the international investor can be determined with certainty at the beginning of the investment horizon, since the forward rate (F) replaces S^*:

7.3
$$Y = (1 + i_f)\left(\frac{F}{S}\right) - 1.$$

However, if interest rate parity holds, the premium (or discount) on the forward rate will represent the interest rate differential between countries. Thus, the apparent advantage of a higher interest rate in a foreign country will be offset by a forward discount on the forward rate. Recall the formula for interest rate parity:

7.4
$$P = \frac{(1 + i_h)}{(1 + i_f)} - 1,$$

where P is the forward premium (negative number implies discount), i_h is the home interest rate, and i_f is the foreign interest rate.

If interest rate parity holds, the yield to an investor who hedges the international money market investment with a forward sale is

7.5
$$Y = (1 + i_f) \left(\frac{F}{S}\right) - 1$$
$$= (1 + i_f)(1 + P) - 1$$
$$= (1 + i_f)\left[1 + \frac{(1 + i_h)}{(1 + i_f)} - 1\right] - 1$$
$$= i_h.$$

Thus, the yield to be earned on a hedged international money market investment is no higher than the yield that can be earned on a domestic investment. The results here suggest that foreign money market securities must be purchased on an unhedged basis to outperform alternative investments in the domestic market, if interest rate parity holds. To achieve the objective of higher returns, one must be willing to accept risk. The term *risk* is used here to represent the potential depreciation in the currency denominating the foreign money market security.

Investors who use the forward rate (F) as a forecast of the future spot rate that will exist at the end of the investment horizon (S^*) do not normally consider investing in foreign money market securities. When the forward rate is used as a forecast of S^*, the forward premium represents the expected percentage change in the spot rate (E). Thus, the expected yield is

7.6
$$Y = (1 + i_f)(1 + E) - 1$$
$$= (1 + i_f)(1 + P) - 1.$$

If interest rate parity holds, eq. 7.6 reduces to i_h, as shown in eq. 7.5. This implies that if the forward rate is used as a forecast of S^* and interest rate parity holds, the expected yield on a foreign money market security is the same as the domestic yield. Furthermore, the yield on the foreign money market instrument is uncertain while the yield on the domestic money market instrument is certain, causing investors to prefer the domestic money market security.

Studies by Bilson (1988) and Hansen and Hodrick (1980) suggest that investment in high interest rate currencies can be beneficial. That is, the forward discount on these currencies implied by interest rate parity overestimates the degree of depreciation, so that the interest rate advantage is not offset on average by exchange rate changes.

Investors who do not use the forward rate as a forecast may still use it to determine whether foreign investing is feasible. We have just shown that when the forward premium (P) is used as a forecast of E, the foreign yield has the same expected value as the domestic yield. Thus, if E is expected to be greater (less) than the quoted P, the effective yield on the foreign investment would be greater (less) than the domestic yield. Using our previous example, in which the U.S. interest rate (i_h) is 9% while the French interest rate (i_f) is 13%, the forward premium could be determined under interest rate parity:

7.7
$$P = \frac{(1 + i_h)}{(1 + i_f)} - 1$$
$$= \frac{1.09}{1.13} - 1$$
$$= -3.54\%.$$

Thus, if the French franc is expected to depreciate by less than 3.54%, or appreciate, the effective yield on the foreign money market security is expected to exceed the domestic yield. Conversely, if the franc is expected to depreciate by more than 3.54%, the effective yield on the foreign money market security is expected to be less than the domestic yield.

Our discussion to this point emphasizes the importance of risk assessment in international money market investing. Using a one-period model, we can measure the risk by the variance of the yield:

7.8
$$VAR(Y) = VAR[(1 + i_f)(1 + E) - 1]$$
$$= (1 + i_f)^2 VAR(E).$$

Thus, two foreign money market instruments with similar interest rates can have significantly different risk simply because the currency denominating one instrument may be much more volatile than the currency denominating the other. U.S.-based investors should assess the market interest rates of non-U.S. securities along with the volatility of foreign currencies (with respect to the dollar) when investing in international money market securities.

For example, the Canadian dollar is more stable than currencies of other industrialized countries against the dollar. Therefore, investment in a Canadian money market security would exhibit lower risk than other foreign money market instruments.

The assessment of exchange rate volatility depends on the investor's perspective. For example, a Canadian money market security has a high degree of risk when assessed by a German investor, since the Canadian dollar's exchange rate with respect to the German mark (or any other European currency) is volatile. To a German investor, the exchange rate risk of a French or Swiss or Italian money market instrument would be significantly lower (because the currencies denominating these investments are somewhat stable relative to the mark).

For international money market portfolio managers, exchange rate risk depends not only on volatility but also on exchange rate correlations. To illustrate, consider the variance of effective yields on an international money market portfolio (Y_P):

7.9
$$VAR(Y_P) = \sum_{j=1}^{n} \sum_{k=1}^{n} w_j w_k COV(Y_j, Y_k).$$

The covariance (COV) term can be measured as

7.10
$$COV(Y_j, Y_k) = COV[(1 + i_j)(1 + E_j) - 1, (1 + i_k)(1 + E_k) - 1]$$
$$= (1 + i_j)(1 + i_k)COV[(1 + E_j),(1 + E_k)]$$
$$= (1 + i_j)(1 + i_k)COV(E_j, E_k).$$

Figure 7.3

Comparison of Effective Yields
between U.S. and British Money
Market Yields to a U.S. Investor

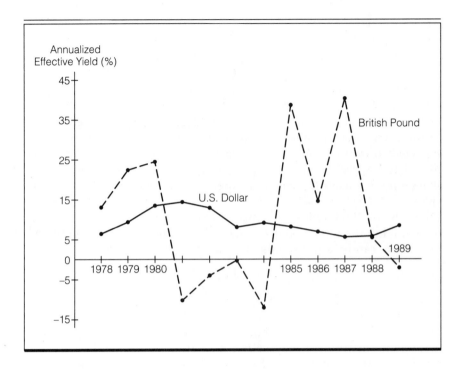

Since the correlation coefficient between currencies j and k is equal to their covariance divided by the respective standard deviations, the correlations between currencies deserve consideration. Some currencies, such as the European currencies, exhibit high correlations. Other currencies have much lower correlations. The Canadian dollar stands out, because its movements appear to be almost independent of other currency movements. A portfolio of money market instruments denominated in currencies with low correlations is desirable, because the likelihood of these currencies simultaneously depreciating substantially against the investor's home currency is low.

The performance of money market investing could be assessed over time by accounting for the actual movement in exchange rates, in order to estimate the periodic effective yield. Figure 7.3 shows the effective yield for a U.S. investor who invests in British money market securities. The effective yield was generally higher than the alternative domestic yields during the 1978–1980 and 1985–1987 periods as a result of the strengthened pound during those periods. Conversely, the effective yield on British money market securities was negative during 1981–1984 and in 1989, when the pound depreciated. Most investors would not invest in foreign money market securities every period, but would choose to do so only when the foreign currency is expected to appreciate. The results displayed in Figure 7.3 show the high potential yields and the risk from investing in foreign money market securities. The risk could be reduced somewhat by spreading the investment across securities denominated in different currencies.

A study by Levy (1981) on international money market portfolios demonstrated the potential gains from diversifying across international securities. An efficient frontier of money market portfolios was created from a multiperiod data base, to show how diversified portfolios could outperform concentration in domestic money market instruments.

Cotner and Seitz (1987) also show that diversified portfolios of international securities can be beneficial to investors. However, they caution that because the variances and covariances of exchange rate movements change over time, so will the optimal portfolios. Thus, international security portfolios identified on an efficient frontier over a previous period will not necessarily be efficient over future periods. Swanson and How (1986) substantiate this claim by identifying efficient international money market portfolios over 25 overlapping six-month periods. Although several efficient portfolios may exist for a given period, Swanson and How focused on the portfolio with minimum risk that could achieve at least a 10% annualized return. They found that the composition of such an efficient portfolio changes significantly over time, which reduces the likelihood of identifying efficient portfolios on an ex ante basis. Even though international money market investors may have difficulty in composing an efficient international portfolio for a future period, they may at least be capable of outperforming any individual foreign money market based on combined return and risk characteristics.

From a multiperiod perspective, investors in international money market securities need to be concerned not only with exchange rate movements but also with interest rate movements. Kirchgassner and Wolters (1987) analyzed the relationship among Eurocurrency market rates over the period 1974–1984. They found that a change in the Eurodollar rate is followed by a somewhat similar change in German and Swiss Eurorates. However, the effects are not always instantaneous; they sometimes occurred only after a lag of up to six months. Swiss and German rates affected each other instantaneously. A reassessment of the interest rate relationships was conducted over two separate subperiods. In the 1974–1978 period, only a weak linkage between interest rates was detected. During the 1980–1984 period, the relationships became much stronger. This evidence carries important implications for participants in international money markets. Investors and borrowers whose securities specify floating rates tied to the market are more susceptible to interest rate risk than before. Diversifying among currencies has limited effectiveness in reducing interest rate risk because interest rates are linked.

FINANCING IN INTERNATIONAL MONEY MARKETS

Financing in international money markets is quite common, as firms attempt to capitalize on lower interest rates in particular countries. Even when the borrower has no use for the foreign currency, it can convert that currency to its home currency to accommodate its financing needs. It will then purchase that foreign currency at the end of the financing horizon to repay the loan. The *effective financing rate* (adjusted for exchange rate) incurred from borrowing a foreign currency can be determined as:

7.11
$$r_f = (1 + i_b) \left(\frac{S^*}{S}\right) - 1,$$

where i_b is the interest rate at which a firm can borrow the foreign currency, S is the spot rate in which the borrowed funds are converted into the borrower's home currency, and S^* is the spot rate at the end of the financing horizon (at which time the borrower purchases the foreign currency to repay the loan).

The effective financing rate can be revised as in eq. 7.12 to illustrate the impact of the percentage change in exchange rates:

7.12
$$r_f = (1 + i_b) \left(\frac{S^*}{S}\right) - 1$$
$$= (1 + i_b)(1 + E) - 1.$$

Although i_b is known, E is not, causing r_f to be uncertain. Forecasts of r_f could be developed from forecasting E.

The uncertainty of E could be avoided by negotiating a forward contract (at the beginning of the financing horizon) to purchase the number of units of foreign currency needed as of the end of the horizon. However, if interest rate parity holds, the forward rate will contain a premium that offsets the lower interest rate of a foreign currency. That is, the amount of savings on interest expenses is offset because the borrower pays a higher rate when purchasing the currency (at the end of the horizon) than the rate at which the currency was initially converted to the borrower's home currency. Borrowers who believe the forward rate (F) is an accurate estimate of the future spot rate (S^*) would not normally borrow foreign currencies, because the expected effective financing rate from borrowing foreign currencies would be equal to the domestic financing rate.

Even if borrowers do not hedge, they can use the forward rate to determine the future spot rate at which the effective financing rate of a foreign currency is equal to the domestic financing rate (assuming that interest rate parity holds). If the expected value of E exceeds (is less than) the quoted forward rate premium, the expected effective financing rate is greater (less) than the domestic financing rate.

Research by Eaker and Lenowitz (1986) assessed the performance from financing in foreign currencies. They found that financing in a currency with the lowest interest rate could significantly reduce financing costs. If interest rate parity holds, and the forward rate was an unbiased forecast of the future spot rate, such a strategy should not have resulted in lower financing costs on average. Although financing in foreign currencies can create exposure to exchange rate risk, some firms may be willing to incur the risk in their attempt to reduce financing costs.

The performance from borrowing in the international money markets could be assessed over time by accounting for the actual movement in exchange rates to estimate the periodic effective financing rate. Figure 7.4 shows the effective financing rate for a U.S. borrower who borrows deutsche marks. The effective financing rate was generally lower than the domestic financing rate during the 1980–1984 period when the mark

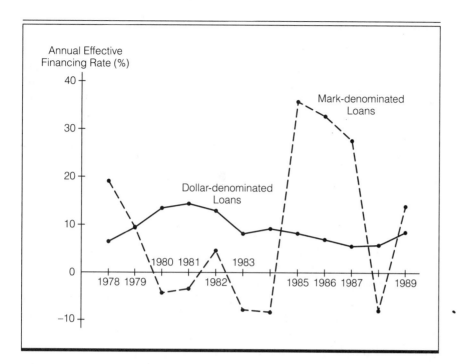

Figure 7.4

Comparison of Effective Financing Rates Between Dollar (from a U.S. Perspective) and Mark Loans

depreciated, but higher during the 1985–1987 period when the mark appreciated. Borrowers would not necessarily borrow in the international money markets in every period, but would choose to do so only when they expect the currency to depreciate. Borrowers of foreign currencies could reduce their exchange rate risk by spreading their foreign financing across several currencies.

The risk involved in borrowing a foreign currency is a positive function of the currency's volatility. The overall level of exchange rate risk when financing with a currency portfolio is influenced not only by individual currency variability but also by currency correlations. Borrowers can reduce their risk by financing with currencies that exhibit low correlations. This reduces the likelihood that all currencies borrowed will simultaneously appreciate to a degree that offsets their relatively low interest rates. Diversifying the foreign financing among European currencies would have only limited risk-reduction capabilities, because these currencies have highly correlated movements against the dollar.

BANK POSITIONS IN INTERNATIONAL MONEY MARKETS

Commercial banks that serve as financial intermediaries in international money markets are commonly susceptible to exchange rate risk. Consider a U.S. bank that receives a one-year German mark deposit worth DM4 million and exchanges them for British pounds at 4 marks per pound to provide a £1 million one-year loan. The rate of return on the loan is

7.13 $$Y = (1 + i_£)(1 + E_£) - 1.$$

The effective cost of funds from the mark deposits is

7.14 $$r = (1 + i_{DM})(1 + E_{DM}) - 1.$$

Thus, the spread between the return on funds loaned (Y) and cost of funds (r) is

7.15   Spread $= Y - r$
$$= [(1 + i_£)(1 + E) - 1] - [(1 + i_{DM})(1 + E_{DM}) - 1]$$
$$= (1 + i_£)(1 + E_£) - (1 + i_{DM})(1 + E_{DM}).$$

Assume that German mark deposits were obtained at a 6% interest rate, while the British pound loan offered a return of 11%. If exchange rates remained constant, the spread would be 5%. However, the spread is reduced if either the mark appreciates or the pound depreciates against the dollar. Assume that over the one-year period, the mark appreciated by 7% while the pound appreciated by 3%. The spread to the U.S. bank would be

7.16   Spread $= (1 + 11\%)(1 + 3\%) - (1 + 6\%)(1 + 7\%)$
$$= 14.33\% - 13.42\%$$
$$= 0.91\%.$$

The reduced spread occurs because the favorable effect of the pound's appreciation was more than offset by the unfavorable effect of the mark's appreciation.

Commercial banks can attempt to reduce their exposure to exchange rate risk by matching long and short positions in the same currency. In the previous example, the bank could have attempted to use the mark deposits to offer mark loans. However, this approach may force the bank to forgo other lending opportunities to borrowers desiring currencies other than marks.

A more appropriate method of reducing exposure to exchange rate risk is to accommodate borrowers, and then attempt to offset the exposure by providing forward rate contracts. Using our example, the bank may attempt to offset its short position in marks by creating a one-year forward contract to purchase marks from a customer. In addition, it may attempt to offset its long position in pounds by creating a one-year forward contract to sell pounds to another customer.

The use of forward contracts can reduce exchange rate risk, but may also prevent opportunities for high returns. Using our example, if the pound appreciated (against the dollar) by more or depreciated by less than the mark, the bank's spread could be enhanced by exchange rate movements. Hedging insulates the bank's spread from both the unfavorable *and* the favorable effects of exchange rate movements. Assuming that interest rate parity obtains, and that British interest rates are higher than U.S. rates, while German interest rates are lower than U.S. rates, the forward rate on the pound would exhibit a discount while the forward rate on the deutsche mark would exhibit a premium. Thus, the actual spread earned by the bank when hedging would be less than the difference between the loan rate on pounds and the deposit rate on marks.

SUMMARY

International money markets allow investors and borrowers to capitalize on perceived advantages in foreign markets. Investors can achieve substantially higher returns in foreign markets than in their domestic markets when investing in currencies that appreciate against their home currency. Given the high degree of volatility, annualized effective yields of 25% or more are not uncommon. However, if these currencies depreciate, the effective yield on the foreign investments will most likely be lower than the domestic yield, and may even be negative. Investors may attempt to capitalize on potentially high effective yields on foreign money market securities, while reducing the exchange rate risk by diversifying the investments across currencies.

International money markets are also used by firms that attempt to finance at a lower cost than what is possible domestically. They normally attempt to borrow currencies that have low interest rates and are expected to depreciate against their own currency. They incur the risk that the currencies borrowed may appreciate, which will increase their cost of financing.

Some commercial banks use an aggressive approach in the international money markets. They take short positions in currencies expected to depreciate, and long positions in currencies expected to appreciate. The potential returns on such positions are very high, but so are the risks. For this reason, commercial banks may impose a maximum limit on the value of short or long positions taken.

Questions and Problems

1. Why would proper regulation in the Eurocurrency market require uniform regulations across all countries where participating banks reside?

2. a. Assume that Bangor Co. invested its excess cash in a one-year CD denominated in Canadian dollars, offering an interest rate of 12%. If the Canadian dollar appreciates by 7% over the year against the U.S. dollar, what is the effective yield earned by Bangor Co.?
   b. Repeat the question, assuming the Canadian dollar depreciates by 9%.

3. Assume that a U.S. investor can invest in either a Canadian CD or a Mexican CD for one year. Assume zero default risk for either investment. Which investment is likely to have a wider dispersion of possible effective yields from the U.S. investor's perspective? Why?

4. What are the implications of interest rate parity for attempting to capitalize on a high-interest foreign security while covering in the forward market?

5. Given that interest rate parity holds, describe the relative magnitude of forward rate premiums (or discounts) on deposits in (1) currencies with interest rates that are similar to U.S. interest rates, (2) currencies with higher interest rates than U.S. interest rates, and (3) currencies with lower interest rates than U.S. interest rates.

6. If one-year-forward rates are reliable forecasts of spot rates one year in advance, compare the performance (from a U.S. investor's perspective) of (1) foreign securities with higher interest rates than U.S. rates, (2) foreign securities with lower interest rates than U.S. rates, and (3) U.S. securities.

7. Assume that the spot rate is a more accurate predictor of the spot rate one year from now than the one-year forward rate. What are the implications for a U.S. investor who invests in foreign securities with higher interest rates?

8. Assume that the British one-year interest rate is 14%, and the U.S. interest rate is 11%. What is the premium or discount on the pound's one-year forward rate if interest rate parity holds?

9. Dalton Co., a U.S. firm, has a money market portfolio diversified across several European currencies in order to reduce exchange rate risk. Comment on whether this strategy will substantially reduce exchange rate risk.

10. Assume that Rezmer Eurobank is planning to convert deutsche mark deposits into French franc loans. The bank pays 6% interest on mark deposits and charges 13% interest on franc loans. The bank is a subsidiary of a U.S. bank, and wants to measure its spread from a U.S. perspective. If the mark is expected to appreciate against the dollar by 11% and the franc is expected to appreciate against the dollar by 5%, determine the spread.

References

Bilson, J. "The Speculative Efficiency Hypothesis." *Journal of Business* (July 1988): 435–51.

Cotner, J., and N. Seitz. "A Simplified Approach to Short-term International Diversification." *Financial Review* (May 1987): 249–66.

Eaker, M., and J. Lenowitz. "Multinational Borrowing Decisions and the Empirical Exchange Rate Evidence." *Management International Review* 1(1986): 24–32.

Garg, R. "Exploring Solutions to the LDC Debt Crisis." *Bankers Magazine* (January/February 1989): 46–51.

Gluck, J. "International Middle-Market Borrowing." *FRBNY Quarterly Review* (Winter 1987): 46–52.

Hansen, L., and R. Hodrick. "Forward Exchange Rates as Optimal Predictors of Future Spot Rates: An Econometric Analysis." *Journal of Political Economy* (October 1980): 829–53.

Kirchgassner, G., and J. Wolters. "U.S.-European Interest Rate Linkage: A Time Series Analysis for West Germany, Switzerland, and the United States." *Review of Economics and Statistics* (November 1987): 675–84.

Laney, L. "The Secondary Market in Developing Country Debt." *Economic Review* (Federal Reserve Bank of Dallas) (July 1987): 1–12.

Levy, H. "Optimal Portfolio of Foreign Currencies with Borrowing and Lending." *Journal of Money, Credit, and Banking* (August 1981): 325–41.

Morgan, J. "Assessing Country Risk at Texas Commerce." *Banker's Magazine* (May/June 1985): 23–29.

Ogilvie, N. "Foreign Banks in the U.S. and Geographic Restrictions on Banking." *Journal of Bank Research* (Summer 1980): 73–79.

Poulsen, A. "Japanese Bank Regulation and the Activities of U.S. Offices of Japanese Banks." *Journal of Money, Credit, and Banking* (August 1986): 366–73.

Radecki, L., and V. Reinhart. "The Globalization of Financial Markets and the Effectiveness of the Monetary Policy Instruments." *FRBNY Quarterly Review* (Autumn 1988): 18–27.

"Recent Innovations in International Banking: The Policy Implications." *World of Banking* (July/August 1986): 4–7.

Ricks, D., and J. Arpan. "Foreign Banking in the United States." *Business Horizons* (February 1976): 84–87.

Severn, A., and D. Meinster. "The Use of Multicurrency Financing by the Financial Manager." *Financial Management* (Winter 1978): 45–53.

Swanson, P. "Interrelationships Among Domestic and Eurocurrency Deposit Yields: A Focus on the U.S. Dollar." *Financial Review* (February 1988): 81–94.

Swanson, P., and W. How. "Portfolio Diversification by Currency Denomination: An Approach to International Cash Management with Implications for Foreign Exchange Markets." *Quarterly Review of Economics and Business* (Spring 1986): 95–103.

"The Bank's Latest Game: Loan Swapping." *Fortune* (December 1983): 111–12.

INTERNATIONAL BOND MARKETS

International bond markets are now commonly used by governments and corporations of numerous countries. The growth is attributed to some unique features offered by international bonds that are not offered by domestic bonds. In this chapter, we explain how international bond markets are used by both bond issuers and investors. First, we explain how international bond markets were developed, and compare yields across markets. Second, we describe how bonds are valued by investors across international markets. Third, we explain the benefits of international bond diversification. Finally, we discuss the use of swaps to hedge possible risks that international bonds exhibit.

DEVELOPMENT OF INTERNATIONAL BOND MARKETS

The development of international bond markets is partially attributed to tax law differentials across countries. Until 1984, foreign investors who purchased bonds that were placed in the United States paid a 30% withholding tax on interest payments. However, various tax treaties between the United States and non-U.S. countries reduced the withholding tax. Even with tax treaties, many firms and governments issued bonds in the Eurobond market, through financing subsidiaries in the Netherlands Antilles. Interest payments paid to non-U.S. investors through the Netherlands Antilles were exempt from the withholding tax, allowing U.S. firms to issue bonds at a higher price (lower cost of financing).

The withholding tax on U.S.-placed bonds was eliminated in 1984, causing a large increase in the foreign demand for U.S.-placed bonds. Figure 8.1 shows the foreign purchases and sales of U.S. bonds over time. Purchases and sales have increased by over 600% over the last eight years.

139

Figure 8.1

Foreign Trading of U.S. Bonds
(in millions of dollars)

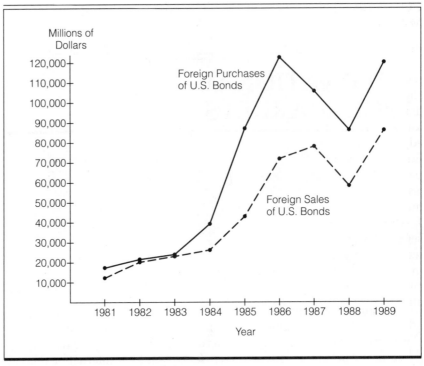

SOURCE: *Federal Reserve Bulletin,* various issues.

As in the U.S. market, bonds placed in the Eurobond market are typically underwritten by a syndicate of investment banking firms. Many underwriters in the Eurobond market are subsidiaries of U.S. banks that have focused their growth on non-U.S. countries, since they were historically banned by the Glass-Steagall Act from underwriting corporate bonds in the United States.

Eurobonds can be denominated in a variety of currencies, with the U.S. dollar being the most common choice. For non-U.S. firms that issued bonds in the mid 1980s, dollar-denominated bonds have been a cheap source of funds, because of the dollar's weakness in the late 1980s. Yet U.S. firms that issued bonds denominated in foreign currencies incurred high financing costs as a result of the dollar's weakness (assuming that their payments were not hedged in any way).

Some recent issuers of bonds in the Eurobond market include Chrysler Financial, Citicorp, General Motors Acceptance Corp., and the World Bank. Chrysler Financial Corp. now obtains about one-fourth of its funds from the Eurobond market. Its bonds have been denominated not only in dollars but also in Swiss francs, German marks, and Australian dollars. Citicorp now borrows about half of its funds overseas. It recently issued 25-year floating-rate Eurodollar bonds that would not have been possible in the United States because of lack of an investor base for long maturities.

COMPARISON OF U.S. AND EUROBOND MARKET YIELDS

Recent research by Kidwell, Marr, and Thompson (1985) compared the issuance of utility bonds in Eurobond versus domestic markets. The researchers found that interest costs paid on Eurodollar bonds are slightly lower than the domestic market, but that Eurodollar bond underwriting fees are higher than domestic issues, and offset the slight interest cost advantage on Eurodollar bonds. However, they acknowledged that underwriting fees were becoming more competitive in the Eurobond market over time. In addition, large Eurodollar bond issues pay "penalty yields" because the Eurobond market cannot absorb the issue as easily as the larger U.S. market could, and an extra premium may be needed to place the entire issue.

A related study by Finnerty and Nunn (1985) assessed the degree of segmentation between the Eurobond market and U.S. bond market. If market imperfections were nonexistent, yields on bonds denominated in the same currency and with similar risk and provisions should be similar. If the yields differed, arbitrage opportunities would be possible, and would force an alignment of yields. However, to the degree that market imperfections such as information inefficiencies and government barriers (such as taxes) exist, bond markets would be segmented. They found that yields of domestic bonds were significantly above yields on Eurobonds for most maturity classes. Finnerty and Nunn suggest that this segmentation of markets is primarily attributed to tax characteristics, such as tax evasion by Eurobond purchasers. Other barriers can also discourage international investment. Information costs may be high in countries where corporate financial reporting is inconsistent, and macroeconomic data about the country may be lacking as well.

ASSESSMENT OF BOND YIELD DIFFERENTIALS ACROSS COUNTRIES

The prices and therefore yields that bonds offer are dependent on the risk-free rate for a similar maturity risk-free bond plus premiums for risk and other provisions, as shown in eq. 8.1:

8.1
$$Y_r = Y_{rf} + Dp + Y_a,$$

where Y_r is the risky bond yield, Y_{rf} is the risk-free bond yield, Dp is the default risk premium, and Y_a is the adjustment in yield due to other factors.

Yield differentials (defined as $Y_r - Y_{rf}$) have been studied in the United States to determine the factors that investors consider when purchasing bonds. Barrett and Kolb (1986) extend this research internationally by examining bond yield differentials in eight different countries. The regression model used for this purpose is specified in eq. 8.2:

8.2
$$YD_t = a_0 + a_1 EMPL_t + a_2 STK_t + a_3 INFL_t + a_4 VARLT_t + e_t,$$

where YD_t is the yield differential, measured as the difference between a long-term corporate index and a long-term government index; $EMPL_t$ is the percentage change in employment index during quarter t (inverse relationship expected); STK_t is the percentage change in the stock market index during quarter t (inverse relationship expected); $INFL_t$ is the inflation rate during quarter t (positive relationship expected); and $VARLT_t$ is the variability in the long-term government interest rate during quarter t (positive relationship expected).

Barrett and Kolb's model is somewhat similar to other models previously applied to explain yield differentials in the United States over time. They found that the variables that have influenced yield differentials in the United States have not had a similar influence on non-U.S. yield differentials. Thus, investors in different countries may use different criteria in assessing the proper risk premium that bonds should exhibit. Consequently, the yield differential that must be offered by a corporation can vary across countries. Thus, it may be to a corporation's advantage to consider various markets before issuing bonds.

INTERNATIONAL BOND VALUATION

Financial institutions such as insurance companies, pension funds, and bond mutual funds consider investing in the international bond market. Many U.S. pension funds began to invest in foreign bonds in the mid-1980s, including those of General Electric Co., United Technologies Corp., IBM, and ITT. Even public pension funds such as the employee retirement systems of California, Hawaii, Kansas, and Massachusetts have invested in foreign bonds. The allure of foreign bonds may be higher coupon payments, or the expected strength of the currency denominating the bonds. For example, General Electric pension fund's attraction to foreign bonds was because of the potentially favorable impact of foreign currency appreciation against the dollar.

The expected cash flows and market value of international bonds are highly influenced by (1) expected interest rate movements of the currency denominating the bond, and (2) expected exchange rate movements. The interest rate movements affect the return required by investors in the secondary market and therefore affect the market value of the bond. The exchange rate movements affect the home currency cash flows received from coupon payments and the sale of the bonds.

Recent research by Lee (1987) demonstrated that the performance of bonds can vary substantially among countries. Lee found that large differences in bond performance are not just a short-term phenomenon but sometimes last for as long as five years. These findings suggest that it is worthwhile for investors to evaluate the potential bond offerings among countries before making the investment decision. Lee showed that performance from purchasing international bonds can be highly dependent on currency movements as well as interest rate movements.

Example

To illustrate the influence of interest rate and exchange rate movements, assume a U.S. company is considering the purchase of British 10-year bonds with a price equal to their par value of £20 million, and annual

Year	British Pound Cash Flows to Be Received	Exchange Rate	Dollar Cash Flows to Be Received
1	£2,400,000	$1.80	$ 4,320,000
2	£2,400,000	$1.80	$ 4,320,000
3	£2,400,000 + £21,947,322	$1.80	$43,825,180

Exhibit 8.1

Estimation of Dollar Cash Flows Received from British Bonds

coupon payments of 12%. Assuming the British pound is presently worth $1.80, the company's investment in these bonds would be $36 million. Assume that the company plans to hold the bonds for only three years. At the end of the third year, the rate of return required by British investors on these bonds is expected to be 10%. The present value of bonds from the U.S. company's perspective can be determined by forecasting dollar cash flows it would receive over the three-year investment horizon. First, the market value of bonds three years from now (present value of remaining cash flows at that time) must be estimated:

8.3

$$\text{Market value of bonds in 3 years} = \sum_{t=1}^{7} \frac{£2,400,000}{(1.10)^t} + \frac{£20,000,000}{(1.10)^7}$$

$$= £11,684,160 + £10,263,162$$

$$= £21,947,322.$$

This market value, along with the annual coupon payments to be received by the U.S. company, must be converted into dollars. Therefore, exchange rate projections are needed for the periods in which British pound payments will be converted. Assume that the existing exchange rate of the pound of $1.80 is used as the forecast for these future periods. The dollar cash flows are derived in Exhibit 8.1. The yield to maturity on these bonds can be determined by solving for the discount rate at which the anticipated cash flows equal the company's initial investment of $36 million. The yield to maturity is estimated to be about 15%. Even though the bonds would be initially purchased at par value, the yield to maturity exceeds the coupon rate, because the expected market value in three years exceeds the par value. Since the required return on these bonds by investors is expected to be lower three years from now, the company expects the value of the bonds to increase.

Impact of Interest Rate Movements

In our example, the lower required return at the end of the third year would typically reflect lower British interest rates at that time. Even if U.S. interest rates are expected to remain stable or increase, British interest rates could decrease, which is beneficial from the U.S. company's point of view.

Exhibit 8.2

Estimation of Dollar Cash Flows
Received from British Bonds
(based on alternative exchange
rate projections)

Year	British Pound Cash Flows to Be Received	Exchange Rate	Dollar Cash Flows to Be Received
1	£2,400,000	$1.75	$ 4,200,000
2	£2,400,000	$1.70	$ 4,080,000
3	£2,400,000 + £21,947,322	$1.65	$40,173,081

If British interest rates had increased by the third year, the required rate of return would most likely have risen, depressing the market value of the bonds. Of course, domestic bonds are also susceptible to interest rate risk, but the degree of risk varies with the currency denominating the bonds. Because interest rates are more volatile in some countries than in others, the potential volatility in the market values of bonds in those countries may be greater as well.

Investors in international bonds can reduce their exposure to interest rate risk by diversifying their investment across bonds denominated in a variety of currencies. The market value of their portfolio would be less sensitive to the interest rate movements of any particular country. The degree to which such diversification can reduce interest rate risk depends on correlations between interest rates across countries. Research by Kool and Tatom (1988) shows that long-term interest rates are somewhat related over time, which implies that prices of bonds denominated in different currencies would be correlated. Nevertheless, the exposure of an internationally diversified bond portfolio to interest rate risk is less than if all bonds were denominated in a single currency.

Impact of Exchange Rate Movements

In the previous example, the spot exchange rate was used as a forecast of the future spot rates. To realize the potential influence of exchange rate movements on the investor's yield to maturity, assume that the pound is expected to depreciate to $1.75 in year 1, $1.70 in year 2, and $1.65 in year 3. The estimated dollar cash flows to be received based on these projections are shown in Exhibit 8.2. The exchange rate effect is especially relevant in the third year, since the principal payment from the sale of bonds is expected to occur in that year. The expected yield to maturity from the U.S. company's perspective would now be about 10%, roughly 5 percentage points less than in the original example.

An international bond's exposure to exchange rate risk can sometimes favorably affect performance. If the pound had appreciated over time, the expected dollar cash flows would be higher, and the yield to maturity would have been enhanced from a U.S. perspective.

Research by Lee (1987) identified currency movements as a key reason for the high returns on international bonds (from a U.S. perspective) in the late 1970s and low returns on international bonds in the early 1980s. The weakened dollar during the 1985–1988 period again enhanced international bond returns for U.S. investors.

Year	British Pound Cash Flows to Be Received	Forward Rate	Dollar Cash Flows to Be Received
1	£2,400,000	$1.79	$ 4,296,000
2	£2,400,000	$1.78	$ 4,272,000
3	£2,400,000 + £21,947,322	$1.76	$42,851,287

Exhibit 8.3

Estimation of Dollar Cash Flows Received from British Bonds when Hedging against Exchange Rate Risk

Hedging Exchange Rate Exposure

Portfolio managers who expect favorable (downward) interest rate swings but unfavorable foreign currency movements may still invest in foreign bonds and hedge their exposure to exchange rate risk. Using the previous example, assume the U.S. company could have sold pounds forward to cover the pounds received in each of the three years it planned to hold the British bonds. Assume that the forward rates for the pound were as follows:

Years from Now	Forward Rate
One year	$1.79
Two years	$1.78
Three years	$1.76

The estimated dollar cash flows when hedging against exchange rate risk are shown in Exhibit 8.3. The cash flows are less than those derived from the original example (Exhibit 8.1), since the forward rates contain a slight discount. However, hedging avoids the exposure to the potential depreciation of the pound (Exhibit 8.2). The yield to maturity on the hedged investment is about 14%, and is insulated from possible exchange rate movements that could have occurred. Of course, the hedged investment would also forgo any favorable effects on dollar cash flows if the pound had appreciated over the three-year period.

A probability distribution of yield to maturities is shown in Figure 8.2 for hedged and unhedged investments in bonds. The probability distribution is more dispersed for the unhedged investment because of exposure to exchange rate movements. The degree of dispersion on an unhedged investment in bonds would be influenced by the volatility of the currency denominating the bond relative to the investor's home currency. For example, the dispersion of possible yields would be less for bonds denominated in Canadian dollars than in British pounds (from a U.S. perspective) because the Canadian dollar's value is more stable. Though a hedged investment in bonds exhibits less dispersion, its yield to maturity is still uncertain (if maturity exceeds the planned investment horizon) because the required rate of return on the bonds at the time the bonds are to be sold is uncertain. The yield to maturity on a planned investment in international bonds can be determined with certainty only

Figure 8.2

Comparison of Yield to Maturity
Distributions for Hedged and
Unhedged Investments

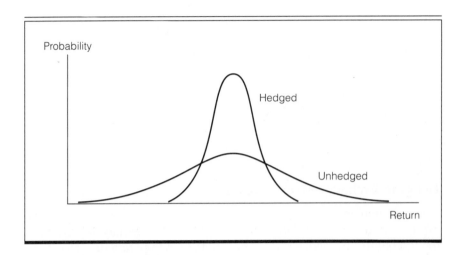

if the foreign cash flows are hedged *and* the bonds are held to maturity
(or if interest rate risk is completely hedged).

Bond portfolio managers may attempt to account for the uncertainty
of future interest rates and exchange rates by using sensitivity analysis.
For each alternative estimate of interest rates and exchange rates, a
distinct forecast of the bond's yield to maturity can be derived. If a
probability can be associated with each possible scenario, a probability
distribution of yield to maturities can be developed. This may facilitate
investment decisions because it measures the expected return *and* risk.

A more elaborate method of accounting for the uncertainty of a bond's
yield to maturity is to use Monte Carlo simulation. A probability distribution of possible interest rates could be determined for the point in
time at which the bonds are sold. In addition, a probability distribution
could be developed for exchange rates at the time each coupon payment
is received, and at the time at which the bonds are sold. A simulation
computer program could then be instructed to generate numerous possible outcomes of the bond's yield based on the possible interest rates
and exchange rates. The outcomes would be transformed into a probability distribution that is used to determine (1) the expected value of the
bond's yield, and (2) the likelihood that the yield will at least achieve
some minimum level desired.

INTERNATIONAL BOND DIVERSIFICATION

Research by Cholerton, Pieraerts, and Solnik (1986) demonstrates the
potential benefits of international bond diversification by estimating the
correlation coefficient of monthly bond returns across currencies. The
researchers found that correlation coefficients were usually less than .50,
indicating potentially large risk reduction benefits from international
bond diversification. They also found that internationally diversified
bond portfolios outperformed the individual bonds when using risk and
return criteria.

Investors can attempt to reduce the international bond portfolio's exposure to exchange rate movements by diversifying among currencies. Because exchange rate movements are not perfectly positively correlated, some degree of exchange rate risk reduction is possible. However, exchange rate movements can still significantly affect the performance of an international bond portfolio.

Research by Cholerton, Pieraerts, and Solnik also shows that hedging the exchange rate risk of international bond investments would have improved performance over the period analyzed. Yet, they suggest that the exposure to exchange rate risk may motivate investment in international bonds if investors expect their home currency to weaken. Over a long-term investment horizon in which expectations of currency movements are periodically revised, investors who purchase international bonds may hedge in some periods and remain exposed to exchange rate risk in others.

Another key reason for international diversification is to reduce credit risk. The investment in bonds issued by corporations from a single country can expose investors to a relatively high degree of credit risk. The credit risk of corporations is highly dependent on economic conditions. Intertemporal shifts in credit risk are likely to be systematically related to the country's economic conditions. Because economic cycles differ across countries, there is less chance of a systematic increase in the credit risk of bonds from different countries.

Because the credit risk of international bonds is influenced by economic characteristics of the country of concern, country risk analysis can be used to assess this risk. Any variables that affect economic conditions may indirectly affect the borrower's cash flow and ability to meet payment obligations. Edwards (1986) analyzed the country risk implied by premiums on international bond yields. He found that the premium is positively related to the debt-output ratio (a measure of a country's debt relative to its total production) and inversely related to the investment-GNP ratio (which represents the potential for future growth and is thought to increase creditworthiness).

A recent study by Levy and Lerman (1988) identified the composition of some efficient bond portfolios (over the 1960–1980 period), which are characterized as exhibiting the minimal risk for various return levels. They used the standard deviation of bond portfolio returns as a proxy for risk. International diversification benefits were demonstrated, as efficient portfolios outperformed individual bond markets in risk-return criteria. Given the graphic display of achievable risk-return combinations by efficient portfolios along with a risk-free interest rate, a capital market line can be applied to bond returns. Figure 8.3 displays achievable risk-return combinations by efficient portfolios as curve AB. These portfolios dominate individual bond markets in risk-return space. Assuming a risk-free rate of R_f, the capital market line can be extended from R_f through point X. The so-called tangency portfolio at point X represents a specific internationally diversified portfolio. International bond portfolio managers could have combined riskless securities (such as Treasury securities denominated in the investor's home currency) with the tangency portfolio to achieve any risk-return combination along

Figure 8.3

Display of Efficient Bond Portfolios

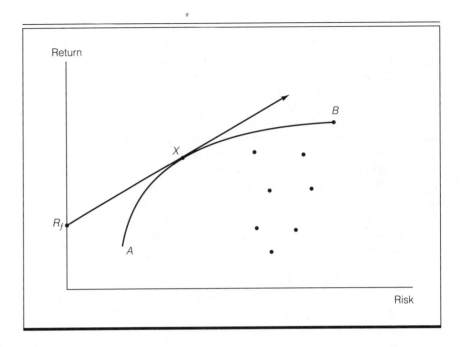

the capital market line. The return from combining Treasury securities with the tangency portfolio is

8.4
$$R_c = W_{rf}R_f + W_pR_p,$$

where W_{rf} is the weight (proportional investment) allocated to risk-free securities, W_p is the weight allocated to the tangency portfolio, R_f is the return on risk-free securities, and R_p is the return on the tangency portfolio.

Given that the Treasury security's term remaining to maturity matches the investor's planned investment horizon, there is no uncertainty about its return. Thus, the standard deviation from combining Treasury securities with the tangency portfolio is

8.5
$$VAR(R_c) = VAR(W_{rf}R_f + W_pR_p)$$
$$= W_{rf}^2 VAR(R_f) + W_p^2 VAR(R_p) + 2COV(R_f, R_p)$$
$$= W_p^2 VAR(R_p).$$

The more weight allocated to Treasury securities, the lower the risk and the lower the return. All points between R_f and X on the capital market line represent

8.6
$$0 < W_{rf} < 100\%, \text{ and } 0 < W_p < 100\%.$$

If bond portfolio managers are allowed to increase their investment of funds by borrowing, the achievable combinations of risk and expected return are depicted along the ray extending outward from point X. The slope of this ray is similar to the slope from R_f to X when assuming portfolio managers can borrow at the rate of R_f. All points on the ray extending from point X represent a zero investment in risk-free Treasury securities and $W_p > 100\%$. That is, all available funds plus additional borrowed funds are used to invest in the tangency portfolio. The greater the amount of funds borrowed relative to the total investment in the tangency portfolio, the higher the risk and expected return.

If the investor's borrowing rate exceeds R_f, the ray extending from point X will be less steep, suggesting less desirable risk-return combinations. If the risk-free rate was lower (higher) than the rate shown in Figure 8.3, the tangency point would be farther to the left (right) along the efficient frontier AB, causing the slope of the capital market line to be more (less) steep.

USE OF SWAPS IN INTERNATIONAL BOND MARKETS

Firms sometimes issue bonds with provisions that differ from what they desired, to assure that the bonds will be easily placed. Various types of swap arrangements can then be executed by these firms to essentially achieve the desired provisions. Two popular swap arrangements are interest swaps and currency swaps.

Using Interest Rate Swaps to Service Bonds

Some corporations issue variable-rate bonds, with interest payments that vary over time in accordance with a proxy for market interest rates. The London Interbank Offer Rate (LIBOR) is a commonly used proxy. Variable-rate bonds can normally be issued at a lower initial cost, but doing so exposes the issuer rather than the investor to interest rate risk.

Corporations that issue bonds in the international bond markets are sometimes better able to place one type of bond than another. For example, consider the following information for two firms attempting to issue bonds:

		Cost of Funds for Different Types of Bonds	
Firm	Objective	Fixed-Rate Bond	Variable-Rate Bond
AAA Corp.	Issue variable-rate bonds	11%	LIBOR + 1%
BBB Corp.	Issue fixed-rate bonds	13%	LIBOR + 2%

Both the fixed-rate and variable-rate bonds contain premiums above the risk-free rate that would not be incurred by a risk-free issuer such as the U.S. Treasury. The rates are higher for BBB Corp. to compensate investors for higher default risk.

The BBB Corp. would pay 1% more on variable-rate bonds and 2% more on fixed-rate bonds. Though it has a comparative advantage in issuing variable-rate bonds, its objective was to issue fixed-rate bonds. The two corporations could engage in an interest rate swap, in which BBB Corp. issues variable-rate bonds while AAA Corp. issues fixed-rate bonds. Then, BBB Corp. can provide fixed-rate payments to AAA Corp. in exchange for variable-rate payments. This type of swap is illustrated in Figure 8.4.

Assume that a swap agreement specifies that BBB Corp. provides fixed interest payments at 12.5% to AAA in exchange for variable-rate payments of LIBOR + 2%. BBB Corp. benefits because the variable-rate payments received cover the payments owed to bondholders, and the fixed-rate payments paid out are 0.5% less than what they would be if BBB Corp. issued fixed-rate bonds. AAA Corp. pays variable-rate payments of 1% more than what it would if it issued variable-rate bonds. However, the fixed payments received from the swap are 1.5% above the amount paid by AAA to bondholders. Each corporation has reduced financing costs by 0.5%. If an investment banking firm served as a financial intermediary for the interest rate swap, a fee would have been charged, reducing the benefits to each corporation.

Using Currency Swaps to Service Bonds

Not only do corporations choose between the variable- and fixed-rate provisions, but they also must choose the currency to denominate the bond. If the corporation wants to denominate the bond in British pounds, it most likely attempts to place the bonds with British investors. For any currency chosen, there is an appropriate market. Yet, if the firm is unknown to them, the market participants corresponding to the chosen currency may not be as willing to purchase the issuing firm's bonds. To resolve the dilemma, some firms issue bonds in other markets and use currency swaps to achieve their desired currency cash flows. For example, consider the following situation:

Company	Objective	Limitation
Smith Co., a French subsidiary of a U.S. corporation	Borrow French francs	French investors are not familiar with Smith Co.
Jacque Co., a U.S. subsidiary of a French corporation	Borrow U.S. dollars	U.S. investors are not familiar with Jacque Co.

A currency swap could be executed between the two companies as shown in Figure 8.5 on page 152. Smith could issue dollar-denominated bonds to U.S. investors who are more familiar with the firm because its headquarters is based in the U.S. Similarly, Jacque Co. can issue French franc-denominated bonds to French investors. Then, periodic currency swaps will allow the respective firms to cover their coupon payments without exposure to exchange rate risk. Smith Co. provides French franc payments (which it receives from its business in France) to Jacque Co. in exchange for U.S. dollar payments, and channels the dollar payments to its bondholders. Conversely, Jacque Co. exchanges U.S. dollar pay-

Figure 8.4 Illustration of an Interest Rate Swap

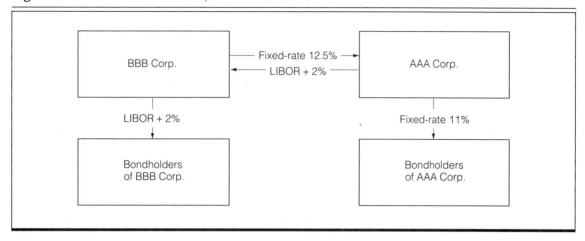

ments (earned from its business in the U.S.) in exchange for French francs, which are channeled to its bondholders.

Chrysler Financial Corp. has been able to obtain funds at a lower cost in the Eurobond market by issuing bonds in foreign currencies and simultaneously executing currency swaps. General Motors Acceptance Corp. has recently issued bonds denominated in Japanese yen and simultaneously executed yen-dollar swaps to avoid exposure to exchange rate risk.

CURRENCY COCKTAIL BONDS

Currency cocktail bonds are denominated in a mix (cocktail) of currencies. Two popular multicurrency units of account used to denominate currency cocktail bonds are Special Drawing Rights (SDRs) and the European Currency Unit (ECU). The SDR represents a weighted average of the U.S. dollar, German mark, Japanese yen, French franc, and British pound. The U.S. dollar is assigned the most weight because of its dominance in international financial transactions. The ECU represents a weighted average of European currencies, and the yield on an ECU bond is based on a weighted average of yields on the currencies constituting the ECU. Bonds issued in ECU amounted to the equivalent of more than $7.5 billion in 1987. Some recent issuers of ECU bonds include the European Investment Bank, Republic of Austria, and Pirelli Financial Services NV.

Investors who purchase currency cocktail bonds achieve currency diversification benefits without having to diversify international bond holdings. However, the degree of currency diversification is somewhat limited. For example, the European currencies included in the ECU are highly correlated. Although the ECU is less volatile than any of its component currencies against the dollar (or any other currency), it may be more volatile than desired by bond portfolio managers. The ECU is

Figure 8.5   Illustration of a Currency Swap to Cover Coupon Payments

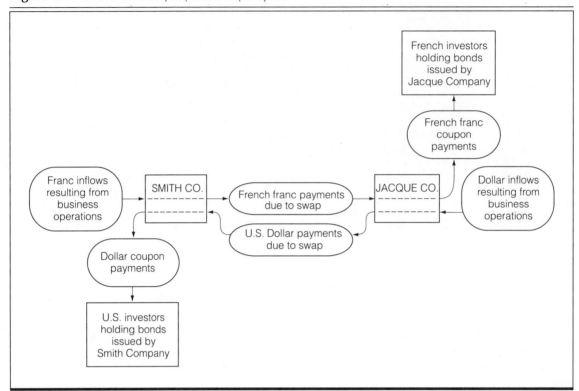

popular among European investors because its value is somewhat stable with respect to any European currency.

Even though the SDR is composed of fewer currencies, it exhibits greater diversity than the ECU because it includes two non-European currencies. However, the SDR's value is quite volatile against European currencies because of the assigned weight to the dollar, which is volatile against European currencies.

Many corporations and governments may prefer to denominate bonds in their invoice currency, so that exchange rate risk is avoided. When issuing bonds denominated in a multicurrency unit of account, the issuer incurs exchange rate risk since the unit of account's value fluctuates against the issuer's primary currency. Even though the unit of account may be less volatile than individual foreign currencies, the issuer may prefer to completely insulate against exchange rate risk by denominating bonds in its primary currency. For the reasons just expressed, currency cocktail bonds do not satisfy everyone, yet they have become more popular in recent years.

SUMMARY

The international bond markets were developed in response to differences in tax laws among countries. Investors were attracted to locations with more favorable tax treatment. Other market imperfections also existed, causing yields to vary among bonds. Furthermore, since the demand for bonds is partially influenced by expectations of the currency denominating them, so is the yield. Research has found large differences in the returns generated by international bonds. The differences are mainly attributed to varied movements in the interest rates and exchange rates for currencies denominating the bonds.

The exchange rate risk of bonds can be hedged by investors to a degree. However, hedging forgoes potential favorable benefits from appreciation of the currency denominating the bonds. Research has found that international bond portfolios have more favorable return and risk characteristics when hedged against exchange rate risk.

Questions and Problems

1. Explain the functions of some large U.S. commercial banks in the Eurobond market.

2. A study by Finnerty and Nunn found that yields on bonds with similar characteristics differed among countries. What does this result imply about the segmentation or integration of bond markets? What types of market imperfections could cause bond yields to differ among countries?

3. Review the regression model for explaining bond yield differentials by Barrett and Kolb. Explain the expected relationship between the employment index and the yield differential.

4. Assume that Mustang Inc., a U.S. insurance company, plans to purchase 20-year bonds denominated in French francs, with a par value of FF 100 million, and a 14% coupon rate (annual coupon payments). The firm would hold the bonds for only two years, and expects the required rate of return on these bonds to be 12% at the time it would sell them. The French franc spot rate is $0.185. Mustang Inc. has forecasted the value of the French franc as follows:

End of Year	Forecast of FF
1	$0.18
2	$0.20

   a. Determine the forecasted market value of the bonds in two years.
   b. Determine the forecasted yield to maturity on the bonds over the two-year period in which the bonds are to be held.
   c. Based on the information, will Mustang Inc. be favorably or unfavorably affected by its exposure to interest rate risk? To exchange rate risk?
   d. Mustang Inc. is aware that it could hedge its exposure to exchange rate risk. Assume that the one-year-forward rate is $0.16 and the two-year-forward rate is $0.18. Should Mustang hedge?

5. Some institutional investors diversify their international bonds across countries in order to reduce exposure to interest rate risk. Is this an effective strategy for reducing exposure to interest rate risk? Explain how correlations

between long-term interest rates of various countries influence the degree to which interest rate risk can be reduced.

6. Jazz Corporation is a U.S. firm that is considering the purchase of Canadian bonds at par value, with a maturity of 30 years and a coupon rate of 14%. It will hold them for eight years, at which time the required rate of return on these bonds will be between 13% and 16%. As Jazz receives annual coupon payments in Canadian dollars, it will convert them to U.S. dollars. It has established ranges for the Canadian dollar at the end of each of the eight years, as follows:

End of Year	Range for Canadian Dollar
1	$0.78–$0.79
2	$0.81–$0.84
3	$0.83–$0.87
4	$0.87–$0.92
5	$0.85–$0.90
6	$0.80–$0.86
7	$0.72–$0.78
8	$0.60–$0.70

Your task as analyst for Jazz Corporation is to determine a probability distribution of yield to maturities over the eight-year horizon, and then compare the distribution to an alternative investment of eight-year U.S. securities that offer a yield to maturity of 12%. Describe how Monte Carlo simulation could be used to develop the probability distribution and help you decide whether to purchase the Canadian bonds.

7. A U.S. pension fund portfolio manager purchased 20-year French Treasury bonds seven years ago because the coupon rate was higher than U.S. Treasury bonds. It just sold the bonds and realized a much smaller gain on these bonds over time than it would have realized if it purchased U.S. Treasury bonds. Assume the reason for this poor performance is not due to default risk or exchange rate risk. How could you explain such poor performance on the French bonds relative to the U.S. bonds over the seven-year period?

8. Quake Inc. is a U.S. financial institution that has purchased British bonds and simultaneously hedged the coupon payments and the principal payment at maturity against exchange rate risk. Explain a scenario that will cause Quake Inc. to earn a lower yield on the bonds (as opposed to if it did not hedge). Also explain how the hedging strategy could backfire if Quake decides to liquidate the bonds prior to maturity.

9. Based on the concepts of portfolio theory described in this chapter, what would be the rationale for diversifying across international bonds and stocks? Would a combined portfolio be likely to exhibit more or less risk than an international bond portfolio? Why?

10. Which bond mutual fund is more exposed to exchange rate risk from a U.S. investor's perspective: (1) a fund containing 20 Canadian bonds with 10-year maturities, or (2) a fund containing 200 bonds, 20 from each of 10 different Western European countries? Explain.

References

Adler, M., and B. Dumas. "The Exposure of Long-Term Foreign Currency Bonds." *Journal of Financial and Quantitative Analysis* (November 1980): 973–94.

Adler, M., and D. Simon. "Exchange Risk Surprises in International Portfolios." *Journal of Portfolio Management* (Winter 1986): 44–53.

Barrett, B., and R. Kolb. "The Structure of International Bond Risk Differentials." *Journal of International Business Studies* (Spring 1986): 107–18.

Cholerton, K., P. Pieraerts, and B. Solnik. "Why Invest in Foreign Currency Bonds?" *Journal of Portfolio Management* (Summer 1986): 4–8.

Edwards, S. "The Pricing of Bonds and Bank Loans in International Markets." *European Economic Review* (1986): 564–89.

Finnerty, J., and K. Nunn. "The Determinants of Yield Spreads on U.S. and Eurobonds." *Management International Review* 2 (1985): 23–33.

Finnerty, J., T. Schneweis, and S. Hedge. "Interest Rates in the Eurobond Market." *Journal of Financial and Quantitative Analysis* (September 1980): 743–55.

Ibbotson, R., R. Carr, and A. Robinson. "International Equity and Bond Returns." *Financial Analysts Journal* (July/August 1982): 61–76.

Kidwell, D., W. Marr, and R. Thompson. "Eurodollar Bonds: Alternative Financing for U.S. Companies." *Financial Management* (Winter 1985): 18–27.

Kool, C., and J. Tatom. "International Linkages in the Term Structure of Interest Rates." *Review* (Federal Reserve Bank of St. Louis) (July/August 1988): 30–43.

Lee, A. "International Asset and Currency Allocation." *Journal of Portfolio Management* (Fall 1987): 68–73.

Levy, H., and Z. Lerman. "The Benefits of International Diversification in Bonds." *Financial Analysts Journal* (September/October 1988): 56–64.

Mahajan, A., and D. Fraser. "Dollar Eurobond and U.S. Bond Pricing." *Journal of International Business Studies* (Summer 1986): 21–36.

Robicheck, A., and M. Eaker. "Debt Denomination and Exchange Risk in International Capital Markets." *Financial Management* (Autumn 1976): 11–18.

Rosenberg, H. "The New Lure of Foreign Bonds." *Institutional Investor* (March 1988): 145–47.

Solnik, B., and B. Noetzlin. "Optimal International Asset Location." *Journal of Portfolio Management* (Fall 1982): 11–21.

9

INTERNATIONAL
STOCK MARKETS

The internationalization of stock markets is relevant from financing and investment perspectives. Firms in need of financing use foreign stock markets as additional sources of funds. Investors use foreign stock markets to enhance their portfolio performance.

In this chapter, we first present a background on international stock markets from both perspectives. Second, we explain the benefits of international diversification, and also identify the risks involved. Finally, we identify methods commonly used to achieve international diversification.

USE OF FOREIGN STOCK MARKETS BY ISSUERS

Some corporations issue stock in foreign markets in order to tap additional sources of funds. This approach may allow them to attract more funds without flooding their home market with stock, so that they can avoid a decline in the market price. The demand for a particular type of stock may be stronger in a country where that type is commonly traded. For example, the U.S. market is the only developed market for preferred stock. In 1989, some non-U.S. firms issued dollar-denominated preferred stock in the U.S. market.

Some markets evaluate a company's characteristics differently, which is another reason for issuing stock in a foreign market. Even if U.S. investors are not interested in a particular stock, non-U.S. investors may still have an interest, owing to a different interpretation of, or emphasis on, financial information. Some firms may issue stock in foreign markets to circumvent regulations, since regulatory provisions differ among markets. Firms may also believe that they can achieve worldwide recognition among consumers if they issue stock in various foreign markets.

In recent years, a Euroequities market has developed and grown at a rapid pace. The stocks issued in the Euroequities market are specifically

Exhibit 9.1

Foreign Listings on Stock
Exchanges

Stock Exchange	Total Number of Stocks Listed	Number of Foreign Stocks Listed	Percentage of Foreign Stocks Listed
Australia	1,506	47	3.1%
France	888	222	25.0
Singapore	326	194	59.5
Switzerland (Zurich)	2,914	1,105	37.9
United Kingdom	2,656	595	22.4
United States (N.Y.)	1,681	74	4.4
West Germany (Frankfurt)	741	329	44.4

SOURCE: *Institutional Investor*, March 1989, pp. 197–204.

designed for distribution among foreign markets. They are underwritten by a group of investment banks, and purchased primarily by institutional investors across several countries. Many of the underwriters are U.S.-based investment banks, such as First Boston, Merrill Lynch, and Salomon Brothers. As an example, the German automobile manufacturer Daimler-Benz AG recently raised $1.5 billion through the Euroequities market. Financial institutions in cities from New York to Tokyo participated in the offering. Other recent issuers of new stock in this market include the Travelers Corp. and American Television & Communication Corp.

Most countries have a telecommunications network to publicize and facilitate new issues of stocks, and stock exchanges to facilitate secondary market trading. The new issues and secondary markets are relatively large in the United States because of (1) corporate expansion in the United States, and (2) tendencies for U.S.-based corporations to use proportionately more equity financing than firms in other countries.

A comparison of foreign listing activity among markets is given in Exhibit 9.1. Foreign listing activity as measured in proportion to total listings varies substantially across markets. The activity is generally higher in European stock markets than in other markets. Yet, some European markets such as Portugal and Spain have no foreign stock listings.

The ability of firms to place new shares in foreign markets depends somewhat on the stock's perceived liquidity in that market. A secondary market for the stock must be established in foreign markets to enhance liquidity, and make newly issued stocks more attractive. Listing stock on a foreign stock exchange not only enhances the stock's liquidity but also may increase the firm's perceived financial standing when the exchange approves the listing application. It can also protect a firm against hostile takeovers because it disperses ownership and makes it more difficult for other firms to gain a controlling interest. There are some costs of listing on a foreign exchange, such as translating its annual report in a foreign currency, and making financial statements compatible with the accounting standards used in that country.

Saudagaran (1988) attempted to determine factors common to firms that list on a foreign stock exchange. He found that the following factors are associated with foreign exchange listings:

- A large absolute size of the firm
- A large relative size of the firm in comparison with its national market
- A large proportion of foreign sales relative to total sales

Because the desire to list on a foreign stock exchange normally coincides with the desire to issue new stocks in that country, the results of Saudagaran's study offer implications about new issues in foreign markets. Perhaps the large firms (in an absolute or relative sense) tap foreign markets for funds because they are more confident that the issue can be absorbed by those markets without a decline in price. In addition, the more internationalized firms (measured as having a high proportion of foreign sales to total sales) may be especially willing to tap foreign markets because their name is already familiar to investors in these markets. Also, these firms may have a greater need for funds denominated in foreign currencies to establish or expand foreign subsidiaries, and issuing stock in foreign markets can achieve such an objective. Dividends to be paid on stock issued in these foreign markets would be denominated in the same currency as that generated by the foreign projects.

If a foreign market lacks interest in a stock, a discrepancy in prices between the foreign and home markets may develop. Foreign market shares can become underpriced and will flow back to the home market, as home investors purchase them from the foreign market. However, this activity can cause a flood of shares in the home market and reduce secondary market activity in the foreign market.

For those stocks that are traded on various international stock markets, trading occurs almost continuously. For example, the stock returns of Exxon and IBM are shown in Figure 9.1 for the period surrounding the stock market crash on 19 October 1987. Notice that for some days preceding the crash, the prices of these two stocks were declining in London and New York markets, but rebounded slightly in the Tokyo market.

USE OF FOREIGN STOCK MARKETS BY INVESTORS

The existence of international mutual funds (IMFs) has resulted in a greater degree of international trading across markets. It allows investors to invest in existing foreign stocks without incurring excessive transaction costs. Furthermore, the foreign securities are selected by the fund's managers, so that individual investment decisions can be left to fund managers who have greater access to information.

The degree to which stock trading is becoming internationalized is illustrated in Figure 9.2, which shows the increase in U.S. stocks purchased and sold by foreign investors. The volume of trading has increased substantially over the last decade.

Cross-border stock transactions between residents and nonresidents are shown in Exhibit 9.2, (on page 161) for four major countries. All

Figure 9.1   Share Price Movements Across Stock Markets

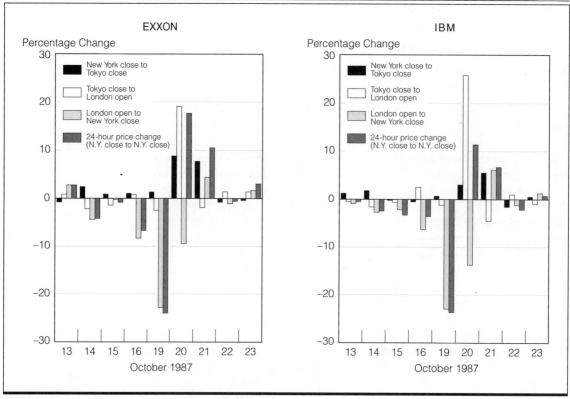

SOURCE: *FRBNY Quarterly Review,* Summer 1988, p. 39.

Figure 9.2

Foreign Trading of U.S. Stocks
(in millions of dollars)

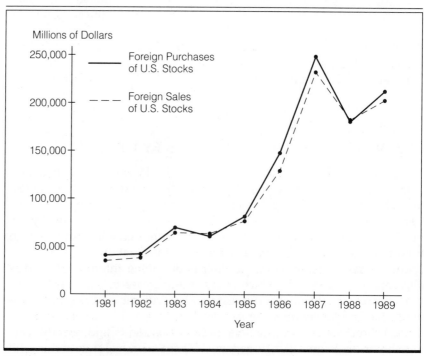

SOURCE: *Federal Reserve Bulletin,* various issues.

Exhibit 9.2
Cross-Border Stock Transactions

Gross Purchases and Sales of Domestic Stocks by Nonresidents
(in Billions of U.S. Dollars)

	United States[a]	Japan[b]	Germany[c]	Canada[d]
1980	75.2	26.2	6.8	12.4
1981	75.5	43.7	6.9	9.2
1982	79.9	34.6	6.3	5.2
1983	134.1	71.5	13.4	8.4
1984	122.6	78.3	12.4	8.8
1985	159.0	81.9	36.9	11.9
1986	277.5	201.6	77.9	20.2
1987	481.9	374.7	76.8	45.7

SOURCE: *FRBNY Quarterly Review*, Summer 1988, p. 22.

[a] U.S. Treasury International Capital data.
[b] Japanese Ministry of Finance.
[c] Deutsche Bundesbank, *Balance of Payments Statistics, Statistical Supplements to the Monthly Reports of the Deutsche Bundesbank*, Series 3.
[d] Statistics Canada, *Security Transactions with Non-Residents and Quarterly Estimates of the Canadian Balance of International Payments*.

transactions are measured in U.S. dollars, so that a comparison among countries is possible. The cross-border transactions involving the U.S. are highest, but Japanese cross-border transactions are increasing at a faster rate.

Characteristics of Stock Markets

A comparison of characteristics across stock markets is provided in Exhibit 9.3. The differences in trading volume are attributed to differences in number of listings, tendencies for investors to invest in stocks versus bonds, and several other factors. Exhibit 9.3 shows that restrictions imposed on foreign investors vary across markets. Many markets impose limits on the proportional foreign investment in a firm's equity, a practice that may not only restrict investments by portfolio managers but also may prohibit foreign acquisitions (unless the foreign government gives approval).

Around-the-Clock Global Security Trading

A major deregulatory event (known as the "Big Bang") that occurred in the London stock market in October 1986 further facilitated progress toward around-the-clock trading. A computerized network called SEAQ (pronounced "see-yak") was established, which is similar to the NASDAQ over-the-counter system in the United States. International traders conduct trading through a telecommunications network. In addition, the London exchange began to allow investment firms that trade in the United States and Japan to trade in London. Consequently, the large investment firms that trade on the New York and Tokyo exchanges have created a nearly 24-hour market, using the New York Stock Ex-

Exhibit 9.3   Characteristics of Stock Exchanges

Stock Exchange	Number of Companies Listed	Market Capitalization (millions of $s)	Average Daily Volume (millions of shares)	Trading Hours	Shares Owned by Individuals (percent)	Shares Owned by Institutions or Funds (percent)	Restrictions on Foreign Ownership
Australia	1,506	$ 164,930	102.8	10:15–12:15 2:00–3:15	10%	90%	Only on strategic industries such as uranium.
Belgium	340	50,535	N/A	10:00–3:30	N/A	N/A	
Canada (Montreal)	1,188	368,917	5.36	9:30–4:00	52	48	Some financial institutions are subject to a maximum limit of equity that can be held by nonresidents.
Canada (Toronto)	N/A	N/A	N/A	9:30–4:00	N/A	N/A	See Montreal exchange.
Canada (Vancouver)	2,334	4,515	14.0	6:30–1:30	80	20	None
France	888	244,998	N/A	10:00–5:00	30	20	Investors in countries outside the European community cannot hold more than 20% of equity without approval.
Hong Kong	308	71,697	N/A	10:00–12:30 2:30–3:30	N/A	N/A	None
Italy	211	135,428	N/A	10:00–1:45	N/A	N/A	None
Japan (Osaka)	N/A	2,747,948	118.9	9:00–11:00 1:00–3:00	N/A	N/A	None
Japan (Tokyo)	N/A	3,191,191	1,040.0	9:00–11:00 1:00–3:00	23.6	72	None
South Korea	N/A	57,007	9.7	9:40–11:40 1:20–3:20	68	29.3	Nonresidents can invest in stocks only through mutual funds and convertible bonds.
Mexico	309	N/A	32.9	10:30–11:30	58.33	41.67	N/A
Netherlands	572	91,720	N/A	10:00–4:30	N/A	N/A	None
New Zealand	387	15,208	6.5	9:30–11:00 2:15–3:30	N/A	N/A	Foreigners must have approval for ownership of 24% or more.
Norway	137	13,090	N/A	10:00–3:00	22.5	15	Limits are imposed on foreign ownership of stocks.
Singapore	326	N/A	N/A	10:00–12.30 2:30–4:00	25	75	Restrictions apply for stocks in some industries.
Switzerland (Basel)	483	N/A	N/A	9:10–1:30	N/A	N/A	No restrictions for bearer shares, but ownership of registered shares is normally restricted to residents.
Switzerland (Geneva)	494	100,032	N/A	9:00–1:15	N/A	N/A	See Basel exchange.
Switzerland (Zurich)	2,914	125,403	N/A	9:30–1:15	10	N/A	See Basel exchange.

Exhibit 9.3 continued

Stock Exchange	Number of Companies Listed	Market Capitalization (millions of $s)	Average Daily Volume (millions of shares)	Trading Hours	Shares Owned by Individuals (percent)	Shares Owned by Institutions or Funds (percent)	Restrictions on Foreign Ownership
Taiwan	N/A	92,008	354	9:00–12:00	40.7	50.1	Foreign investors are required to apply for a remittance permit.
United Kingdom	2,656	2,659,707	N/A	9:00–5:00	20	80	None
United States	1,681	2,400,000	161	9:30–4:00	N/A	N/A	None
West Germany	741	186,601	7,354	11:30–1:30	N/A	N/A	None

SOURCE: *Institutional Investor*, March 1989, pp. 197–204.

change from 9:30 A.M. to 4 P.M. Eastern time, the Tokyo Stock exchange from 7 P.M. to 1 A.M. Eastern time, and the London Stock Exchange from 4 A.M. to 10:30 A.M. Eastern time. Shares that are traded on each exchange could be bought or sold almost any time of the day. As more companies are having their stocks listed on the various exchanges, stock market trading will be almost continuous without the interruptions that result from exchange closings.

The Big Bang also allowed the commissions paid on stock transactions in London to be competitive (similar to the deregulated commissions in the United States in 1975). As a result, profit margins of brokerage firms have been reduced, and the market has become more cost effective for investors.

BENEFITS FROM INTERNATIONAL DIVERSIFICATION

If correlations between stock returns of different countries are lower than correlations of stock returns within a country, investors may be able to reduce portfolio risk through international diversification. Assuming that similar returns can be achieved, international portfolios should outperform domestic portfolios because of lower portfolio risk. This point can be illustrated with the use of efficient frontiers, which depict potentially achievable risk-return characteristics for a variety of portfolios. Any points along a given frontier dominate other possibly achievable points in that they either have a lower risk for a given return, or a higher return for a given risk level. A comparison of efficient frontiers is shown in Figure 9.3. The efficient international portfolios (lying along the international efficient frontier) should dominate the efficient domestic portfolios if returns on securities of different countries exhibit lower correlations.

Figure 9.3

Comparison of International and
Domestic Efficient Frontiers

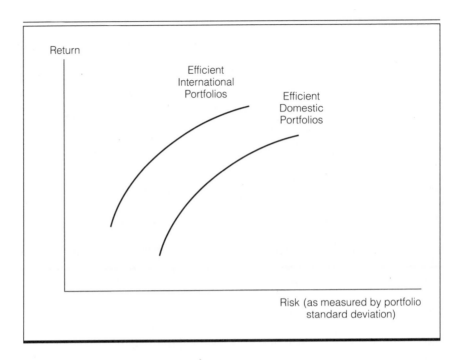

Evidence of Diversification Benefits

Several studies have applied the mean-variance model to historical returns on country stock indices, to identify the composition of a portfolio
that would have achieved minimum variance of returns (a proxy for risk)
for a given return level. The actual shape of the efficient frontier varies
with the time period analyzed. Yet, studies by Levy and Sarnat (1970),
Grubel and Fadner (1971), and others consistently confirm that the frontier of internationally diversified stock indices dominates individual indices, as shown in Figure 9.4.

Levy and Sarnat (1970) emphasized the importance of correlations
between particular country stock returns in determining how best to
capitalize on international diversification. The correlations of returns
among industrialized countries were relatively higher, suggesting that
markets with fewer restrictions are more integrated, and therefore offer
fewer risk-reduction benefits.

Although most studies on benefits from international diversification
have focused on a U.S. perspective, some studies (Biger 1979) assessed a
non-U.S. perspective. Biger's study was especially insightful because it
compared risk-reduction benefits among various country perspectives.
He showed that although benefits existed from all perspectives, the
degree of potential risk reduction varied among perspectives, because
exchange rate effects cause differences in pairwise correlations of stock
returns among perspectives.

In a famous study, Solnik (1974) assessed the degree of risk reduction
attributable to the addition of foreign securities to a portfolio. Solnik's
study differs from many other related studies because he analyzed ac-

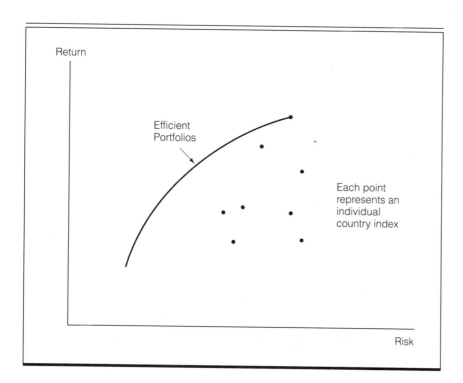

Figure 9.4
Benefits from International
Diversification

tual stocks instead of stock market indices. If the correlations between foreign and U.S. stock returns are lower than those among pairs of U.S. stocks, we would expect that the inclusion of foreign securities would offer favorable risk-reduction benefits, as shown in Figure 9.5. Solnik found that the degree of risk reduction when including international securities was clearly greater than when including only U.S. securities. A well-diversified international portfolio exhibited about one-half the variability of a well-diversified portfolio of U.S. stocks.

Impact of European Integration on Diversification Benefits

To the extent that stock markets in Europe are affected by economic conditions, and their economies become more integrated, their market returns should become more highly correlated. In addition, the increased capital mobility resulting from reduced capital restrictions is likely to increase the influence of one member's stock market conditions on the others. Exhibit 9.4 on page 167 discloses correlations of stock market returns (based on indices measured in local currency units) for the European countries over two subperiods. The vast majority of correlations among stock returns have increased significantly. Given that stock prices are driven by expectations of future performance, these results imply that expectations of corporate performance among countries are more similar than before.

For institutional investors that construct international stock portfolios, the likely increasing correlations among European stock returns offers relevant implications. Benefits from geographical diversification across

Figure 9.5

Risk Reduction from Increasing
Portfolio Size: International Versus
Domestic

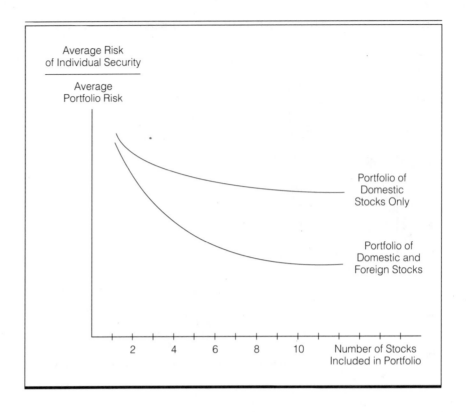

European countries would be reduced as stocks within these countries become more systematically influenced by expectations of underlying conditions.

Because of the increasing integration across EC countries, stock portfolio managers may view European countries as one market. While this market would still be attractive, it may not by itself achieve the degree of diversification benefits desired. For this reason, portfolios may be revised to replace some European securities with non-European securities.

COMPARISON OF INTERNATIONAL STOCK AND BOND PORTFOLIOS

Are the benefits from international bond diversification greater or less than those of international stock diversification? Levy and Lerman (1988) derived the achievable risk-return combinations of efficient bond portfolios. Then, using a risk-free rate, they developed a capital market line for bonds and for stocks. All points along the bond market line tend to dominate the points along the stock market line up to returns of 11 percent. However, some stock portfolios offered greater potential returns that could only be achieved by bond portfolios if borrowing (leveraging the portfolios) was allowed.

	Belgium	Denmark	France	Ireland	Italy	Nether.	Spain	UK
Denmark	−.26							
	.27							
France	.16	−.37						
	.68	.35						
Ireland	−.26	−.08	.07					
	.66	.39	.62					
Italy	−.02	.36	.11	.09				
	.45	.22	.69	.41				
Nether.	.15	.43	−.20	.07	.16			
	.18	.30	.27	−.02	.47			
Spain	.12	.51	−.01	−.36	.22	.45		
	.00	.52	.26	−.07	.08	.41		
UK	.12	.25	−.02	.46	.17	.30	.11	
	.72	.20	.66	.61	.33	.17	.08	
WG	−.21	.16	−.22	.51	−.02	.67	.03	.44
	.65	.52	.66	.46	.52	.29	.29	.66

Exhibit 9.4

Correlations among Stock Index Movements

NOTE: The coefficient in the top of each cell represents the subperiod from the first quarter of 1977 to the third quarter of 1982 while the coefficient in the bottom of each cell represents the subperiod from the fourth quarter of 1982 through 1988.

International Diversification of Stocks and Bonds

Up to this point, the concept of international portfolio diversification has been applied separately to bonds and stocks. Yet, many large institutional investors would likely construct both types of portfolios. Because stock and bond returns are not highly correlated, a combined investment in international stocks and bonds may achieve additional risk reduction. Levy and Lerman combined stocks and bonds, and derived an efficient frontier of portfolios containing both types of securities. Based on risk/return criteria, these portfolios dominated efficient stock portfolios and efficient bond portfolios. The capital market line applicable to the combined stock and bond portfolios dominated the respective capital market lines for stock portfolios and bond portfolios.

Related research by Solnik and Noetzlin also compared the risk/return characteristics of combined portfolios to bond portfolios and stock portfolios. They demonstrate significant risk reduction benefits from combining international stocks and bonds, which reinforces the results of Levy and Lerman.

Portfolio managers that consider international diversification of stocks and bonds must determine the optimal portfolio combination or *asset allocation*. Solnik and Noetzlin identify three possible asset allocation methods that can be used by practitioners. First, the *extrapolative approach* represents the construction of a portfolio based on the historical covariance matrix (of historical stock and bond returns). This matrix can be used to develop minimum risk portfolios. The minimum risk portfolio in the historical period may not necessarily be efficient in the future period, as the covariance structure is intertemporally unstable. Nevertheless, this extrapolative approach may still be useful for identifying portfolios that will perform well in the future.

A second approach, referred to as the *simplified approach,* allocates an equal amount of investment to all securities. This implies the expectation that correlations among all security pairs are similar. While correlations are not necessarily similar, this approach avoids the potential error in allocating more funds to securities whose returns exhibited relatively low correlations in the past, but which may become relatively highly correlated in the future.

A third approach, referred to as the *passive approach,* allocates funds in accordance with the degree of market concentration. That is, securities of larger countries would be allocated more funds at the expense of smaller countries.

Solnik and Noetzlin find that the extrapolative approach consistently outperforms the alternative approaches. This implies that even though the covariance matrix is not perfectly stable over time, it can be useful for indicating pairs of securities that will exhibit relatively low or high correlations.

ESTIMATING RETURN AND RISK FROM INTERNATIONAL DIVERSIFICATION

To the extent that foreign securities can offer a high return or low risk, they are attractive to investors. A foreign stock's return (R_j) can be estimated as

9.1 $$R_j = (1 + R_d)(1 + E) - 1,$$

where R_d is the stock return in the domestic market (without an exchange rate adjustment), and E is the percentage change in the value of the currency denominating the stock with respect to the investor's home currency.

Foreign stocks may be desirable if either the expected value of R_d or E is high. Because exchange rate movements are so volatile, they can significantly affect R_j.

Foreign stocks generated very large returns to U.S. investors during the 1985–1988 period, primarily because of the strength of foreign currencies relative to the dollar. Consider a U.S. investor who purchased a British stock for £30 per share and sold it for £33 per share at the end of the period. Also assume that the pound was worth $1.50 at the time of purchase and $1.80 at the time of the sale. The stock's domestic return (R_d) is 10%, and the percentage change in the pound's value (E) is 20%. Thus, the return to the U.S. investor is

9.2 $$\begin{aligned} R_j &= (1 + R_d)(1 + E) - 1 \\ &= (1 + 0.1)(1 + 0.2) - 1 \\ &= 32\%. \end{aligned}$$

In some periods, exchange rate movements adversely affect R_j. For example, if the pound's value at the time of the sale was $1.38, the pound would have depreciated by 8% over the investment horizon, causing the U.S. investor's return to be

9.3
$$R_j = (1 + 0.1)[1 + (-0.08)] - 1$$
$$= 1.2\%.$$

The returns on foreign stocks to U.S. investors were generally lower during the 1981–1984 period, because foreign currencies weakened against the dollar.

In addition to exchange rate risk, other risks of investing in foreign securities also deserve some attention. Foreign securities may be subject to different liquidity characteristics than domestic securities, which can affect their volatility. For example, the price of a non-U.S. security is likely to exhibit more day-to-day volatility because the trading activity is less, and the market price is more sensitive to individual transactions.

The risk of a security is often measured by the variance of returns over time. The variance of a foreign security is

9.4
$$VAR(R_j) = VAR[(1 + R_d)(1 + E) - 1]$$
$$\simeq VAR(R_d) + VAR(E) + 2COV(R_d, E),$$

where COV represents the covariance. Although the covariance between R_d and E is often thought to be negligible, exchange rate variation can cause $VAR(R_j)$ to be more than double $VAR(R_d)$.

The impact of correlations between stock returns on a stock portfolio's risk can be illustrated by eq. 9.5, representing the variance of a two-stock portfolio (R_p):

9.5
$$VAR(R_p) = W_A^2 VAR(R_A) + W_B^2 VAR(R_B) + 2COV(R_A, R_B),$$

where W_A is the weight (proportional investment) allocated to stock A, W_B is the weight (proportional investment) allocated to stock B, $VAR(R_A)$ is the variance of stock A's returns, $VAR(R_B)$ is the variance of stock B's returns, and $COV(R_A, R_B)$ is the covariance of returns between stocks A and B.

Since the covariance is equal to the product of the correlation coefficient and respective standard deviations of the pair of stocks, the portfolio's variance can be rewritten as

9.6
$$VAR(R_p) = W_A^2 VAR(R_A) + W_B^2 VAR(R_B) + 2(CORR(R_A, R_B)),$$

where VAR represents the variance and $CORR$ represents the correlation coefficient of returns between stocks A and B. To the extent that one can find stocks with low (or ideally negative) correlations, the stock portfolio's variability can be reduced. At an extreme, a perfectly negative correlation (equal to -1) would cause $VAR(R_p)$ to be zero (if weights were equally distributed, and standard deviations were similar). The ability to find low or negatively correlated stocks in a given country is limited by the systematic influence of the local economy on all the local stocks. Diversifying among stocks of different countries can possibly achieve lower portfolio variability because the stocks are influenced by different markets. The correlations of stocks of separate markets are normally expected to be less than correlations of stocks within the same market.

Even for portfolios containing several stocks, portfolio risk is significantly influenced by the pairwise correlations of stock returns of all stocks included in the portfolio. Thus, international diversification is plausible for large stock portfolios as well.

OPERATIONALIZING INTERNATIONAL DIVERSIFICATION

U.S. investors attempt to achieve international diversification by using any one of the following methods:

- Direct investment in foreign stocks
- American depository receipts (ADRs)
- Investment in U.S.-based multinational corporations (MNCs)
- International mutual funds (IMFs)

A description of each method follows.

Direct Investment in Foreign Stocks

Foreign securities are sometimes purchased directly by institutional portfolio managers for inclusion in their respective portfolios. Though information and other transaction costs are relatively high, they may be less significant (on a percentage basis) for large institutional transactions. However, the costs can be overwhelming for individual and small institutional investors. Therefore, some investors desiring international diversification need an alternative method.

American Depository Receipts

American depository receipts (ADRs) are certificates representing ownership of foreign stocks. An ADR typically represents 1 to 10 shares of the underlying stock. Dividends on stocks represented by ADRs are received by a depository bank and are transferred to investors holding ADRs. The bank charges a fee for transactions involving the payment of dividends or the exchange of ADRs for the underlying shares. Most ADRs are traded over the counter, although as of 1989, 79 ADRs were traded on the New York Stock Exchange. The list of available ADRs has been growing over time.

Some well-known firms for which ADRs are available include Porsche (Germany), Phillips Lamp (Netherlands), Hachette (France), Jaguar (United Kingdom) and Jardine Matheson (Hong Kong). Companies represented by ADRs are required by the Securities and Exchange Commission (SEC) to file financial statements consistent with the generally accepted accounting principles in the United States. Therefore, the financial information on such foreign companies is compatible with information on U.S. companies. ADRs are also desirable because reliable

The Uniqueness of U.S. Investors

Novo Industri is a Danish Biotechnology company for which ADRs were available in the 1980s. It was known to have excellent public relations with Wall Street investment firms. However, in 1984, Novo learned a lesson about how U.S. investors are short-term-oriented. Novo announced a 2% decline in quarterly earnings, and stated that it may have low earnings for the year. Novo's ADR prices declined substantially. One U.S. stockholder with 60 ADR shares sued the company for deceit. Non-U.S. investors tend to focus more on long-term expectations, and may not have reacted as strongly to short-term problems experienced by Novo. In fact, some non-U.S. firms that historically provided semiannual reports in their home countries have begun to offer quarterly reports to satisfy U.S. investors.

Other non-U.S. firms are less willing to incur the substantial costs of providing quarterly statements, even if it means less interest by U.S. investors. For example, some German companies do not consolidate their subsidiary reports, and some Dutch firms provide only abridged reports.

Differences in accounting procedure can complicate any assessment of foreign financial reports. For example, Swedish companies use a reserve system that protects some earnings from taxation. This system may cause some investors to believe such companies have lower earnings than they actually had.

In general the only way for a non-U.S. firm to attract a strong U.S. demand for its shares is to provide frequent information in a form that U.S. investors can follow. The investment community in the United States is often highly specialized and focuses on numbers. Such a focus tends to result in abrupt sales or purchases of stock in response to information about unusually high or low performance in a single quarter.

Source: *Institutional Investor*, February 1989, pp. 189–192.

quotes on ADR prices are consistently available, with existing currency values accounted for to translate the price in dollars.

Some disadvantages of ADRs also need to be considered. Some of the reporting rules are looser for the foreign firms. For example, foreign firms need to provide financial reports to shareholders only semiannually, and they are not required to disclose salaries of top management. In addition, foreign firms can issue non-voting stock. The number of available ADRs is limited and ADRs are generally less liquid than other stocks. Because ADRs generally represent more established conservative non-U.S. companies, they may not satisfy investors desiring to invest in growth stocks of smaller non-U.S. firms.

In a recent study, Officer and Hoffmeister (1987) assessed the viability of ADRs as a means of international diversification. They found that whereas ADR returns were more volatile than U.S. stock returns, combined portfolios of ADRs and U.S. stocks exhibit significantly lower variability than portfolios composed solely of U.S. stocks. Thus, ADRs could effectively enable U.S. investors to reduce risk. In related research, Tucker (1987) compared the benefits of ADRs to foreign stocks, by contrasting the marginal benefits from adding ADRs to a U.S. stock portfolio to the benefits of adding foreign stocks. The degree of risk reduction when using ADRs was quite similar to that when using foreign stocks. These results imply that ADRs are an effective means of international diversification, and therefore that investment in ADRs may be an adequate substitute for direct investment in foreign stocks. However, the limited number of ADRs available, and the relatively high transaction costs, may encourage some investors to use an alternative approach.

Investment in U.S.-based MNCs

A multinational corporation (MNC) essentially represents a portfolio of international operations. Thus, its performance is only partially susceptible to its home market. U.S.-based MNCs should be somewhat insulated from U.S. market downturns, because a substantial portion of their operations are in non-U.S. countries. Even though the stock of a U.S.-based MNC is not international, it could possibly serve as an adequate substitute for an international stock portfolio.

If MNC stocks behave like an international portfolio, then they should be sensitive to the stock markets of the various countries in which they operate. Jacquillat and Solnik (1978) assessed the sensitivity of MNC returns to various stock market movements during the 1966–1974 period using the following regression model:

9.7 $\qquad R_{mnc} = a_0 + a_1 R_L + b_1 R_{I1} + b_2 R_{I2} + \cdots + b_n R_{I,n} + u,$

where R_{mnc} is the average return on a portfolio of MNCs from the same country, a_0 is the intercept, R_L is the return on the local stock market, $R_{I,1}$ through $R_{I,n}$ are returns on foreign stock indices I_1 through I_n, and u is an error term. The regression coefficient a_1 measures the sensitivity of MNC returns to their local stock market, and coefficients b_1 through b_n measure the sensitivity of MNC returns to the various foreign stock markets. The results of the time-series regression analysis showed that MNCs based in a particular country were typically affected only by the local stock market and were not strongly affected by other stock market movements. This same result occurred for the MNC portfolio of each country.

As a complementary test, Jacquillat and Solnik applied a simple regression model to each MNC portfolio using the local stock market returns as the independent variable, and the explanatory power of this model was compared to that of the multiple regression model specified earlier. The multiple regression model exhibited very little additional explanatory power (based on a comparison of the adjusted coefficients of determination), suggesting that the MNC stock movements are solely attributable to the local market movements. The results imply that the returns of MNCs behave similar to non-MNCs. Therefore, investment in a portfolio of MNCs does not sufficiently achieve international diversification.

In a recent study, Madura (1989) reassessed the sensitivity of MNC returns to various stock markets over the 1974–1987 period. A reassessment was necessary because many MNCs have significantly increased their international operations since the period used by Jacquillat and Solnik in evaluating MNCs. The increased international involvement of MNCs could have caused them to behave more like an internationally diversified stock portfolio. Based on a procedure similar to that of Jacquillat and Solnik, the results again showed that MNC stock returns respond principally to the local stock market returns and not to the movements of any other markets. Thus, MNCs continue to be poor substitutes for direct international diversification.

Brewer (1982) assessed both risk and return aspects of MNC and non-MNC stocks by deriving separate security market lines (based on returns over time) for MNCs versus non-MNCs. He found no statistically significant difference between the two security market lines, and therefore concluded that MNCs offer no advantage over non-MNCs.

Agmon and Lessard (1977) grouped MNC portfolios according to degree of international business (measured by foreign sales as a percentage of total sales) and estimated the betas of these portfolios. They found that portfolios of MNCs with a greater degree of international business typically exhibited lower betas. This relationship suggests that investors may be able to reduce systematic risk by investing in firms with a greater degree of international business. However, several other studies have less favorable implications for investing in MNCs. Hughes, Logue, and Sweeney (1975) found that although MNCs tend to exhibit lower systematic risk, they also exhibit lower returns.

Michel and Shaked (1986) used the Sharpe and Treynor indexes to combine the measures of return and risk for non-MNCs and MNCs, as defined in eq. 9.8:

9.8
$$\text{Sharpe index} = \frac{\text{mean return} - \text{risk-free rate}}{\text{standard deviation}}$$

$$\text{Treynor index} = \frac{\text{mean return} - \text{risk-free rate}}{\text{beta}}$$

Both the Sharpe and Treynor indexes were higher for domestic companies than for MNCs. This result suggests that the favorable risk characteristics of MNCs were more than offset by lower returns.

Senchack and Beedles (1980) assessed the risk reduction from increasing the number of MNC stocks in randomly selected portfolios. The procedure was then repeated for non-MNCs, so that the degree of risk reduction achievable due to the increased number of stocks could be compared between MNCs and non-MNCs. The authors found that the degree of risk reduction in portfolios of non-MNCs exceeded that exhibited by portfolios of MNCs. Specific results may vary, but most of the studies on diversifying with MNCs imply that investing in MNCs does not generate significant international diversification benefits.

International Mutual Funds (IMFs)

Perhaps the most efficient method of diversifying internationally is to employ international mutual funds (IMFs), which are created by various investment firms. Investors can purchase shares of an IMF with a small minimum investment, such as $1,000. The IMFs are managed by the sponsoring investment firm's portfolio managers, which limits the investor control over investment performance. Yet, investors can choose from several kinds of IMFs. Some IMFs include stocks across several continents; others focus on a specific country or continent. For example, Fidelity offers the following IMFs:

- Fidelity Overseas Fund, representing stocks all over the world
- Fidelity Pacific Basin Fund, representing stocks in Japan, Hong Kong, Singapore, Australia, and other Far East countries

- Fidelity International Growth and Income Fund, representing stocks and bonds mostly outside the United States
- Fidelity Europe Fund, representing stocks in Western Europe
- Fidelity United Kingdom Fund, representing stocks in the United Kingdom
- Fidelity Canada Fund, representing stocks in Canada

An IMF focusing on a specific country may be less effective than a more geographically dispersed portfolio, for reasons stated earlier. However, it provides an efficient means for investors from other countries to invest in that particular market. For example, if investors wanted to create a portfolio composed of 30% investment in Australian stocks, 50% in South Korean stocks, and 20% in Singapore stocks, they could allocate the appropriate proportions to purchase three existing IMFs, each concentrating on a specific market.

Performance of IMFs Essayyad and Wu (1988) assessed the performance of 18 international mutual funds over the 1977–1984 period. Fifteen of the 18 IMFs exhibited a higher mean monthly return than the Standard & Poor's (S&P) 500 index. In addition, 16 of the IMFs exhibited a lower coefficient of variation (defined as standard deviation of returns divided by mean return) than the S&P 500 index, suggesting a lower level of risk per unit of return.

To further assess risk, the authors measured the betas of the IMFs, using the S&P 500 index as a proxy for the market. Four of the 18 IMFs had a beta that was not statistically different from zero. For the 18 IMFs, the average percentage of variation in returns explained by market movements was only about 24%. This finding confirms that IMF return patterns differ substantially from U.S. market returns, which is a desirable attribute for portfolio diversification.

Rao and Aggarwal (1987) examined the sensitivity of IMF returns to the U.S. market (with the S&P 500 index as a proxy for the market). Using regression analysis, they found that the betas estimated for IMFs were less than 1.00. Furthermore, the degree of variation in each IMF's returns that could be explained by market movements (as measured by R^2) averaged 30%, supporting the findings by Essayyad and Wu. This result is significantly below the average R^2 on similar regression applications to domestic mutual funds. Therefore, IMFs appear to offer U.S. investors some degree of insulation from U.S. market movements, and therefore serve as a useful means of international diversification.

Gains from Diversifying Among IMFs If IMFs were completely diversified across all industries of all countries, a single IMF should offer sufficient diversification benefits. However, because some IMFs are focused on a particular country or continent, they may exhibit low correlations with other IMFs, and investors may benefit from diversifying across IMFs.

The correlation coefficients for nine IMFs were estimated, based on quarterly returns from the third quarter of 1976 to the second quarter of 1984. The correlations were generally found to be low, as verified by an

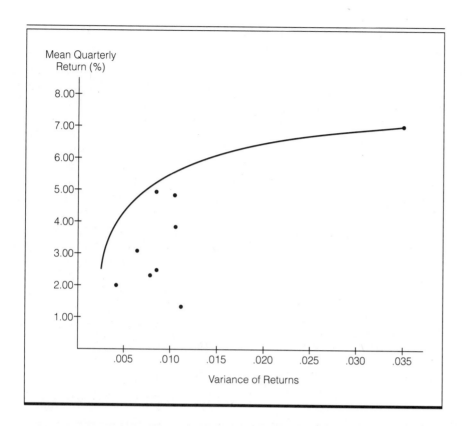

average correlation coefficient of 0.387. Thus, IMF returns do not normally follow a similar pattern over time. Because IMF return patterns are dissimilar, a portfolio of IMFs may achieve more stable returns to the investor than a single IMF.

To assess the potential gains from diversifying across IMFs, the mean-variance program has been applied to the mean IMF returns, variances of IMF returns, and covariances of IMF returns. The efficient IMF portfolios are graphically displayed in Figure 9.6, connected by the efficient frontier curve. Note that only the IMF with the highest mean return is positioned on the efficient frontier. All other individual IMFs are dominated by portfolios. That is, particular portfolios of IMFs were able to achieve the same return as the individual IMFs while reducing risk. The minimum variance portfolio of IMFs exhibited a risk level (measured by variance) approximately 83% less than that of the average variance of an individual IMF.

To assess the possibility of realistically achieving a reduction in risk to the degree previously demonstrated, consider that efficient portfolios were generated from mean return, variability, and pairwise correlation inputs not available until after the period of concern. The potential to truly realize the lower risk from such an ex post analysis depends largely on whether the pairwise correlations of IMF returns are intertemporally stable. To further investigate this issue, the data set has been segmented into two subperiods: (1) third quarter 1976 through fourth quarter 1979,

Exhibit 9.5   Correlation Coefficients of IMF Pairs for Two Separate Subperiods[a]

International Mutual Fund	Axe-Houghton Income Fund	Calvin Bullock Canadian Fund	Int'l. Investors Fund	Massachusetts Financial Int'l. Trust	Putnam Int'l. Equities Fund	Scudder Int'l. Fund	Templeton Growth Fund	United Int'l. Growth Fund	Vanguard Invest. Fund
Axe-Houghton Income Fund	1.00								
	1.00								
Calvin Bullock Canadian Fund	0.01	1.00							
	0.62[b]	1.00							
Int'l. Investors Fund	0.13	0.22	1.00						
	0.01	0.40	1.00						
Massachusetts Financial Int'l. Trust	−0.25	0.59	0.15	1.00					
	0.55[b]	0.89[b]	0.50	1.00					
Putnam Int'l. Equities Fund	0.13	0.45	0.01	−0.03	1.00				
	0.45	0.60	0.28	0.47	1.00				
Scudder Int'l. Fund	0.20	0.31	0.13	−0.14	0.66	1.00			
	0.62	0.43	0.00	0.48[b]	0.38	1.00			
Templeton Growth Fund	0.29	0.23	0.36	0.00	0.23	0.61	1.00		
	0.27	0.69	0.53	0.79[b]	0.33	0.28	1.00		
United Int'l. Growth Fund	0.39	0.67	0.18	0.12	0.65	0.60	0.53	1.00	
	0.41	0.36	0.16	0.58	0.26	0.59	0.30	1.00	
Vanguard Invest. Fund	−0.24	0.70	0.09	0.43	0.52	0.59	0.23	0.54	1.00
	0.06	0.59	0.52	0.61	0.72	0.20	0.54	0.33	1.00

a. Earlier subperiod results represented in top of each cell; more recent subperiod results represented in bottom of each cell.
b. Indicates a statistically significant change at the 0.10 level.

and (2) first quarter 1980 through the beginning of second quarter 1984. Correlation coefficients of IMF pairs have been computed for each subperiod, with the results shown in Exhibit 9.5 (earlier subperiod represented in top of each cell; more recent subperiod represented in the bottom of each cell). Twenty-three of the 36 (64%) IMF pairs exhibited a higher correlation in the more recent subperiod, and the remaining 13 pairs exhibited a reduced correlation. Based on a correlation comparison test, five (22%) of the rising correlations were statistically significant and none of the decreasing correlations were significant. The average correlation coefficient of the 36 IMF pairs was 0.285 in the first subperiod and 0.538 in the second subperiod. The general increase in correlations may be due to a reduction in barriers to international capital flows over time, thereby allowing for greater economic integration between countries. Such a scenario would force one IMF to be more closely linked to other IMFs, even when the IMFs specialize in different countries. A second possible reason for higher intertemporal correlations in IMF returns is that some IMFs have been spreading out into additional foreign markets. Thus, the degree of emphasis in a particular country by each IMF is reduced as funds are spread into other available territories, and the intercountry composition of each IMF may have become more similar.

The preceding analysis provides two reasons why we would typically not be able to achieve the 83% reduction in risk (demonstrated earlier) from holding an IMF portfolio versus an individual IMF. First, the identification of the minimum-risk portfolio of IMFs required the correlations and variances that would not have been available at the time the portfolio was established. The evidence that correlations are not perfectly stationary over time suggests that an ex post minimum-risk IMF portfolio does not necessarily continue to exhibit minimum risk in the future. For this reason, the degree of risk reduction realistically achievable may be overestimated. In addition, evidence that correlations have been increasing over time may further dampen the degree to which IMF portfolios can reduce risk in the future.

We can conduct a more accurate assessment of risk reduction realistically achievable through IMF portfolio composition by comparing the variance of a naive (equal weighted) IMF portfolio to the average variance of an individual IMF. Such a comparison is not "rigged" in any way, since composing the naive portfolio does not necessitate information about correlations and variability over the period of concern. To account for the recent general increase in correlations, we conduct the comparison over the two separate subperiods. The naive IMF portfolio exhibits 69.2% less risk than an individual IMF in the earlier subperiod and 68.7% less risk in the more recent subperiod. The degree of risk reduction is only marginally less in the more recent subperiod, when pairwise correlations were generally higher. Thus, even if individual IMF returns become more highly correlated with each other in the future, there is still much to be gained from diversifying among IMFs. Moreover, the risk reduction may be realized to a greater degree if portfolio managers have the ability to construct IMF portfolios that exhibit less risk than does the naive IMF portfolio.

MANAGING EXCHANGE RATE RISK

The exchange rate risk resulting from foreign stock holdings can be reduced by diversifying among stocks of different countries. For example, a U.S. investor can reduce the exchange rate risk by spreading whatever funds are to be used for foreign investments across various non-U.S. countries. In this way, the variability of portfolio returns attributable to exchange rate movements can be reduced. Exchange rate risk can be most effectively reduced through diversification if correlations between foreign currency movements (against the U.S. dollar) are low or negative.

Many foreign currencies move in tandem against the dollar, especially the European currencies that are pegged to the European Currency Unit (ECU). Because these currencies are essentially fixed relative to one another (within boundaries), they are forced to move by a similar magnitude and direction against the dollar. Thus, if one of these currencies depreciates substantially against the dollar, the others will as well, and all foreign stocks denominated in these currencies are adversely affected to a similar degree. Investors would achieve more effective diversification of currencies by spreading the foreign investment across continents.

Another method of reducing exchange rate risk is to take short positions in the foreign currencies denominating the foreign stocks. For example, a U.S. investor holding British stocks who expects the stocks to be worth £200,000 one year from now could sell forward contracts (or futures contracts) representing £200,000. The stocks could be liquidated at that time and the British pounds could be exchanged for dollars at a locked-in price. The return on this hedged foreign investment (R_h) depends on (1) the spot rate at which the pounds were purchased (S), (2) the domestic return on the stock (R_d), and (3) the forward rate at which the pounds are to be sold (F), as shown in eq. 9.9:

9.9
$$R_h = [(1 + R_d)(F/S)] - 1$$
$$= (1 + R_d)(1 + P) - 1,$$

where P represents the forward rate premium. Since S and F (and therefore P) are known at the time the investment is undertaken, the only uncertain variable is R_d. Thus, the risk of R_h is primarily attributable to the risk of R_d.

Limitations of Hedging

Hedging the exchange rate risk of an international stock portfolio can be effective, but it has three limitations. First, the number of foreign currency units to be converted to dollars at the end of the investment horizon is unknown. If the units received from liquidating the foreign stocks are more (less) than the amount hedged, the investor has a net long (short) position in that foreign currency, and the return will be unfavorably affected by its depreciation (appreciation). Though investors may not perform a perfect hedge for this reason, they should normally be able to hedge most of their exchange rate risk.

A second limitation of hedging exchange rate risk is that the investors may decide to retain the foreign stocks beyond the initially planned investment horizon. Of course, they can create another short position after the initial short position is terminated. If they ever decide to liquidate the foreign stocks before the forward delivery date, the hedge will be less effective. They could use the proceeds to invest in foreign money market securities denominated in that foreign currency in order to postpone conversion to dollars until the forward delivery date. But this approach prevents them from using the funds for other opportunities in the United States until that delivery date.

A third limitation of hedging is that forward rates for some currencies may not exist, or may exhibit a large discount. This limitation generally does not apply to the widely traded currencies.

Research on Hedged International Portfolios

Madura and Reiff (1985) estimated the returns of country stock indices with and without hedging (from a U.S. perspective), to determine the degree of risk reduction achievable from hedging. They developed an ex post efficient frontier of unhedged portfolios and compared it to an efficient frontier of hedged portfolios. The hedged portfolios generally exhibited about half the variance for a given return level. These results are due to higher variances of unhedged stock index returns, and higher covariances between the unhedged stock index returns.

Although the development of ex post efficient portfolios shows potential risk-return levels that could have been achieved, such optimal results are difficult to achieve in reality. Eun and Resnick (1988) assessed the performance of hedged and unhedged portfolios on an ex ante basis. That is, only information acquired before the decision dates was used to compose the portfolios. Their study showed that the hedged portfolios resulted in much lower risk than the unhedged portfolios, even on an ex ante basis. The hedged portfolios consistently outperformed unhedged portfolios, suggesting that the benefits of international diversification are best realized by hedging against exchange rate risk.

Related research by Perold and Schulman (1988) suggests that hedging the exchange rate risk of foreign investments can substantially enhance diversification benefits. They state that over the long run, the effect of hedging on returns would be negligible, while the variability of the stock portfolio would be significantly reduced as a result of international diversification. If the forward rate is an unbiased estimator of the future spot rate in the long run, stock portfolio returns would not be adversely affected by hedging. Since much of the variation in international stock returns is attributed to exchange rate movements, the variation in these returns could be reduced substantially by hedging.

SUMMARY

Stock markets have become more accessible to foreign investors and issuers as explicit and implicit barriers have been removed. International stock portfolios can generate diversification benefits beyond those of purely domestic portfolios. Research has clearly documented substantial gains from an internationally diversified portfolio. The returns and risk of foreign stocks are highly influenced by the currency of denomination. Most of the volatility of foreign stock returns is normally attributable to the volatility of exchange rate movements.

Of the popular methods used for international diversification, the most efficient method is to invest in international mutual funds. They allow investors to invest in a well-diversified portfolio with a small investment. Numerous international mutual funds are available, so that investors can even diversify among them.

The exchange rate exposure resulting from investment in foreign stocks can be hedged by large investors. However, hedging forgoes the potential benefits if the currency of denomination appreciates. In addition, a perfect hedge requires that investors accurately assess the future stock price to estimate the amount of the currency to sell forward. Although hedging has its limitations, research indicates that hedged international stock portfolios have generally outperformed their unhedged counterparts.

Questions and Problems

1. What are some possible advantages for a U.S. firm that lists its stock on a foreign stock exchange?

2. Why was the "Big Bang" important to U.S. investment firms?

3. In what way did the Big Bang intensify competition in the brokerage industry?

4. Explain why efficient portfolios that include foreign stocks typically dominate efficient portfolios of U.S. stocks.

5. Over the period from February 1985 to February 1988, some currencies appreciated by 50% or more against the U.S. dollar. If a U.S. investor held foreign stocks over this three-year period denominated in these currencies, and the stock prices stayed constant, what would have been the return over the three-year period to the U.S. investor?

6. Assume you purchased a German stock today for DM50 per share, which pays no dividends. You expect the mark to appreciate from today's spot rate of $0.55 to $0.62 in one year. You also expect the stock to be worth DM59 per share in one year. What is the expected return on this stock from your perspective?

7. A U.S. portfolio manager considers purchasing a Mexican stock that is expected to increase in price by 130% in one year. However, the peso is expected to depreciate against the U.S. dollar by 40% over the year. What is the expected return on the Mexican stock from the U.S. investor's perspective?

8. Would a portfolio of German stocks generate the same returns to a U.S. investor as to a British investor or a German investor? Explain.

9. Would you expect correlations of stock returns to be higher between the United States and industrialized country stocks, or between the United States stocks and less-developed country (LDC) stocks? Why? What implications would this finding have for constructing an optimal international portfolio?

10. In some years, the stock returns of less developed countries such as Mexico have been very high.
    a. Does this necessarily imply that U.S. investors would have earned superior returns by investing in Mexican stocks?
    b. Does it mean that Mexican investors investing in Mexican stocks will have increased their purchasing power more than U.S. investors investing in U.S. stocks?

11. What are some disadvantages of using ADRs as a means of achieving international diversification?

12. Studies by Jacquillat and Solnik and by Madura assessed the sensitivity of returns on MNCs to stock index returns. Summarize the results, and offer implications for investors that invest in MNCs as a means of international diversification.

13. Assume that a particular mutual fund consists of over 100 stocks, representing companies based in Great Britain. Is this fund likely to be more or less risky than a portfolio of 10 U.S. stocks for U.S. investors?

14. An international mutual fund (IMF) offered to U.S. investors contained stocks of firms from 10 different European countries. Is the exchange rate risk of this IMF to U.S. investors substantially less than an IMF concentrated on stocks in a single European country (from a U.S. perspective)? Explain.

15. A U.S. investor purchases a French stock for FF200 and expects the stock to be worth FF280 at the end of one year. What would be the return if the investor's expectations were correct and a one-year-forward sale of francs was negotiated as of the day of the stock investment at a forward discount of 3%?

16. Review the components that determine the volatility of unhedged foreign stock returns and hedged foreign stock returns. Why would you normally expect unhedged foreign stock returns to be more volatile? Under what conditions would unhedged stock returns possibly be less volatile?

References

Adler, M., and D. Simon. "Exchange Risk Surprises in International Portfolios." *Journal of Portfolio Management* (Winter 1986): 44–53.

Agmon, T. "The Relations among Equity Markets: A Study of Share Price Co-Movements in the United States, United Kingdom, Germany, and Japan." *Journal of Finance* (September 1972): 839–55.

Agmon, T., and D. Lessard. "Investor Recognition of International Diversification." *Journal of Finance* (September 1977): 1049–55.

Bertoneche, M. "An Empirical Analysis of the Interrelationship among Equity Markets under Changing Exchange Rate Systems." *Journal of Banking and Finance* (December 1979): 397–405.

Bicksler, J. "Gains from Portfolio Diversification into Less Developed Countries' Securities: A Comment." *Journal of International Business Studies* (Spring/Summer 1978): 113–15.

Biger, N. "Exchange Risk Implications of International Portfolio Diversification." *Journal of International Business Studies* (Fall 1979): 64–74.

Brewer, J. "Investor Benefits from Corporate International Diversification." *Journal of Financial and Quantitative Analysis* (March 1982): 113–25.

Errunza, V. "Gains from Portfolio Diversification into Less Developed Countries' Securities." *Journal of International Business Studies* (Fall/Winter 1977): 83–99.

Essayyad, M., and H. Wu. "The Performance of U.S. International Mutual Funds." *Quarterly Journal of Business and Economics* (Autumn 1988): 32–46.

Eun, C., and B. Resnick. "Exchange Rate Uncertainty, Forward Contracts, and International Portfolio Selection." *Journal of Finance* (March 1988): 197–215.

Finnerty, J., and T. Schneeweis. "The Comovement of International Asset Returns." *Journal of International Business Studies* (Winter 1979): 66–78.

Grubel, H. "Internationally Diversified Portfolios: Welfare Gains and Capital Flows." *American Economic Review* (December 1968): 1299–1314.

Grubel, H., and K. Fadner. "The Interdependence of International Equity Markets." *Journal of Finance* (March 1971): 89–94.

Hilliard, J. "The Relationship between Equity Indices on World Exchanges." *Journal of Finance* (March 1979): 103–114.

Hughes, J., D. Logue, and R. Sweeney. "Corporate International Diversification and Market-Assigned Measures of Risk and Diversification." *Journal of Financial and Quantitative Analysis* (November 1975): 627–37.

Jacquillat, B., and B. Solnik. "Multinationals are Poor Tools for Diversification." *Journal of Portfolio Management* (Winter 1978): 8–12.

Jorion, P. "International Portfolio Diversification with Estimation Risk." *Journal of Business* (July 1985): 259–78.

Joy, M., D. Panton, F. Reilly, and S. Martin. "Comovements of Major International Equity Markets." *Financial Review* (1976): 1–20.

Levy, H., and Z. Lerman. "The Benefits of International Diversification in Bonds." *Financial Analysts Journal* (September/October 1988): 56–64.

Levy, H., and M. Sarnat. "Exchange Rate Risk and the Optimal Diversification of Foreign Currency Holdings." *Journal of Money, Credit, and Banking* (November 1978): 453–63.

———. "International Diversification of Investment Portfolios." *American Economic Review* (September 1970): 668–75.

Madura, J. "International Portfolio Construction." *Journal of Business Research* (Spring 1985): 87–95.

———. "Influence of Foreign Markets on Multinational Stocks: Implications for Investors." *International Review of Economics and Business* (Oct. 1989): 1009–18.

Madura, J., and W. Reiff. "A Hedge Strategy for International Potfolios." *Journal of Portfolio Management* (Fall 1985): 70–74.

Maldonado, R., and A. Saunders. "International Portfolio Diversification and the Inter-Temporal Stability of International Stock Market Relationships, 1957–78." *Financial Management* (Autumn 1981): 54–63.

McDonald, J. "French Mutual Fund Performance: Evaluation of Internationally Diversified Portfolios." *Journal of Finance* (December 1973): 1161–80.

Michel, A., and I. Shaked. "Multinational Corporations vs. Domestic Corporations: Financial Performance and Characteristics." *Journal of International Business Studies* (Fall 1986): 89–100.

Mikhail, A., and H. Shawky. "Investment Performance of U.S.-based Multinational Corporations." *Journal of International Business Studies* (Spring/Summer 1979): 53–66.

Officer, D., and R. Hoffmeister. "ADRs: A Substitute for the Real Thing?" *Journal of Portfolio Management* (Winter 1987): 61–65.

Perold, A., and E. Schulman. "The Free Lunch in Currency Hedging: Implications for Investment Policy and Performance Standards." *Financial Analysts Journal* (May/June 1988): 45–50.

Rao, R., and R. Aggarwal. "Performance of U.S.-based International Mutual Funds." *Akron Business and Economic Review* (Winter 1987): 98–106.

Rugman, A. "Risk Reduction by International Diversification." *Journal of International Business Studies* (Fall/Winter 1976): 75–80.

Saudagaran, S. "An Empirical Study of Selected Factors Influencing the Decision to List on Foreign Stock Exchanges." *Journal of International Business Studies* (Spring 1988): 101–127.

Senchak, A. Jr., and W. Beedles. "Is Indirect International Diversification Desirable?" *Journal of Portfolio Management* (Winter 1980): 49–57.

Shaked, I. "International Equity Markets and the Investment Horizon." *Journal of Portfolio Management* (Winter 1985): 80–84.

———. "Are Multinational Corporations Safer?" *Journal of International Business Studies* (Spring 1986): 83–106.

Solnik, B. II. "Why Not Diversify Internationally Rather Than Domestically?" *Financial Analysts Journal* (July/August 1974): 48–54.

Solnik, B., and B. Noetzlin. "Optimal International Asset Location." *Journal of Portfolio Management* (Fall 1982): 11–21.

Thomas, L. III. "Currency Risks in International Equity Portfolios." *Financial Analysts Journal* (March/April 1988): 68–70.

Tucker, A. "International Investing: Are ADRs an Alternative?" *AAII Journal* (November 1987): 10–12.

Watson, J. "The Stationarity of Inter-country Correlation Coefficients: A Note." *Journal of Business, Finance, and Accounting* (Spring 1980): 297–303.

INTERNATIONAL STOCK VALUATION

The potential benefits from international diversification demonstrated in Chapter 9 motivate portfolio managers to continually search for undervalued foreign stocks. For this reason, portfolio managers apply valuation techniques to the stocks of foreign companies.

In this chapter we describe techniques that can be used to value foreign stocks. We then assess the degree of integration between stock markets, to offer inferences about international stock valuation. Next, we suggest how international stock valuation techniques could be applied by firms considering foreign acquisitions. Finally, we describe differences in stock market efficiency across countries.

INTERNATIONAL STOCK VALUATION TECHNIQUES

A variety of stock valuation procedures are used by analysts to search for undervalued or overvalued stocks. Valuation leads to buy/sell decisions by portfolio managers and recommendations for investors. A simplified valuation framework follows, to emphasize additional considerations when assessing foreign stocks.

Dividend Discount Model

One common method used for valuing stocks is to determine the present value of future expected dividends. The dividend-discount model given in eq. 10.1 is used for such a purpose:

10.1
$$p = \frac{D_1}{(1 + k)} + \frac{D_2}{(1 + k)^2} + \cdots + \frac{D_n}{(1 + k)^n}$$

where D_1 is the dividend payment at the end of period 1, k is the required rate of return, and n is the planned liquidation date. If the growth rate of dividends (called g) is known, eq. 10.1 can be simplified to

10.2
$$p = \frac{D_1}{(k - g)}.$$

When valuing a foreign stock, the cash flow to the investor depends on future exchange rates, as shown in eq. 10.3:

10.3
$$p = \frac{D_1(ER_1)}{(1 + k)} + \frac{D_2(ER_2)}{(1 + k)^2} + \cdots + \frac{D_n(ER_n)}{(1 + k)^n},$$

where ER represents the anticipated exchange rate in the period of concern. Thus, even if investors from different countries had similar expectations about a foreign stock's dividend stream, they may value the stock differently because of disparate exchange rate effects on their respective cash flows. A foreign stock is especially attractive to investors whose home currency is expected to weaken against the currency denominating the stock.

Stock valuation enables investors to compare values in order to identify preferred investments for their portfolios. Yet, valuation comparisons of stocks among countries must account for intercountry differences in financial characteristics. For example, the dividend streams of stocks in countries where government support is common have less downside risk. Thus, firms of two different countries could have identical firm-specific risk characteristics, but a firm may be perceived by investors as less risky if its government is more likely to back it. The investor's required rate of return on the firm whose dividend stream exhibits less downside risk would be lower, causing the value of that stock to be higher.

Capital Asset Pricing Model (CAPM)

Barriers to international investment can result from government-imposed policies (such as capital flow controls and taxation), transaction costs, and information costs. Consequently, investors may make different portfolio choices than they would if these barriers did not exist. Because of barriers, the various investment markets of different countries are thought to be segmented. If there were sufficient barriers to prevent all international investment, all securities markets would be completely segmented. Therefore, security returns (R_j) could be modeled using a national index as a proxy for the market, as described by the traditional form of the capital asset pricing model:

10.4
$$R_j = R_f + \beta_j(r_m - R_f),$$

where R_j is the required return on asset j, R_f is the risk-free rate, r_m is the market return, and β_j = beta of stock j:

$$\beta_j = COV(R_j, r_m)/VAR(r_m).$$

According to this model, the required return on a firm's stock is based on its perceived degree of systematic risk, which is estimated by the beta. The CAPM offers a method of determining what the return of an asset should be, based on the beta and market return. For example, if the risk-free rate is 9%, the market return is 14%, and a firm's beta is 1.2, the return on the stock is 15 percent:

10.5
$$\begin{aligned} R_j &= R_f + \beta_j(r_m - R_f) \\ &= 9\% + 1.2\,(14\% - 9\%) \\ &= 15\%. \end{aligned}$$

If international stock markets are segmented, any stock's required returns can be modeled as a function of its national risk-free interest rate and national stock market return.

Use of the CAPM to Explain Market Return Differentials

A segmented market's version of the capital asset pricing model could explain why expected stock returns to investors in some countries would be higher than in others. Risk-averse investors should be willing to invest in stocks only if they expect to receive a premium beyond the risk-free rate that compensates them for the risk incurred. In countries where the risk-free rate is very high, stock must be priced to offer even higher returns to the local residents. Investors would not purchase stocks that offer an expected annual return of 10% when the annualized interest rate on a risk-free security is 60%. Such high risk-free rates are prevalent in some less-developed countries, where high inflation discourages saving and encourages borrowing. The equilibrium nominal interest rate must be sufficiently high to compensate for the anticipated inflation and therefore retain purchasing power.

Even if stock markets are accessible to foreign investors, the high expected stock returns in some less developed countries (LDCs) do not necessarily offer excessive returns to investors outside those countries. For example, consider a U.S. investor who expects the price of a Mexican stock to rise by 60% over the next year. Assume that expected inflation in the United States is 5%, and expected inflation in Mexico is 55%. If the exchange rate of the Mexican peso was influenced solely by purchasing power parity (PPP) conditions, the peso's exchange rate would be expected to depreciate by 32.26%:

10.6
$$\begin{aligned} \frac{\%\Delta}{\text{in Peso}} &= \frac{(1 + 0.05)}{(1 + 0.55)} - 1 \\ &= -32.26\%. \end{aligned}$$

Thus, the expected exchange rate-adjusted return of the Mexican stock to the U.S. investor is

10.7
$$\begin{aligned} R_j &= (1 + 0.60)[1 + (-0.3226)] - 1 \\ &= 8.38\%. \end{aligned}$$

In reality, exchange rate movements are responsive to other factors in addition to inflation rate differentials. Yet, other factors may not necessarily dampen the influence of inflation differentials and could even cause more pronounced depreciation of a highly inflated country's currency.

The U.S. investor could possibly insulate against the peso's exchange rate movement by selling pesos forward for a future date that corresponds to the planned liquidation of the stock. Yet, interest rate parity forces the forward rate of the peso to exhibit a large discount, because of the relatively high Mexican interest rate. Consequently, the U.S. purchase of Mexican stock with a simultaneous hedge does not necessarily achieve higher returns than are possible in the U.S. stock market.

International Pricing Models

If securities markets are not completely segmented, the returns of any security may be affected not only by the national market but also by the world market. A world market beta would represent an additional degree of nondiversifiable risk of the security as related to world market returns.

In the extreme case where markets were fully integrated, investors would be expected to earn the same risk-adjusted return on stocks from different national markets. The returns of any securities would not be uniquely affected by national market-specific variables. All stocks would be systematically affected by world market movements. If stocks were not uniquely sensitive to their respective national market conditions, then correlations of returns on stocks across countries should be just as high as on stocks within countries. In that case, international diversification would not be expected to outperform domestic diversification.

Several researchers have attempted to determine whether an international capital asset pricing model (ICAPM) may be more appropriate for modeling security returns. In a comprehensive study, Cho, Eun, and Senbet (1986) used international arbitrage pricing theory (IAPT) to test the viability of the ICAPM. Arbitrage pricing theory uses relative pricing on any set of assets that adhere to a specific return-generating process. It can be tested by determining whether subsets of the universe of assets are driven by the same factors. The authors used a sample of 349 stocks spanning 11 different countries to derive monthly returns from January 1973 through December 1983. They used factor analysis to estimate the international common factors. Fifty-five pairs of country groups were created, to determine whether the number of influential factors for one country's stocks was similar for another country's stocks. The authors found that the number of factors tends to vary among countries. For example, the U.S. group generally had more factors than the other groups. There appear to be about three or four worldwide common factors. The United States and Singapore were most highly integrated with other countries, and Australia and Canada were least integrated. Overall, the authors rejected the joint hypothesis that capital markets are integrated and that the IAPT holds.

In a separate analysis, Errunza and Losq (1985) found some degree of segmentation across markets. Jorion and Schwartz (1986) tested the viability of the ICAPM by applying it to Canadian stocks. They found that the ICAPM does not model Canadian returns well, because national factors not embedded in the world index strongly influenced Canadian stock returns. This finding again confirms some degree of segmentation, because the stocks were affected by national market-specific conditions.

Partial segmentation of markets results from two types of barriers to international investment:

- Indirect barriers, such as lack of information, variations in accounting disclosure requirements and reporting procedures, and differences in language
- Legal barriers, such as government restrictions or taxes on investor ownership of foreign securities

Over time, these so-called market imperfections may be reduced, which could result in less market segmentation, more highly correlated markets, and therefore reduced benefits from international diversification.

Since markets appear to be partially segmented, it is possible that a national index and a world index are needed to model stock returns. Such a two-factor model is specified in eq. 10.6:

10.8
$$R_j = \beta_0 + \beta_1 R_{Nm} + \beta_2 R_{Wm} + u,$$

where R_{Nm} is the return on the national market, R_{Wm} is the return on the world market (defined in a manner that is statistically unrelated to R_{Nm}), β_0 is a constant, β_1 is a coefficient measuring the sensitivity of R_j to R_{Nm}, β_2 is a coefficient measuring the sensitivity of R_j to R_{Wm}, and u is an error term.

Agmon and Lessard (1977) used regression analysis to test this type of model on portfolios of U.S. multinational stocks. They found that the estimates of β_1 and β_2 were usually statistically significant, implying that both R_{Nm} and R_{Wm} can influence returns. This finding suggests that stock returns can best be described by a two-factor model rather than by the sole use of either a national index or a world index.

Agmon and Lessard hypothesized that the sensitivity of multinational corporations (MNCs) to the national or world market would depend on their degree of multinationality. MNCs with a greater degree of international business are expected to be less sensitive to the national market and more sensitive to the world market than other MNCs. The authors found that β_1 was lower and β_2 was higher for portfolios of MNCs with a higher proportion of international business. These results support their hypothesis, and suggest that the two-factor model described here may be especially appropriate for MNCs with a high degree of international business.

In a related study, Yang, Wansley, and Lane (1985) also found that the sensitivity of MNCs to the world market is an increasing function of their degree of international business. In addition, they found that returns of domestic U.S. companies are significantly related to the world market.

INTEGRATION AMONG STOCK MARKET MOVEMENTS

Price movements among international stock markets may be somewhat related since some underlying economic factors reflecting the world's general financial condition may systematically affect all markets. To the degree that one country's economy can influence others, expectations about economies across countries may be somewhat similar. Thus, stock markets across countries may respond to some of the same expectations. Integration is an important concept because of its implications about benefits from international diversification. A high degree of integration implies that stock returns of different countries would be affected by common factors. Therefore, the returns of stocks from various countries would move in tandem, allowing only modest benefits from international diversification.

Integration between Each National Market and a World Market

Thomas (1988) assessed the sensitivity of each stock market to a world market. If stock markets are related, each national market would most likely be somewhat sensitive to the world market. Thomas suggests that for portfolios of international stocks only the systematic risk of the securities is relevant, since unsystematic risk can be diversified away. He applied the following regression model to monthly data on 15 national markets:

10.9
$$ER_{Nm} = \beta_0 + \beta_1 ER_{Wm} + u,$$

where ER_{Nm} is the excess return (above the risk-free rate) of a particular national market, ER_{Wm} is the excess return (above the risk-free rate proxy) of the world market, β_0 is the intercept, β_1 is the slope coefficient estimating the sensitivity of the national market to the world market, and u is an error term.

The so-called betas estimated by β_1 were positive and significantly different from zero for all national markets. This result implies that each given national market is somewhat influenced by the world market. The average market beta estimated by applying the regression model separately to each national market was about 0.53. The adjusted R^2 ranged from 0.02 (for Spain) to 0.46 (for Canada). It was less than 0.20 for 12 of the 15 markets, suggesting that the world market could explain only a small percentage of the variation in most national equity market returns.

Timing of Integration between Markets

Research by Agmon (1972) offers some interesting implications about the degree and timing of integration between stock markets. Agmon assessed the responsiveness of non-U.S. stock market prices to the U.S. stock market. Regression analysis was applied as follows:

10.10
$$\begin{aligned}
\ln R_{j,t} = \beta_0 &+ \beta_1 \ln R_{U.S.,t+3} + \beta_2 \ln R_{U.S.,t+2} \\
&+ \beta_3 \ln R_{U.S.,t+1} + \beta_4 \ln R_{U.S.,t} \\
&+ \beta_5 \ln R_{U.S.,t-1} + \beta_6 \ln R_{U.S.,t-2} \\
&+ \beta_7 \ln R_{U.S.,t-3} + u,
\end{aligned}$$

where $\ln$ is the natural logarithm, $R_{j,t}$ is monthly return on the jth foreign country index during period t, $R_{U.S.}$ is monthly return on the U.S. index,

Figure 10.1   Stock Market Movements around the Crash

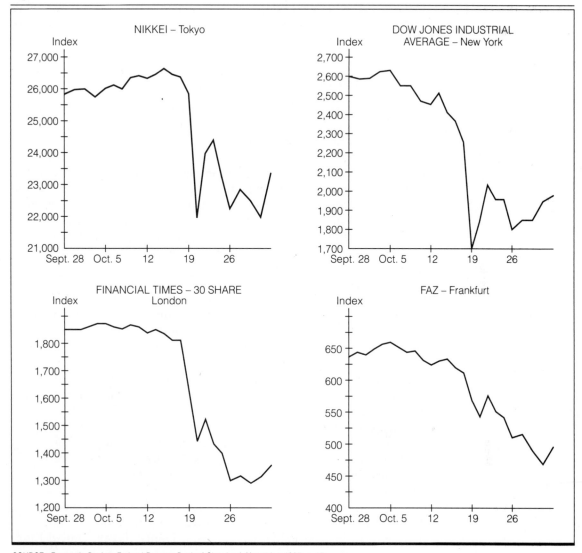

SOURCE: *Economic Review*, Federal Reserve Bank of Cleveland, November 1987, p. 17.
NOTE: Indexes are closing values for business days.

β_0 is the intercept, β_1 to β_7 are regression coefficients measuring the responsiveness of the foreign stock market return to the U.S. stock market return, and u is an error term.

The inclusion of stock returns over different periods allows for an assessment of the lead-lag relationship between the United States and foreign markets. This regression model was separately applied to three foreign markets: Japan, the United Kingdom, and Germany. The lead and lag coefficients contained within each model were not found to be significant. The variable $R_{U.S.,t}$ was positive and statistically significant for all three models, suggesting a positive relationship between the U.S.

market and each of the foreign markets analyzed. The results suggest that there is some integration between markets, and that the impact of one market on another is contemporaneous.

Stock Market Integration during the Crash

We can obtain further evidence on the integration among stock markets by assessing market movements during the stock market crash in October 1987. Figure 10.1 shows the stock market movements for four major countries during the crash. Though the magnitude of the decline was not exactly the same, all four markets were adversely affected. When institutional investors anticipated a general decline in stocks, they sold some stocks from all markets, rather than just the U.S. market. In addition, the concern about the U.S. economy apparently caused concern about the foreign economies that are influenced by the U.S. economy, causing investors in various countries to react to unfavorable expectations about the U.S. economy.

Many stock markets experienced larger declines in prices than did the United States. For example, during the month of October 1987, the U.S. market index declined by about 21%, the German market index declined by about 23%, and the United Kingdom index declined by 26%. The stock market indices of Australia and Hong Kong decreased by more than 50% over this same month.

Some critics have suggested that the institutional forces in the United States (such as computer-assisted trading, specialists, and concurrent trading in stock-index futures), along with a strong U.S. influence on the world, were reasons for a worldwide crash. Yet, a study by Roll (1988) gives no evidence that the United States was the sole culprit. Roll shows that during October 1987, country stock-indices became more highly correlated than normal, which was most likely caused by some underlying factor that could disrupt all markets. Even if computerized trading did not precipitate the crash, it could have caused a more pronounced decline. Roll compared the markets in which computerized trading was prevalent during the 1987 crash (Canada, France, Japan, United Kingdom, United States) to other markets. In local-currency terms, the five markets with computerized trading had an average decline of about 21% over October 1987, versus a 28% average decline for the other markets. This comparison suggests that computerized trading may even have reduced market volatility. Asian markets such as Hong Kong, Malaysia, and Singapore experienced substantial market declines on Black Monday (19 October 1987) several hours *before* the U.S. market even opened. In fact, other markets throughout Europe also experienced declines before the United States did. It appears that the non-U.S. markets could have caused paranoia in the U.S. market rather than the other way around. Thus, institutional factors such as computerized trading in the United States did not precipitate the worldwide crash.

Roll also assessed the possible impact of liquidity on declines across markets in October 1987. He used market capitalization as a proxy for liquidity, since larger markets are generally perceived as more liquid.

Day Begins in United States —U.S. Market's Impact on:	Estimated Slope Coefficient
Japan volatility	0.74*
United Kingdom volatility	0.88*
Germany volatility	0.81*
Day Begins in Japan —Japan Market's Impact on:	
United Kingdom volatility	0.88*
United States volatility	0.82*
Germany volatility	0.85*
Day Begins in United Kingdom —U.K. Market's Impact on:	
Japan volatility	0.86*
United States volatility	0.90*
Germany volatility	0.79*

Exhibit 10.1

Transmission of International Stock Market Volatility

SOURCE: Results are drawn from *FRBNY Quarterly Review*, Summer 1988, p. 21.

* Significant at the 0.05 level.

Roll found no statistical relationship between market capitalization and the magnitude of decline across markets. Therefore, liquidity did not influence market performance during the crash.

Integration and Stock Market Volatility Levels

The impact of volatility in one stock market on another has been assessed by Bennett and Kelleher (1988), using the following regression model:

10.11
$$ln\ S_M = a_0 + a_1\ ln\ S_{MX} + u,$$

where ln is the natural logarithm, S_{MX} is the standard deviation of daily U.S. market returns for a 30-day period, S_M is the standard deviation of daily non-U.S. market returns, a_0 is a constant, a_1 is a slope coefficient, and u is an error term.

The analysis was applied separately to test the impact on stock markets in Japan, the United Kingdom, and Germany, using nonoverlapping 30-day periods extending from January 1980 to September 1987. Then the analysis was revised to determine the impact of Japanese stock market volatility on the volatility in the other markets, and finally to determine the impact of British market volatility. Results are disclosed in Exhibit 10.1. If there is a positive relationship between a given market's volatility and volatility in the other markets, the slope coefficient should be positive and significant. Exhibit 10.1 shows a positive relationship between U.S. market volatility and non-U.S. markets. Furthermore, the non-U.S. market volatility appears to be influential as well. The results suggest that market volatility is commonly transmitted across countries.

INTERTEMPORAL ASSESSMENT OF STOCK MARKET INTEGRATION

Since some stock market risk characteristics have been changing over time, it is worthwhile to assess the direction and magnitudes of those changes so that implications about the degree of risk reduction from international diversification can be drawn.

Bennett and Kelleher (1988) assessed the sensitivity of daily stock returns in non-U.S. markets to stock returns in U.S. markets for two separate subperiods: (1) January 1972 to December 1979, and (2) January 1980 to September 1987. They found that the sensitivity of non-U.S. markets has increased in the more recent subperiod, suggesting greater integration among markets.

The intertemporal stability of correlation coefficients may be affected by the investment horizon of concern. Shaked (1985) found that correlations among market returns are intertemporally unstable when using a short-term investment horizon. However, the correlation structure was more stable for longer-term investment horizons. Thus, portfolio managers with a long-term investment perspective may be able to effectively use past correlation data to compose international portfolios with low risk.

A study by Madura and McDaniel (forthcoming) assesses stock market correlations before and after the October 1987 crash (using weekly data). The authors found that correlations after the crash were generally higher than before the crash. This result implies that the worldwide crash could have caused investors to more closely monitor other markets when assessing their home markets. If market volatility did not change, the higher correlations would have implied reduced benefits from international diversification. However, because market volatilities increased after the crash, the potential to reduce risk is greater. A naive (equally weighted) international portfolio was almost as effective in reducing risk (relative to a single market) after the crash as before the crash.

Since correlations can be intertemporally unstable, there is some question as to how international portfolio managers should forecast correlations as they construct their portfolios. Eun and Resnick (1984) assessed 12 different methods for forecasting correlations between securities considered for an international portfolio. They found that the best method is the use of a national historical mean correlation to serve as a forecast for all securities of that particular country. This method slightly outperformed the use of individual historical security correlations as forecasts for the future. These two methods were superior to the other 10 methods considered. This study suggests that although correlations are not perfectly stable over time, historical correlations appear to serve as reasonable forecasts of the future.

IMPLICATIONS OF PARTIALLY SEGMENTED MARKETS FOR PORTFOLIO MANAGEMENT

Because markets are at least somewhat segmented, international portfolio managers should consider the unique influence of each national market. That is, a portfolio manager may first develop general forecasts for each national market, and use this information to determine how funds should be allocated across countries. The assessment of stocks within each national market that deserve to be considered may be dependent on the forecast for the corresponding market. Those stocks that are highly responsive to national market conditions may be considered only if the outlook for their respective national markets is favorable, and less responsive stocks may be preferred in national markets with less favorable outlooks. Some foreign stocks may be included in the portfolio simply to benefit from the expectation of favorable currency movements against the portfolio manager's home currency. Although an international asset pricing model has not replaced the traditional CAPM, investors are more closely monitoring the potential sensitivity of stock returns to foreign markets.

INTERNATIONAL ACQUISITIONS

In this chapter, we have described international investing from the perspective of a portfolio manager. However, international stock valuation is sometimes performed for acquisitions rather than portfolio management. The valuation must then be revised because the future performance of the target firm's stock may differ if acquired, since operations and management organization would most likely be restructured.

Some of the concepts introduced earlier also apply here. Foreign acquisitions expose the acquirer to two general forms of exchange rate risk: (1) the risk that the foreign currency denominating the target's shares appreciates before the acquisition date, and (2) the risk that the foreign currency denominating future earnings of the target depreciate against the acquiring firm's home currency. The first form of risk can be hedged by forward contracts to lock in the exchange rate as of the acquisition date. However, this strategy assumes that the deal is guaranteed. If a firm requested forward contracts and its acquisition attempt failed, it would be exposed to exchange rate risk because of its forward contract commitment. As discussed in Chapter 15, the acquiring firm may instead employ currency options to control this exchange rate risk.

The second form of exchange risk results after the acquisition and is common to many MNCs. The financing decision of the acquisition may influence the acquiring firm's degree of exposure. If the acquisition is financed with debt denominated in the acquiring firm's currency, exchange rate risk is normally substantial. The acquisition generates cash inflows in the foreign currency, which differs from the currency needed to cover debt payments that resulted from the financing. Alternatively, if the acquisition is partially financed with debt denominated in the target's home currency, subsequent cash inflows can be used to cover debt payments, and exchange rate risk could be reduced.

All countries have one or more agencies that monitor mergers and acquisitions. The acquisition activity in any given country is influenced somewhat by the regulations enforced by agencies. For example, in France, the Treasury can reject any deal if the acquirer is based outside the European Economic Community (ECC). It can also reject a deal if the target is in some closely monitored industries, such as defense or health care. The Monopolies Commission of France also reviews acquisitions to prevent any combined firms from controlling more than 25% of an industry or from severely reducing competition.

Acquisitions in Japan are reviewed by the Fair Trade Commission, acquisitions in Germany are examined by the Antitrust Authority, and acquisitions in the United Kingdom are reviewed by several regulatory agencies. Acquisitions in the United States are also reviewed by several agencies, including the Securities and Exchange Commission (SEC), which regulates the conduct of acquisitions, and the Justice Department and Federal Trade Commission, which analyze the potential impact on competition.

Japan is a prime example of a country with barriers to foreign acquisitions. Cultural differences cause the Japanese market to be less attractive than the more liberal U.S. market. The acquisition process is much slower in Japan, and hostile bids are not welcomed. Yet, some foreign acquisitions of Japanese firms have been successful. Eastman Kodak, Corning Glass Works, and Motorola are among the U.S. companies that have acquired Japanese firms.

More U.S. companies are evaluating Japanese firms as potential targets. The Japanese government has reduced most restrictions on foreign investment and is no longer likely to prevent a foreign takeover as long as the Japanese target approves. The declining reluctance to foreign takeovers in Japan is partially because some Japanese firms may feel the need to merge in order to compete.

Doukas and Travlos (1988) recently assessed U.S. acquisitions of non-U.S. firms. They found that on an aggregate basis, there is no significant market reaction to news of these acquisitions. However, when disaggregating the acquiring firms according to specific characteristics, the results varied by group. For U.S. MNCs acquiring firms in countries where they were previously not operating, there was a significant positive market reaction to the news. For U.S. MNCs acquiring firms in countries where they were previously operating, there was no significant market reaction. Doukas and Travlos also found that the foreign acquisition was perceived more favorably by the market when (1) it reflected business diversification by the acquiring firm, and (2) the economy of the acquired firm's country is substantially less developed than the U.S. economy.

INTERNATIONAL STOCK MARKET EFFICIENCY

Numerous researchers have studied stock market efficiency in the United States. Research has supported the hypothesis that stock markets are weak-form efficient, implying that stock prices fully reflect all publicly available information. However, results differ when efficiency tests are applied to non-U.S. markets. For example, Haugen, Ortiz, and Arjona (1985) assessed the reaction of stock prices in Mexico to quarterly earnings per share (EPS) reports. They found a market reaction to such reports, with a significant lag. This finding suggests that excess returns can be earned by reacting to EPS reports of Mexican companies before the Mexican stock market's reaction.

Rubio (1988) assessed the Spanish stock market and found that small market capitalization stocks earned 0.58% per month more than what is suggested by the CAPM, whereas larger market capitalization stocks earned less than suggested by the CAPM. The difference in excess returns between groups of the smallest and largest stocks averaged about 6.9% per year. In the month of January alone the difference in groups was 3.2%, which represents 47% of the average excess returns per year. The size effect detected by Rubio could not be explained by a liquidity premium nor by trading distortions.

In a recent study, Kamarotou and O'Hanlon (1989) tested the informational efficiency of the U.S., U.K., Canadian, and Japanese stock markets. Informational efficiency implies that new information is reflected immediately in the stock market. The authors' analysis supports informational efficiency for the U.S., Canadian, and Japanese stock markets, but rejects informational efficiency for the U.K. market.

Rosenthal (1983) assessed the efficiency of foreign stocks traded in the United States (American depository receipts). The possibility of arbitrage should cause the share price of ADRs to be similar to the share price of the underlying stock, after accounting for the exchange rate. However, there is little simultaneous trading between the foreign stock markets and the ADR market. The ADRs are traded after the European markets close and before the Japanese markets open. In addition, there are some market imperfections that could create share price discrepancies between the markets (such as tax credits allowed for local investors but not for foreign investors). Rosenthal examined 54 ADRs and detected some degree of serial correlation, which suggests that investors may be able to capitalize on the time-series tendencies. However, he also determined that significant excess abnormal returns would most likely not be achievable when attempting to capitalize on these tendencies. Therefore, he concluded that there is some support for a weak-form efficient ADR market.

SUMMARY

International stock diversification has been advocated for three decades because of the low correlations between stock returns of different countries. However, as stock markets become more integrated, the correlations between stock returns are likely to increase. Consequently, benefits from international diversification will be reduced. Research has shown that some significant international stock market barriers still exist, causing some degree of market segmentation. One form of evidence of segmentation is the relatively strong sensitivity of stocks to their local market index, and relatively weak or no sensitivity of stocks to other foreign indices or a world index.

Although stocks are most responsive to their respective local market conditions, there is some evidence of integration between stock market indices. The markets appeared to be especially integrated during the 1987 crash. This finding may suggest that though international diversification can reduce portfolio risk, the portfolio is still susceptible to much downside risk in the event of a crash. Because the crash of 1987 was transmitted across all stock markets, international portfolios were just as susceptible to it as domestic portfolios.

Non-U.S. stock markets are not yet as developed as the U.S. stock market. Consequently, there may be opportunities to capitalize on market inefficiencies. Most studies tend to support market efficiency in the United States, but some research has detected inefficiencies in non-U.S. markets. The inefficiencies will very likely dissipate as more institutional investors attempt to trade in these markets.

Questions and Problems

1. A U.S. investment firm has a U.S. and a British subsidiary that provide brokerage services. Both subsidiaries generally use the same forecasts provided by the centralized research department. Yet, the U.S. firm subsidiary is recommending BUY for several U.S. stocks in which the British firm is recommending SELL. Explain how both subsidiaries could use the same information but have different recommendations (assume transaction costs are negligible).

2. Explain how the downside risk of two stocks with very similar characteristics except country of origin may vary distinctly (assume exchange rate risk is negligible).

3. Errunza and Losq (1985) and Jorion and Schwartz (1986) have tested the international CAPM. Summarize their results and offer implications.

4. In a 1977 study, Agmon and Lessard assessed the sensitivity of MNC returns to a national market index and a world market index. Summarize how the sensitivity to each index was related to the MNC's degree of international business. What are the implications for the viability of a two-factor pricing model?

5. If stock markets are becoming increasingly integrated over time, what are the implications for stock correlations and benefits from international stock diversification?

6. Thomas (1988) used regression analysis to assess the sensitivity of individual market returns to the returns of a world index. What were the results and implications of this study?

7. Assume that you wish to test whether daily U.S. market returns are significantly affected by returns on a British market during the same day and the previous day. Specify the regression model to achieve this objective.

8. Some critics say program trading caused the crash of October 1987. Describe Roll's (1988) response to the criticism.

9. Some critics say program trading caused the stock price decline during October 1987 to be more pronounced. Describe Roll's (1988) response to this criticism.

10. Describe Roll's assessment of whether less liquid stock markets experienced larger declines during the 1987 crash.

11. Bennett and Kelleher (1988) used regression analysis to determine whether the stock volatility in one stock market can affect the volatility in other markets. Summarize the results and implications of this study.

12. What is a limitation of using historical correlations of international stocks to construct an international stock portfolio?

References

Aderhold, R., C. Cumming, and A. Harwood. "International Linkages among Equities Markets and the October 1987 Market Break." *FRBNY Quarterly Review* (Summer 1988): 34–46.

Agmon, T. "The Relations among Equity Markets: A Study of Share Price Co-Movements in the United States, United Kingdom, Germany, and Japan." *Journal of Finance* (September 1972): 839–55.

Agmon, T., and D. Lessard. "Investor Recognition of Corporate International Diversification." *Journal of Finance* (September 1977): 1049–55.

Bennett, P., and J. Kelleher. "The International Transmission of Stock Price Disruption in October 1987." *FRBNY Quarterly Review* (Summer 1988): 17–33.

Cho, C., C. Eun, and L. Senbet. "International Arbitrage Pricing Theory: An Empirical Investigation." *Journal of Finance* (June 1986): 313–29.

Doukas, J., and N. Travlos. "The Effect of Corporate Multinationalism on Shareholder's Wealth: Evidence from International Acquisitions." *Journal of Finance* (December 1988): 1161–75.

Elliot, J. "The Expected Return to Equity and International Asset Prices." *Journal of Financial and Quantitative Analysis* (December 1978): 987–1002.

Errunza, V., and E. Losq. "International Asset Pricing under Mild Segmentation: Theory and Test." *Journal of Finance* (March 1985): 105–124.

Essayyad, M., and H. Wu. "The Performance of U.S. International Mutual Funds." *Quarterly Journal of Business and Economics* (Autumn 1988): 32–46.

Eun, C., and S. Janakiramanan. "A Model of International Asset Pricing with a Constraint on the Foreign Equity Ownership." *Journal of Finance* (September 1986): 897–914.

Eun, C., and B. Resnick. "Estimating the Correlation Structure of International Share Prices." *Journal of Finance* (December 1984): 1311–24.

Grauer, R., and N. Hakansson. "Gains from International Diversification: 1968–85 Returns on Portfolios of Stocks and Bonds." *Journal of Finance* (July 1987): 721–41.

Hardouvelis, G. "Evidence on Stock Market Speculative Bubbles: Japan, The United States, and Great Britain." *FRBNY Quarterly Review* (Summer 1988): 4–16.

Haugen, R., E. Ortiz, and E. Arjona. "Market Efficiency: Mexico Versus the U.S." *Journal of Portfolio Management* (Fall 1985): 28–32.

Jorion, P. "International Portfolio Diversification with Estimation Risk." *Journal of Business* (July 1985): 259–78.

Jorion, P., and E. Schwartz. "Integration vs. Segmentation in the Canadian Stock Market." *Journal of Finance* (July 1986): 602–616.

Kamarotou, H., and J. O'Hanlon. "Informational Efficiency in the U.K., U.S., Canadian, and Japanese Equity Markets: A Note." *Journal of Business, Finance, and Accounting* (Spring 1989): 183–92.

Madura, J., and W. McDaniel. "Impact of the 1987 Crash on Gains from International Diversification." *Journal of International Finance.* Forthcoming.

Roll, R. "The International Crash of October 1987." *Financial Analysts Journal* (October 1988): 19–35.

Rosenthal, L. "An Empirical Test of the Efficiency of the ADR Market." *Journal of Banking and Finance* 7 (1983): 17–29.

Rubio, G. "Further International Evidence on Asset Pricing." *Journal of Banking and Finance* (1988): 221–42.

Senchak, A. Jr., and W. Beedles. "Is Indirect International Diversification Desirable?" *Journal of Portfolio Management* (Winter 1980): 49–57.

Shaked, I. "International Equity Markets and the Investment Horizon." *Journal of Portfolio Management* (Winter 1985): 80–84.

Solnik, B. "International Arbitrage Pricing Theory." *Journal of Finance* (May 1983): 449–57.

———. "Testing International Asset Pricing: Some Pessimistic Views." *Journal of Finance* (May 1977): 503–517.

Stehle, R. "An Empirical Test of the Alternative Hypotheses of National and International Pricing of Risky Assets." *Journal of Finance* (May 1977): 493–502.

Thomas, L. III. "Currency Risks in International Equity Portfolios." *Financial Analysts Journal* (March/April 1988): 68–70.

Yang, H., J. Wansley, and W. Lane. "Stock Market Recognition of Multinationality of a Firm and International Events." *Journal of Business, Finance, and Accounting* (Summer 1985): 233–74.

11

INTERNATIONAL LOAN MARKETS

As regulations across Europe, Japan, and the United States are standardized, the markets for loans and other financial services are becoming more globalized. As a result, some financial institutions are attempting to achieve greater economies of scale on the services they offer. Even financial institutions that are not planning global expansion are experiencing increased foreign competition in their home markets. In this chapter we explain the globalization of financial services, with a focus on loans. We first provide a background on international lending, followed by a description of recent regulations pertaining to international loan markets. Then we discuss the international competition between market participants. Finally, we describe the international debt crisis, with special emphasis on how various commercial banks are reducing their exposure to the debt, and conclude with a discussion of international credit analysis.

BACKGROUND ON INTERNATIONAL LENDING

International lending evolved as commercial banks and other lending institutions attempted to capitalize on opportunities in other countries. U.S. banks were particularly interested in foreign markets, because U.S. regulations prohibited banks from spreading throughout the country.

Banks from all countries perceived international lending as a means of diversification. A portfolio of loans to borrowers across various countries would be less susceptible to a recession in the bank's home country. International lending also allowed banks to develop relationships with foreign firms, which created a demand for the banks' other services.

During the 1960s and 1970s, numerous banks established subsidiaries in the so-called Eurocurrency market in response to the lack of regulations. The absence of reserve requirements and deposit insurance fees allowed banks to improve their profit margins. In addition, the absence of interest rate ceilings on deposits allowed banks to more aggressively compete for deposits. The Eurocurrency market is currently served by large banks from several different countries. Participating banks accept deposits and offer loans in numerous currencies.

Commercial banks that offer foreign loans commonly have less information about the borrowers than what is aviarable for domestic loans, even when they have subsidiaries in the countries where the loans are offered. The amount of information disclosure required by regulators varies among countries. Even if the bank is able to obtain additional information, the industry norms on financial ratios vary significantly among countries. Thus, banks may be unsure of the proper benchmarks to use when assessing loan applicants.

Exchange Rate Risk of International Loans

Commercial banks that provide international loans in a foreign currency may become exposed to exchange rate risk. Unless they engage in currency swaps or some alternative strategy to offset the future receipts in a foreign currency, the banks are susceptible to the risk that the currency to be received may depreciate against their home currency.

Even if banks use currency swaps or other techniques to hedge loans denominated in foreign currencies, they can be exposed to exchange rate risk if the loan is not repaid on time. For example, assume New York Bank provides a 10-year loan of 20 million British pounds to Brit Company. It simultaneously executes with another financial institution a currency swap agreement in which it will exchange £20 million 10 years from now for dollars at some specified exchange rate. If Brit Company either defaults on the repayment of its principal or requests an extension of its loan, New York Bank will not receive the £20 million needed to fulfill its swap obligation. Thus, it will have to purchase pounds in the spot market which will be swapped for dollars. If the spot rate of the pound at that time exceeds the exchange rate specified in the swap contract, the bank incurs an exchange rate loss.

Many banks involved in international lending tend to require loan denomination in their local currency, so that they are not exposed to exchange rate risk. Yet, they have insulated against exchange rate risk by shifting that risk to foreign debtors. Any attempts by lending institutions to avoid exchange rate risk can increase their credit risk, because the debtor country's ability to repay loans becomes more dependent on exchange rate movements. For example, loans provided by U.S. banks to less developed countries (LDCs) were commonly denominated in dollars, thereby avoiding exchange rate risk. Yet, since the dollar had typically strengthened against many LDC currencies by over 50% per year, the repayment problems for LDCs became more pronounced.

Trends in International Lending

The term *international lending* is often immediately associated with international loans to the governments of LDCs. Yet a much more popular form of international lending in recent years has been to support international acquisitions. Commercial banks and investment banks serve not only as advisors but also as financial intermediaries by placing stocks and bonds or by providing loans. One common form of participation has been to provide direct loans for financing acquisitions, especially for leveraged buyouts (LBOs) by management or some other group of investors.

Since LBOs are financed mostly with debt, they resulted in a large demand for loanable funds. Many LBOs are supported by debt from an international syndicate of banks. In this way, each bank limits its exposure to any particular borrower.

Because the firms engaged in LBOs are in diversified industries, a problem in any given industry does not create a new lending crisis. In addition, the debt of each individual firm is relatively small, so that most borrowers would not have sufficient bargaining power to reschedule debt payments. For this reason, international bank financing of LBOs is perceived to be less risky than providing loans to LDCs.

Although lending for LBOs is distinctly different from lending to LDCs, there is one striking similarity. Both types of loans are exposed to a worldwide recession. Just as a worldwide recession in 1982–1983 was a primary reason for the international debt crisis, a worldwide recession in the 1990s could cause an LBO-debt crisis. Since the lenders are from numerous countries, the crisis would be globalized. Although any corporate loan is more likely to default during a recession, loans supporting LBOs are even more likely to default because of the high degree of financial leverage.

INTERNATIONAL REGULATIONS

The globalization of markets for loans and other financial services is motivated by the standardization of regulations around the world. Three significant regulatory events allowing for a more competitive global playing field are (1) the International Banking Act, which placed U.S. and foreign banks operating in the United States under the same set of rules; (2) the Single European Act, which placed all European banks operating in Europe under the same set of rules; and (3) the uniform capital adequacy guidelines, which forced banks of 12 industrialized nations to abide by the same minimum capital constraints. A discussion of each of these key events follows.

Uniform Regulations for Banks Operating in the United States

A key act related to international banking was the International Banking Act (IBA) of 1978, which was designed to impose similar regulations across domestic and foreign banks doing business in the United States. Before the act, foreign banks had more flexibility to cross state lines in the United States than did U.S.-based banks. The IBA required foreign banks to identify one state as their home state, so that they would be regulated in the same way as other U.S.-based banks residing in that state. Aharony, Saunders, and Swary (1985) assessed the reaction of U.S. bank stock prices during the time period surrounding this act. Large money center banks experienced abnormal returns of 1.48% during the announcement week and 2.35% in the following week. Regional banks did not experience a significant stock price reaction. This may have resulted from provisions in the IBA that would allow foreign banks to become more competitive in the United States at the retail level. Such provisions are of more concern to regional banks than wholesale-oriented money center banks, and could offset any favorable consequences of other IBA provisions on regional banks.

Uniform Regulations across Europe

One of the most significant events affecting the international banking markets is the Single European Act, to be phased in by 1992 throughout the European Economic Community (EEC) countries. Some relevant provisions of the act for the banking industry are

- Capital can flow freely throughout Europe.
- Banks can offer a wide variety of lending, leasing, and securities activities in the EEC.
- The regulations regarding competition, mergers, and taxes will be similar throughout the EEC.
- A bank established in any one of the EEC countries has the right to expand into any or all of the other EEC countries.

As a result of the act, the European banks are already consolidating to expand across countries. Efficiency in the European banking markets will increase as banks can more easily cross countries without concern about country-specific regulations that prevailed in the past.

Another key provision of the act is that banks can enter Europe and receive the same banking powers as other banks there. Similar provisions are allowed for non-U.S. banks that enter the United States.

Even some European savings institutions will be affected by more uniform regulations across European countries. Savings institutions throughout Europe are now evolving into full-service institutions, expanding into services such as insurance, brokerage, and mutual fund management. A merger among Spain's savings institutions will create Spain's biggest financial institution, with assets of about $47 billion and 1,650 branches.

Uniform Capital Adequacy Guidelines around the World

Before 1987, capital standards imposed on banks varied across countries, allowing some banks to have a comparative global advantage over others. As an example, consider a bank in the United States that is subject to a 6% capital ratio, twice that of a foreign bank. The foreign bank could achieve the same return on equity as the U.S. bank by generating a return on assets that is only one-half that of the U.S. bank. In essence, the foreign bank's equity multiplier (assets divided by equity) would be double that of the U.S. bank, which would offset the low return on assets. Given these conditions, foreign banks could accept lower profit margins while still achieving the same return on equity. This affords them a stronger competitive position. In addition, growth is more easily achieved since a relatively small amount of capital is needed to support an increase in assets.

Some analysts would counter that these advantages are somewhat offset by the investors' perception that banks with low capital ratios represent higher risk. Yet, if the governments in those countries are more likely to back banks that experience financial problems, banks with low capital may not necessarily be too risky. Therefore, some non-U.S. banks had globally competitive advantages over U.S. banks, without being subject to excessive risk. In December 1987, 12 major industrialized countries attempted to resolve the disparity by proposing uniform bank standards. In July 1988, central bank governors of the 12 countries agreed on standardized guidelines. We provide specific details of the global capital adequacy guidelines in the appendix to this chapter. Briefly, capital was classified as either tier 1 ("core") capital, or tier 2 ("supplemental") capital. Tier 1 capital must be at least 4% of risk-adjusted assets. The use of risk weightings on assets implicitly caused a higher capital ratio for riskier assets, since those assets were assigned lower weights. Off-balance-sheet items were also accounted for, so that banks could not circumvent capital requirements by focusing on services (such as letters of credit and interest rate swaps) that are not explicitly shown on a balance sheet. Even with uniform capital requirements across countries, some analysts may still contend that U.S. banks are at a competitive disadvantage because they are subject to different accounting and tax provisions. Nevertheless, the uniform capital requirements represent significant progress toward a more level global field.

INTERNATIONAL COMPETITION

As the markets for loans and other financial services become more integrated, banks from any given country are recognizing that their main competition may be foreign banks. U.S. banks have always had a competitive advantage in technology, such as devising new products and services. For example, U.S. banks are advanced in their creation of interest rate swaps and currency swaps. They also dominate the market for selling packaged loans. However, their growth is somewhat constrained by the low U.S. savings rate. U.S. banks have experienced problems because of some poor investment decisions, such as their heavy involvement in lending to less developed countries. In addition, their acquisitions of British securities firms during the period in which British financial markets were deregulated ultimately backfired. Furthermore, U.S. banks have been adversely affected by U.S. regulations, which tend to cause costly reporting procedures and some inefficiencies because of geographical and product restrictions. Reserve requirements and deposit insurance premiums imposed on U.S. banks are relatively high.

Competition in Foreign Markets

U.S. banks have reduced their international lending in recent years. The largest U.S. banks have divested some foreign operations and are focusing on specific niches in foreign countries. Chase Manhattan is creating a niche in the credit card business overseas, Chemical is focusing on mortgage-backed securities, and J.P. Morgan is heavily involved in underwriting. Citibank is concentrated in consumer banking and some other services. Many of the super-regional banks in the United States are focusing their growth within the United States.

Whereas the U.S. banks have taken a cautious stance in foreign markets, non-U.S. banks have been more aggressive in penetrating the U.S. market. Japanese banks have a significant presence in the United States. They control about 25% of the California market. One major reason for their growth is very competitive corporate loans. They also have been known to provide letters of credit for lower fees than those charged by U.S. banks. Another reason for their growth is a relatively low cost of capital, which allows them to take on more ventures that might not be feasible to U.S. banks. Furthermore, the high savings rate of the Japanese allows for substantial growth in deposits in Japan, which may then be channeled to support operations in the United States.

Competition for Investment Banking Services

In addition to loans, a variety of financial services have become globalized. Some obvious examples of global participation are in services such as foreign exchange, swaps, and investment banking services such as underwriting and brokerage. Global competition exists not only *within* each industry but also *across* the industries, because some financial institutions offer a full range of services around the world. In fact, some commercial banks were initially able to offer a complete range of services by establishing subsidiaries in countries with less regulation.

One of the most common examples of commercial banks circumventing regulations by migration to other countries is in the securities industry. In most non-U.S. countries, commercial banks can participate in securities activities such as underwriting and full-service brokerage. In the United States, securities and banking activities continue to be somewhat separated, although commercial banks have recently been allowed some underwriting and brokerage privileges in the United States. Non-U.S. commercial banks are more able to diversify across services and products because of fewer regulatory barriers. U.S. banks have attempted to diversify across products by establishing subsidiaries in foreign markets. However, this is an inconvenient approach for smaller banks that would prefer to focus on a region of the United States. In addition, the U.S. restrictions prevent U.S. commercial banks from fully capitalizing on economies of scale in securities activities.

Since 1988, the barriers between securities and traditional banking activities have diminished, allowing U.S. commercial banks to behave more like non-U.S. banks. In 1988, some money center banks in the United States filed applications requesting that specific subsidiaries be allowed to underwrite and deal in corporate debt. In January 1989, the Federal Reserve Board approved the applications contingent on specific requirements, including that the revenues from debt underwriting be limited to 5% of the banks subsidiary's total revenues. The generation of fee income from underwriting has become more desirable since the more stringent capital requirements have been imposed. Underwriting allows banks to boost their revenues without significantly altering their asset size. Therefore, entry into the underwriting business does not necessarily require an increase in the required capital. The underwriting activities by banks could also lead to closer relationships with corporate clients, and allow them to facilitate mergers and acquisitions for additional fee income.

Some critics suggest that entrance into securities activities will increase the risk of U.S. banks. This argument is based on the premise that U.S. banks do not have the necessary expertise to fully participate in securities activities. However, this argument is dampened by the evidence of numerous U.S. banks that have successfully offered securities activities in other countries.

Because U.S. bank entrance into the U.S. securities industry has been somewhat limited, there has been little empirical research on its effects on bank performance. Saunders and Smirlock (1987) measured the risk-return characteristics of money center banks in response to a regulatory ruling to allow discount brokerage services. They found no significant impact of the ruling on either bank returns or risk. Kwast (1989) assessed the historical returns on securities and other activities, and determined that diversification between these two types of activities could be beneficial. In general, momentum is increasing to remove the barriers between traditional banking and securities activities in the United States. In 1991, this momentum continued as U.S. banks complained that they were unable to compete in international banking because of excessive regulations.

INTERNATIONAL DEBT CRISIS

In the 1970s, many large commercial banks aggressively pursued lending to governments of various countries. The expected returns on these loans were high, and the risk was thought to be negligible. Furthermore, the overall default risk of each bank's portfolio of international loans was thought to be reduced by geographic diversification. Many of the loans were to LDCs.

During the late 1970s and early 1980s, many LDCs began to experience financial problems. In August 1982, the Mexican government requested that loan repayments be rescheduled. Mexico's request was followed by requests of numerous LDC governments. This chain of events marked the beginning of the international debt crisis, which continues to exist today.

On 19 August 1982, Mexico announced that it would be unable to meet its principal payments on existing debt. Bruner and Simms (1987) assessed the market reaction to this announcement by measuring abnormal stock returns surrounding the announcement date. They found an average abnormal return on the announcement day of about −1.6%, which was followed by four consecutive days of declines in stock prices. These results suggest that the market was not fully aware of the degree of Mexico's financial problems. Furthermore, Cornell, Landsman, and Shapiro (1986) and Smirlock and Kaufold (1987) found that the market reaction to news about the LDC crisis was more unfavorable for banks that were more highly exposed to LDC debt. Thus, the market used comparative exposure data when penalizing banks with outstanding loans to LDCs.

Mansur, Cochran, and Cahill (1989) assessed the market reaction to the 20 February 1987 announcement of Brazil's interest payments moratorium. They detected an unfavorable market response, implying that this announcement contained adverse information about LDC debt that was not fully embedded in share prices. Even though the market had already substantially discounted Brazilian debt, the news reflected further deterioration of the debt's perceived value. Musumeci and Sinkey (1990) also assessed the market reaction to Brazil's announcement. They also detected a negative market reaction to the announcement, and found that the bank share price response was greater for banks with a high degree of exposure.

Mansur, Cochran and Seagers (1990) assessed the market reaction to a tentative debt-rescheduling agreement between Argentina and commercial banks on 14 April 1987. They found significant abnormal returns on two different days before the announcement for banks exposed to Argentine debt. Results of the study imply that the debt rescheduling will result in reduced cash flows to the banks over time.

There are many reasons for the international debt crisis. We summarize some commonly cited reasons in the text that follows.

International Liquidity

In the 1970s, international banks had an abundant supply of loanable funds because of recycled petrodollars—more than enough to accommodate the demand for funds by industrialized countries. Lending to LDC governments was a viable alternative. Not only were potential returns high, but the transactions costs incurred by large banks lending a large amount to a particular LDC government were relatively small.

During the late 1970s, inflationary pressures increased the demand for loanable funds. In addition, more restrictive monetary policies in the United States and other industrialized countries were imposed, further reducing liquidity in the banking system. Consequently, interest rates rose to their highest levels by 1980. Since many LDC loans contained floating-rate provisions, debt payments required of LDCs had increased.

The high interest rates combined with a continued tight monetary policy contributed to the 1982 worldwide recession. The recession severely reduced demand by industrialized countries for LDC exports. By that time, the U.S. dollar had begun to strengthen and oil prices declined. The events just described can be consolidated to present a cash flow analysis of an oil-exporting LDC. Cash inflows declined due to (1)

Indicator	Change in Real GDP[b] (percent)	Change in Consumer Prices (percent)	Trade Balance ($billion)	Debt/Export Ratio (percent)[c]
1969–1978[a]	6.1%	28.5%	NA[d]	NA
1979	6.1	40.8	$-1.9	182.3%
1980	5.0	47.4	4.4	167.1
1981	0.5	53.2	-7.5	201.4
1982	-0.4	57.7	3.2	269.8
1983	-3.4	90.8	28.3	289.7
1984	2.2	116.4	43.2	272.1
1985	3.1	126.9	40.8	284.2
1986	3.5	76.2	22.9	337.9
1987	3.2	86.3	18.8	349.6

SOURCE: World Bank, World Debt Tables: 1987–1988 (1988) and Federal Reserve Bank of Cleveland.

Notes: a. Compound annual rates of change unless otherwise noted
    b. Gross domestic product
    c. Ratio of debt or debt-service payments to exports of goods and services
    d. NA = information not available

lower oil revenues to oil-exporting LDCs resulting from lower prices and (2) lower revenues generated from other exports. Debt obligations to the United States increased due to (1) high interest rates and (2) a strengthening dollar.

In a recent study, Billingsley and Lamy (1988) assessed the market reaction to news concerning possible additional aid to LDCs. On 7 March 1983 a bill was proposed to increase the U.S. quota to the International Monetary Fund (IMF) by $8.5 billion. For each of the two days preceding this proposal, stocks of U.S. banks experienced an abnormal return of about 1%. Based on a cross-sectional analysis of the abnormal returns among banks, the authors found that there was no significant reaction for banks without Latin American loan exposure. Yet, the other banks with Latin American loan exposure experienced a large favorable reaction to their stock price. This finding implies that the market anticipated that the efforts of the IMF should favorably affect bank values. Some critics may claim that the bill reflects a wealth transfer from U.S. taxpayers to banks with high LDC debt exposure, with the IMF simply serving as an intermediary. Nevertheless, the market appears to believe that IMF funding may help mitigate the LDC crisis. As the IMF provided funding, it imposed economic reforms across LDCs. Some LDCs were able to meet the reforms; others requested more time, funds, or both in order to improve their financial condition.

Economic Trends since the International Debt Crisis

Exhibit 11.1 shows the average economic indicators for 15 countries experiencing debt repayment problems. Real (inflation-adjusted) gross domestic product has grown since 1983, and the trade balance has im-

Exhibit 11.2

Shares of U.S. Banks' Exposure to Troubled LDCs by Size of Bank (Millions of Dollars; Percent of Total)

Year	Total*	% of Total	Nine Money Center Banks	% of Total	Next 14 Largest Banks	% of Total	All Other Banks	% of Total
1977	$50699.4	100	$30757.0	60.7	$ 9389.5	18.5	$10552.9	20.8
1978	54116.7	100	32585.3	60.2	10155.8	18.8	11375.6	21.0
1979	63715.7	100	39482.7	62.0	11320.3	17.8	12912.7	20.3
1980	74738.8	100	44388.0	59.4	13273.2	17.8	17077.6	22.8
1981	87707.8	100	50099.5	57.1	16565.1	18.9	21043.2	24.0
1982	92033.3	100	51925.2	56.4	18249.9	19.8	21858.2	23.8
1983	93896.8	100	53571.3	57.1	18594.1	19.8	21731.4	23.1
1984	93819.2	100	56004.5	59.7	18492.3	19.7	19322.4	20.6
1985	87257.0	100	54084.3	62.0	15496.7	17.8	17676.0	20.3
1986	81112.0	100	50884.0	62.7	14521.0	17.9	15707.0	19.4
Mean				59.7		18.7		21.6
Standard deviation				2.1		0.8		1.6

SOURCE: Country Exposure Lending Survey, Federal Reserve Board, and *Economic Review*, Federal Reserve Bank of San Francisco, Spring 1988, p. 19.

Note: *Figures may not add due to rounding.

proved. However, debt has also grown, causing an increase in the debt/ export ratio since 1983.

Bank Exposure to LDC Debt

Exhibit 11.2 shows the allocation of U.S. bank international loans by country group over time. Notice that the proportion of international loans by U.S. banks to the 15 principal LDC debtors has increased consistently over time. Yet, the absolute dollar amount of loans to these countries has declined since 1985. Lending exposure as a percent of assets (Figure 11.1) or as a percent of capital (Figure 11.2, page 212) declined since 1982. There is also evidence that banks have reduced their LDC debt exposure in 1988 and 1989.

Nine money center banks represent over 60% of the total U.S. bank exposure to troubled LDCs. Although the exposure is concentrated within a small group of banks, these banks are the largest. The failure of even a single money center bank could potentially cause a panic within the financial system.

The exposure of several money center banks to the debt of three prominent LDCs is disclosed in Exhibit 11.3 on page 212. Their exposure to Argentine debt is clearly less than their exposure to Brazilian or Mexican debt. The degree of exposure to any country's debt varies distinctly across banks.

Over the past several years, commercial banks have attempted to reduce their default risk resulting from the international debt crisis. One common method of reducing exposure was to sell existing loans. A secondary loan market facilitates the sale of loans. The values of existing loans to five LDCs as of October 1989 (and the previous year) are shown

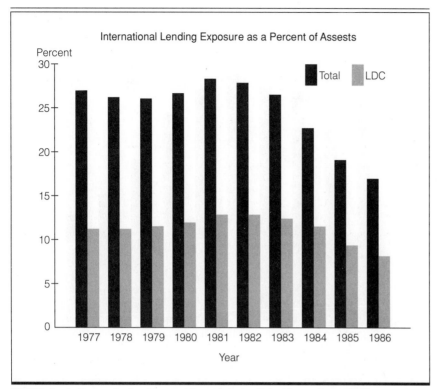

Figure 11.1

Bank Exposure to LDC Debt (as a Percent of Assets)

SOURCE: Country Exposure Lending Survey, and *Economic Review*, Federal Reserve Bank of San Francisco, Spring 1988, p. 18.

in Exhibit 11.4 on page 213. The size of the discount implies the market's confidence (or lack of confidence) that the loans will be repaid. The prices are discounted substantially for all loans. Yet, the wide divergence among discounts indicates that the market is much more confident in some LDCs resolving their financial problems than others.

An alternative method of reducing exposure to LDC loans is the so-called *debt-equity swaps*, in which a bank swaps the debt in exchange for some assets owned by the borrower. As an example, Citicorp swapped claims on Chilean debt in exchange for an equity investment in Chile's gold mining. Many swaps have been conducted through nonbank multinational corporations (MNCs). U.S.-based MNCs including General Electric and Chrysler purchased LDC loans at a discount in the secondary market, and then exchanged the debt for companies or other assets owned by the borrower.

Initially, the debt-equity swap had only limited use, because U.S. banks were not able to invest in equity of other firms. In August 1986, the Federal Reserve Board amended Regulation K to allow bank holding companies to swap LDC government debt for the equity in nationalized foreign nonfinancial firms. The debt-equity swap has been frequently used by U.S. banks since this amendment. There may be some concern that the U.S. banks are not capable of managing the nationalized firms

Figure 11.2

Bank Exposure to LDC Debt (as a
Percent of Capital)

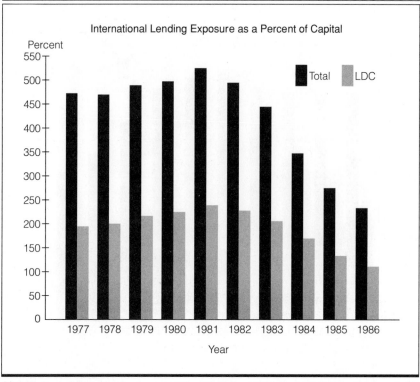

SOURCE: Country Exposure Lending Survey, and *Economic Review*, Federal Reserve Bank of San Francisco, Spring
1988, p. 20.

Exhibit 11.3

Exposure of Money Center Banks
To Selected LDC Debt[a] (Year-End
1988)

Bank Holding Company	Debt Exposure					
	Argentina		Brazil		Mexico	
	Amount (in millions)	% of Total Assets	Amount (in millions)	% of Total Assets	Amount (in millions)	% of Total Assets
Bank America	$ 672	0.71%	$2,928	3.10	$2,338	2.50%
Bankers Trust	270	0.47	901	1.55	1,328	2.30
Chase Manhattan	940	0.96	2,660	2.70	1,510	1.50
Chemical	436	0.65	1,547	2.30	1,703	2.53
Citicorp	1,300	0.91	3,951	2.76	2,288	1.60
Continental	383	1.25	426	1.39	384	1.25
J.P. Morgan	772	0.93	1,824	2.20	789	0.95
Manufacturers Hanover	1,417	2.12	2,014	3.02	1,695	2.54
Security Pacific	NR[b]	NR	623	0.80	670	0.86
Wells Fargo	NR	NR	231	0.50	80	0.20

Notes: a. Data compiled from 1988 annual reports.
       b. NR = not reported, implying that the debt is less than 1% of total assets.

	Value per Dollar of Principal	
	30 October 1989	30 October 1988
Brazil	24¢	29¢
Mexico	37	41
Argentina	16	17
Venezuela	39	41
Chile	60	62

Exhibit 11.4
Value of LDC Debt in the Secondary Market

they acquire. Yet, these firms may have more upside potential value than LDC debt.

Security Pacific is a primary example of a U.S. bank that has reduced its exposure to future loan losses. It reduced its exposure to developing countries by more than 40% in 1988, mainly by selling loans in the secondary market and executing debt-equity swaps. It has revamped its strategy to concentrate on a smaller number of countries. In this way, it can restructure its resources to provide additional trade-related services to the countries it continues to serve. In essence, it has reduced its geographical diversification in favor of product (or service) diversification.

Some banks recently reacted to their large LDC debt exposure by increasing their loan loss reserves. Because income is used to build the loan loss reserve account, an increase in reserves causes a reduction in reported earnings. In May 1987, Citicorp announced a $3 billion increase in loan loss reserves. Over the following months, several other money center and regional banks followed this strategy. These actions signal anticipation that some of the LDC loans will default, or that only a portion of the loans will ultimately be repaid.

Some studies have assessed market reaction to the loan loss reserve announcement. Musumeci and Sinkey (1988) found a favorable market reaction to banks that boosted their loan loss reserves. This reaction may suggest that the market had already fully penalized the banks for their exposure to LDC debt. The boost in loan loss reserves indicates the bank's recognition that some of the loans will not be recovered. Yet, it may signal that banks will soon write off some of the debt, which will provide cash flows in the form of tax benefits.

In September 1989, another round of increases in loan loss reserves began for some money center banks. The most publicized announcement was J. P. Morgan's increase in loan loss reserves by $2 billion, which boosted its loan loss reserve account to match its total LDC debt exposure. The total loan loss reserves at other money center banks represented only between 35% and 50% of medium- and long-term LDC debt. As a result of its strategy, J. P. Morgan was in a more flexible position, from which it could discontinue negotiations with LDCs and write off the LDC debt.

Use of the Brady Plan to Reduce LDC Debt Exposure

Over the period from 1985 to 1988 the so-called Baker Plan was endorsed as a means of mitigating the LDC debt crisis. The plan was based on voluntary actions by lenders to reduce their exposure. In December 1988, the World Bank proposed a gradual implementation of the Baker Plan, along with its commitment to provide loans to LDCs in place of bank loans and impose economic reforms on the LDCs. During 1989, the plan gained momentum as the IMF signalled its willingness to replace LDC debt maintained by banks. In what then became known as the Brady Plan, negotiations between banks and individual LDCs were encouraged in order to provide banks with the option of having their debt replaced by the World Bank and IMF by trading it in at a discount. In July 1989, banks reached an agreement with Mexico, in which they were given the following options: (1) agree to a 35% cut in the principal or interest on loans, or (2) grant new loans equal to 25% of the Mexican loans. Essentially, the tradeoff involves either recognizing losses on previous loans while reducing exposure or increasing investment in LDCs without incurring immediate losses. The agreement could improve Mexico's position because it reduces the amount Mexico owes on existing debt and also allows for additional loans from banks. In this way, Mexico may be more able to improve its debt-servicing, which would enhance the investor's perceptions of Mexican debt maintained by banks. The agreement between banks and Mexico is encouraging because it could pave the way for agreements with other countries.

A dilemma involved in resolving the crisis is that if all banks prefer to discontinue loans to LDCs by writing off all or a portion of existing loans, the LDCs may be unable to secure adequate financing to improve economic conditions. Their only chance to repay existing loans is by economic reform, which requires more loans. Yet, many banks may believe that providing additional loans amounts to throwing good money after bad. For this reason, the use of World Bank and IMF funds to assume commercial bank debt at some discounted price could help resolve the continuing crisis.

ASSESSING CREDIT RISK OF INTERNATIONAL LOANS

The international debt problems of LDCs have precipitated efforts by money center banks to effectively assess the credit risk of countries. Various techniques are available for assessing the credit risk of loans to foreign governments. One popular technique is the use of *discriminant analysis,* which is a statistical model that attempts to identify factors that can correctly discriminate between two or more groups. To illustrate, we consider two groups of countries: (1) financially sound, and (2) financially troubled. If financial and political data were available in previous years in both groups, discriminant analysis could be applied to determine which characteristics could properly differentiate between the two groups. This type of information may be useful for predicting whether a given country will be financially sound or financially troubled in the future. In some cases, discriminant analysis is much more accurate in an ex post sense than in an ex ante sense. That is, the analysis was able to detect factors that historically distinguished between groups, but it cannot always accurately predict whether a country will be financially sound in the future.

When assessing the risk of international loans, banks must measure *country risk*, which can be broadly defined as any type of risk within a country that could adversely affect the cash flows. From a lending bank's perspective, country risk reflects any factors prevailing in the country that may cause a borrower (whether a government or company) to default on its loans. The degree to which country risk can be properly assessed depends on the ability to forecast economic and political conditions that affect risk. For example, discriminant analysis may have determined that negative growth in gross national product (GNP) precedes financial problems, but if a bank cannot properly forecast GNP, it may provide loans to countries that will experience financial problems.

Proper prediction of country risk also depends on the sensitivity of a country's financial condition to specific factors. For example, countries that rely heavily on oil exports may have experienced strong financial performance when oil prices were relatively high. Yet if oil prices decline, these countries would be more susceptible to financial problems.

Much research has attempted to identify indicators that could discriminate between countries that experience debt-repayment problems versus those that do not. Frank and Cline (1971) assessed eight indicators for 26 countries over the 1960–1968 period. Of the variables assessed, three variables were found to significantly influence the debt-repayment capabilities of the countries: (1) debt service ratio, (2) amortization-to-debt ratio, and (3) imports-to-reserves ratio. These variables were later confirmed as being relevant by related research performed by Feder and Just (1977). Using these three variables, Frank and Cline were able to correctly identify 10 of 13 debt reschedulings and 118 of 132 nonreschedulings.

Sargen (1977) assessed 44 countries over the 1960–1975 period, and found that the inflation and the debt service ratio were the most important variables for signalling debt-repayment problems. A study by Cline (1984) of 58 countries over the 1967–1982 period identified the most relevant indicators to be the debt service ratio, a reserves/imports ratio, and the ratio of debt to reserves.

A review of these studies over time suggests that the significance of any variable can vary with the period studied, which reduces the ability of lending institutions to use an ex post analysis for future lending decisions. To illustrate, consider the study by Morgan (1986) that applied the models by Frank and Cline (1971) and Feder and Just (1977) to the 1975–1982 period. Frank and Cline's model had an overall accuracy of about 62%. The model exhibited an "overestimation bias," frequently predicting debt rescheduling problems that did not exist. Morgan also found that Feder and Just's model exhibited an "underestimation bias," correctly predicting only 8 of the 40 debt reschedulings. Morgan tested nine variables over the 1975–1982 period and found that total debt to exports and real economic growth were the most significant variables during this period for discriminating between countries that experienced debt-repayment problems versus those that did not.

SUMMARY

The globalization of financial services has evolved in response to the standardization of regulations across countries. The International Banking Act of 1978 imposed similar regulations among U.S. and non-U.S. banks conducting business in the United States. The provisions of the Single European Act, to be phased in through 1992, call for more uniform banking regulations across European countries. The uniform capital adequacy guidelines agreed on in 1988 force banks that compete internationally to meet the same minimum capital requirements. All these regulatory events prevent banks in any particular country from having an unfair competitive advantage.

The international debt crisis is still a major topic in international banking, since it continues to adversely affect the performance of money center banks. Over time, various strategies have been used by banks to reduce their exposure to the debt of LDCs. Some commonly used strategies include selling the debt in the secondary market, and swapping the debt for equity in firms owned by the governments of those countries.

In 1989, the Brady Plan was developed as a means of mitigating the international debt crisis. The Brady Plan prescribes an arrangement whereby banks either cut the principal and interest on existing debt, or grant additional loans. The specifics of the arrangement vary with the country of concern. The success of the plan depends on whether banks and the LDCs can agree on restructuring the terms of the previous debt arrangement.

Questions and Problems

1. Why do more standardized bank regulations across countries tend to promote the globalization of the banking industry?

2. Explain the main objective of the International Banking Act of 1978.

3. Explain the main theme of the Single European Act regarding the banking industry.

4. Why might you expect banks in Europe to more easily capitalize on economies of scale as a result of the Single European Act?

5. Explain how a bank would have competitive advantages in global markets if it were subject to looser capital requirements.

6. What are some limitations in using discriminant analysis to assess potential credit problems in foreign countries?

7. Describe how debt-equity swaps can enable commercial banks to reduce their LDC debt exposure.

8. In what way can the savings behavior in a given country influence the potential growth of banks in that country? Since markets are internationalized, couldn't banks attract any funds needed from foreign sources if necessary?

9. Boston Bank provided a seven-year loan of 60 million French francs to Pierre Company. To protect against the exchange rate risk, Boston Bank executed currency swap agreements for all interest payment dates and for repayment

of principal seven years from now. Under what circumstances could Boston Bank still be subject to exchange rate risk?

10. Many money center banks boosted loan loss reserves in the late 1980s because the debt-repayment capabilities of LDCs did not improve significantly. Why would a bank's increase in loan loss reserves possibly have a favorable effect on bank share prices?

References

Aharony, J., A. Saunders, and I. Swary. "The Effects of the International Banking Act on Domestic Bank Profitability and Risk." *Journal of Money, Credit, and Banking* (November 1985): 493–506.

Aliber, R. "International Banking: A Survey." *Journal of Money, Credit and Banking* (November 1984): 661–712.

———. "International Banking: Growth and Regulation." *Columbia Journal of World Business* (Winter 1975): 9–15.

———. "Monetary Aspects of Offshore Markets." *Columbia Journal of World Business* (Fall 1979): 8–16.

———. "The Integration of Offshore and Domestic Banking Systems." *Journal of Monetary Economies* (October 1980): 509–526.

Billingsley, R., and R. Lamy. "The Regulation of International Lending, IMF Support, the Debt Crisis, and Bank Stockholder Wealth." *Journal of Banking and Finance* 12 (1988): 255–74.

Bruner, R., and J. Simms, Jr. "The International Debt Crisis and Banking Security Returns in 1982." *Journal of Money, Credit and Banking* (February 1987): 46–55.

Chrystal, A. "International Banking Facilities." *Review*, Federal Reserve Bank of St. Louis (April 1984): 5–11.

Cline, W. *International Debt: Systemic Risk and Policy Response.* Cambridge MA. MIT Press, 1984.

Cornell, B., W. Landsman, and A. Shapiro. "The Impact on Bank Stock Prices of Regulatory Responses to the International Debt Crisis." *Studies in Banking and Finance* 3 (1986): 161–78.

Dale, B. "The Slow Road to Investment Banking." *Bankers Magazine* (May/June 1989): 26–32.

Eisenbeis, R., R. Harris, and J. Laconishok. "Benefits of Bank Diversification: The Evidence from Shareholder Returns." *Journal of Finance* (July 1984): 881–94.

Eisenbeis, R., and L. Wall. "Bank Holding Company Diversification and Risk." *Proceedings of the Conference on Bank Structure and Competition*, Federal Reserve Bank of Chicago (1984).

Feder, G., and R. Just. "A Study of Debt Servicing Capacity Applying Logit Analysis." *Journal of Development Economics* (March 1977): 23–58.

Fieleke, N. "International Lending on Trial." *New England Economic Review* (May/June 1983): 5–13.

Frank, C., and W. Cline. "Measurement of Debt Servicing Capacity: An Application of Discriminant Analysis." *Journal of International Economics* (August 1971): 327–44.

Kwast, M. "The Impact of Underwriting and Dealing on Bank Returns and Risks." *Journal of Banking and Finance* (March 1989): 101–125.

Madura, J. and W. McDaniel. "Market Reaction to Loan Loss Reserve Announcements at Money Center Banks." *Journal of Financial Services Research* (December 1989): 359–69.

Mansur, I., S. Cochran, and D. Cahill. "The Relationship between Equity Returns and the Brazilian Interest Payments Moratorium." *Journal of Applied Business Research* (Winter 1988–89): 52–58.

Mansur, I., S. Cochran, and D. Seagers. "The Relationship between the Argentinean Debt Rescheduling Announcement and Bank Equity Returns." *Financial Review* (May 1990): 321–34.

Morgan, J. "A New Look at Debt Rescheduling Models." *Journal of International Business Studies* (Summer 1986): 37–54.

Musumeci, J., and J. Sinkey, Jr. "The International Debt Crisis and Bank Security Returns Surrounding Citicorp's Loan-Loss-Reserve Decision on May 19, 1987." *Proceedings of the Conference on Bank Structure and Competition*, Federal Reserve Bank of Chicago (May 13, 1988).

Musumeci, J., and J. Sinkey Jr., "The International Debt Crisis, Investor Contagion, and Bank Security Returns in 1987: The Brazilian Experience." *Journal of Money, Credit, and Banking* (May 1990): 209–20.

Poulsen, A. "Japanesse Bank Regulation and the Activities of U.S. Offices of Japanese Banks." *Journal of Money, Credit, and Banking* (August 1986) 366–73.

Rose, P. "Diversification of the Banking Firm." *Financial Review* (May 1989): 251–80.

Sargen, N. "Economic Indicators and Country Risk Appraisal." *Economic Review*, Federal Reserve Bank of San Francisco (Fall 1977): 19–39.

Saunders, A. "Bank Safety and Soundness and the Risk of Corporate Securities Activities." In *Deregulating Wall Street*, ed. Ingo Walter. New York: John Wiley and Sons, 1985.

Saunders, A., and M. Smirlock. "Intra- and Interindustry Effects of Bank Securities Market Activities: The Case of Discount Brokerage." *Journal of Financial and Quantitative Analysis* (December 1987): 467–82.

Smirlock, M., and H. Kaufold. "Bank Foreign Lending, Mandatory Disclosure Rules, and the Reaction of Bank Stock Prices to the Mexican Debt Crisis." *Journal of Business* 60, no. 3 (1987): 347–64.

Swary, I. "Bank Acquisition of Mortgage Firms and Stockholders Wealth." *Journal of Banking and Finance* (June 1981): 201–215.

Appendix 11.A

BREAKDOWN OF TIER 1 AND TIER 2 CAPITAL

Tier 1 capital = Common shareholder's equity
+ disclosed reserves (including retained earnings)
+ perpetual noncumulative preferred stock
− goodwill

Tier 2 capital = Undisclosed reserves
+ 45% of revaluation reserves
+ general loan loss reserves (up to a maximum of 1.25% of assets)
+ hybrid debt capital instruments
+ subordinated debt (up of a maximum of 50% of Tier 2 capital)
− investments in unconsolidated subsidiaries

Part Three

DERIVATIVE SECURITY MARKETS

In Part III of this book, we provide a treatment of derivative securities related to international investment and financing. In Chapter 12 we detail the operations of the foreign exchange forward and futures markets, and in Chapter 13 we describe the pricing and applications of currency forward and futures contracts. We provide analogous information for the expanding currency options market in Chapters 14 and 15. Finally, in Chapter 16 we provide a more rigorous treatment of the marketing and pricing of currency and interest rate swaps. The markets and instruments detailed in Part III are particularly useful for reducing exchange rate risk and interest rate risk.

CURRENCY FORWARD AND FUTURES MARKETS

A *currency forward or futures contract* entails an obligation to trade an underlying currency at a specified rate of exchange, which is determined today, on a specified future delivery date. The specified rate of exchange is known as the *forward price* or *futures price*. Future delivery dates may be *nearby* or *deferred* in time. If the contract calls for the purchase of the underlying foreign exchange, the trader is said to hold a *long* position in the contract. A *short* position represents an obligation to sell currency in the future.

Currency forward and futures contracts are *derivative securities*. They are "written on" the underlying foreign exchange, and the forward and futures prices depend critically on the underlying currency's spot rate of exchange. Currency forward and futures contracts offer investors and multinational corporations (MNCs) the ability to better manage their exchange exposure. These contracts can also be employed for speculative purposes or for future price discovery.

In this chapter we analyze currency forward and futures contracts and markets. We highlight the important differences between these closely related instruments. We also provide illustrations of how these contracts can be used to estimate subsequent spot rates, to speculate on currency movements, and to immunize against unanticipated changes in rates of exchange.

MARKETS

The currency forward market offers private contracts that are tailored to the specific needs of customers. Large banks and private currency brokers network and trade electronically to meet the customer's needs. For instance, an MNC may require a forward contract for two or more years. It can obtain such a contract through direct negotiations with its bank. Often the negotiating is done over the telephone, and the bank may

Exhibit 12.1

Contract Specifications for IMM
Currency Futures Contracts

Currency	Contract Months	Contract Size	Minimum Price Fluctuations
Australian dollar	Jan/Mar/Apl Jne/Jly/Spt Oct/Dec/Spot Month	100,000 AD	$0.0001/AD
British pound	"	25,000 BP	$0.0005/BP
Canadian dollar	"	100,000 CD	$0.0001/CD
Deutsche mark	"	125,000 DM	$0.00001/DM
French franc	"	250,000 FF	$0.00005/FF
Japanese yen	"	12,500,000 JY	$0.000001/JY
Swiss franc	"	125,000 SF	$0.0001/SF
European Currency Unit (ECU)	Mar/Jne/Spt Dec	125,000 ECU	$0.0001/ECU

Notes: There are no daily price limits. The IMM removed all daily price limits on currency futures in February 1985. Trading hours are approximately 7:20 A.M. to 1:20 P.M. central time. Delivery takes place on the third Wednesday of the contract month. The last trading day is the second business day before delivery.

require compensating balances or lines of credit to insure the MNC's obligation. These currency forward contracts often are valued at $1 million or more to facilitate the transactions of large MNCs.

Forward contracting in currencies (and other underlying assets) has existed for centuries. Currency futures contracts represent an institutionalized form of currency forward contracting. Currency futures are traded on an *organized market*, which is a physical trading floor where standardized or listed contracts are traded face to face. The first *listed* currency futures contracts began trading on the International Monetary Market (IMM) division of the Chicago Mercantile Exchange on 16 May 1972. This was about the time that the floating exchange rate system emerged. Also, the advent of currency futures trading represented the first-ever trading of financial futures contracts. Before 1972, only agricultural and metallurgical futures were traded on organized exchanges. Today financial futures trading, including that on stock indices and treasury securities as well as currency, represents the majority of all futures trading.

The IMM is the largest trader of listed currency futures contracts. Exhibit 12.1 presents contract sizes and other details for the currency futures contracts traded on the IMM. Exhibit 12.2 presents total and relative trading volumes for these contracts for the calendar year 1989.

Listed futures contracts on foreign exchange traded on the IMM and other organized futures exchanges may not appeal to MNCs desiring longer-term and otherwise less standardized contracts. Instead, currency futures appeal more to individual traders and speculators and smaller firms unable to transact in the currency forward market.

Currency	Contract Volume	Percent of Total Volume
Australian dollar	113,972	0.43%
British pound	2,518,232	9.68
Canadian dollar	1,263,664	4.86
Deutsche mark	8,186,221	31.48
French franc	2,030	0.01
Japanese yen	7,823,739	30.08
Swiss franc	6,092,885	23.44

Exhibit 12.2
IMM Currency Futures Total and Relative Trading Volume for 1989

Exhibit 12.3 provides a comprehensive comparison of the currency forward and IMM currency futures markets. Highlighting this exhibit are the following differences:

- Contract sizes and delivery dates are standardized for currency futures but are negotiated and tailored for currency forward contracts.
- Qualified public speculation is encouraged for futures but not for forwards.
- Currency futures trading entails posting a small security deposit.
- Currency forward contracts are accessible only to large creditworthy customers who deal in foreign trade.
- The majority of forward contracts are settled by actual delivery of the underlying currency, whereas the majority of futures contracts are settled via reversing trades (discussed later) such that delivery never occurs.

Currency Futures Trading

Besides the IMM, currency futures contracts are traded on the Philadelphia Board of Trade, the London International Financial Futures Exchange, the Singapore International Monetary Exchange, the Sydney Futures Exchange, and several other organized exchanges worldwide. At each of these exchanges trading occurs in areas called *pits*. Traders in the pits offer to buy or sell through a system of open outcry or, often, by using sophisticated hand signals.

These traders may be members of the exchange who trade for their own accounts, typically called locals. Locals attempt to profit from their expertise in forecasting future spot exchange rates. Exchange members hold seats in the exchange, which is often organized as a not-for-profit association of its members. These memberships (seats) can be traded. A recent price commanded for a full seat on the Chicago Mercantile Exchange was $490,000 (4 May 1990).

Traders in the pits may also be representatives of trading firms (e.g., Merrill Lynch) that act as *commission brokers,* trading for their clients.

Exhibit 12.3

A Comparison of Currency
Forward and Futures Markets

Characteristic	Forward	Futures
Size of contract	Tailored to individual needs.	Standardized.
Delivery date	Tailored to individual needs.	Standardized.
Method of transaction	Established by the bank or broker via telephone contact with limited number of buyers and sellers.	Determined by open auction among many buyers and sellers on the exchange floor.
Participants	Banks, brokers, and MNCs. Public speculation not encouraged.	Banks, brokers, and MNCs. Qualified public speculation encouraged.
Commissions	Set by "spread" between bank's buy and sell price. Not easily determined by customer.	Published small brokerage fee and negotiated rates on block trades.
Security deposit	None as such, but compensating bank balances required.	Published small security deposit required.
Clearing operation (financial integrity)	Handling contingent on individual banks and brokers. No separate clearinghouse function.	Handled by exchange clearinghouse. Daily settlements to the market.
Marketplace	Over the telephone worldwide.	Central exchange floor with worldwide communications.
Economic justification	Facilitate world trade by providing hedge mechanism.	Same as forward market. In addition, provides a broader market and an alternative hedging mechanism via public participation.
Accessibility	Limited to very large customers who deal in foreign trade.	Open to anyone who needs hedge facilities, or has risk capital to speculate with.
Regulation	Self-regulating.	April 1975: Regulated under the Commodity Futures Trading Commission.
Frequency of delivery	More than 90% settled by actual delivery.	Theoretically, no deliveries in a perfect market. In reality, less than 1%.
Price fluctuations	No daily limit.	No daily limit.
Market liquidity	Offsetting with other banks.	Public offset. Arbitrage offset.

Such clients may be speculators, or hedgers seeking to immunize against adverse exchange rate movements. Some commission brokers trade for their own accounts as well. When traders in the pits trade for themselves as locals and for others as commission brokers, we have what is known as *dual trading*. Currently such dual trading is criticized by many who feel that the trader somehow gives priority or favorable treatment to his own trading at the expense of outside clients. Such favorable treatment is known as *frontrunning*.

To illustrate a trade, assume that you (the client or principal) want to undertake a long position in the June British pound (BP) futures contract traded on the IMM. You are willing to assume the long position *at market*, meaning that you are seeking the best currently available price. The process begins with a phone call to your agent (account executive or broker), who must trade through an exchange member, typically a commission broker whose seat is financed by the agent's trading firm. Your agent places the order with the commission broker, who executes the trade in the BP futures pit in return for a commission fee. Once the trade is executed, the commission broker confirms the trade with your agent, who then notifies you of the completed transaction and the futures price. You must then deposit an initial margin with a member firm of the clearinghouse (discussed later) by the start of trade the next morning. Typically, your broker or account executive handles this process, withdrawing funds from your established account.

The commission broker may have transacted in the pit with another commission broker who represented another public client. Alternatively, he may have transacted with a local. Locals trade for their own accounts, buying contracts at a *bid price,* and selling contracts at a higher *ask price.* Locals are sometimes called scalpers, day traders, or position traders, depending on their trading behavior. Scalpers trade actively, holding their position for no more than a few minutes. They attempt to profit from volume trading and provide market liquidity. Day traders hold comparatively longer-term positions, but less than a full trading session. They attempt to profit on price movement but do not wish to assume the risk of holding longer-term positions. Position traders assume contract positions ranging from overnight to weekly or monthly periods.

Types of Orders

Besides placing a market order, a public currency futures trader can place any of the following order types:

- A *limit order,* which stipulates a specific price at which you will contract. A limit order can be good only for a trading session (a *day order*), or until cancelled (an *open order*).

- A *fill-or-kill order,* which instructs the commission broker to fill an order immediately at a specified price. The order is cancelled if it cannot be transacted quickly.

- An *all-or-none order,* which allows the commission broker to fill part of the order at one specified price, and the remainder at another price.

- An *on-the-open* or *on-the-close order,* which represent orders to trade within a few minutes of opening or closing, respectively.

- A *stop order,* which triggers a reversing trade when prices hit a prescribed limit. Stop orders are used to protect against losses on existing positions.

Transaction Costs

Transaction costs in currency futures markets are very small, especially for exchange members. Currently it costs locals about 24 cents per futures contract traded. Of course, public traders incur other costs. The following transaction costs are realized from futures trading:

- *Floor trading and clearing fees.* These are the small fees charged by the exchange and its associated clearinghouse (discussed later). If a trade is executed through a commission broker, these fees are built into the broker's commission. Locals pay the fees directly.

- *Commissions.* A commission broker charges a commission to transact a public order: This commission is paid at the order's inception and covers both the opening and reversing trades.

- *Bid-ask spreads.* Locals simultaneously quote bid and ask prices. The bid-ask spread represents a transaction cost when effecting a trade with a local. The spread represents the cost of obtaining trading immediacy, since locals offer the public trading liquidity. A bid-ask spread is typically equal to the value of the contract's minimum price fluctuation, called a *tick.*

- *Delivery costs.* A trader who holds a position until delivery is exposed to delivery costs. However, as previously noted, the overwhelming majority of currency futures contracts never entail actual delivery of the underlying foreign exchange.

Taxes

Determining the tax consequences of currency futures trading can be complex, especially when spreads (discussed later) are involved. Following are a few generally applicable tax guides:

- *Marking to the market.* At the end of the calendar year, every futures contract is marked to the market so that any unrealized gains or losses are treated, for tax purposes, as though they were actually realized during the tax year.

- *Gains.* The realized and unrealized gains from currency futures trading are taxed at the ordinary personal income tax rate.

- *Losses.* The realized and unrealized losses are deductible by offsetting them against any other investment gains. Losses exceeding gains by up to $3,000 can be deducted against ordinary income.

- *Commissions.* In general, brokerage commissions are tax deductible.

Price Quotes

Chapter 4 offered an exhibit indicating various currency forward prices. Exhibit 12.4 presents *settlement prices* for currency futures contracts traded on the IMM on 16 November 1988. Presented are the day's high, low, and settlement prices, as well as other information such as each contract's daily volume and current *open interest,* the number of contracts outstanding. For example, the settlement futures price for Canadian dollars, December 1988 delivery, was $0.8115/CD, up $0.0027/CD from the previous day's settlement. Open interest in all CD futures was 17,370 contracts.

All organized futures exchanges report their settlement prices in a similar manner. The reported prices are called settlement prices rather

Exhibit 12.4

Settlement Prices for IMM
Currency Futures Contracts

FUTURES

- CURRENCY FUTURES -

	Open	High	Low	Settle	Change	Lifetime High	Lifetime Low	Open Interest
JAPANESE YEN (IMM) 12.5 million yen; $ per yen (.00)								
Dec	.8156	.8208	.8143	.8205	+ .0064	.8530	.7115	46,936
Mr89	.8250	.8297	.8230	.8296	+ .0068	.8590	.7439	3,393
June	.8350	.8399	.8340	.8399	+ .0072	.8400	.7500	697
Sept	.8445	.8490	.8445	.8501	+ .0076	.8490	.7690	246
Est vol 45,934; vol Tues 24,165; open int 51,272, −2,692.								
W. GERMAN MARK (IMM) – 125,000 marks; $ per mark								
Dec	.5768	.5834	.5752	.5831	+ .0078	.6610	.5252	49,374
Mr89	.5879	.5890	.5800	.5887	+ .0079	.6240	.5304	3,278
June	.5900	.5950	.5900	.5950	+ .0082	.5950	.5434	704
Est vol 42,411; vol Tues 19,793; open int 52,856, −787.								
CANADIAN DOLLAR (IMM) – 100,000 dlrs.; $ per Can $								
Dec	.8101	.8129	.8093	.8115	+ .0027	.8340	.7390	13,915
Mr89	.8060	.8097	.8057	.8075	+ .0029	.8309	.7570	2,308
June	.8070	.8047	.8020	.8035	+ .0031	.8285	.7670	1,036
Est vol 7,727; vol Tues 5,324; open int 17,370, −183.								
BRITISH POUND (IMM) – 62,500 pds.; $ per pound								
Dec	1.8080	1.8244	1.8030	1.8238	+ .0220	1.9000	1.6374	18,097
Mr89	1.7970	1.8150	1.7906	1.8120	+ .0224	1.8150	1.6320	1,126
Est vol 11,900; vol Tues 7,153; open int 19,333, −432.								
SWISS FRANC (IMM) 125,000 francs-$ per franc								
Dec	.6885	.6962	.6855	.6940	+ .0085	.8210	.6286	35,733
Mr89	.6956	.7040	.6935	.7026	+ .0088	.7735	.6300	1,497
June	.7070	.7118	.7025	.7118	+ .0090	.7118	.6450	116
Est vol 33,154; vol Tues 16,091; open int 36,751, −865.								
AUSTRALIAN DOLLAR (IMM) – 100,000 dlrs.; $ per A.$								
Dec	.8490	.8550	.8480	.8542	+ .0047	.8550	.7450	2,291
Est vol 303; vol Tues 326; open int 2,353, +93.								

than closing prices, although in most cases the two prices are nearly the same. If volume in a particular contract was very thin (e.g., in a deferred contract), a settlement committee would determine a representative price to publish. This representative price is established by observing price changes that day for the more active (nearby) contract, and extrapolating to determine a rational price change for the inactive (deferred) contract.

Clearinghouses

A central part of any organized futures exchange is its *clearinghouse*, which guarantees contract performance to all market participants. The clearinghouse guarantees performance by breaking down every futures contract into two distinct contracts: one contract between the buyer (i.e., long position) and the clearinghouse acting as the seller, and one contract between the seller (i.e., short position) and the clearinghouse acting as a buyer. All traders have obligations to the clearinghouse, but not to each other. Also, the two traders need only be concerned with the reliability of the clearinghouse. However, clearinghouses have never defaulted on a contract. To do so would tear down the confidence of the market and ultimately the market itself.

Since the clearinghouse can match its long and short positions perfectly, it is said to be *perfectly hedged*. That is, its net position in all futures contracts is zero. The clearinghouse merely acts as an intermediary or dealer that facilitates trade and liquidity, and is exposed to little risk. The clearinghouse may be part of the futures exchange or, often, is incorporated separately. The clearinghouse charges a small transaction fee for its role.

Margins

Currency futures traders represent a source of credit risk to the clearinghouse. For instance, the long futures trader may have insufficient funds to purchase the underlying foreign exchange. To cover the risk, the

Exhibit 12.5

Margin Requirements for IMM
Currency Futures Contracts

Contract	Margins	
	Initial	Maintenance
British pound	$2,000	$1,500
Canadian dollar	900	700
Deutsche mark	2,000	1,500
Japanese yen	1,500	1,000
Swiss franc	2,000	1,500

Notes: The margin on spreads is zero. Hedge margins are usually lower than speculative margins shown here.

trader is required to post *margin*, usually with a member firm of the clearinghouse. This margin often is a cash deposit, but a bank letter of credit or liquid securities can be used. For instance, U.S. Treasury bills can be posted to cover at least part of the initial margin.

The initial margin varies from market to market. Exhibit 12.5 presents current margin requirements for the major currency futures contracts traded on the IMM. These are the margin requirements for pure speculators. Requirements for hedgers are typically lower. The initial margin is returned upon completion of the contract and, if securities are posted, the interest earned is paid to the trader.

Daily Resettlement

The initial margin represents a small fraction of the underlying currency's total value. This is attributable to a procedure known as daily resettlement. *Daily resettlement*, or *marking to the market*, is a futures market requirement that traders realize losses daily.

Consider a specific example of daily resettlement using a British pound futures contract with futures price $1.25/£ and one month until expiration. Assume that the contract settles today at $1.22, down $0.03/£ from yesterday's settlement price. Since there are 25,000 pounds per contract traded on the IMM (see Exhibit 12.1), this represents a one-day loss of $750 ($0.03 × 25,000) to the long futures trader. At the end of the trading day, the $750 is deducted from the trader's margin deposited with the member firm. Then there is a *margin call*; that is, the trader must replenish the margin in order to resume the contract the next day. This is daily resettlement; the contract is now said to be marked to the market.

The trader may not need to replenish the entire $750. In general, the trader must deposit funds to restore a *maintenance margin*. This maintenance margin often is about 75% of the initial margin. From Exhibit 12.5, for BP futures the initial margin is $2,000 but the maintenance margin is just $1,500. Here the long futures trader must deposit only $250

Exhibit 12.6

Daily Resettlement in the Currency
Futures Market

Suppose that on Monday, 16 November, you assume a long position in one March Deutsche mark futures contract at the futures price of $0.5887/DM. The initial margin is $2,000, and the maintenance margin is $1,500. For simplicity, you do not withdraw excess monies from your margin balance. All margin requirements are met with cash. You hold your long position through Friday, 20 November. Then you short the contract (a reversing trade) at the opening price on Monday, 23 November. Following is a schedule of assumed DM futures prices and the associated margin requirements. Your gross profit on the entire transaction is −$812.50.

Trading Date	Settlement Price	Marked to the Market	Other Entries	Account Balance
Nov. 16	$0.5892	+$ 62.50	+$2,000.00[a]	$2,062.50
Nov. 17	0.5800	− 1,150.00	+ 587.50[b]	1,500.00
Nov. 18	0.5808	+ 100.00		1,600.00
Nov. 19	0.5817	+ 112.50		1,712.50
Nov. 20	0.5815	− 25.00		1,687.50
Nov. 21	0.5822[c]	+ 87.50	− 1,775.00[d]	0.00
			+$ 812.50[e]	

Notes: a. $2,000 initial margin deposit.
 b. $587.50 deposit to meeting $1,500 maintenance margin.
 c. $0.5822 opening futures price on 21 November.
 d. Entire account balance withdrawn after reversing trade.
 e. Deposits less withdrawals. A positive amount indicates a loss. Also note that $812.50 = ($0.5887 − 0.5822) (125,000).

[$1,500 − ($2,000 − $750)] in order to resume trading. This $250 deposit is known as the *variation margin*, which is usually paid in cash. To smooth this daily process, the broker or account executive typically has permission to draw the required deposit from the trader's established account.

The daily resettlement procedure facilitates low margin requirements. Because losses are realized daily, the margin has to cover only one-day price changes, which are typically very small. The overall effect of the daily resettlement procedure is to create a safer futures market, allowing less creditworthy investors to participate. To see this, compare the currency futures and forward markets with respect to the timing of cash flows. In the forward market no daily resettlement exists, so the only cash flow that can occur is at delivery of the forward contract. Clearly, big price fluctuations can occur over the life of forward contracts. For instance, recall that currency forward contracts often have maturities of two or more years. Exchange rates can change dramatically over such long periods. Consequently, the potential risk exhibited by forward contracts is greater than that exhibited by futures contracts, where daily resettlement ensures small price changes between cash flows. As a result, only very large and creditworthy MNCs can participate in the currency forward market. Exhibit 12.6 provides another, self-contained illustration of the daily resettlement process.

Reversing Trades

In the currency forward market, the vast majority of contracts are settled by actual delivery of the underlying foreign exchange. In contrast, nearly all currency futures contracts are settled by *reversing trades* such that delivery never occurs. A reversing trade effectively makes a trader's net futures position equal to zero. For instance, suppose a trader had agreed to buy British pounds for delivery next December. A reversing trade is accomplished by assuming a short position in the same BP futures contract with December delivery. The trader's net position is now zero. The clearinghouse recognizes this position, so the trader is absolved from any future trading requirements. A long trader can enter into a reversing trade instead of taking delivery of the pounds. A short trader can assume a reversing trade instead of delivering pounds.

Market Growth

The continuing integration of international capital markets and the increasing volume of international trade have resulted in an explosive growth of currency forward and futures trading. The currency forward market is substantially larger than the currency futures market when measuring market size by the U.S. dollar amount of underlying currency traded. Most estimates place the forward market at about twenty times larger. However, the currency futures market is growing more rapidly when measured in percentages. Figure 12.1 displays the growth in currency futures trading on the IMM. Over the 14-year period 1975 through 1989, contract volume increased over a hundredfold.

Market Regulation

Organized futures markets are regulated to ensure performance and to preclude illegal activities such as insider trading and price manipulation. U.S. futures markets, including those offering contracts on foreign exchange, are regulated by the Commodity Futures Trading Commission, which is federal agency empowered to approve new contracts, set maximum daily price limits, ensure the competency of brokers, and the like. Also, the National Futures Association was recently established as a type of self-regulatory agency. The London International Financial Futures Exchange, which is the second largest currency futures trading market, is regulated by the International Commodities Clearing House.

USING CURRENCY FORWARD AND FUTURES CONTRACTS

Investors and MNCs typically employ currency forward and futures contracts for one of the following three reasons: price discovery, speculation, or hedging exchange exposure. In this section we discuss each reason, providing illustrations throughout.

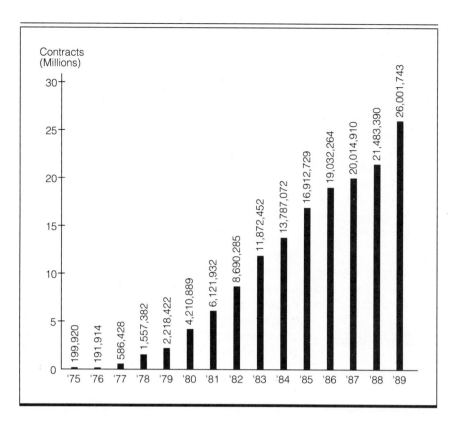

Figure 12.1
Annual IMM Currency Futures
Contract Volume, 1975–1989

Price Discovery

Trading a currency forward or futures contract implies the receipt or delivery of the underlying foreign exchange at a specified rate of exchange. Such a rate is largely determined by investors' expectations about the spot rate of exchange at contract delivery. Consequently, a forward or futures price may serve as an indicator of future currency values.

Currency forward and futures prices are not perfect forecasts of actual future currency values, and most contend that forward and futures rates are biased estimators, although the magnitude of the bias appears to be small. Still, the usefulness of currency forward and futures prices for price discovery depends largely on the availability, cost, and accuracy of alternative forecasting techniques and services. Viewed in this context, currency forward and futures prices are relatively attractive estimators. They are readily available, inexpensive to obtain, and many empirical studies find that alternative estimators are not, on average, more accurate (Levich 1983).[1]

To exemplify the relative forecast accuracy of currency forward and futures prices, consider the results presented in Exhibit 12.7 on page

---

[1] However, see the discussion in Chapter 4 concerning the finding that the current spot rate may be a superior predictor of future rates than is the contemporaneous forward rate.

Futuresgate 1989

In January of 1989 the FBI disclosed a massive, ongoing investigation of abusive futures trading practices at both the Chicago Board of Trade (CBOT) and Chicago Mercantile Exchange (CME). The investigation centered on the Japanese yen and Swiss franc futures pits at the CME, and the U.S. Treasury bond and soybean futures pits at the CBOT. FBI agents, posing as independent floor brokers and traders under assumed names, found several abusive practices, especially an illegal trading scheme known as bucket trading.

Bucket trading occurs when two traders conspire to exploit profits on public market orders by delaying the order's execution. Here is how a bucket trade can be executed:

■ First, an independent floor broker receives a client's market order, which is an order to execute a trade at the best currently available market price. For instance, suppose that the order is to buy 25 Swiss franc futures contracts.

■ Second, the floor broker signals a confederate, called a "bagman," to buy the contracts. Presume the bagman buys the 25 contracts at $87,500 per contract, or $2,187,500. The floor broker continues to hold the client's market order.

■ Third, suppose the price rises shortly to $87,550. The floor broker now executes the client's order. The client believes that $87,550 was the best available price. The bagman sells the 25 contracts at $87,550 for a profit of $1,250. This profit, which should have been the client's, is "bucketed" into the bagman's account. The bagman and the broker later split the monies. If the Swiss franc futures price had fallen, the customer would have purchased the contracts from the bagman at the $87,500 price. Hence, the loss is bucketed into the client's account and the two illegal traders do not exhibit any losses.

The FBI's investigation is still unfolding. The federal government has issued dozens of subpoenas and is reportedly not offering full immunity for cooperation into the investigation. Although it is too early to draw meaningful inferences, many feel that Futuresgate 1989 will lead to several operating changes, including more trading surveillance, more computerized trading, and especially the banning of dual trading. Such a ban would help to reduce or eliminate abusive practices like bucket trading. Notice that the bagman in preceding illustration must be a dual trader.

235, which provides percentage forecast errors for four exchange rate forecasting services and the simple currency forward rate obtained from the *Wall Street Journal*. Forecasts are for 30-day forward rates, nonoverlapping for the 5-year period 1985 through 1989. The forward rate has a lower average percentage forecast error than any of the more expensive forecasting services. With the two exceptions of Harris Bank's $/CD forecast and Chemical Bank's $/JY forecast, the forward rate exhibits smaller forecast errors. Arguably, none of the average errors are statistically distinguishable.

Speculation

Currency futures contracts can be used to speculate on forecasted changes in rates of exchange. Consider a simple speculative trade involving British pound futures. Suppose that the current spot rate is $1.8300/£, and that the futures price for December delivery is $1.8238/£ (see Exhibit 12.4). If a position trader believes that the pound will not depreciate to the degree implied by the futures price, he will buy the futures contract and subsequently undertake a reversing trade to close his long position. To gain, the speculator must be able to reverse at a new futures price, for December delivery, of $1.8238/£1 or higher.

Figure 12.2, on page 236, presents a contingency graph summarizing the strategy. If the position trader is correct and the subsequent futures

	Percentage Forecast Errors			
	Exchange Rates			
Forecaster	$/CD	$/DM	$/JY	Average Error
Chemical Bank	6.2%	20.4%	21.4%	16.0%
Citibank	6.1	18.3	23.0	15.8
Harris Bank	5.7	17.9	22.3	15.3
Security Pacific	6.2	19.2	23.2	16.2
Forward Rate	5.9	17.7	21.7	15.1

Exhibit 12.7

Forecast Errors for Four Services and the 30-Day Forward Rate

price is, say, $1.8300/£, then his proceeds are $0.0062/£, or $387.50 per contract [($1.8300 − $1.8238) × 62,500 pounds per contract]. Of course, these proceeds must be sufficient to cover the trader's transaction costs. These costs are nominal for locals, but can be important for public speculators. The round-trip brokerage fee for public futures traders is currently about $30.00 per contract at discount brokerage firms.

Speculative strategies can be more elaborate than the one just described. Consider an *intracurrency spread*, which involves the purchase and sale of futures contracts on the same underlying currency but with two different delivery dates. Suppose you observe the following rates (see Exhibit 12.4):

	$/£
Spot:	1.8301
December Futures:	1.8238
March Futures:	1.8150

Also suppose that you believe the pound will depreciate by more than implied by these futures prices. You could short the deferred contract (March 1989), but a spread is less risky. To establish the intracurrency spread, you short the deferred contract at $1.8150, and take a long position in the nearby contract (December 1988) at $1.8238. To profit, you must be able to reverse these trades, before the December expiration, such that the price difference between the new December and March futures is $0.0088 or greater. For instance, suppose that you reverse at the following futures prices: $1.8200 for the December contract and $1.8000 for the March 1989 contract. The pound has depreciated, consistent with your forecast; also, the resulting price difference, $0.0200 = $1.8200 − $1.8000, is greater than the original difference, $0.0088 = $1.8238 − $1.8150, so you profit. Here your profit is $0.0112/£, or $700.00 per contract [($0.0200 − $0.0088) × 62,500] ignoring transaction costs and taxes. Figure 12.3, on page 237, provides a contingency graph for this intracurrency spread.

Figure 12.2

Contingency Graph for a Long
British Pound Futures Position

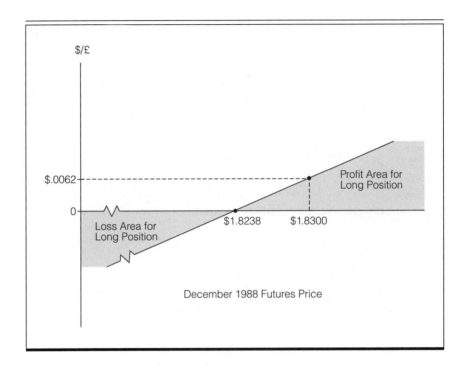

Another more elaborate speculative trading strategy is the *intercurrency spread*, which involves the purchase and sale of futures contracts with the same delivery dates but with two different underlying currencies. Suppose a position trader observed the following rates (see Exhibit 12.4):

	$/£	$/CD	Cross Rate (£/CD)
Spot:	1.8301	0.8165	0.4462
December Futures:	1.8238	0.8115	0.4450

The *cross rates* (£/CD) are generated by dividing $/CD by $/£. These cross rates represent prices implied by the $/£ and $/CD rates.

Now suppose the position trader feels that the CD will depreciate, relative to the BP, by less than that implied by the December futures cross rate, £0.4450/CD. For instance, the speculator may feel that the CD will actually appreciate against the BP during the period. She can try to profit from this forecast through an intercurrency spread. Specifically, she will write the December pound futures and buy the December CD futures. She must be careful to match the position sizes such that the numbers of BP and CD are equal. If she can reverse these trades such that the futures price difference is less than $1.0123 ($1.8238/BP − $0.8115/CD), then profits (ignoring taxes and transaction costs) are realized. For example, suppose that she can reverse at the following futures prices: $1.8238 for the December pound contract, and $0.8150 for the December CD contract. The CD has appreciated against the BP, consis-

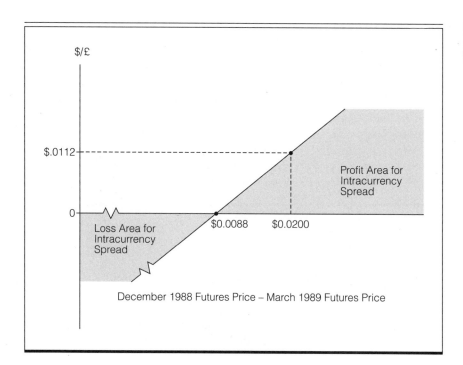

Figure 12.3
Contingency Graph for an
Intracurrency Spread

tent with her forecast (the new December futures cross rate is £0.4469/
CD); also, the resulting price difference is $1.0088 = $1.8238 − $0.8150,
which is less than $1.0123, so she profits. Here the position trader's
profit is $0.0035 per unit of foreign currency. Figure 12.4 provides a
contingency graph for this intercurrency spread.

Hedging Exchange Exposure[2]

Although currency forward and futures contracts can be used for price
discovery and speculation, the primary reason for their existence is to
facilitate the hedging of exchange rate risk. By providing an efficient
means of risk transfer, currency forward and futures markets contribute
to social welfare. They serve as insurance markets, allowing participants
to reduce the disutility associated with price and revenue variability
attributable to unexpected exchange rate movements. This in turn enhances stability and promotes international trade. Moreover, the existence of these contracts can be argued to contribute to market completion, in the Arrow-Debrue sense.

---

[2] In this subsection we assume that the goal of hedging is to minimize variability attributable to exchange rate movements. The *minimum variance hedge ratio* for foreign exchange is
assumed to be ±1, meaning that a one-to-one correspondence between the number of
foreign currency units in the spot and futures markets will minimize the hedger's exchange exposure. See Appendix 12.A for a discussion of these assumptions.

A Winning Speculative Strategy with Currency Futures?

Thomas (1985) analyzed the following speculative trading strategy involving currency futures. In each period futures on discount currencies were purchased, and futures on premium currencies were sold. If the currency futures price was, on average, an unbiased estimator of the future spot exchange rate at contract settlement, Thomas' strategy would yield zero profits on average. However, Thomas found large profits on average from his speculative strategy. This finding suggested that discount currencies did not depreciate on average to the degree implied by the futures price, and that premium currencies did not appreciate to the degree implied during Thomas' sample period. Alternatively, his results may suggest that the futures price is not an unbiased predictor of the actual future spot rate. As we will show in Chapter 13, the currency futures price may not be unbiased if interest rates are nonconstant, or if investors are not risk-neutral, or if both conditions occur.

A Long Hedge   For our first hedging illustration, assume that a U.S. auto dealer contracts on February 1 to take delivery of ten Mercedes, at DM100,000 each, on May 15. The importer must pay DM1,000,000 on delivery, and wishes to immunize against an unexpected appreciation in the mark relative to the U.S. dollar. The current $/DM spot rate is $0.5780.

Since marks will be paid in May, the U.S. auto dealer uses the June DM futures contract. Assume that this contract is currently priced at $0.5950/DM (see Exhibit 12.4). At 125,000 marks per contract, the price of one contract is $74,375 ($0.5950 × 125,000). The importer wants to hedge marks currently worth $578,000 ($1,000,000 × 0.5780) with con-

Figure 12.4

Contingency Graph for an Intercurrency Spread

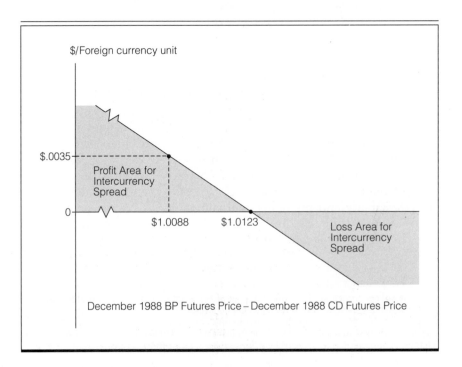

tracts priced at $74,375 each. Thus, the number of contracts is 7.8 ($578,000/74,375). The dealer decides to take a long position in eight DM futures contracts with June delivery.

Suppose that on May 15 the $/DM spot rate is $0.6000. Consequently, the mark appreciated and the auto dealer must pay more for the Mercedes: $0.6000/DM × DM1,000,000 = $600,000. Fortunately, however, the mark futures price increased to $0.6189/DM, or $77,362.50 per contract (assumed). For eight contracts the dealer's profit is $23,900 (8 × ($77,362.50 − 74,375.00)). Thus, the long futures position covered all of the Mercedes' additional cost ($600,000 − 578,000 = $22,000) due to the mark's increased value. Also, the importer realized a profit of $1,900 ($23,900 − 22,000) on the entire transaction.

The degree of losses due to the mark's appreciation that is covered by the long futures position depends on the subsequent spot and futures rates on May 15. However, as long as the spot and futures rates move in the same direction, the hedge will succeed in reducing at least part of the dealer's loss on the Mercedes import. If the mark depreciated over the period, there would have been a loss on the futures position that would have offset some or all of the gain on the Mercedes import.

February 1:	Spot rate is $0.5780/DM.
	Cost of ten Mercedes is $578,000.
	June DM futures price is $0.5950.
	Buy (long) eight June DM futures contracts.
May 15:	Spot rate is $0.6000/DM.
	Cost of ten Mercedes is $600,000.
	June DM futures price is $0.6189.
	Enter a reversing trade (sell eight contracts).
Results:	Profit on Mercedes import is −$22,000.
	Profit on futures transaction is $23,900.
	Net profit is $1,900.

A Short Hedge For our second illustration of hedging exchange exposure, assume that a U.S. corporation has a U.K. subsidiary that is expected to generate earnings of £1,020,000 at the end of the operating quarter, March 31. The U.S. firm wishes to repatriate the pounds, perhaps to pay domestic shareholders a quarterly dividend. Let the current spot rate (January 20) be $1.8301/£. The current April BP futures price is $1.8010. The U.S. firm would like to hedge against an unexpected depreciation in the pound, since such a depreciation will result in fewer U.S. dollars upon repatriation. The firm can do so by shorting BP futures contracts for April delivery.

Since there are £62,500 per futures contract traded on the IMM, each contract's price is currently $112,562.50 ($1.8010 × 62,500). The firm wants to hedge pounds currently worth $1,866,702 ($1.8301 × 1,020,000) with contracts priced at $112,562.50 each. The number of contracts is therefore 16.6 ($1,866,702/112,562.50). The firm decides to take a short position in 16 June BP futures contracts.

Suppose that on March 31 the $/£ spot rate is $1.7500. The pound depreciated and the U.S. firm receives fewer dollars upon repatriation:

$1,785,000 = $1.7500/£ × £1,020,000. Fortunately, however, the BP futures price decreased to $1.7250, or $107,812.50 per contract (assumed). The U.S. firm can enter a reversing trade, realizing a profit on the sixteen contracts of $76,000 (−16 × ($107,812.50) − 112,562.50)). Consequently, the short futures position covered most of the loss on the spot position (−$81,702 = 1,785,000 − 1,866,702) due to the pound's decreased value.

January 20:	Spot rate is $1.8301/£.
	Anticipate repatriating £1,020,000 on March 31.
	April BP futures price is $1.8010.
	Short 16 April BP futures contracts.
March 31:	Spot rate is $1.7500/£.
	April BP futures price is $1.7250.
	Enter a reversing trade (buy 16 contracts).
Results:	Profit on repatriation is −$81,702.
	Profit on futures transaction is $76,000.
	Net profit is −$5,702.

SUMMARY

A currency forward or futures contract obligates a trader to buy or sell an underlying currency in the future at a specified rate of exchange. Forward contracts are tailored to the specific needs of customers, and futures contracts are standardized and traded in pits located on the trading floors of organized futures exchanges. Some of the differences between these contracts and markets were detailed in Exhibit 12.3. An especially noteworthy difference concerns daily resettlement in the currency futures market. Daily resettlement is a procedure that requires futures traders to realize losses each day. This process allows traders to post a small fraction of the underlying currency's value (the margin) in order to contract. The resettlement procedure also creates a safer futures market, allowing smaller customers to transact.

Although currency forward and futures contracts can be used for price discovery and speculation, their major purpose is to facilitate the hedging of exchange rate risk. Investors and MNCs can employ these contracts to help immunize against exchange exposure.

Volume and open interest in these contracts has been growing rapidly over the last decade. In the next chapter we examine the determination of currency forward and futures prices, and examine extant empirical evidence concerning these markets.

Questions and Problems

1. How do currency forward and futures contracts differ with respect to the following: maturity; settlement; cash flows?
2. What is the primary role of a clearinghouse?

3. What agencies regulate U.S. futures trading?

4. What is maintenance margin? A variation margin?

5. Why are initial margins so low?

6. Exhibit 12.5 reports that initial margins vary by currency. Why do you suppose this occurs?

7. From Exhibit 12.4, what was the settlement price for Swiss francs with June 1989 delivery? What was the settlement price for the nearby contract?

8. What are the three purposes of currency forward and futures markets? What is the major social welfare provided by these markets?

9. Suppose that a currency speculator believes that the German central bank will soon begin expanding its money supply rapidly in an attempt to stimulate its economy. What can this speculator do to exploit this belief?

10. Assume that it is now November and a U.S. importer has agreed to purchase 100,000 bottles per month of a fine French wine for three months beginning in January. The U.S. importer has agreed to pay the French exporter 88 francs per bottle. Also, the U.S. importer has contracted to distribute the 300,000 bottles to various interests for $16.50 per bottle. There is a $0.50 per bottle import duty, and shipping costs are $0.05 per bottle. There are no other costs. The importer has obtained the following $/FF forward rates:

Month	Forward Rate
January	$0.1252
February	$0.1247
March	$0.1241

If the importer is fully hedged, how much profit does he earn?

11. On September 11 a U.S.-based MNC with a German subsidiary decides to transfer DM3,000,000 from an account in Stuttgart to an account at a New York bank. The currency spot rate is $0.5950/DM. The transfer cannot occur until December 10, and the current DM futures price for December delivery is $0.6075/DM. How many futures contracts should the U.S. MNC short in order to hedge? What is the MNC's net profit on December 10 if the new spot rate is $0.5900/DM and the reversing trade occurs at a new futures price of $0.6012/DM?

12. Assume that a position trader forecasts an appreciation of the German mark relative to the dollar. To profit, the trader undertakes the following intracurrency spread: long the June DM futures contract at $0.5498/DM, and short the March DM futures contract at $0.5450/DM. Suppose that in mid-March the trader lifts the spread by engaging in reversing trades at the new futures prices of $0.5535/DM (March) and $0.5625/DM (June). What is the position trader's profit per mark, ignoring taxes and transaction costs?

13. Using the price information contained in Exhibit 12.4, create an intercurrency spread for a forecasted increase in the short-term pound-mark cross rate. Provide a contingency graph for your spread position.

References

Carlton, D. "Futures Markets: Their Purpose, Their History, Their Growth, Their Successes and Failures." *Journal of Futures Markets* 4 (Fall 1984): 237–71.

Chiang, R., G. Gay, and R. Kolb. "Commodity Exchange Seat Prices." *Review of Future Markets* 6 (1987): 1–12.

Chiang, T. "The Forward Rate as a Predictor of the Future Spot Rate—A Stochastic Coefficient Approach." *Journal of Money, Credit, and Banking* (May 1988): 212–32.

Doukas J., and A. Rahman. "Unit Root Tests: Evidence from the Foreign Exchange Futures Market." *Journal of Financial and Quantitative Analysis* 22 (March 1987): 101–108.

Easterbrook, F. "Monopoly, Manipulation, and the Regulation of Futures Markets." *Journal of Business* 59 (1986): 103–127.

Edwards, F. "The Clearing Association in Futures Markets: Guarantor and Regulator." *Journal of Futures Markets* 3 (Winter 1983): 369–92.

Eun C., and B. Resnick. "Exchange Rate Uncertainty, Forward Contracts, and International Portfolio Selection." *Journal of Finance* (March 1988): 197–215.

Fischel, D. "Regulatory Conflict and Entry Regulation of New Futures Contracts." *Journal of Business* 59 (1986): 85–102.

Fishe R., and L. Goldberg. "The Effects of Margins on Trading in Futures Markets." *Journal of Futures Markets* 6 (Summer 1986): 261–71.

Grossman, S. "An Analysis of the Role of "Insider Trading" on Futures Markets." *Journal of Business* 59 (1986): 129–46.

Kolb, R., G. Gay, and J. Jordan. "Futures Prices and Expected Future Spot Prices." *Review of Futures Markets* 2 (1983): 110–23.

Hartzmark, M. "The Effects of Changing Margin Levels on Futures Market Activity, the Composition of Traders in the Market and Price Performance." *Journal of Business* 59 (1986): 147–80.

Hill, J., and T. Schneeweis. "The Hedging Effectiveness of Foreign Currency Futures." *Journal of Financial Research* 5 (Spring 1982): 95–104.

Kahl, K., R. Rutz, and J. Sinquefield. "The Economics of Performance Margins in Futures Markets." *Journal of Futures Markets* 5 (Spring 1985): 103–112.

Kane, E. "Market Incompleteness and Divergences between Forward and Futures Interest Rates." *Journal of Finance* 35 (May 1980): 221–34.

Levich, R. "Currency Forecasters Lose Their Way." *Euromoney* (August 1983): 140–47.

Maldonado R., and A. Saunders. "Foreign Exchange Futures and the Law of One Price." *Financial Management* 12 (Spring 1983): 19–23.

Silber, W. "Marketmaker Behavior in an Auction Market: An Analysis of Scalpers in Futures Markets." *Journal of Finance* (December 1984): 937–53.

Thomas, L. "A Winning Strategy for Currency-Futures Speculation." *Journal of Portfolio Management* (Fall 1985): 65–69.

Appendix 12.A

THE MINIMUM VARIANCE HEDGE RATIO FOR FOREIGN EXCHANGE

The objective of hedging often is to obtain the lowest level of risk. Define the profit from a short currency hedge as

12.A.1
$$\pi = \Delta S + \Delta F N_F,$$

where π is profit, ΔS is the change in the spot exchange rate, ΔF is the change in the forward/futures price, and N_F = the number of forward/futures contracts.

The variance of the profit is

12.A.2
$$\sigma^2_\pi = \sigma^2_{\Delta S} + \sigma^2_{\Delta F} N^2_F + 2\sigma_{\Delta S \Delta F} N_F,$$

where σ^2_π is the variance of the hedged profit, $\sigma^2_{\Delta S}$ is the variance of the change in the spot rate, $\sigma^2_{\Delta F}$ is the variance of the change in the forward/futures rate, and $\sigma_{\Delta S \Delta F}$ is the covariance of the change in the spot rate and the change in the forward/futures rate.

Our objective is to determine N_F such that σ^2_π is minimized. Differentiating σ^2_π with respect to N_F gives

12.A.3
$$\partial \sigma^2_\pi / \partial N_F = 2\sigma^2_{\Delta F} N_F + 2\sigma_{\Delta S \Delta F}.$$

Setting eq. 12.A.3 equal to zero and solving for N_F gives

12.A.4
$$N_F = -\sigma_{\Delta S \Delta F}/\sigma^2_{\Delta F}.$$

A check of the second derivative confirms that this is a minimum. The negative sign implies that the hedger should sell currency forward/futures. The sign would have been positive if we formulated the problem as a long currency hedge.

The effectiveness of the minimum variance hedge is determined by examining the amount of exchange rate risk reduced. Define h as the percentage of unhedged risk that the short currency hedge eliminates:

12.A.5
$$h = (\sigma^2_{\Delta S} - \sigma^2_\pi)/\sigma^2_{\Delta S}.$$

Substituting eq. 12.A.2 and 12.A.4 into 12.A.5 yields.

12.A.6
$$h = (N^2_F \sigma^2_{\Delta F})/\sigma^2_{\Delta S}.$$

Equation 12.A.6 is the coefficient of determination from a regression relating currency forward/futures prices and currency spot rates. If the coefficient of determination is one, indicating perfect positive correlation between spot and forward/futures rates, then, from eq. 12.A.5, $\sigma^2_\pi = 0$; and from eq. 12.A.4, $N_F = -1$ since $\sigma_{\Delta S \Delta F} = \sigma^2_{\Delta F}$. Thus, the minimum variance hedge ratio is simply -1 ($+1$ for a long currency hedge) if spot and forward/futures rates are perfectly positively correlated. This can be confirmed by using eq. 12.A.2 and recognizing that $\sigma^2_{\Delta S} = \sigma^2_{\Delta F}$ when $h = 1$.

It can also be shown that $\sigma^2_{\Delta S} = \sigma^2_{\Delta F}$ if interest rates are constant. Suppose that the instantaneous spot rate change relative is given by the following standard Itô process:

12.A.7 $d\tilde{S} = \mu S dt + \sigma S d\tilde{Z},$

where μ is the expected instantaneous spot rate change relative and $d\tilde{Z}$ is a standard Wiener process increment. Also, let the forward/futures rate by given by the interest rate parity theorem:

12.A.8 $F = Se^{(r-r_f)(T-t)},$

where the U.S. (r) and foreign (r_f) rates of interest are assumed constant. From Itô's lemma:

12.A.9
$$d\tilde{F} = [(\partial F/\partial S)\mu S + (\partial F/\partial t) + (1/2)(\partial^2 F/\partial S^2)\sigma^2 S^2]dt + (\partial F/\partial S)\sigma S d\tilde{Z},$$

where $\partial F/\partial S = e^{(r-r_f)(T-t)}$, $\partial F/\partial t = -(r-r_f)Se^{(r-r_f)(T-t)}$, and $\partial^2 F/\partial S^2 = 0$. Substituting for the partial derivatives yields

12.A.10
$$\begin{aligned} d\tilde{F} &= [e^{(r-r_f)(T-t)}\mu S - (r-r_f)Se^{(r-r_f)(T-t)}]dt + e^{(r-r_f)(T-t)}\sigma S d\tilde{Z} \\ &= (\mu - r + r_f)Fdt + \sigma F d\tilde{Z}. \end{aligned}$$

Thus, the instantaneous volatilities of currency spot and forward/futures price changes are equal under constant rates of interest (compare eqs. 12.A.7 and 12.A.10). Under the notation used in deriving the minimum variance hedge ratio, $\sigma^2_{\Delta S} = \sigma^2_{\Delta F}$. Finally, notice that the instantaneous drifts of spot and forward/futures rates differ by $r - r_f$. This result occurs since the spot and forward/futures rates converge at contract maturity.

The preceding proof demonstrates that $\sigma^2_{\Delta S} = \sigma^2_{\Delta F}$ if interest rates are constant. Thus, it must be that $N_F = \pm 1$ when interest rates are constant and the interest rate parity theorem holds continuously. However, in reality interest rates are nonconstant, implying that currency spot and forward/futures rates may not be perfectly positively correlated and, thus, the minimum variance hedge ratio may not be ± 1.

Empirically, we investigate the correlation structure between spot and forward/futures rates by regressing spot currency returns onto contemporaneous "returns" (percentage changes) on nearby futures contracts. The analysis uses closing prices for the first trading day of each week for futures contracts on British pounds, Deutsche marks, and Japanese yen traded on the IMM between January 1981 and June 1988. Spot exchange rates are obtained from 3:00 P.M. Eastern time quotes by Bankers Trust Company. The sample is divided into two subsets. The first, January 1981 through May 1985, reflects a strong U.S. dollar period; the second, June 1985 through June 1988, reflects a weak U.S. dollar period.

The correlation coefficients for each currency for both periods are reported in the following table. In all cases the correlation between returns on spot and futures, ρ_{SF}, is large, suggesting that a hedge ratio of

±1 is a reasonable ratio to employ in order to minimize return variance attributable to exchange rate fluctuations.

Correlation Coefficients (ρ_{SF})		
Currency	Strong Dollar	Weak Dollar
British pound	0.94	0.98
Deutsche mark	0.96	0.98
Japanese yen	0.98	0.91

CURRENCY FORWARD AND FUTURES PRICING AND EVIDENCE

Currency forward and futures markets are similar in many respects. As a consequence, close relations must hold between prices in the two markets in order to prevent arbitrage. Differences in prices may arise, however, particularly because of the different cash flow patterns exhibited by currency forward and futures contracts. In this chapter we analyze currency forward and futures pricing. Specifically, we present a discussion of how interest rate parity (IRP) represents the currency market's version of the standard carrying charge model of forward and futures prices. We then discuss how currency forward and futures prices may differ. This discussion focuses on expectations of subsequent spot rates of exchange under various assumptions regarding investor risk preferences and the nature of interest rates. Finally, a body of empirical evidence concerning these contracts is summarized.

PRICE VERSUS VALUE

It is important to distinguish between price and value when dealing with currency forward and futures contracts. The forward or futures price is the exchange rate at which the contract parties agree to trade the underlying currency in the future. As such, it simply represents an observable figure on a contract. It is not the contract value. In general, the contract value is determined by unanticipated changes in the currency's spot rate, which in turn cause subsequent changes in forward and futures prices.

In this chapter we are vitally concerned with the process of determining prices. That is, we are concerned with how market participants go about determining the exchange rate at which they agree to trade currency in the future. However, it is now useful to make some statements about contract value.

Contract Value at Inception

The value of a currency forward or futures contract is zero at the contract's inception. This follows from the fact that neither party to the contract pays or receives anything of monetary value. The long position (the buyer) does not pay for the contract, and the short position (the seller) does not receive any money for the contract. Indeed, with a forward contract no cash flow occurs until contract expiration, and the futures margin represents only a performance bond, not a contract "payment." Provided that the forward or futures price does not change, neither party can profit. Thus, the contract generates value only when prices subsequently change, and has no value when the contract is initially written.

Forward Contract Value at Expiration

At expiration, the forward contract calls for immediate delivery of the underlying currency. Thus, the forward price at contract expiration must be equal to the prevailing spot exchange rate, ignoring delivery costs. Since no cash flow has occurred before expiration, the value of the forward contract at expiration must equal the spot rate at expiration minus the original forward price.

Forward Contract Value Before Expiration

Assuming that no default risk exists, the value of a currency forward contract before expiration is the difference between the new forward price and the original forward price, discounted at the domestic risk-free rate of interest over the remaining time to contract expiration. To illustrate this principle, assume that you buy a forward contract today with a forward price of $1.00 per unit of foreign currency. This contract expires in six months. Now suppose that in four months there exist new forward contracts expiring at the same time (in two months) that are written at a forward price of $1.05. Assuming that the risk-free rate is 8%, the value of your forward contract is $0.04934:

$$\$0.04934 = (\$1.05 - \$1.00)e^{(2/12)(-0.08)}.$$

This value follows from arbitrage restrictions. When both forward contracts expire in two months, you can buy the underlying currency for $1.00 (per unit) with the first contract and sell it for $1.05 with the second contract. Your proceeds are $0.05. Since no default risk is assumed to exist, and the forward prices are known, these proceeds are discounted at the domestic risk-free rate to yield a present value of $0.04934. Any other contract value would result in riskless profit, ignoring market frictions.

Futures Contract Value

As noted previously, the value of a currency futures contract is zero at contract inception. However, the contract value is also zero each time the contract is marked to the market. Suppose that you buy a British pound futures contract. Its current value is zero. By later in the trading session, however, the futures price has increased. At that point you can profit by selling the contract (a reversing trade). The contract has value. Once the trading session is over, however, the contract is marked to the market and any proceeds are credited to your margin account. Thus, the contract's value reverts to zero.

THE CARRYING CHARGE MODEL

The *carrying charge model* posits that any forward or futures price must equal the current spot price plus the costs of carrying the spot asset forward to the delivery date. An arbitrage trading strategy, known generally as *cash and carry arbitrage*, ensures this pricing relation.

Carrying an asset forward in time incurs three costs:

- *Storage costs.* These include the costs of warehousing and insuring the asset in question.
- *Transportation costs.* These are the costs of delivering the asset.
- *Financing costs.* These are the costs of financing the asset. Most financial futures traders pay the repo rate when financing the asset.[1]

Let C represent the sum of the these costs, expressed as a percentage of the spot price. By arbitrage, the forward or future price, F, must be less than or equal to the spot price of the asset, S, plus the carrying charges needed to carry the spot asset forward to delivery:

13.1
$$F \le Se^{CT},$$

where T is the maturity of the forward or futures contract expressed as a fraction of a year. If $F \le Se^{CT}$, representing a violation, an arbitrageur can profit by undertaking the following cash-and-carry trading strategy:

Buy S	$-\$S$
Sell (short) the forward/futures contract	0
Carry the asset forward for T	$-S(e^{CT}-1)$
Deliver the asset against the contract	$+F$
Proceeds	$\$F - Se^{CT} > 0.$

The arbitrageur's proceeds are positive, representing a certain profit if transaction costs are ignored. This profit is guaranteed by the sale of the forward or futures contract. Also, there is no investment because the funds needed to undertake the trading strategy were borrowed and the cost of using these funds was incorporated in C. As arbitrageurs conduct

---

[1] The *repo rate* is the interest rate on repurchase agreements, which are agreements to sell assets at a specified time and to repurchase them at a specified price at a later time, often just one day later. Typically, the repo rate is slightly higher than the rate on short-term U.S. Treasury bills.

these trades, the values S and F (and, potentially, C) will be altered until the violation no longer exists.

A similar arbitrage argument ensures that F must be greater than or equal to S plus the necessary carrying charges:

13.2 $$F \geq Se^{CT}.$$

If $F < Se^{CT}$, representing a violation, an arbitrageur can profit by undertaking the following trading strategy, known as a *reverse cash and carry*:

Sell S short	$+\$S$
Invest the proceeds for T	$+S(e^{CT}-1)$
Buy (long) the forward/futures contract	0
Take delivery and reverse the short position	$-F$
Proceeds	$\$Se^{CT} - F > 0$

The arbitrageur's proceeds are positive, representing a certain profit if transaction costs and restrictions on short selling are ignored. The profit is guaranteed by the purchase of the forward or futures contract. These arbitrage trades will alter S and F (and, potentially, C) until the violation no longer exists.

By combining eqs. 13.1 and 13.2, we have the following equality:

13.3 $$F = Se^{CT}.$$

Equation 13.3, which is the carrying charge model of forward and futures prices, states that the forward or futures price must equal the spot price plus the costs of carrying the spot asset forward to the delivery date of the contract.

Interest Rate Parity and the Carrying Charge Model

Interest rate parity (IRP) is a special case of the general carrying charge model. To understand this principle fully, it is useful to classify underlying assets as either physical assets, which are agricultural or metallurgical, or financial assets, such as currency or Treasury securities. There are important differences in storage and transportation costs across these assets. Consequently, there are important differences in carrying charges applicable to physical and financial assets.

With regard to storage costs, there are obvious differences for physical and financial assets. For physical assets, such as wheat or corn, warehousing is necessary and costly. Financial assets are warehoused as well (typically with depository banks), but the costs of warehousing financial securities are nominal. Also, many financial assets generate cash flows while held in storage. Treasury securities pay interest, stocks pay dividends, and currency can be used to purchase interest-bearing foreign assets. Hence, financial assets often exhibit a negative cost of storage, which may result in an overall negative cost of carry.

There are also important differences between physical and financial assets with respect to transportation costs. For instance, it may be costly to ship corn from Iowa to Chicago, but it costs almost nothing to transfer foreign exchange by wire to settle a currency forward or futures contract.

Let SC, TC, and FC represent the costs, expressed as a percentage of the spot asset price, of storage, transportation, and financing, respectively:

13.4 $$C = SC + TC + FC.$$

For currency, SC is the negative of the foreign rate of interest, r_f. The cost of warehousing currency is, for all intents and purposes, zero, and the currency can be invested in foreign interest-bearing assets. Currency therefore exhibits a negative cost of storage. TC is zero for currency since, again, it is nearly costless to transfer foreign exchange by wire to settle the contract. Finally, let $FC = r$, the U.S. rate of interest applicable to finance the purchase of the foreign exchange. For currency we therefore have

13.5 $$C = -r_f + 0 + r = r - r_f.$$

Substituting eq. 13.5 into the carrying charge model, eq. 13.3, yields the IRP formula:

13.6a $$F = Se^{(r-r_f)T}.$$

Therefore, IRP is a special case of the carrying charge theory of forward and futures prices. IRP represents the currency market's version of the standard cost-of-carry pricing model. Covered interest arbitrage is merely a unique arbitrage trading strategy that ensures that eq. 13.6a holds in well-functioning markets. Covered interest arbitrage is the currency market's version of the standard cash-and-carry strategy. If a currency sells at a future discount ($F < S$), it exhibits an overall negative cost of carry ($r < r_f$), while a premium currency ($F > S$) exhibits an overall positive cost of carry ($r > r_f$).

Transaction Costs and Restrictions on Short Selling

Transaction costs and restrictions imposed on short selling prevent arbitrage from working perfectly and therefore complicate the carrying charge theory of forward and futures prices. A broker can retain up to 50% of the proceeds from a short sale to help insure against default risk by the short seller. If we define TC^* as the dollar transaction costs to arbitrage, and p as the fraction of usable proceeds derived from a short sale, then the IRP formula becomes

13.6b $$pSe^{(r-r_f)T} - TC^* \leq F \leq Se^{(r-r_f)T} + TC^*.$$

Thus, a range of currency forward or futures prices exists within which arbitrage is profitless because of transaction costs and restrictions on short selling. Figure 13.1 portrays this range.[2]

---

[2] Transaction costs and restrictions on short-sale proceeds are very small for large institutional traders. We can expect these traders to ensure that eq. 13.6a holds closely.

Figure 13.1

Interest Rate Parity with
Transaction Costs and Restrictions
on Short Selling

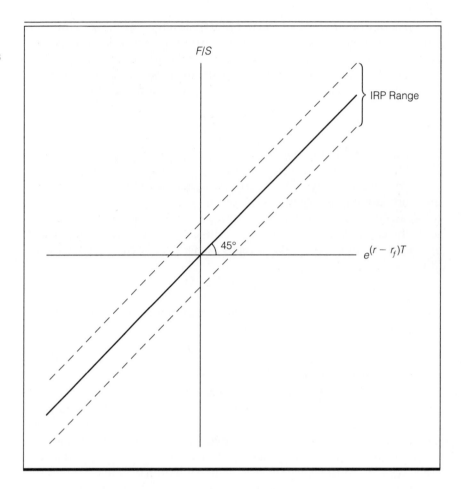

Also due to these market imperfections, the currency forward or futures price may only approximately equal the expected future spot exchange rate. A discrepancy between the contract price and expected future spot rate may arise because of these frictions. For instance, suppose the expected spot rate at contract maturity is \$1.7000/£ while the observed futures price is currently \$1.7002/£. Arbitrageurs may not attempt to profit from this small discrepancy because of the transaction costs involved.

CURRENCY FORWARD AND FUTURES PRICES

The IRP theorem implies that currency forward and futures prices are equal if interest rates are constant and investors are risk-neutral. These assumptions were implicit in the preceding analysis. However, forward and futures prices for foreign exchange can differ because of nonconstant interest rates and risk aversion on the part of market participants. Also for these reasons, both forward and futures prices may differ from the expected future spot exchange rate at contract delivery. In this section we analyze pricing when interest rates change intertemporally and investors are risk-averse. This analysis, which is based largely on the works of Cox, Ingersoll, and Ross (1981) and Richard and Sundaresan (1981), stresses the role of market expectations in determining prices.

Forward Prices under Risk Neutrality

Suppose we are considering buying a foreign currency in T years. Also suppose that the current yield to maturity on U.S. riskless bonds is $_TY_0$, if these bonds exhibit a maturity of T years. Further, suppose that we purchase $(1 + {_TY_0})^T$ forward contracts today, where each contract obligates us to buy one unit of the foreign exchange at the forward price. Additionally, we buy $\$_TF_0$ of riskless U.S. bonds with T years to maturity, where $_TF_0$ is the currency forward price. Our initial investment is therefore $\$_TF_0$, since the forward price is set so that the initial value of the forward contract is zero.

In T years the forward contracts expire and their value is

13.7
$$\$(1 + {_TY_0})^T(\tilde{S}_T - {_TF_0}),$$

where $\tilde{S}_T$ is the exchange rate at contract delivery, which is currently unknown. The payoff from the bond investment is

13.8
$$\$_TF_0(1 + {_TY_0})^T.$$

Combining eqs. 13.7 and 13.8 gives the total proceeds from the investment:

13.9
$$\$(1 + {_TY_0})^T(\tilde{S}_T - {_TF_0}) + {_TF_0}(1 + {_TY_0})^T = \$(1 + {_TY_0})^T\tilde{S}_T.$$

Thus we invest $\$_TF_0$ and receive $\$(1 + {_TY_0})^T\tilde{S}_T$. It must therefore be true that the current forward price is equal to the present value of $(1 + {_TY_0})^T\tilde{S}_T$.

To determine this present value, we discount the expected proceeds of the investment: $E[(1 + {_TY_0})^T\tilde{S}_T]$. We can discount at the domestic risk-free rate of interest if investors are risk-neutral. Since $E[(1 + {_TY_0})^T\tilde{S}_T] = (1 + {_TY_0})^T E(\tilde{S}_T)$, the present value is

13.10
$$\frac{(1 + {_TY_0})^T E(\tilde{S}_T)}{(1 + {_TY_0})^T} = E(\tilde{S}_T) = {_TF_0}.$$

Hence, the currency forward price is equal to the expected spot exchange rate at contract delivery if investors are risk-neutral. Under this assumption, the forward price is an unbiased predictor of $\tilde{S}_T$.

Currency Futures Prices under Risk Neutrality

For currency futures we must adjust our trading strategy to reflect the daily marking to the market procedure. We now purchase one-day bonds and futures contracts, reinvesting the cash flows at the end of each trading day into new one-day bonds and purchasing futures contracts as they unwind. Specifically, at the beginning of the initial trading day, we buy an amount of bonds equal to the current futures price $_TF^*_0$. We then purchase $(1 + {_1Y_0})$ futures contracts, where $_1Y_0$ is the yield to maturity on a current one-day riskless bond. At the end of the day the proceeds from the bond investment will be

13.11 $$\$_T F^*_0 (1 + {}_1 Y_0).$$

The amount credited (or debited) to our futures margin account will be

13.12 $$\$(1 + {}_1 Y_0)({}_{T-1}\tilde{F}^*_1 - {}_T F^*_0).$$

Combining eqs. 13.11 and 13.12 gives our total proceeds from the one-day investment:

13.13 $\$_T F^*_0 (1 + {}_1 Y_0) + (1 + {}_1 Y_0)({}_{T-1}\tilde{F}^*_1 - {}_T F^*_0) = \$(1 + {}_1 Y_0){}_{T-1}\tilde{F}^*_1.$

In turn, these proceeds are reinvested in one-day bonds at the new (but currently unknown) rate of ${}_1 \tilde{Y}_1$. We also buy more futures contracts; namely, we buy $(1 + {}_1 Y_0)(1 + {}_1 \tilde{Y}_1)$ contracts. Thus, our proceeds at the end of the second day are

13.14 $\$(1 + {}_1 Y_0){}_{T-1}\tilde{F}^*_1 (1 + {}_1 \tilde{Y}_1) + (1 + {}_1 Y_0)(1 + {}_1 \tilde{Y}_1)({}_{T-2}\tilde{F}^*_2 - {}_{T-1}\tilde{F}^*_1)$

$$= \$(1 + {}_1 Y_0)(1 + {}_1 \tilde{Y}_1){}_{T-2}\tilde{F}^*_2.$$

Continuing the process (and recognizing the pattern emerging from payoffs in eqs. 13.13 and 13.14), at any day t the proceeds from our investment strategy will be

13.15 $$\$(1 + {}_1 Y_0)(1 + {}_1 \tilde{Y}_1)(1 + {}_1 \tilde{Y}_2) \ldots (1 + {}_1 \tilde{Y}_t){}_{T-t}\tilde{F}^*_t.$$

Finally, since at contract delivery the futures price must equal the prevailing exchange rate, $\tilde{S}_T$, we have proceeds at delivery equal to

13.16 $$\$(1 + {}_1 Y_0)(1 + {}_1 \tilde{Y}_1)(1 + {}_1 \tilde{Y}_2) \ldots (1 + {}_1 \tilde{Y}_T)\tilde{S}_T.$$

Thus we invest $\$_T F^*_0$ and receive $\$\tilde{R}\tilde{S}_T$, where $\tilde{R}$ is the product of 1 plus the one-day interest rates through delivery:

13.17 $$\tilde{R} = (1 + {}_1 Y_0)(1 + {}_1 \tilde{Y}_1)(1 + {}_1 \tilde{Y}_2) \ldots (1 + {}_1 \tilde{Y}_T).$$

It must therefore be true that the current futures price is equal to the present value of $\tilde{R}\tilde{S}_T$.

To determine this present value, we discount the expected proceeds of the investment: $E(\tilde{R}\tilde{S}_T)$. We can discount at the domestic risk-free rate if investors are risk-neutral:

13.18 $$_T F^*_0 = \frac{E(\tilde{R}\tilde{S}_T)}{(1 + {}_T Y_0)^T}.$$

Since no liquidity premiums exist in the term structure under risk neutrality, $(1 + {}_T Y_0)^T = E(\tilde{R})$. Thus, we have:[3]

---

[3] Equation 13.19 follows from the mathematical identity: $E(AB) = E(A)E(B) + COV(A,B)$. Specifically:

$$_T F^*_0 = \frac{E(\tilde{R}\tilde{S}_T)}{(1 + {}_T Y_0)^T} = \frac{E(\tilde{R})E(\tilde{S}_T) + COV(\tilde{R},\tilde{S}_T)}{(1 + {}_T Y_0)^T}$$

$$= \frac{(1 + {}_T Y_0)^T E(\tilde{S}_T) + COV(\tilde{R},\tilde{S}_T)}{(1 + {}_T Y_0)^T}$$

$$= E(\tilde{S}_T) + \frac{COV(\tilde{R},\tilde{S}_T)}{(1 + {}_T Y_0)^T}.$$

13.19
$$_T F^*_0 = E(\tilde{S}_T) + \frac{COV(\tilde{R}, \tilde{S}_T)}{(1 + _T Y_0)^T}.$$

Equation 13.19 states that under risk neutrality, the currency futures price is a biased estimate of the expected spot exchange rate at delivery and, thus, is also not equal to the currency forward price. There exists an additional term that depends on the covariance between $\tilde{R}$, the product of one-day interest rates, and $\tilde{S}_T$, the rate of exchange.

This additional term is called the *reinvestment rate premium,* and it drives a wedge between the current forward and futures prices. It arises because of the different cash flow patterns exhibited by currency forward and futures contracts. This additional term also derives from the nonconstant nature of interest rates. If rates, and thus yields, were constant, then the covariance term in eq. 13.19 would be zero, since $\tilde{R}$ would no longer be random. Thus we can conclude that currency forward and futures prices differ under risk neutrality because of (1) the daily resettlement procedure that exists in the futures market, and (2) the nonconstant nature of interest rates.

The Economics Underlying the Reinvestment Rate Premium   To understand why the reinvestment rate premium occurs, suppose you are long a DM futures contract. If the U.S. interest rate falls and the $/DM rate rises (negative covariance), then you can reinvest your day's margin credit only in a lower-interest-bearing U.S. asset. In a sense, your gain from the long DM futures position is somewhat offset by the lower reinvestment rate experienced. This offset would not occur in the DM forward market, because no cash flows occur until contract delivery. Thus, you will demand a futures price that is below the forward price (the expected future spot rate) to compensate for your reinvestment loss. Conversely, under positive covariance you are willing to accept a higher futures price since any daily gains on the futures contract can be reinvested at a higher rate of interest.

Whether the covariance term $COV(\tilde{R}, \tilde{S}_T)$ is positive or negative for currencies is somewhat vague, and constitutes an empirical issue. For instance, one can argue that the covariance term is negative in the short run. As U.S. interest rates rise, Germans will purchase dollars in order to buy higher-yielding U.S. securities. Such purchases will tend to drive up the dollar's value, lowering the $/DM exchange rate. On the other hand, higher U.S. interest rates can cause a dollar depreciation in the longer run. Higher rates presumably reflect greater expected U.S. inflation, and more expensive U.S. goods and services will lower the foreign demand for dollars.[4]

Currency Forward Prices under Risk Aversion

Recall the original investment strategy for determining currency forward prices under risk neutrality. If market participants are now risk-averse, we cannot determine currency forward prices by discounting expected

---

[4] See Chapters 2 through 4 for a discussion of the various determinants of exchange rates.

payoffs at the riskless rate of interest. Instead, we must account for the risk associated with the initial investment.

In equilibrium, the market value of the investment now must be such that the foregone utility associated with the investment is equal to the expected utility gained from the payoff:

13.20
$$U_0[_TF_0] = \sum_{i=1}^{n} h_i\{\tilde{U}_{T,i}[(1 + {}_TY_0)^T\tilde{S}_{T,i}]\}.$$

In eq. 13.20, the term $U_0[_TF_0]$ represents the total utility lost by making the investment. U_0 denotes the utility associated with each dollar increase in our current consumption. Multiplying U_0 by our initial outlay, $_TF_0$, gives us the total loss in our current utility associated with making the investment. The term $\tilde{U}_{T,i}$ denotes the utility associated with increasing our consumption by a dollar in the ith state of nature at contract delivery T. This utility is currently unknown, since the investment's payoff is currently uncertain. Given n possible states of nature, the right-hand side of eq. 13.20 yields the expected increase in utility from the investment.

Dividing both sides of eq. 13.20 by U_0 and taking expectations yields

13.21
$$_TF_0 = (1 + {}_1Y_0)^T E(\tilde{M}_{T,i}\tilde{S}_{T,i}),$$

where $M_{T,i} = \tilde{U}_{T,i}/U_0$. The term $\tilde{M}_{T,i}$ is the *marginal rate of substitution* of consumption at delivery T for current consumption. For instance, if $\tilde{M}_{T,i} = 0.70$, then we would be indifferent between $1.00 of consumption at T in state i and $0.70 of consumption now.

Applying the mathematical identity previously described in footnote 3 to eq. 13.21 gives

13.22
$$_TF_0 = (1 + {}_TY_0)^T[E(\tilde{M}_T)E(\tilde{S}_T) + COV(\tilde{M}_T,\tilde{S}_T)].$$

$E(\tilde{M}_T)$ is the expected marginal rate of substitution over all n states of nature. Intuitively, it is the expected value for the implicit rate of discount relating consumption now to future consumption at delivery T. Thus:

13.23
$$E(\tilde{M}_T) = [(1 + {}_TY_0)^T]^{-1}.$$

Substituting eq. 13.23 into 13.22 gives the following result:

13.24
$$_TF_0 = E(\tilde{S}_T) + (1 + {}_TY_0)^T COV(\tilde{M}_T,\tilde{S}_T).$$

Equation 13.24 states that under risk aversion, the currency forward price is equal to the expected future spot exchange rate at contract delivery plus a *hedging premium*, also known as a *risk premium*, that is a function of $COV(\tilde{M}_T,\tilde{S}_T)$, the covariance between the marginal rate of substitution and the exchange rate at delivery. The forward price is no longer an unbiased estimate of $\tilde{S}_T$. Under risk neutrality, investors have linear utility functions and, thus, constant marginal rates of substitution. Consequently, the covariance term $COV(\tilde{M}_T,\tilde{S}_T)$ would be zero, and eq. 13.24 reduces to eq. 13.10. Again, under risk neutrality the

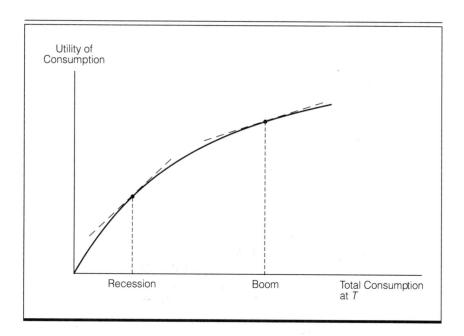

Figure 13.2

A Utility Function for a Representative Risk-Averse Investor

currency forward price is equal to the spot exchange rate expected to prevail at contract delivery.

The Economics Underlying the Hedging Premium A representative utility function for a risk-averse investor is shown in Figure 13.2. As consumption increases, utility increases at a decreasing rate (a positive first derivative and negative second derivative). Also, the marginal rate of substitution (and the marginal utility of consumption) is greater when consumption is low (a recessionary state of nature) than when consumption is high (a boom state). This condition occurs if the level of consumption is greater in booms, which is likely. The marginal utilities are given by the slopes of the utility function at different levels of consumption.

If you are long the currency forward contract and the covariance term $COV(\tilde{M}_T, \tilde{S}_T)$ is positive, then the contract is more likely to yield positive payoffs when the marginal rate of substitution is high, as in a recessionary state. Thus, the payoff on the forward contract is negatively correlated with the payoffs on your other investments from which you draw wealth for consumption. The forward contract represents insurance. You are consequently willing to enter into the contract at a forward price that is greater than your expected spot exchange rate at contract delivery. When this situation occurs (covariance is positive and the forward rate is greater than $E(\tilde{S}_T)$), we have what is known as *contango*. If $COV(\tilde{M}_T, \tilde{S}_T) < 0$, then we have what is known as *normal backwardation* $(_TF_0 < E(\tilde{S}_T))$.

Whether the covariance term $COV(\tilde{M}_T, \tilde{S}_T)$ is positive or negative for currencies is somewhat vague, and represents an empirical issue. Also, the magnitude of the covariance term largely depends on an investor's overall portfolio from which wealth is drawn for consumption.

Currency Futures Prices under Risk Aversion

Recall the original investment strategy for determining currency futures prices under risk neutrality. If market participants are risk-averse, then the futures price is likely to change (in much the same way that the currency forward price changed under risk aversion).

If we apply the expected utility argument used previously, the expected value of the investment strategy now is

13.25 $$_T F^*_0 = E(\tilde{M}_T \tilde{R} \tilde{S}_T).$$

By applying our mathematical identity that the expected value of a product is equal to the product of the expected values plus their covariances, we have

13.25 $_T F^*_0 = E(\tilde{M}_T)[E(\tilde{R})E(\tilde{S}_T) + COV(\tilde{R}, \tilde{S}_T)] + COV(\tilde{M}_T, \tilde{R}\tilde{S}_T).$

Using eq. 13.23 gives

13.27 $_T F^*_0 = E(\tilde{S}_T)\left[\dfrac{E(\tilde{R})}{(1 + {}_T Y_0)^T}\right] + \dfrac{COV(\tilde{R}, \tilde{S}_T)}{(1 + {}_T Y_0)^T} + COV(\tilde{M}_T, \tilde{R}\tilde{S}_T).$

Equation 13.27 states that the current futures price, $_T F^*_0$, differs from the expected spot exchange rate at contract delivery because of three premia. The first premium, $E(\tilde{R})/(1 + {}_T Y_0)^T$, represents a term premium, which is constant across all currencies. It arises from the existence of liquidity premia in the term structure when investors are risk-averse. There is a reduction in the average maturity (duration) of the cash flows associated with the process of marking to the market. The second premium, $COV(\tilde{R}, \tilde{S}_T)/(1 + {}_T Y_0)^T$, represents a reinvestment rate premium associated with daily resettlement and nonconstant rates of interest. It is the same premium that occurs in eq. 13.19. The third premium, $COV(\tilde{M}_T, \tilde{R}\tilde{S}_T)$, is a hedging or risk premium that derives from the relation between the futures payoff and an investor's marginal rate of substitution. It is analogous to the premium appearing in eq. 13.24 for currency forward prices under risk aversion.

Again, the signs and magnitudes of these premia represent an empirical issue. Also, the last two premia in eq. 13.27 may be nonconstant over time.

The Impact of the Premia   Equation 13.27 yields the currency futures price under the conditions that investors are risk-averse and interest rates are nonconstant. These are very realistic conditions. As a result of these conditions, currency forward and futures prices differ, and the futures price differs from the expected future spot rate because of three premia. The magnitudes and signs of these premia are vague, and two of these premia are likely to be nonstationary.

The impact of these premia on international investment and international financial management is threefold. First, the futures price cannot be used blindly as an indicator of the market's expected future spot exchange rate. It is a biased estimate. Second, the expected return on a futures contract may be negative. If the contract has a tendency to reduce risk, then a hedging premium will be commanded in the marketplace. And third, multinational corporations that employ currency futures should not necessarily anticipate a share price appreciation from

Regression Estimates of the Unbiased Forward Rate Hypothesis

Equation 13.10 can be expressed in regression form as

$$ln(S_t^j) = \alpha + \beta ln(F_{t-1}^j) + \varepsilon_t^j,$$

where S_t^j is the spot rate for currency j at time t, F_{t-1}^j is the forward rate for currency j at time $t - 1$, α and β are time-invariant parameters, and ε_t^j is an error term. Under the assumption that the forward rate is an unbiased predictor of the subsequent spot exchange rate, $\alpha = 0$, $\beta = 1$, and ε_t^j is white noise. Failure to reject this joint hypothesis implies that F_{t-1}^j contains all the relevant information for the prediction of S_t^j.

The preceding regression is estimated using monthly exchange rate data over the floating rate period January 1974 to August 1983. All data are end-of-period values from Data Resources, Inc. for the Canadian dollar, French franc, deutsche mark, and British pound. Both spot and forward rates are expressed as U.S. dollar prices per unit of foreign currency, and 30-day forward rates are used to avoid the potential serial correlation involved with overlapping data.

The results of the regression analysis follow. The method of estimation is ordinary least squares, although similar results are obtained when using Zellner's seemingly unrelated regression technique. The high R^2 values suggest that all equations perform very well. With the exception of the constant term (α) for the mark, neither the individual hypotheses that $\alpha = 0$ and that $\beta = 1$ nor the joint hypothesis that $\alpha = 0$ and $\beta = 1$ can be rejected

at the 5% significance level. The Durbin-Watson (D.W.) statistics indicate the absence of first-order correlation.

These results generally support the unbiased hypothesis of the forward foreign exchange market, at least for the in-sample fit. The results do not necessarily imply that a hedging premium does not exist. However, they do suggest that any such premium is likely to be very small.

	Estimated Coefficients				
Currencies	α	β	R^2	$F(2,113)$[b]	D.W.
Canadian dollar	−0.002 (0.002)[a]	0.989 (0.015)	0.97	0.455	2.133
French franc	0.006 (0.028)	1.005 (0.017)	0.97	0.168	2.054
Deutsche mark	−0.037 (0.018)	0.958 (0.022)	0.94	2.289	1.976
British pound	0.005 (0.014)	0.990 (0.021)	0.95	0.245	1.761

a. The numbers in parenthesis are standard errors.
b. $F(2,113)$ is for testing the joint hypothesis that $\alpha = 0$ and $\beta = 1$. The critical value for $F(2,113)$ is 3.09 at the 5% significance level.

hedging. If the currency futures contract indeed reduces the riskiness of the MNC's stock, hedging will result in a commensurate cost that reduces the stock's expected return such that market value is unchanged. This condition occurs if markets are integrated and risk is priced uniformly across all market participants.

EMPIRICAL EVIDENCE

The preceding analysis implies that (1) currency forward and futures prices may differ from the expected future spot rate, and (2) currency forward and futures prices may differ from one another. These results in turn imply that currency forward and futures contracts may offer different degrees of hedging effectiveness. We now summarize a body of empirical evidence that addresses these issues.

Forward and Futures as Predictors of the Future Spot Rates

Equation 13.10 implies that the forward rate is an unbiased predictor of the actual future spot exchange rate under risk neutrality. The conventional test of this unbiased forward rate hypothesis uses a regression estimation by fitting the current spot rate on the one-period lagged forward rate. This test involves the joint hypothesis that the constant term does not differ from zero, that the coefficient on the one-period lagged forward rate does not differ from one, and that the error term is free of serial correlation. Empirical work by Edwards (1982; 1983), Kohlhagen (1975), Longworth (1981), and Cornell (1977) supports this unbiased forward rate hypothesis, suggesting that the hedging premium in eq. 13.24 is nonexistent. Since a similar hedging premium applies to currency futures (see eq. 13.27), these empirical studies also imply that the futures hedging premium is nonexistent.

More recent tests conducted by Hansen and Hodrick (1980), Fama (1984), and Chiang (1986) show that the previous evidence supporting the unbiased forward rate hypothesis is weak. These authors employ more sophisticated econometric analyses and demonstrate the existence of a nonconstant hedging premium present in several major foreign exchange markets. However, it appears that the magnitude of this premium is very small, implying that its modelling and incorporation into forecasts will result in nominal gains in predictive accuracy.

Euromoney recently conducted an examination of the accuracy of professional exchange rate forecasting services vis-à-vis the simple forward rate. Exhibit 13.1 reports the results of this examination. If the hedging premium is large and behaves systematically, such professional forecasters should be able to incorporate the premium and generate predictions superior to the simple forward rate. However, only five of the 16 services surveyed exhibited an average forecast error smaller than the forward rate forecast. Also, the best professional forecast outperformed the forward rate by just one percentage point over the sample period.

Differences between Forward and Futures Prices

Cornell and Reinganum (1981) and Park and Chen (1985) examined the pricing of foreign exchange forward and futures contracts, reporting no statistical or economic evidence of pricing differences between the two types of contracts. Also, Kohers and Simpson (1987) tested the relative forecasting accuracy of currency forward versus futures contracts for five major trading currencies. They reported that forecast errors were statistically significantly different but had little economic significance. This finding also implies that currency forward and futures prices are very similar.

The similarity of currency forward and futures prices implies that the term premium and the reinvestment rate premium in eq. 13.27 are nominal (or, perhaps, tend to cancel each other).

Hedging Effectiveness of Forward and Futures

Hill and Schneeweis (1982; 1984) compared the hedging effectiveness of 90-day and 180-day forward contracts with the hedging effectiveness of corresponding futures contracts and reported no distinguishable differences when employing weekly data. Swanson and Caples (1987) investi-

	$/JY	$/CD	$/£	$/DM	Average Error
1. Berkely Consulting Group	7.4	1.2	15.1	29.1	13.2
2. European American Bank/Forex Research	3.5	1.2	17.2	31.2	13.2
3. Henley Centre/Manufacturers Hanover	7.4	6.0	11.5	28.3	13.3
4. Economic Models	8.3	4.5	14.1	28.7	13.9
5. Amex Bank	5.2	1.2	19.3	30.0	13.9
6. BI Metrics	—	1.2	10.9	32.9	15.0
7. Brown Brothers Harriman	9.6	4.5	16.7	30.4	15.3
8. Chemical Bank	7.4	6.0	18.3	31.2	15.7
9. Predex	12.3	3.6	18.3	29.1	15.8
10. Citibank	12.7	8.0	14.1	29.1	15.8
11. ContiCurrency	9.6	8.0	17.8	30.0	16.3
12. Phillips and Drew	12.7	8.0	17.8	29.1	16.9
13. Marine Midland	16.2	4.5	19.3	29.1	17.2
14. Data Resources	22.0	6.0	18.8	29.5	19.0
15. Harris Bank	12.3	8.0	25.6	33.3	19.8
16. Security Pacific	13.2	4.5	29.8	32.9	20.1
Forward rate:	4.0	6.0	18.8	28.3	14.2

Exhibit 13.1.

Percentage Forecasting Errors for 16 Exchange Rate Forecasting Services and the 30-Day Forward Rate

SOURCE: *Euromoney*, August 1981, p. 45. Euromoney Publications PLC.

gated minimum-risk hedge ratios and the hedging effectiveness of forward and futures contracts using daily data for the British pound and the Deutsche mark. The authors found that optimal hedge ratios and hedging effectiveness were again similar for the two contracts.

SUMMARY

Currency forward and futures prices are obtained from two related approaches. First, these prices arise from an application of the carrying charge theory of forward and futures prices. Interest rate parity (IRP) represents the currency market's version of the more general carrying charge model. Second, currency forward and futures prices arise from expectations concerning actual future spot exchange rates. For instance, the currency forward price represents an unbiased estimator of the actual future spot rate when investors are indifferent toward risk.

Since currency forward and futures markets are similar, close relations must be obtained between forward and futures prices. Differences arise because of the daily resettlement feature observed in the futures market and because of the nonconstant nature of rates of interest.

Under risk aversion, the forward rate differs from the expected spot rate because of a hedging premium. Under risk neutrality, the futures prices differs from the forward price and, thus, expected future spot rate, because of a reinvestment rate premium associated with daily resettlement. Under risk aversion, the futures price deviates from the expected spot rate by three premia, a constant term premium, a time-variant reinvestment premium, and a time-variant hedging premium.

Most empirical studies find that these premia are small. Currency forward and futures prices are very similar, as are the effectiveness of hedging strategies based on the two contracts. Also, currency forward and futures prices exhibit similar predictive accuracy and, in general, alternative forecasting techniques do not offer superior fit. Finally, the modelling and quantifying of the premia are confounded by the existence of market frictions such as transaction costs and restrictions on short selling.

Questions and Problems

1. Explain how the interest rate parity formula is a special case of the carrying charge theory of forward and futures prices.

2. Derive eq. 13.27 from eq. 13.25.

3. Under what conditions does eq. 13.27 collapse to eq. 13.10? Explain your answer.

4. Suppose that the covariance between the marginal rate of substitution and the exchange rate at delivery is negative. What is the current forward rate relative to the expected spot rate at delivery if investors are risk-averse?

5. What would be the relation between currency forward and futures prices if investors were risk-averse but interest rates were constant?

6. Describe three premia that result in differences between the expected future spot rate and the currency futures price.

7. If investors were risk-neutral and interest rates were constant, could forward and futures prices differ from expected future spot rates at contract delivery? How?

8. Cornell and Reinganum (1981) and Park and Chen (1985) find that currency forward and futures prices are very similar. What does this finding imply about the term premium and reinvestment rate premium in eq. 13.27?

9. How do marginal utilities of consumption differ under risk neutrality and risk aversion?

10. What are the assumptions that underlie the interest rate parity theorem?

11. Explain how covered interest arbitrage represents the currency market's version of the general cash-and-carry strategy.

12. Define normal backwardation and contango in the currency market.

13. What is the value of a currency futures contract at contract inception?

14. What is the value of a currency forward contract before expiration?

15. Define the repo rate.

References

Agmon, T., and Y. Amihud. "The Forward Exchange Rate and the Prediction of the Future Spot Rate." *Journal of Banking and Finance* (September 1981): 425–37.

Chiang, T. "On the Predictors of the Future Spot Rates—A Multi-Currency Analysis." *Financial Review* (February 1986): 69–83.

———. "The Forward Rate as a Predictor of the Future Spot Rate—A Stochastic Coefficient Approach." *Journal of Money, Credit, and Banking* (May 1988): 212–32.

Cornell, B. "Spot Rates, Forward Rates and Exchange Market Efficiency." *Journal of Financial Economics* (August 1977): 55–65.

Cornell, B., and M. Reinganum. "Forward and Futures Prices: Evidence from the Foreign Exchange Markets." *Journal of Finance* (December 1981): 1035–45.

Cox, J., J. Ingersoll, and S. Ross. "The Relation Between Forward and Futures Prices." *Journal of Financial Economics* (December 1981): 321–46.

Edwards, S. "Exchange Rates and 'News': A Multi-Currency Approach." *Journal of International Money and Finance* (December 1982): 211–14.

———. "Foreign Exchange Rates, Expectations and New Information." *Journal of Monetary Economics* (May 1983): 321–26.

Eun, C., and B. Resnick. "Exchange Rate Uncertainty, Forward Contracts, and International Portfolio Selection." *Journal of Finance* (March 1988): 197–215.

Fama, E. "Forward and Spot Exchange Rates." *Journal of Monetary Economics* (November 1984): 319–38.

Grammatikos, T. "Intervalling Effects of the Hedging Performance of Foreign Currency Futures." *Financial Review* (February 1986): 21–36.

Grammatikos, T., and A. Saunders. "Stability and the Hedging Performance of Foreign Currency Futures." *Journal of Futures Markets* (Fall 1983): 295–305.

Hansen, L., and R. Hodrick. "Forward Exchange Rates as Optimal Predictors of Future Spot Rates: An Econometric Analysis." *Journal of Political Economy* (October 1980): 829–53.

Hill, J., and T. Schneeweis. "The Hedging Effectiveness of Foreign Currency Futures." *Journal of Financial Research* (Spring 1982): 95–104.

———. "Reducing Volatility with Financial Futures." *Financial Analysts Journal* (November/December 1984): 34–40.

Hodrick, R., and S. Srivastava. "An Investigation of Risk and Return in Forward Foreign Exchange." *Journal of International Money and Finance* (December 1984): 5–29.

Huang, R. "An Analysis of Intertemporal Pricing for Forward Foreign Exchange Contracts." *Journal of Finance* (March 1989): 183–94.

Kohers, T., and W. Simpson. "A Comparison of the Forecast Accuracy of the Futures and Forward Markets for Foreign Exchange." *Applied Economics* (July 1987): 961–67.

Kohlhagen, S. "The Performance of Foreign Exchange Markets: 1971–1974." *Journal of International Business Studies* (Fall 1975): 33–39.

———. "The Forward Rate as an Unbiased Predictor of the Future Spot Rate." *Columbia Journal of World Business* (Winter 1979): 77–85.

Longworth, D. "Testing the Efficiency of the Canadian-U.S. Exchange Market Under the Assumption of No Risk Premium." *Journal of Finance* (March 1981): 43–49.

Panton, D., and M. Joy. "Empirical Evidence on International Monetary Market Currency Futures." *Journal of International Business Studies* (Fall 1978): 59–68.

Papadia, F. "Forward Exchange Rates as Predictors of Future Spot Rates and the Efficiency of the Foreign Exchange Market." *Journal of Banking and Finance* (June 1981): 217–40.

Park, H., and A. Chen. "Differences Between Futures and Forward Prices: A Further Investigation of the Marking-to-Market Effects." *Journal of Futures Markets* (Spring 1985): 77–88.

Richard, S., and M. Sundaresan. "A Continuous Time Equilibrium Model of Forward Prices and Futures Prices in a Multigood Economy." *Journal of Financial Economics* (December 1981): 347–71.

Stein, J., M. Rzepcznski, and R. Selvaggio. "A Theoretical Explanation of the Empirical Studies of Futures Markets in Foreign Exchange and Financial Instruments." *Financial Review* (February 1983): 1–32.

Swanson, P., and S. Caples. "Hedging Foreign Exchange Risk Using Forward Foreign Exchange Markets: An Extension." *Journal of International Business Studies* (Spring 1987): 75–82.

14

CURRENCY OPTION MARKETS

The *buyer* of an option on foreign exchange has the right, but not the obligation, to purchase or sell a specified currency at a specified rate of exchange on or before a specified expiration date. The specified rate of exchange is the option's *exercise price*, and the specified expiration date represents the option's *maturity*. If the option buyer has the right to purchase the underlying currency, then the buyer holds a *call* option. For example, the buyer may have the right to purchase (call) 62,500 Swiss francs, at $0.64/SF1, in three months. Alternatively, if the buyer can sell the currency at the prescribed exercise price, then he is said to own a currency *put* option. For instance, the buyer may have the right to sell (put) 31,250 British pounds, at $1.75/£1, in six months. Of course, whether the option buyer exercises his right is contingent on the rate of exchange at (or before) option expiration. Thus, options often are called *contingent claims*.

The option buyer can call (put) the foreign exchange from (onto) the currency option *writer*. The writer has contracted to sell (buy) the underlying currency, at the exercise price, to (from) the option buyer. The writer charges a premium for offering the option. Determining this premium is the subject of Chapter 15.

The option contract may be *European* or *American*. A European currency option can be exercised only at expiration, whereas an American option can be exercised prematurely. It may be in the buyer's interest to exercise a currency option before its maturity. Thus, an American currency option typically commands a greater price than a similar European currency option. This price difference, known as the *early exercise premium*, is analyzed in Chapter 15.

In this chapter we describe the various currency option markets: the listed currency option market, the interbank currency option market, the market for futures-style currency options, and the currency futures option market. We also examine how these derivative securities can be employed to hedge exchange exposure, to speculate on currency forecasts, and for price discovery.

THE LISTED CURRENCY OPTION MARKET

Beginning in December 1982, the Philadelphia Stock Exchange (PHLX) began the trading of listed American currency options on the British pound. Today the PHLX offers American options trading on seven foreign currencies: the Australian dollar (AD), British pound (BP), Canadian dollar (CD), deutsche mark (DM), French franc (FF), Japanese yen (JY), and Swiss franc (SF). The PHLX also provides side-by-side trading of European options on these seven currencies. The PHLX began side-by-side trading of European currency options on 27 August 1987, when the Chicago Board Options Exchange (CBOE) turned its currency option operations over the PHLX. Before this date the CBOE listed European currency options, but volume and open interest were low. Over the 487 days during which European currency options were traded on the CBOE, 825,870 contracts were executed. This number compares with 22,566,852 American contracts traded on the PHLX during this same period. The PHLX also currently trades options on the European Currency Unit, but trading volume for ECU options has been negligible.

Listed currency options are standardized contracts that are cleared and guaranteed by the Options Clearing Corporation (OCC). When a currency option trade is initiated, the OCC acts as a dealer creating two distinct contracts: one currency option between the buyer and the OCC acting as a writer, and one option between the writer and the OCC acting as the buyer. The OCC guarantees both sides of the contract. This procedure allows the buyer to close a position by simply selling the currency options held. The writer can buy into a previous position. The difficulty and costs of finding someone willing to assume an existing, specific contract are therefore minimized. Also, should the buyer decide to exercise the currency option, the OCC randomly selects a writer to accept exercise. The OCC charges a fee for facilitating trade. Currency option *market makers* at the PHLX pay a fee of $0.05 per contract.

The currency option writer represents a source of credit risk to the OCC. For instance, the writer of a put option may not have sufficient funds to purchase the underlying currency should the put be exercised. To cover this risk, the OCC requires the writer to post margin, typically a cash margin. The OCC requires that a currency option writer maintain a cash margin equal to the current market price of the option plus a percentage of the underlying currency's value. This percentage changes as the option's price varies.

Exhibit 14.1 presents the contract specifications for the currency options traded on the PHLX. Contracts exhibit different (but standardized) sizes, exercise price intervals, and the like. If an option is exercised then traders must deposit currency to OCC bank accounts.

Executing Trades

To illustrate the execution of a listed currency option trade, presume a client places a *market order* to purchase a CD call option with exercise price $0.825 and December expiration. The process begins with a phone call to the client's broker, who is a member of the PHLX. The broker

Exhibit 14.1

Contract Specification for
PHLX-Traded Currency Options[a]

Currency	Symbols[b]	Exercise Price Intervals	Underlying Units	Premium Quotations
Australian dollar	CAD XAD	$0.0100	50,000	Cents per unit
British pound	CBP XBP	$0.0250	31,250	Cents per unit
Canadian dollar	CCD XCD	$0.0100	50,000	Cents per unit
Deutsche mark	CDM XDM	$0.0100	62,500	Cents per unit
French franc	CFF XFF	$0.0050	125,000	Tenths of a cent per unit
Japanese yen	CJY XJY	$0.0010	6,250,000	Hundredths of a cent per unit
Swiss franc	CSF XSF	$0.0100	62,500	Cents per unit
ECU	ECU	$0.0200	62,500	Cents per unit

Notes: a. For all contracts: (1) Expiration months are March, June, September, and December, plus two additional near-term months. (2) The expiration date is the Saturday before the third Wednesday of the expiration months. (3) The expiration settlement date is the third Wednesday of the month. (4) The margin for an uncovered writer is the option premium plus 4% of the underlying contract value less out-of-the-money amount, if any, to a minimum of the option premium plus ¾% of the underlying contract value, which equals the spot price times the number of units per contract. (5) The position limit is 50,000 contracts. (6) The delivery method requires the call buyer (seller) to deliver dollars (foreign currency) to an OCC domestic (foreign) bank account; the opposite is true for puts.

b. C is for European options; X is for American options. Only American ECU options are traded.

then places the order by booking and clocking the order and relaying it electronically to the broker's booth on the exchange floor. The broker's floor trader then shouts a bid of, say, $0.01. The floor trader's bid is then countered by offers to sell from other traders. These counteroffers may be $0.0150, $0.0140, and $0.0120. The floor trader takes the lowest offer, $0.0120, implying a contract price of $600.00 ($0.0120 × 50,000 Canadian dollars per contract).

Next the two traders match tickets, confirming the trade in pencil on slips of paper. The buying trader hands these slips of paper to the specialist, who quickly checks them and passes them to an exchange employee, who then enters the trade information into the PHLX's computerized reporting system. This information is flashed onto the trading floor screens and private wire service screens. The floor traders monitor these screens throughout the trading day. The time from the price agreement (trade) to the time the information is flashed is less than 90 seconds. Finally, the floor trader wires confirmation of the trade back to the broker, who then notifies the client as to the trade completion and price. The entire execution process typically takes place in a few minutes.

The offers ($0.0150, $0.0140, $0.0120) may have come from market makers, other floor brokers, or specialists. As their titles implies, market makers exist to ensure trading. They are member firms who trade for their own account, and who must make a bid or offer on a client's order if the specialist orders them to do so. Thus market makers may trade when it is not in their interest. For this, market makers enjoy reduced margins and transaction costs. Specialists exist to maintain order on the floor and to manage *limit orders,* which are client orders to execute trades only when prices hit certain levels. The specialist coordinates these limit orders.

Option Quotes

Exhibit 14.2 illustrates quotations for PHLX-traded currency options. Reported are the closing prices of various currency options, categorized by exercise price and expiration, for trading on Tuesday, 28 June 1988. Also reported are the closing interbank spot exchange rates, as well as daily trading volume and open interest. For example, the closing (2:30 P.M. eastern time) $/£ exchange rate for June 28 was $1.7150/£1. Call option volume for the day was 16,431 contracts. *Call open interest* (the total number of currency calls outstanding) was 484,335 contracts.

To understand the exhibit, consider the first price entry for British pounds. This is 3.30. This means that the last traded call option for pounds, with exercise price $1.7000 and July expiration, had a price of 3.30 cents ($0.0330) per pound. Since there are £31,250 per contract, this option contract had a price of $1,031.25 ($0.0330 × 31,250). Currency options at the PHLX expire on the Saturday before the third Wednesday of the contract month (here July). Thus, this American option expired on 16 July 1988. Finally, it is important to note that this last traded option may have traded well before closing. Indeed, the surveillance department of the PHLX reported that this option traded at 1:49 P.M. The other prices reported in Exhibit 14.2 are similarly interpreted.

Market Growth

The volume of listed currency options trading has grown tremendously since 1983. Figure 14.1, on page 270, portrays this growth. For the period 1983 to 1988, annual volume has increased more than 25-fold. As Figure 14.2, on page 270, illustrates, the most liquid contracts are those on the DM and JY, which together account for over 60% of total volume. On one recent record-setting day (15 July 1987), the PHLX traded nearly 114,000 contracts representing $4.5 billion in underlying value. On that day alone, when the U.S. trade deficit figures were released and the July options were one day from expiration, 65,216 JY put options were traded.

Growth in currency options trading is also exemplified by the recent advent of evening and early morning trading sessions at the PHLX. On 16 September 1987 the PHLX initiated an evening trading session (6:00 to 10:00 P.M.) to accommodate market participants in Asian-Pacific time zones. On 29 January 1989, the PHLX extended its morning trading session, pushing the new opening time back to 4:30 A.M. to accommodate market participants in Western European time zones. With these ex-

Exhibit 14.2
Currency Option Quotes

FOREIGN CURRENCY OPTIONS

Tuesday, June 28, 1988

Philadelphia Exchange

Option & Underlying	Strike Price	Calls—Last			Puts—Last		
		Jul	Aug	Sep	Jul	Aug	Sep
50,000 Australian Dollars-cents per unit.							
ADollr	...78	r	r	2.77	r	r	r
80.69	...79	r	r	1.83	r	0.95	r
80.69	...80	0.95	r	1.53	0.83	r	r
80.69	...81	0.43	r	1.15	r	r	r
80.69	...82	0.32	r	0.85	r	r	r
80.69	...83	0.24	r	0.80	r	r	r
80.69	...84	r	0.20	r	r	r	r
80.69	...85	r	r	0.43	r	r	r
50,000 Australian Dollars-European Style.							
80.69	...80	1.30	r	0.41	r	r	r
12,500 British Pounds-cents per unit.							
BPound	165	s	s	s	s	s	1.30
171.50	.170	3.30	s	4.40	1.05	1.85	3.00
171.50	172½	1.55	2.50	2.85	2.42	s	3.90
171.50	.175	s	s	1.84	s	s	5.65
171.50	177½	s	s	1.20	s	s	7.06
171.50	.180	s	s	s	s	8.35	9.45
12,500 British Pounds-European Style.							
171.50	172½	s	2.35	s	s	s	s
50,000 Canadian Dollars-cents per unit.							
CDollr	...81	1.67	s	s	s	s	s
82.84	.81½	s	s	0.06	s	s	s
82.84	...82	0.98	s	0.21	s	s	s
82.84	.82½	0.59	0.76	s	s	s	s
82.84	...83	0.32	0.52	s	s	s	s
82.84	.83½	s	0.33	s	s	s	s
50,000 Canadian Dollars-European Style.							
CDollar	...81	s	s	1.97	s	s	s
82.84	.81½	s	s	s	s	0.17	s
82.84	...84	s	0.14	s	s	s	s
62,500 West German Marks-cents per unit.							
DMark	.. 50	s	s	s	s	s	0.04
55.08	...51	s	s	s	s	s	0.07
55.08	...52	s	s	s	s	s	0.11
55.08	...53	s	s	s	s	s	0.26
55.08	...54	s	s	s	s	0.24	0.36
55.08	...55	0.67	1.00	s	0.42	0.72	0.88
55.08	...56	0.25	0.65	0.84	1.02	s	1.20
55.08	...57	0.10	0.28	0.54	1.71	1.55	1.84
55.08	...58	0.04	s	s	2.58	s	s
55.08	...59	s	s	0.19	3.86	s	3.40
55.08	...60	s	s	0.08	s	s	s
55.08	...63	s	s	0.04	s	s	s
62,500 West German Marks-European Style.							
55.08	...56	s	s	0.90	s	s	s
55.08	...59	s	s	s	s	s	3.36
6,250,000 Japanese Yen-100ths of a cent per unit.							
JYen	... 72	s	s	s	s	s	0.10
75.91	...73	s	s	s	s	s	0.19
75.91	...74	s	s	s	s	s	0.25
75.91	...75	s	s	0.19	s	0.34	0.43
75.91	...76	0.84	s	1.82	0.53	0.56	0.96
75.91	...77	0.30	0.56	1.00	s	1.08	1.25
75.91	...78	0.14	0.35	0.70	s	s	2.18
75.91	..79	0.07	s	0.38	2.94	s	2.60
75.91	.. 80	s	0.10	0.25	3.70	3.80	4.00
75.91	...81	s	s	s	4.31	s	s
62,500 Swiss Francs-cents per unit.							
SFranc	..65	s	s	s	0.19	s	0.54
66.67	...66	s	s	s	s	0.54	0.75
66.67	...67	s	s	1.47	0.56	0.84	1.21
66.67	...68	0.28	0.63	s	1.13	1.35	s
66.67	...69	0.13	0.41	s	1.95	1.93	s
66.67	...70	0.05	0.25	s	s	s	s
66.67	...71	s	s	0.30	s	s	3.98

Total call vol. 16,431 Call open int. 484,335
Total put vol. 29,015 Put open int. 459,896
r—Not traded. s—No option offered.
Last is premium (purchase price).

Figure 14.1

Annual Trading Volume for
Currency Options

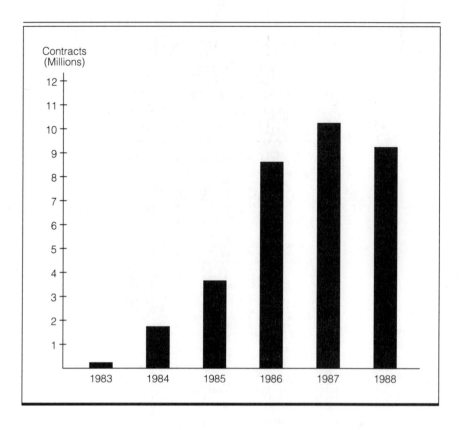

Figure 14.2   Relative Currency Option Volume and Open Interest

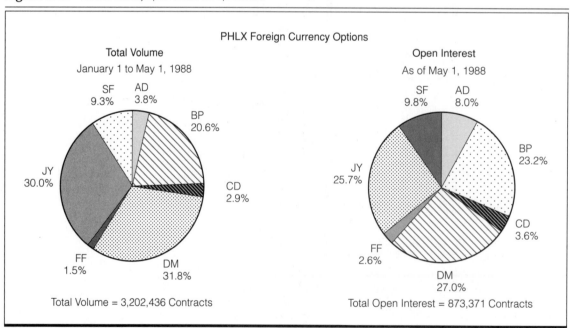

SOURCE: *FX Exchange,* The Philadelphia Stock Exchange, Vol. 4, No. 2 (May 20, 1988).

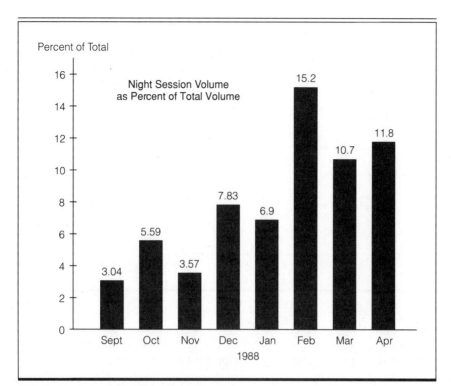

SOURCE: *FX Exchange*, The Philadelphia Stock Exchange, Vol. 4, No. 2 (May 20, 1988).

Figure 14.3
Currency Option Evening Session Volume

tended sessions, the PHLX now trades currency options 14 hours each trading day. Figure 14.3 portrays evening session volume as a percentage of total volume for a recent time period.

THE INTERBANK CURRENCY OPTION MARKETS

A sizeable interbank market for European currency options presently exists. This market, centered in London and New York, exhibits open interest that is about 20-fold that of PHLX-listed currency options. Over-the-counter currency options traded on the interbank market differ substantially from listed currency options, including:

- Over-the-counter options are usually much larger, typically involving $1,000,000 or more of foreign currency.
- Over-the-counter options are European, whereas most listed-options trading involves American currency options.
- Over-the-counter options are available for a wider variety of foreign currencies, including many South American currencies.
- Over-the-counter options are tailored to the specific needs of the client; since these options are tailor-made, little secondary trading occurs.

Figure 14.4
Payoff Graph for a Bounded Payoff
Put

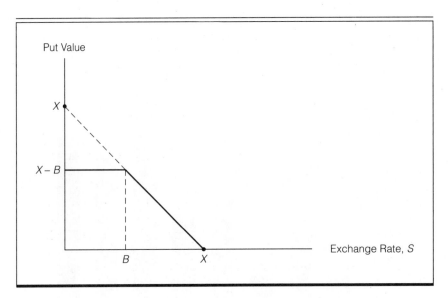

Commercial banks, investment banks, and brokerages write over-the-counter options for clients, often multinational firms. To offset their exposure, these banks and brokerages often trade currency options listed on the PHLX. Also, many banks rely on currency option brokers, like Bierbaum-Martin and Exco International, to help manage exposure.

Some Unique Over-the-Counter Currency Options

These banks and brokerages create tailor-made currency options by trading standardized options and repackaging them to the client's specifications. For example, Citibank and Salomon Brothers both offer a popular instrument known as a range forward. A *range forward* contract is a combination of a purchased currency put and a written currency call such that a zero price results at contract inception. Here the U.S. exporter and bank agree on two exchange rates, S_1 and S_2, at inception. At contract maturity the bank purchases the currency at S_1 if the current spot rate is less than S_1, or at S_2 if the spot rate is greater than S_2. At any rate between S_1 and S_2, the currency is purchased at the prevailing spot rate. S_1 and S_2 can be set so that no money changes hands at contract inception.

Another example of a unique over-the-counter currency option is the *bounded payoff put*, which is a currency put option with a limit on the payoff. Figure 14.4 displays the payoff graph for a bounded payoff put. If at maturity the spot rate lies between the exercise price X and the limit B, the payoff is that of a regular put ($X - S$). If the spot rate lies below B, however, the payoff is bounded at $X - B$. Clearly this option should command a lower price than a corresponding ordinary currency put. The bounded payoff put may be attractive to a corporate treasurer who anticipates a modest decline in the exchange rate.

Other unique options are offered by banks and brokerages, including currency cylinder options, proportional coverage puts, and the like. Each of these unique instruments can be thought of as financially engineered, replicable by combinations of listed currency options.

FUTURES-STYLE CURRENCY OPTIONS

American *futures-style currency options* are presently traded on the London International Financial Futures Exchange (LIFFE). These options are unique in that both the option buyer and writer post margin representing a small fraction of the option's value, and each trading day the loser must post additional capital. In other words, the traders engage in a type of futures contract that is written on the currency option. Each day the contract is marked to the market. Cash flows occur daily, whereas the buyer of an ordinary currency option has no further cash flow until the option is sold or exercised. Unlike a mere futures contract, however, the buyer of a futures-style option can exercise the option. Thus, this unique instrument is part ordinary currency option and part futures contract. It conveys the same rights and obligations as an American currency option traded on the PHLX, but exhibits cash flows like a futures contract. The daily resettlement procedure allows players to engage in currency option trading while posting only a fraction of the contract's value.

THE CURRENCY FUTURES OPTION MARKET

The International Monetary Market (IMM) division of the Chicago Mercantile Exchange currently trades listed American options on currency futures contracts. The futures contracts are written on the BP, CD, DM, JY, and the SF.[1] Exhibit 14.3, on page 275, illustrates closing price quotations for these options for trading on Tuesday, 28 June 1988. The information reported is analogous to that reported in Exhibit 14.2 for PHLX-traded currency spot options. For instance, the closing price of a BP call futures contract, with exercise price $1.7000 and July expiration, was 1.70 cents ($0.0170) per pound on 28 June 1988. Since there are £62,500 per contract traded, this futures option exhibits a closing contract price of $1,062.50 ($0.0170 × 62,500).

Volume and open interest of currency futures options are similar to those of PHLX-traded spot options. Two reasons underlie the popularity of currency futures options. First, individuals who held memberships in the IMM division of the Chicago Mercantile Exchange, which entitled them to trade IMM-listed currency futures, could not easily trade cur-

---

[1]The IMM also trades options on AD futures, but volume is very low. Also, the LIFFE trades options on BP futures, but with little open interest. Finally, the Financial Instrument Exchange, a division of the New York Cotton Exchange, trades options on U.S. Dollar Index futures. Again, volume is negligible.

Creating Unique Currency Option Contracts

A range forward is created by the simultaneous purchasing of currency puts and the selling of currency calls with a higher exercise price. The net cost of the strategy is zero. The result is a floor, below which the foreign exchange is protected, and a ceiling, above which further gains are foregone, as shown in the following figure.

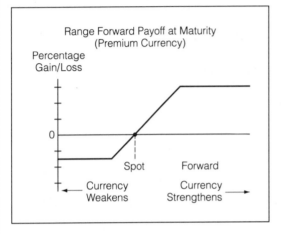

Between the floor and ceiling, returns depend on the level of the prevailing spot rate. Either the floor or the ceiling must be decided upon initially. The other is then determined by the exercise price of the currency option that offsets the cost (or revenue) from the first.

Many floor-ceiling combinations are possible by simply altering the exercise prices. For instance, the range forward strategy provides protection for the foreign currency holder but truncates all further gains after a certain point (the call options' exercise price). A modification can overcome this penalty if the currency should appreciate strongly.

Specifically, by lowering the ceiling somewhat (selling higher-priced calls with lower exercise prices) and using the proceeds to buy high exercise price calls, the return profile can be altered to appear as follows. This example is called a breakout pattern.

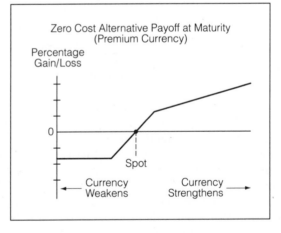

Another variation is to sell currency calls for which the exercise price equals the current spot rate. Since these options are more expensive, fewer need to be sold to cover the costs of the puts. The result is the following payoff pattern.

rency options on the PHLX. If they wished to trade options, they had to place orders through brokers who would execute trades on the PHLX. When options on currency futures were introduced in 1984, however, they gave currency futures traders the opportunity to trade both futures and options. At the IMM the trading pits for the options and underlying currency futures are adjacent. This arrangement facilitates the contemporaneous trading of the option and the underlying futures. Interest-

Exhibit 14.3

Currency Futures Option Quotes

– FINANCIAL –

BRITISH POUND (IMM) 62,500 pounds; cents per pound

Strike Price	Calls – Settle			Puts – Settle		
	Jly-c	Aug-c	Sep-c	Jly-p	Aug-p	Sep-p
1650	....	....	....	....	0.60	2.80
1675	...	....	....	0.32	1.10	3.76
1700	1.70	2.74	4.76	0.96	1.98	4.84
1725	0.62	1.58	3.74	2.34	3.30	6.24
1750	0.18	0.92	2.84	4.38	5.08	7.76
1775	0.06	0.54	2.10	6.78	7.14	9.48

Est. vol. 1,729, Mon vol. 2,785 calls, 792 puts
Open Interest Mon: 16,244 calls, 12,345 puts

W. GERMAN MARK (IMM) 125,000 marks; cents per mark

Strike Price	Calls – Settle			Puts – Settle		
	Jly-c	Aug-c	Sep-c	Jly-p	Aug-p	Sep-p
54	..	1.74	1.96	0.05	0.25	0.47
55	0.73	1.03	1.30	0.23	0.53	0.80
56	0.21	0.51	0.79	0.71	1.01	1.29
57	0.05	0.25	0.47	1.55	1.74	1.96
58	0.02	0.13	0.27	2.51	2.61	2.75
59	0.00	0.06	0.15	3.50	3.53	3.63

Est. vol. 14,788, Mon vol. 7,964 calls, 10,172 puts
Open Interest Mon; 72,684 calls, 61,259 puts

SWISS FRANC (IMM) 125,000 francs; cents per franc

Strike Price	Calls – Settle			Puts – Settle		
	Jly-c	Aug-c	Sep-c	Jly-p	Aug-p	Sep-p
65	....	2.47	....	0.04	0.24	0.47
66	....	...	1.98	0.11	0.45	0.74
67	0.64	1.05	1.38	0.40	0.81	1.14
68	0.23	0.61	0.93	0.98	1.36	1.67
69	0.07	0.34	0.61	1.80	2.07	2.33
70	0.02	0.18	0.39	2.77	2.92	3.11

Est. vol. 7,519, Mon vol. 5,250 calls, 5,445 puts
Open Interest Mon: 32,334 calls, 28,263 puts

JAPANESE YEN (IMM) 12,500,000 yen; cents per 100 yen

Strike Price	Calls – Settle			Puts – Settle		
	Jly-c	Aug-c	Sep-c	Jly-p	Aug-p	Sep-p
75	...	...	....	0.12	0.33	0.59
76	0.93	1.21	1.53	0.32	0.61	0.90
77	0.36	0.68	0.93	0.76	1.08	1.33
78	0.13	0.34	0.58	1.52	1.74	1.98
79	0.04	0.17	0.35	2.44	2.58	2.71
80	0.02	0.09	0.21	3.42	3.50	3.56

Est. vol. 20,240, Mon vol. 7,756 calls, 17,504 puts
Open Interest Mon; 55,374 calls, 73,022 puts

CANADIAN DOLLAR (IMM) 100,000 Can.$, cents per Can.$

Strike Price	Calls – Settle			Puts – Settle		
	Jly-c	Aug-c	Sep-c	Jly-p	Aug-p	Sep-p
815	1.11	1.23	1.44	0.04	0.18	0.38
820	0.68	0.87	1.13	0.12	0.32	0.54
825	0.35	0.58	0.84	0.28	0.53	0.76
830	0.14	....	0.62	0.58	....	1.02
835	0.06	0.21	0.44	....	....	....
840	....	....	0.30	....	....	....

Est. vol. 1,241, Mon vol. 765 calls, 440 puts
Open Interest Mon: 9,339 calls, 5,959 puts

ingly, the PHLX recently (1986) began the side-by-side trading of currency futures with its spot currency options.

Second, capital constraints for currency futures options are lower than those for spot options. To exercise an option on foreign exchange, the trader must have the entire cash value of the exercise price. However, to exercise an option on a currency futures contract the trader needs only the futures margin. When a put or call futures option is exercised, settlement is in a currency futures contract priced at the option's exercise price. This futures contract matures after the option. For example, an investor exercising a call receives a long position in the underlying currency futures contract. At the end of the day this contract is marked to the market, and the investor receives cash equal to the difference between the settlement price for the futures contract and the exercise price of the exercised option. The call writer is assigned a corresponding short position in the futures contract and pays the difference between the settlement and exercise prices.

HEDGING WITH CURRENCY OPTIONS

Firms with open positions in foreign exchange may employ currency options to hedge these positions from adverse exchange rate movements. For instance, suppose a U.S. firm orders British goods requiring it to send pounds to the British exporter on delivery. The U.S. importer could use BP call options. The option contracts specify the maximum exchange rate (the option's exercise price) the U.S. firm must pay to obtain the pounds. If the $/£ exchange rate remains below the exercise price, the U.S. firm can purchase the pounds at the lower prevailing spot rate. The options are allowed to expire. Should the spot rate increase (a dollar depreciation), however, the U.S. firm will exercise its options, purchasing the required pounds at the specified exercise price.

In the preceding example, the U.S. firm had offsetting positions in pounds and pound options. Specifically, it had a short position in pounds and a long position in the call option contracts. If the BP appreciated, the U.S. firm lost on its short position but gained on its long position in BP call options. Thus, we can say that the two positions were negatively correlated. Such negative correlation helps to reduce exchange exposure.

As another example, consider a firm that bids on a Swiss government project. If its bid is accepted, the firm will require approximately SF312,500 for purchasing Swiss materials. However, the firm presently does not know the bid's outcome, which will be revealed in six months. The firm can purchase five SF call option contracts, with six-month maturities, to hedge its potential exchange exposure. If the bid is accepted, the contracts will guard against a dollar depreciation over the period.

Currency put options also can be used to immunize foreign exchange positions. The following example illustrates how foreign exchange put options can be used to immunize a contingent international trade agreement against exchange rate risk.

Immunizing with Currency Puts

For domestic companies to be competitive in securing contracts for business overseas, it may be important for them to submit bids in the foreign currency. When the company submits bids in a foreign currency, however, it is exposed to fluctuations in foreign exchange markets before knowing whether the bid has been accepted. If the company hedges this exposure using forward or futures contracts and its bid is rejected, the company risks exchange rate losses that will not be offset, because no business follows. The use of currency options can prove to be an effective tool when international trade agreements are contingent, as in the submission of contract bids in the foreign currency.

For example, assume that a U.S. firm is preparing a bid in September for a contract in Germany that can be awarded anytime until December. To generate a profit on the contract, the U.S. firm must receive $10,000,000 after the German marks (DM) are converted to U.S. dollars. By using December DM put options, the U.S. company can create differ-

Exhibit 14.4
Contract Bids

A	B	C	D	E	F
		Effective Exchange Rate	Projected Bid in Marks	Number of Contracts	Premium B × $10,000,000 × 0.0125/Bias
Strike	Premium	(A) – (B)	$10,000,000/C	D/62,500	Point × E
$0.4900	$0.0158	$0.4742	DM21,088,148	338	$333,775.00
0.4800	0.0110	0.4690	21,321,961	342	235,125.00
0.4700	0.0073	0.4672	21,612,275	346	157,862.50

Notes: A = Strike price defined as $/mark
      B = Premium per put option contract
      C = Effective exchange rate in $/mark
      D = Bid in Deutsche marks (10,000,000/C)
      E = Number of option contracts (rounded)
      F = Total premium cost in dollars

ent bids, at different costs, that will protect its revenue target against unfavorable exchange rate fluctuations.

In September, the following price quotes are assumed to exist:

Exercise Prices	Prices, December DM Puts
$0.4900/DM	$0.0158/DM
0.4800/DM	0.0110/DM
0.4700/DM	0.0073/DM

The various bids can be determined by taking the exercise price and subtracting the option price per contract and then dividing this rate into the target revenue figure, $10,000,000. This calculation results in the bid for the project. The number of options contracts required to hedge the bid is obtained by dividing the bid by the number of currency units per option contract. The total cost of hedging is determined by multiplying the option price (per DM) by the value of the bid. Exhibit 14.4 presents the bids that are associated with the three exercise prices. These bids are DM21,088,148, DM21,321,961, and DM21,612,275.

In reviewing Exhibit 14.4, notice that the U.S. company's bid is inversely related to the exercise price; however, with each consecutively lower bid the company pays a higher total premium cost. This is because it costs more to obtain a higher exchange rate; that is, the more insurance the higher the premium. This premium must be paid up front in dollars and may not be recouped if the bid is rejected. If the bid is rejected, the firm may be able to recover some funds or even profit, however, depending on how the option price changes over time. Finally, the premium is recovered if the bid is accepted.

Exhibit 14.5 presents the revenue outcomes for three assumed spot rates at option expiration: $0.5100/DM, $0.4900/DM, and $0.4700/DM.

Exhibit 14.5

Revenue Outcomes At
Option Expiration

	1	2	3	4	5
	Futures Price = Spot Price	Final Options Value	Initial Options Value	Revenue if Bid is Rejected[a] (2) − (3)	Revenue if Bid is Accepted[a] DM Bid × (1) + (2) − (3)
Case 1					
Buy $0.4900 put	(A) $0.5100	$ 0	$333,775.00	$(0.334)	$10.421
Bid DM21,088,148	(B) 0.4900	0		(0.334)	9.999
Premium = $333,775.00	(C) 0.4700	422,500[b]		0.089	10.000
Case 2					
Buy $0.48000 put	(A) $0.5100	$ 0	$235,125.00	$(0.235)	$10.639
Bid DM21,321,961	(B) 0.4900	0		(0.235)	10.213
Premium = $235,125.00	(C) 0.4700	213,750		(0.021)	9.999
Case 3					
Buy $0.4700 put	(A) $0.5100	$ 0	$157,862.50	$(0.158)	$10.869
Bid DM21,622,275	(B) 0.4900	0		(0.158)	10.437
Premium = $157,862.50	(C) 0.4700	0		(0.158)	10.005

Notes: a. Rounded to millions
        b. For example, ($0.4900 − 0.4700) × DM62,500/option contract × 338 contracts

Buying the $0.4900 exercise-price put options represents the most conservative strategy. The U.S. firm buys more insurance than in the other two cases and can bid the lowest price (DM21,088,148). As a result, the company is most likely to bid successfully for the contract. If the company gets the contract, it faces the narrowest range of revenue outcomes: $10.421 million to $9.999 million. If the bid fails, the firm's revenue is simply the gain or loss on the puts: −$0.334 million to $0.089 million.

Buying the $0.4700 exercise-price put options represents the most aggressive strategy. The firm makes the highest bid (DM21,622,275) and is consequently less likely to win the contract. However, if the firm is awarded the contract and the dollar depreciates, net income is substantially greater ($10.869 million) than in the other two cases.

Ultimately, the choice of option depends on (1) management's forecast of exchange rate movements, and (2) management's appetite for the business. But whichever option is chosen, the U.S. firm protects its target revenue figure from exchange rate risk. Options, which are contingent claims, are useful immunization tools for any contingent trade agreements.

Futures versus Options

The preceding example utilizing DM puts demonstrates an important distinction between currency futures contracts and currency option contracts. Specifically, suppose that the U.S. firm naively entered into a DM

Figure 14.5   Contingency Graphs for Currency Spot Options

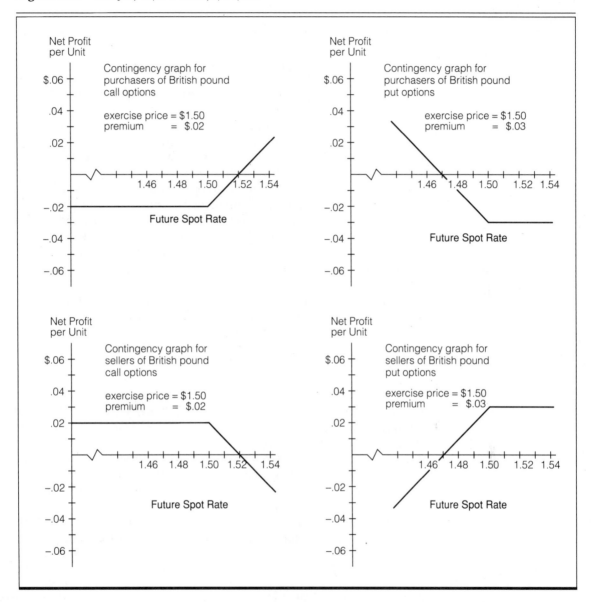

futures contract, with December expiration, to sell marks. If the firm lost the bid and the dollar depreciated greatly, then the firm would lose money on its short futures position. Since the firm does not receive marks, it effectively holds a naked futures position. Its potential losses are unlimited (in theory), since the mark could appreciate without bound. Instead, the employment of DM put options ensures a limited downside loss for the firm. For instance, if the aggressive strategy were undertaken and the firm's bid was rejected, its losses are at most $157,862.50, the initial premium. The options represent the superior hedging vehicle in this case, since the trade agreement itself is contingent on the resolution of the bidding process.

SPECULATING WITH CURRENCY OPTIONS

Although the primary reason for the existence of currency options is to help firms and investors immunize against exchange exposure, these options can be employed to speculate on exchange rate forecasts. For instance, a speculator who anticipates a large BP depreciation can purchase BP put options. Should the forecast be accurate, the put options can be exercised or sold for a profit.

Figure 14.5 presents the payoffs to option buyers and writers, ignoring transaction costs. These contingency graphs represent payoffs for European British pound options with an exercise price of $1.50/£1. The call option has a price of $0.02/£1, and the put option price is $0.03/£1. Similar contingency graphs can be created for other options.

The contingency graphs in Figure 14.5, on page 279, present the payoffs associated with various $/£ exchange rates at option expiration. In the graph at top left, the call buyer loses money (negative net profit) when the exchange rate at option expiration is less than $1.52/£1. At rates lower than $1.50/£1, the buyer does not exercise. Also notice that the call buyer's profit potential is, in theory, unlimited, since the pound can appreciate without bound.

In the graph at top right, the put buyer has positive net profit only when the exchange rate is less than $1.47/£1 at expiration. Here the buyer's net profit potential is limited to $1.47/£1, since the pound can depreciate to a zero value only. This buyer's loss potential is limited to the option price ($0.03/£1).

The two lower graphs in Figure 14.5 show the writer's payoffs. For the call option, the writer has a net profit when the future spot rate is less than $1.52/£1. Here the writer's net profit potential is $0.02/£1, and the net loss potential is unbounded. For the put option, the writer profits when the future spot rate is greater than $1.47/£1. The writer's liability is limited to $1.47/£1, which is the put buyer's net profit potential.

More Advanced Speculative Strategies

Currency options can be combined to create more advanced speculative strategies. One such combination is the *currency butterfly spread*. It is constructed by combining currency call options written on the same currency, with the same expiration, but with three different exercise prices. A speculator uses a butterfly spread when he feels that the range of future spot exchange rates is narrower than that implied by current option prices. In other words, the speculator uses this spread when he feels that the underlying currency's volatility is less than that perceived by the general marketplace.

Suppose the current $/FF exchange rate is $0.15/FF1. Let the investor undertake the following option combination:

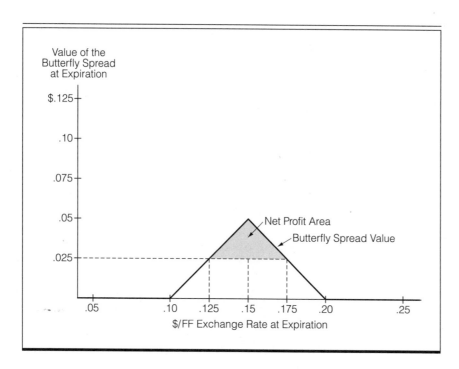

Figure 14.6
Contingency Graph for a Currency Butterfly Spread

	Price
Buy 1 call with exercise price $0.10:	−$0.052
Sell 2 calls with exercise price $0.15:	+$0.015 × 2
Buy 1 call with exercise price $0.20:	−$0.003
	−$0.025

The total cost of this combination is $0.025/FF.

Figure 14.6 portrays the value of the butterfly spread, at option expiration, for various $/FF exchange rates. If the exchange rate is less than $0.10/FF1 at expiration, then none of the call options is exercised and the value of the butterfly spread is zero. If the future spot rate is $0.20/FF1 or higher, then the value of the spread is also zero. Here the losses incurred from writing the two $0.15 exercise-price call options are exactly offset by the profits from the two purchased call options. For future spot rates between $0.10/FF1 and $0.20/FF1, the spread has positive value. The spread's maximum possible value is $0.05/FF1.

Notice that the butterfly spread strategy yields net profits whenever the future spot rate is close to the original spot rate, or $0.15/FF1. Consequently, the spread is profitable when the range of future spot rates is narrow. Here the investor exhibits positive net profit if the spot rate at option expiration lies between $0.125/FF1 and $0.175/FF1.

The *currency straddle* represents another currency option combination. It is constructed by combining an equal number of put and call options exhibiting the same underlying currency, exercise price, and maturity

Figure 14.7

Contingency Graph for a Currency Straddle

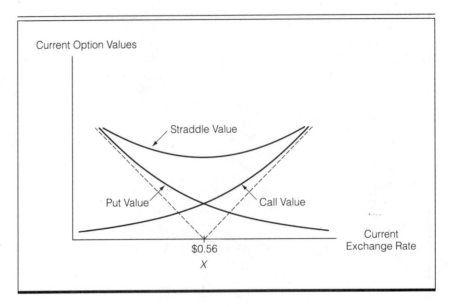

date. In general, a currency straddle can be used when a speculator feels that the underlying currency's volatility is *greater* than that implied by current option prices. The straddle can be thought of as an opposite speculative strategy to the butterfly spread.

Assume that a speculator can purchase a European DM call, with exercise price $0.56/DM1 and three-month maturity, for $0.01/DM1. Assume that the current spot rate is also $0.56/DM1. The speculator also can purchase a corresponding DM put option (with exercise price $0.56/DM1 and three-month expiration) for the $0.01/DM1. The currency straddle therefore costs $0.02/DM1.[2]

The payoffs to this straddle are portrayed in Figure 14.7. At expiration, the value of the straddle will be positioned on one of the two 45-degree lines emanating from the exercise price, $0.56/DM1. The speculator profits only if the resulting spot rate at expiration is below $0.54/DM1 or above $0.58/DM1. For instance, if the rate is $0.52/DM1, then the call option expires worthless but the put's value is $0.04/DM1 ($0.56 − 0.52), generating a net profit of $0.02/DM1 on the straddle (ignoring taxes and transaction costs). If the rate is $0.59/DM1, the put is worthless but the call's value of $0.03/DM1 generates a net profit of $0.01/DM1. For spot exchange rates between $0.54 and $0.58, the speculator exhibits a net loss.

<hr>

[2]As shown in Chapter 15, these two currency options can have the same price ($0.01/DM) only if we assume that domestic and foreign interest rates are zero. This assumption does not influence our discussion here.

USING CURRENCY OPTIONS FOR PRICE DISCOVERY

Unlike currency futures or forward contracts, currency options are not typically thought of as useful instruments for price discovery. Still, underlying exchange rates can be inferred from currency option prices and an appropriate valuation model, to make inferences about subsequent exchange rate movements. Using PHLX-traded call currency options, Peterson and Tucker (1988) inferred underlying exchange rates. That is, they generated *implied exchange rates* from observed option values. These implied rates can be thought of as the currency option market's assessment of equilibrium underlying rates.

Peterson and Tucker used these implied rates to make predictions about subsequent rate movements in the foreign exchange market itself. They argued that informed traders will trade in the options market first because options are more leveraged instruments. The informed investor can maximize the returns to her information by trading currency options. Thus, information enters the option market first, before it flows to the foreign exchange market.

Peterson and Tucker found that implied rates are indeed good predictors of subsequent changes in actual exchange rates, and remain so up to about one day. They concluded that currency option prices tend to lead exchange rates. Currency option values observed in the marketplace may therefore be useful in discovering information about short-term exchange rate changes. Tucker (1987) also found that the information implied from currency option prices is useful in predicting subsequent changes in 30-day forward rate movements.

SUMMARY

Currency options are derivative securities that allow investors to lay claim to the underlying foreign exchange without paying its full purchase price. The popularity of these securities is growing rapidly, especially because of the opportunities currency options provide to hedge foreign exchange exposure. Many firms now employ these options regularly to manage their exchange rate risk. For instance, Chrysler Corporation uses currency options for about one-half of its hedging transactions, with forward contracts used for the other half. Currency options also can be used to speculate on exchange rate movements and for some limited price discovery.

In the next chapter, we examine the valuation of currency options, and provide a discussion of the extant empirical evidence concerning market efficiency and the accuracy of currency option pricing models.

Questions and Problems

1. From Exhibit 14.2, what was the closing value of a Japanese yen call option contract with exercise price $0.0077/JY1 and August 1988 expiration?

2. Suppose you make a bet with a foreigner. If you win, you will be paid a specified number of units of foreign exchange in three months. How can

you use currency options to immunize against exchange rate risk? Why wouldn't you use currency forward or futures contracts?

3. Provide two arguments for the popularity of currency futures options.

4. What differentiates an American currency option from a European currency option?

5. How is a futures-style option like both an ordinary currency option and a futures contract?

6. Suppose you write European British pound put options at a price of $0.05/£1, with exercise price $1.20/£1 and three months to expiration. Determine your net profit (loss) per pound if the spot rate in three months is $1.05/£1; $1.10/£1; $1.14/£1; $1.20/£1; $1.25/£1; $1.30/£1.

7. What is the fundamental reason for the existence and popularity of currency options? Explain your answer.

8. From Exhibits 14.4 and 14.5, what are the potential revenue outcomes of the conservative strategy if the spot rate at expiration is $0.45/DM1?

9. From Figure 14.5, what is the net profit from the butterfly spread if the spot rate at expiration is $0.135/FF1?

10. Using Exhibit 14.2, what is the closing price of the Swiss franc put option with exercise price $0.67/SF1 and August expiration?

11. Suppose a U.S. exporter was using this SF put option to hedge a contract bid in Swiss francs. For simplicity, assume that the contract decision, franc payment, and option expiration are contemporaneous. If the U.S. firm's target revenue figure is $1,000,000, then what will be its bid in francs?

12. How many put option contracts must the firm buy to fully immunize itself against exchange exposure?

13. What is the firm's insurance premium?

14. If the bid fails and the spot rate at option expiration is $0.68/SF1, what is the firm's revenue?

15. What is the firm's revenue if the bid is successful and the spot rate at expiration is $0.66/SF1?

References

Agmon, T., and R. Eldon. "Currency Options Cope with Uncertainty." *Euromoney* (May 1983): 227–28.

Biger, N., and J. Hull. "The Valuation of Currency Options." *Financial Management* (Spring 1983): 24–28.

Briys, E., and M. Crouhy. "Creating and Pricing Hybrid Foreign Currency Options." *Financial Management* (Winter 1988): 59–65.

Chang, J., and L. Shanker. "Hedging Effectiveness of Currency Options and Currency Futures." *Journal of Futures Markets* (April 1986): 289–306.

Feiger, G., and B. Jacquillat. "Currency Option Bonds, Puts and Calls on Spot Exchange, and the Hedging of Contingent Foreign Earnings." *Journal of Finance* (December 1979): 1129–39.

Gendreau, B. "New Markets in Foreign Currency Options." *Business Review* (July/August 1984): 3–12.

Goodman, L. "How to Trade in Currency Options." *Euromoney* (January 1983): 73–74.

Lesniowski, M. "Mastering Currency Options." *Euromoney* (August 1983): 78–81.

Madura, J., and T. Veit. "Use of Currency Options in International Cash Management." *Journal of Cash Management* (January/February 1986): 42–48.

Peterson, D., and A. Tucker. "Implied Spot Rates as Predictors of Currency Returns: A Note." *Journal of Finance* (March 1988): 247–58.

Sender, H. "The New Case for Currency Options." *Institutional Investor* (January 1986): 245–47.

Shepard, S. "Forwards, Futures, and Currency Options as Foreign Exchange Risk Protection." *Canadian Banker* (December 1983): 22–25.

Tucker, A. "Foreign Exchange Option Prices as Predictors of Equilibrium Forward Exchange Rates." *Journal of International Money and Finance* (September 1987): 283–94.

Appendix 14.A

SYNTHETIC CURRENCY FUTURES CONTRACTS

Options on foreign exchange can be held in combinations to create *synthetic currency futures contracts*. A combination that consists of a written currency call and a purchased currency put, with the same exercise price and expiration, behaves in a manner identical to a short position in a currency futures contract. A long position in a synthetic currency futures contract is created by purchasing currency calls and writing corresponding puts.

To illustrate this concept, suppose a U.S. firm that will receive DM6,250,000 in September purchases 10 September DM put option contracts with exercise price $0.56/DM1, and simultaneously writes 10 corresponding call option contracts. Assume that these European put and call contract prices are $0.010/DM1 and $0.015/DM1, respectively. The result is that the firm can always sell its marks at $0.56/DM1, regardless of how the $/DM exchange rate moves from now until September contract expiration. Consequently, the firm has created a short position in synthetic DM futures.

Since synthetic futures can be created by currency option combinations, we should expect to observe intimate pricing relations between options and actual futures. Arbitrage restrictions should ensure that the payoffs obtained from actual ad synthetic currency futures strategies are inextricably linked. Differences that arise must be attributable to transaction costs or other frictions if markets are operating efficiently.

In the preceding illustration, a DM futures contract, with the same maturity as the options, should exhibit a futures price of $0.565/DM1 in order to preclude riskless arbitrage. The U.S. firm received $31,250 from its options trades:

Purchased put: −$0.010/DM1 × DM62,500 × 10 contracts = −$62,500
Written call: +0.015/DM1 × DM62,500 × 10 contracts =+$93,750
Proceeds =+$31,250

In equilibrium, therefore, the difference between the synthetic futures price (the options' exercise price) and the actual futures price must be −$0.005/DM1:

$$(\$0.560 - \$0.565) = -\$0.005/DM \times DM6,250,000 = -\$31,250.$$

In effect, the U.S. firm's proceeds from its option trades exactly offset its foregone proceeds from shorting the actual DM futures with its greater futures price of $0.565/DM1.

This exercise is really a representation of the law of one price. Arbitrage ensures this law. For example, suppose that the actual DM futures price was, say, $0.55/DM1. Here an arbitrageur could create a synthetic short DM futures and simultaneously take a long position in the actual futures contract. The profit realized would be $93,750, regardless of the spot exchange rate at contract expiration. For instance, suppose that the spot rate at expiration is $0.55/DM1. The profits realized on the three positions are

---

DM futures (purchased at $0.55 and settles at $0.55)	$ 0
DM puts (purchased at $0.010 and settles at $0.010)	$ 0
DM calls (written at $0.015 and expires worthless)	+$93,750
	+$93,750

If the spot rate at expiration is $0.53/DM1, the profits realized on the three positions are

---

DM futures (purchased at $0.55 and settles at $0.53)	−$125,000
DM puts (purchased at $0.010 and settles at $0.030)	+$125,000
DM calls (written at $0.015 and expires worthless)	+$ 93,750
	+$ 93,750

Finally, if the spot rate at expiration is above the futures price, say at $0.57/DM1, the profits realized on the three positions are

---

DM futures (purchased at $0.55 and settles at $0.57)	+$125,000
DM puts (purchased at $0.010 and expires worthless)	−$ 62,500
DM calls (written at $0.015 and settles at $0.010)	+$ 31,250
	+$ 93,750

As arbitrageurs conduct these trades, equilibrium should be restored.

The ability to create a currency futures contract through currency option combinations may imply that currency futures are redundant instruments, a type of financial "excess." However, futures contracts appear to exhibit lower transaction costs than option combinations. Thus, actual currency futures offer less costly exchange risk insurance than synthetic currency futures. Chang and Shanker (1986) explicitly accounted for differential transaction costs and reported that synthetic currency futures contracts have less hedging effectiveness than actual currency futures contracts, implying that the actuals are not redundant instruments.

Appendix 14.B

DYNAMIC HEDGING WITH CURRENCY FUTURES

It is possible to replicate the behavior of a currency-put combination by continuously adjusting a position in the currency and its futures contract. This replication technique is known as dynamic hedging. *Dynamic hedging* entails selling a number of currency futures contracts such that the currency-futures combination responds to exchange rate changes exactly as the currency-put combination would respond. The number of currency futures contracts to sell is defined by the hedge ratio N_F. This ratio must be continually adjusted because its determinants are time variant. Dynamic hedging can be employed to help ensure against exchange rate risk if no viable currency put option is available. This situation may occur in the deferred contracts.

N_F is given by the following equation:

14.B.1 $$N_F = [(V/S) - (V/S + P^E)(1 + \partial P^E/\partial S)]e^{(r_f - r)T},$$

where V is the value of the currency-put combination, S is the spot exchange rate, P^E is the European currency option price, r is the U.S. riskless rate of interest, r_f is the foreign riskless rate of interest, and T is the option's maturity expressed as a fraction of a year.

To derive the dynamic hedge ratio, consider a currency-put combination of N units of foreign currency and N puts, which is initially worth V:

14.B.2 $$V = N(S + P^E), \text{ where } N = V/(S + P^E).$$

The change in V for a small exchange rate change is given by

14.B.3 $$\partial V/\partial S = N(1 + (\partial P^E/\partial S))$$
$$= (V/(S + P^E))[1 + (\partial P^E/\partial S)].$$

If the currency put is unavailable, we replicate the position with a combination of N_S units of foreign exchange and N_F currency futures contracts (short). Thus:

14.B.4
$$V = N_S S - N_F V^F,$$

where V^F is the value of the futures contract. Since $V^F = 0$ at contract inception, $N_S = V/S$. The change in V for a small change in S now is

14.B.5
$$\partial V/\partial S = N_S - N_F(\partial F/\partial S), \text{ where } \partial F/\partial S = \partial V^F/\partial S.$$

By interest rate parity, $\partial F/\partial S = e^{(r-r_f)T}$. By substitution we have

14.B.6
$$\partial V/\partial S = V/S - N_F[e^{(r-r_f)T}].$$

Since we want the currency-put and currency-futures combinations to respond equally to changes in S, we set eqs. 14.B.3 and 14.B.6 equal to each other:

14.B.7
$$(V/(S + P^E))[1 + (\partial P^E/\partial S)] = V/S - N_F[e^{(r-r_f)T}].$$

Solving for N_F gives us eq. 14.B.1.

15

CURRENCY OPTION PRICING AND EVIDENCE

Given the popularity of currency options, it is important to possess a fundamental understanding of their valuation. In this chapter we introduce a basic framework to value these options. We start with a discussion of boundaries that govern currency option prices. Next we discuss the valuation of European currency options, followed by a discussion of early exercise and the valuation of American options. We also analyze the relation between spot and corresponding currency futures option prices. Finally, we summarize a body of empirical literature about currency options.

CURRENCY OPTION BOUNDS

Foreign exchange option prices exhibit certain limits or bounds that should not be violated in efficient markets. This section presents some important bounds.

Floors and Ceilings

We begin with the lower bound, or *floor*, for an American currency call options. Before option maturity, the call's price should be at least zero or the spread between the underlying exchange rate and the exercise price, whichever is greater. That is,

$$C^A \geq MAX(0, S - X),$$

where C^A is the American call option's price, S is the underlying rate of exchange, and X is the option's exercise price. This floor is depicted by the bold line in Figure 15.1. The floor results from arbitrage restrictions. For instance, suppose that $C^A = \$0.01/£1$, $S = \$1.75/£1$, and $X = \$1.73/£1$ such that a violation on the floor exists. Arbitrageurs can profit by (a)

Figure 15.1

Boundaries for American Currency
Call Options

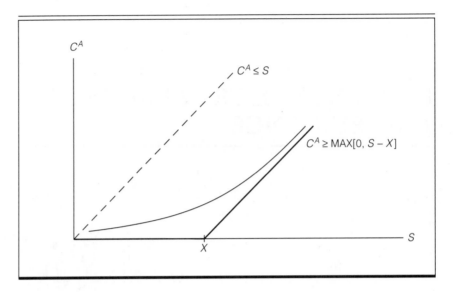

purchasing the undervalued call (−$0.01), (b) immediately exercising it
(−$1.73), and (c) selling the currency thus acquired (+$1.75). Here the
riskless profit is $0.01/£1, ignoring taxes, transaction costs, and the like.
As arbitrageurs enter the market and conduct such trading, the call
(currency) price is bid up (down) until the violation is eliminated and
equilibrium (the floor) is restored. By a similar arbitrage argument, the
American currency put option's floor is given by

$$P^A \geq MAX(0, X - S),$$

where P^A is the put's price. The put's floor is depicted by the bold line in
Figure 15.2.

The currency call option's price also has an upper bound, or *ceiling*,
that if violated implies a riskless arbitrage profit opportunity. Specifically, $C^A \leq S$. This ceiling is depicted by the broken line in Figure 15.1.
Suppose that $C^A = \$1.80/£1$ and $S = \$1.75/£1$ such that a violation of the
ceiling exists. Arbitrageurs can profit by (a) writing the call (+$1.80) and
(b) buying the underlying currency (−$1.75). Here the proceeds are
$0.05/£1. Should the written call option ever be exercised, then the
writer simply turns over the underlying foreign exchange owned. The
writer has a *covered call* option; a naked currency option is one in which
the writer holds no position in the underlying currency. Again, as arbitrageurs execute these trades the call (currency) price is bid down (up)
until the violation is eliminated. This ceiling also holds for European
currency options.

A currency put's ceiling is given by the option's exercise price, or $P^A \leq
X$. This is because the put option writer can never lose more than X
upon option exercise, since $S \geq 0$. The currency put option's ceiling is
depicted by the broken line in Figure 15.2. To exploit a violation of this
ceiling, which also holds for European puts, the arbitrageur simply
writes the overvalued put.

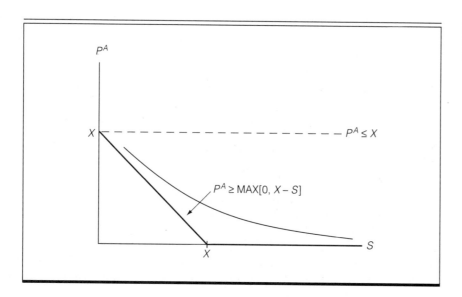

Figure 15.2
Boundaries for American Currency
Put Options

The actual market values of currency calls and puts lie somewhere between these floors and ceilings. For instance, recall the British pound spot call option, with exercise price $1.7000/£1 and July expiration, from Exhibit 14.2 in Chapter 14. This option had a closing price of $0.0330/£1, which is lower than its ceiling ($S = \$1.7150/£1$) and greater than its floor ($MAX(0, S - X) = \$0.0150/£1$). The market prices of currency options are depicted in Figures 15.1 and 15.2 by the convex curves. All option prices vary with the underlying exchange rate along a curve similar to those shown in these exhibits. As the S/X ratio falls, the currency call price asymptotically approaches zero. This call option is said to be deeply *out of the money*. The probability that this option will expire *in the money* ($S > X$) is low. Still, there is a positive probability, so the currency option maintains some small nonzero value before expiration. On the other hand, as S/X increases, the call price asymptotically approaches $S - X$. This currency option is deeply in the money and almost surely will be exercised. Therefore the call price approaches $S - X$. For similar reasons, the currency put market price function also is convex, as seen in Figure 15.2. For instance, as S/X falls the currency put becomes more in the money with its price approaching the option writer's limited liability, X.

Put-Call Parity

Another important option boundary concerns the relationship between European puts and calls exhibiting the same common maturity, exercise price, and underlying currency. This bound is known as *put-call parity* and, for currencies, is given by the following equation:

15.1 $$P^E = C^E + Xe^{-rT} - Se^{-r_fT},$$

where P^E and C^E are the corresponding European currency put and call prices respectively, r is the U.S. riskless rate of interest, r_f is the foreign riskless rate of interest, and T is the options' common maturity expressed as a fraction of a year.

Equation 15.1 follows from an elegant arbitrage argument. To illustrate this argument, suppose we observe the following variables:

$$P^E = \$0.01/SF1, \ C^E = \$0.04/SF1, \ X = \$0.67/SF1, \ S = \$0.67/SF1,$$
$$r = 0.10, \ r_f = 0.03, \text{ and } T = 0.50.$$

Here we have a violation of put-call parity:

$$\$0.01 < \$0.04 + (\$0.67)e^{-0.10(0.50)} - (\$0.67)e^{-0.03(0.50)} = \$0.0173.$$

When such a violation occurs, the appropriate arbitrage trading strategy is to (a) buy the put ($-\$0.01$), (b) write the call ($+\$0.04$), and (c) buy the underlying currency ($-\$0.67$). To do so, we raise the required capital ($\$0.64$) by borrowing at the U.S. riskless rate for time T. Thus, in six months we owe \$0.6728 [$\$064e^{0.10(0.50)}$]. Since we now own one Swiss franc, we deposit it to earn the Swiss riskless rate for T. Thus, in six months we have SF1.0151 [$SF1e^{0.03(0.50)}$]. We invest in the foreign riskless asset to ensure that our arbitrage strategy is risk free. This trading strategy ensures us a profit of \$0.0072/SF1, ignoring transaction costs and taxes, regardless of the resulting spot rate of exchange at option expiration.

For instance, suppose that the spot rate at option expiration (six months) is still \$0.67/SF1. Here both the SF put and SF call options expire worthless. Also, we can convert our SF1.0151 to generate \$0.68 (SF1.0151 × \$0.67/SF1). Paying off our domestic loan (\$0.6728) leaves us with a profit of \$0.0072/SF1. Now suppose that the spot rate at expiration is less than \$0.67/SF1, say \$0.65/SF1. Here the call is worthless, but our put option is worth \$0.02/SF1. Also, we can convert our SF1.0151 to generate \$0.66 (SF1.0151 × \$0.65/SF1), giving us \$0.68. Paying off our loan again yields a profit of \$0.0072/SF1. If the dollar should depreciate, then we will again profit. For instance, suppose that the spot rate at expiration is \$0.69/SF1. Here the put is worthless, and we lose \$0.02/SF1 on the written call that is exercised. However, we can convert our SF1.0151 to generate \$0.70 (SF1.0151 × \$0.69/SF1), again yielding a net inflow of \$0.68, and a gross profit of \$0.0072/SF1 after our domestic loan is satisfied. As we (arbitrageurs) exploit this violation, the security prices P^E, C^E, and S will be altered until put-call parity is restored. Finally, if a violation occurs such that $P^E > C^E + Xe^{-rT} - Se^{-r_fT}$, then to profit we simply reverse our trading strategy. Again, we are assured of a risk-free profit and our trading will tend to restore parity.

Put-call parity for corresponding American currency options differs a bit from that for corresponding European currency options, because American options can be exercised prematurely. Thus, the arbitrageur must undertake strategies that account for the possibility that the written options may be exercised before T. Also, Ball and Torous (1986) generated the following two parity conditions for American currency *futures* options:

15.2a $$C_F^A \leq P_F^A + F - Xe^{-rT}$$

15.2b $$C_F^A \geq P_F^A + Fe^{-rt} - X.$$

Here F refers to the underlying currency futures price, and the futures options, denoted C_F^A or P_F^A, mature before the underlying futures contract. Equations 15.2a and 15.2b result from more complex arbitrage restrictions than does eq. 15.1.

Arbitraging European and American Currency Options

Our final boundary concerns the relation between corresponding European and American currency options. The bounds $C^A \geq C^E$ and $P^A \geq P^E$ follow from simple arbitrage restrictions. For example, suppose we observe $C^A = \$0.012/DM1$ and $C^E = \$0.015/DM1$. We can exploit this violation by (a) buying the American option, and (b) writing the European option. Our proceeds are $\$0.003/DM1$. The written European call option cannot be exercised until it matures. However, at that time $C^A \equiv C^E$ since both options have no remaining life. By holding our American currency option until maturity, therefore, we can never lose our proceeds, $\$0.003/DM1$. A similar arbitrage restriction ensures that $P^A \geq P^E$.

To demonstrate empirically the relation between corresponding American and European currency option values, consider the two BP calls, with exercise price $\$1.7250/£1$ and August expiration, in Exhibit 14.2 from Chapter 14. The American BP call had a closing price of $\$0.0250/BP1$, while the corresponding European BP call had a closing price of $\$0.0235/BP1$. This price difference, $\$0.0015/BP1$, represents the early exercise premium associated with the American option (assuming these two reported options traded at approximately the same time).

EUROPEAN CURRENCY OPTION PRICING

Black and Scholes (1973) developed a closed-form analytic model to value European options given the following assumptions: (1) there are no taxes, transaction costs, or restrictions on short selling; (2) the underlying asset exhibits no dividends or other leakages and its returns are log-normally distributed with constant variance; (3) markets operate continuously; and (4) interest rates are constant and risk free.

Given these assumptions, Black and Scholes derive their valuation model by forming a riskless hedged portfolio consisting of a long position in the underlying asset and a short position in its European call option. The payoff to this hedged portfolio, which in equilibrium should be the domestic riskless rate of interest, represents a partial differential equation. The solution to this equation, subject to boundary conditions, yields their pricing model.

Merton (1973) extended the Black and Scholes model to underlying assets that exhibit a continuous dividend leakage. Foreign exchange exhibits such a leakage. When forming the riskless hedged portfolio, the portfolio manager takes a long position in the underlying currency. This currency can be invested in the foreign risk-free asset, thus earning a constant and continuous dividend yield given by the foreign riskless rate of interest. Thus, the European currency option pricing model follows directly from Merton's extension. Appendix 15.A provides a derivation of the currency call option pricing model. This model is

15.3
$$C^E = e^{-r_f T}SN(d) - e^{-rT}XN(d - \sigma\sqrt{T}),$$
$$d = \frac{ln(S/X) + [r - r_f + (\sigma^2/2)]T}{\sigma\sqrt{T}},$$

where

σ^2 = the instantaneous variance of the underlying currency's annual rate of return, and

$N(\cdot)$ = the standard normal cumulative probability distribution function.

Although this model appears rather ominous at first, its application is quite simple. To take an example, suppose we want to value a European call currency option where $S = \$1.75/£1$, $X = \$1.70/£1$, $r = 0.08$, $r_f = 0.12$, $T = 0.25$, and $\sigma^2 = 0.10$. The first step in valuing this option is to compute the probability terms $N(d)$ and $N(d - \sigma\sqrt{T})$. Here d and $d - \sigma\sqrt{T}$ represent the upper limits of integration of the standard normal cumulative probability distribution function, $N(\cdot)$, and are given by

$$d = \frac{ln(1.75/1.70) + [0.08 - 0.12 + (0.10/2)](0.25)}{\sqrt{0.10}\sqrt{0.25}}$$
$$= 0.1991$$
$$d - \sigma\sqrt{T} = 0.1991 - \sqrt{0.10}\sqrt{0.25} = 0.0410.$$

We obtain $N(0.1991)$ and $N(0.0410)$ by employing Exhibit 15.1 and interpolating: $N(0.1991) = 0.5789$ and $N(0.0410) = 0.5163$. Alternatively, we may have used the following power series function to approximate these probabilities:

15.4 $$N(d) \approx 1 - 1/2(1 + a_1d + a_2d^2 + a_3d^3 + a_4d^4)^{-4},$$

where $a_1 = 0.196854$, $a_2 = 0.115194$, $a_3 = 0.000344$, $a_4 = 0.019527$, and obtaining $N(d)$ for $d < 0$ by symmetry.

Notice that the probability $N(d) = 0.5789$ is fairly high. It is easily demonstrated that $N(d)$ is the probability that the call option will expire in the money. Thus, this currency option's probability of being exercised is presently over 57%. We expect a high probability since this call option is currently in the money $(S > X)$.

Given $N(d) = 0.5789$ and $N(d - \sigma\sqrt{T}) = 0.5163$, the next step to compute this option's price is to employ eq. 15.3:

$$C^E = e^{-0.12(0.25)}1.75(0.5789) - e^{-0.08(0.25)}1.70(0.5163)$$
$$= 0.9813 - 0.8603 = \$0.1228/£1.$$

Notice that the option's price ($\$0.1228/£1$) is below its ceiling ($S = \$1.75/£1$) and above its floor $(MAX(0,S - X) = \$0.05/£1)$. Finally, a corresponding BP put option has a price of $\$0.0909/£1$. This put price follows from eq. 15.1, put-call parity:

$$P^E = \$0.1228 + (\$1.70)e^{-0.08(0.25)} - (\$1.75)e^{-0.12(0.25)}$$
$$= \$0.0909/£1.$$

d	N(d)	d	N(d)	d	N(d)
		−1.00	0.1587	1.00	0.8413
−2.95	0.0016	−0.95	0.1711	1.05	0.8531
−2.90	0.0019	−0.90	0.1841	1.10	0.8643
−2.85	0.0022	−0.85	0.1977	1.15	0.8749
−2.80	0.0026	−0.80	0.2119	1.20	0.8849
−2.75	0.0030	−0.75	0.2266	1.25	0.8944
−2.70	0.0035	−0.70	0.2420	1.30	0.9032
−2.65	0.0040	−0.65	0.2578	1.35	0.9115
−2.60	0.0047	−0.60	0.2743	1.40	0.9192
−2.55	0.0054	−0.55	0.2912	1.45	0.9265
−2.50	0.0062	−0.50	0.3085	1.50	0.9332
−2.45	0.0071	−0.45	0.3264	1.55	0.9394
−2.40	0.0082	−0.40	0.3446	1.60	0.9452
−2.35	0.0094	−0.35	0.3632	1.65	0.9505
−2.30	0.0107	−0.30	0.3821	1.70	0.9554
−2.25	0.0122	−0.25	0.4013	1.75	0.9599
−2.20	0.0139	−0.20	0.4207	1.80	0.9641
−2.15	0.0158	−0.15	0.4404	1.85	0.9678
−2.10	0.0179	−0.10	0.4602	1.90	0.9713
−2.05	0.0202	−0.05	0.4801	1.95	0.9744
−2.00	0.0228	0.00	0.5000	2.00	0.9773
−1.95	0.0256	0.05	0.5199	2.05	0.9798
−1.90	0.0287	0.10	0.5398	2.10	0.9821
−1.85	0.0322	0.15	0.5596	2.15	0.9842
−1.80	0.0359	0.20	0.5793	2.20	0.9861
−1.75	0.0401	0.25	0.5987	2.25	0.9878
−1.70	0.0446	0.30	0.6179	2.30	0.9893
−1.65	0.0495	0.35	0.6368	2.35	0.9906
−1.60	0.0548	0.40	0.6554	2.40	0.9918
−1.55	0.0606	0.45	0.6736	2.45	0.9929
−1.50	0.0668	0.50	0.6915	2.50	0.9938
−1.45	0.0735	0.55	0.7088	2.55	0.9946
−1.40	0.0808	0.60	0.7257	2.60	0.9953
−1.35	0.0885	0.65	0.7422	2.65	0.9960
−1.30	0.0968	0.70	0.7580	2.70	0.9965
−1.25	0.1057	0.75	0.7734	2.75	0.9970
−1.20	0.1151	0.80	0.7881	2.80	0.9974
−1.15	0.1251	0.85	0.8023	2.85	0.9978
−1.10	0.1357	0.90	0.8159	2.90	0.9981
−1.05	0.1469	0.95	0.8289	2.95	0.9984

Exhibit 15.1

Values for d and N(d)

The value of a European currency put option also can be obtained independently of its corresponding call option value. Using a derivation similar to that contained in Appendix 15.A, the put valuation model is

15.5 $P^E = e^{-rT}X[1 - N(d - \sigma\sqrt{T})] - e^{-r_fT}S[1 - N(d)].$

Factors Affecting Currency Option Prices

As evidenced by eqs. 15.3 and 15.5, there are six parameters influencing currency option values: S, X, r, σ^2, T, and r_f. Clearly, the value of a currency call (put) option increases (decreases) with S/X. The change in currency option value for a unit change in S is called the option's *delta*. A simple proof demonstrates that delta is $N(d)$. The influence of each of the remaining four variables on option value is discussed in the following list:

- *Domestic interest rate.* As r increases, the financing cost of purchasing a foreign currency also increases. Options are leveraged instruments, allowing an investor to lay claim to the underlying currency without paying its full purchase price S. This option feature implies that currency call option value increases with r.

- *Volatility.* An option buyer prefers a more volatile underlying currency. This is because she can never lose more than the option's price, but may realize large profits. This asymmetry implies that option value increases with σ^2. The change in option value for a unit change in volatility is often called the option's *lambda*.

- *Maturity.* As the option's maturity is increased, there is an increasing probability of a large change in S. This change is desirable since an option buyer exhibits a large profit potential with a limited lose potential. Time also compounds the interest rate effect described earlier. Therefore, currency option value increases with T. An inspection of Exhibit 14.2 from Chapter 14 affirms this relation. The option's *theta* represents a change in option value with respect to time. Figure 15.3 portrays a currency option's time-value-decay pattern.

- *Foreign interest rate.* By interest rate parity, a larger foreign interest rate implies a lower future spot exchange rate at currency option expiration. In turn, this result implies a lower (higher) currency call (put) option price.[1]

---

[1] To see this result more clearly, plug the interest rate parity equation, $F = Se^{(r-r_f)T}$, into eq. 15.3. The resulting pricing equation is $C^E = e^{-rT}FN(d_1) - e^{-rT}XN(d_1 - \sigma\sqrt{T})$, where $d_1 = \{[ln(F/X) + (\sigma^2/2)T]/\sigma\sqrt{T}\}$. European currency options on the spot and on currency futures (forwards) have identical prices when the options and futures (forward) contracts expire simultaneously. This result is obvious when one considers that the spot and futures (forward) prices are identical at contract expiration and that early exercise is prohibited when the option is European. From this equation, one sees that a higher r_f lowers F and, thus, C^E. The opposite is true for currency puts.

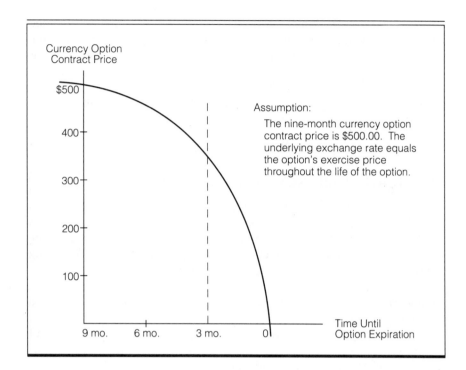

Figure 15.3
A Currency Option's
Time-Value-Decay Pattern

Quantifying Currency Return Variance

Of these option parameters, only σ^2 is not readily observable. There are two popular ways to estimate this volatility measure. The first is to use historical currency return data. For instance, we can use the most recent six months of daily currency returns to compute a daily return variance. We then generate an annualized variance measure by multiplying the daily variance by 365. Recall that eqs. 15.3 and 15.5 require an annualized variance input. This technique assumes that exchange rates continue to fluctuate on nontrading days and that successive changes in rates are uncorrelated. We want to use the most recent data because the pricing model assumes that σ^2 remains constant over the option's remaining life. Finally, we may want to adjust our σ^2 estimate if we anticipate the underlying currency's risk to change substantially during the option's life, or if we employ Box-Jenkins analysis and detect patterns in the time series of σ^2.

The second technique to estimate volatility is to impute σ^2 from a similar currency option's price. For example, suppose we want to price a Deutsche mark call option with $X = \$0.57/DM1$ and $T = 0.25$. Also suppose that we can observe the current market price of a DM call with $X = \$0.56/DM1$ and $T = 0.25$. Using this observed price and the call option pricing model, we can impute σ^2. That is, we can use the observed price and eq. 15.3, and solve for the unknown variance. The *implied variance* is that unique variance equating the model and market prices, and it represents the currency option market's assessment of σ^2 for the mark over the next three months. Thus, we can use this implied measure to price our focal DM option with exercise price $0.57/DM1. Imputing σ^2 requires computer routines since it is a slow, iterative process. However, studies have shown that implied currency volatilities are superior predictors of actual future volatilities than are historically estimated volatilities (Scott and Tucker 1989). Intuitively, implied σ^2s are superior since they reflect current exchange rates and market expectations, whereas historically estimated σ^2s do not.

AMERICAN CURRENCY OPTION PRICING

It may be optional to prematurely exercise an American currency option. For calls, there are two necessary conditions for premature exercise to occur. First, the option must be deeply in the money ($S \ggg X$), and second, the underlying currency must be selling at a future discount or parity ($r \le r_f$). To obtain this result, notice that as S/X increases, the probability terms $N(\cdot)$ in eq. 15.3 approach one. The deeply in the money option will almost surely be exercised. As $N(\cdot) \to 1$, from eq. 15.3 we have

$$C \to e^{-r_f T} S - e^{-rT} X.$$

Now if $r \le r_f$, the call option's price may be less than $S - X$, the option's exercisable proceeds. Therefore, the option holder should exercise; the proceeds from exercising, $S - X$, are greater than the current market value of the option. Intuitively, the option has little remaining *time value*, and exercising it would entitle you to the underlying currency and the associated interest-bearing foreign asset. This deeply in the money option is said to be worth more dead than alive. More generally, there exists a critical exchange rate above which premature exercise of the American currency call option is optimal, given $r \le r_f$.

For currency puts, the two necessary conditions for premature exercise are (1) a deeply in the money put ($S \lll X$), and (2) a premium or parity currency ($r \ge r_f$). Since here $N(\cdot) \to 0$ (the probability of exercising the corresponding call is almost surely zero so that the probability of exercising the put is almost surely one), from eq. 15.5 we have

$$P \to e^{-rT} X - e^{-r_f T} S.$$

Now if $r \ge r_f$, the put option's price may be less than its exercisable proceeds, $X - S$. Therefore, the option holder may exercise. There exists a critical exchange rate below which premature exercise of the American currency put option is optimal, given $r \ge r_f$.

Since it may be optimal to prematurely exercise a currency option, an American currency option typically commands a greater price than a corresponding European currency option. As discussed in Appendix 15.A, however, quantifying this early exercise premium is difficult. No closed-form, analytic model exists for pricing American currency options. Instead, the price may be obtained by numerical techniques (Schwartz 1977), or by model approximations (Barone-Adesi and Whaley 1987). Appendix 15.B provides an approximating model to price American foreign exchange options. Unfortunately, the application of

Panel A			Panel C		
$r - r_f$	$C^A - C^E$	$P^A - P^E$	T	$C^A - C^E$	$P^A - P^E$
0.06	0.000	0.067	30	0.007	0.020
0.02	0.000	0.031	120	0.033	0.067
−0.02	0.033	0.000	210	0.066	0.180

Panel B			Panel D		
S	$C^A - C^E$	$P^A - P^E$	σ	$C^A - C^E$	$P^A - P^E$
0.54	0.314	0.003	0.10	0.033	0.067
0.50	0.033	0.067	0.20	0.038	0.075
0.46	0.001	0.083	0.30	0.046	0.089

Exhibit 15.2

Differences in Model Prices of American and European Currency Spot Call (Put) Options

Notes: a. For all panels the base values of the parameters are $S = \$0.50$, $X = \$0.50$, $T = 120$ days, $\sigma = 0.10$, $r = 0.08$, and $r_f = 0.10$ (0.02) for calls (puts).
b. The European option prices are given by eqs. 15.3 and 15.5. The American option prices are given by a quadratic approximation developed by Barone-Adesi and Whaley (1987).
c. All differences in model prices are reported in U.S. cents per unit of foreign exchange.

such techniques and approximations is beyond the intended scope of this book.

An Illustration of the Early Exercise Premium

To provide you with a sense of the magnitude of this early exercise premium, we have simulated the differences in model prices of American and European currency options. The results of this simulation, provided in Exhibit 15.2, show that the early exercise premium increases with option maturity and volatility. For calls, the premium increases with the exchange rate S and the foreign interest rate r_f. The opposite occurs for puts. The largest premium is $0.00314, representing nearly 8.5% of the price of the European currency option. Shastri and Tandon (1986a) report similar early exercise premia for simulated American and European currency option prices. Also, Jorion and Stoughton (1988) and Tucker (1989) find that currency option traders place a statistically significant premium on the value of American currency options.

PRICING CURRENCY FUTURES OPTIONS

Currency futures contracts do not pay dividends or interest per se. However, the futures price does exhibit a continuous leakage as the contract matures and the spot and futures prices converge. The daily resettlement (marking to the market) of a currency futures contract means that there is a series of cash flows associated with a position in the futures market. These resettlement cash flows represent a continu-

Market Premiums for American Currency Options

From September 1985 to August 1987, the CBOE traded European currency options and the PHLX traded American currency options. Since September 1987, the PHLX trades both options side by side. Such trading represents, remarkably, the only contemporaneous trading of both European and American options on the same underlying instrument in the history of U.S. securities markets.

Tucker (1989) exploited this unique situation, and documented what the marketplace determines to be the early exercise premia on American currency options. Specifically, Tucker used transactions data and generated over 48,000 matched European and American currency option trades. These option pairs have the same underlying currency, exercise price, and maturity. On average, the pairs trade less than 10 minutes apart.

The results of Tucker's analysis show that the market assigns a statistically significant premium to American currency options. Overall, the average premium for call options is 1.62% of the European option's value, and the average premium for puts is 1.54%. The average premiums for each of the five currencies studied are reported in the following table.

	Average Premium	
Currency	Calls	Puts
British pound	2.90%	0.43%
Canadian dollar	2.88%	0.59%
Deutsche mark	1.94%	1.60%
Japanese yen	0.77%	1.26%
Swiss franc	1.01%	2.51%

ous leakage when valuing currency futures options. The continuous leakage factor is given by the U.S. riskless rate of interest, r. Thus, Merton's (1973) extension of the Black and Scholes (1973) model is also applicable to currency futures options. Black (1976) recognized this application. The resulting formula to price European call currency futures options is

15.6 $$C_F^E = e^{-rT}FN(d_1) - e^{-rT}XN(d_1 - \sigma\sqrt{T}),$$

where

$$d_1 = \frac{ln(F/X) + (\sigma^2/2)T}{\sigma\sqrt{T}}, \text{ and}$$

C_F^E = the European call currency futures option price.

Recall from footnote 1 that eq. 15.6 gives the same price as a European call currency spot option (eq. 15.3), provided that the futures contract, the currency spot option contract, and the currency futures option contract all expire simultaneously. This result relies on the assumptions that underlie the Black-Scholes model. Most critically, interest rates must be constant, implying that currency forward and futures prices are identical (Cox, Ingersoll, and Ross 1981); see also Chapter 13. Constant interest rates also imply that the variances of currency spot and futures returns are identical. In Appendix 15.C we offer a proof. Therefore, σ^2 applies to both spot and futures exchange rates.

The value of a corresponding European put currency futures option, P_F^E, can be obtained from the following parity condition, which follows from arbitrage restrictions:

15.7 $$P_F^E = C_F^E + Xe^{-rT} - Fe^{-rT}.$$

Alternatively, P_F^E can be obtained independently of C_F^E:

15.8 $\qquad P_F^E = e^{-rT}X[1 - N(d_1 - \sigma\sqrt{T})] - e^{-rT}F[1 - N(d_1)].$

To illustrate the valuation of a currency futures option, suppose that we want to determine C_F^E where $F = \$1.7326/£1$, $X = \$1.7000/£1$, $\sigma^2 = 0.10$, $T = 0.25$, and $r = 0.08$:

$$d_1 = [ln(1.7326/1.700) + (0.10/2)(0.25)]/\sqrt{0.10}\sqrt{0.25}$$
$$= 0.1991;$$
$$d_1 - \sqrt{0.10}\sqrt{0.25} = 0.0410;$$
$$N(0.1991) = 0.5789;$$
$$N(0.0410) = 0.5163;$$
$$C_F^E = e^{-0.08(0.25)}1.7326(0.5789) - e^{-0.08(0.25)}1.700(0.5163)$$
$$= \$0.1228/£1.$$

The resulting BP futures option price is $0.1228 per pound, which is the same as the price of our earlier BP spot option where $r_f = 0.12$. Given our preceding argument that European currency spot and futures options command the same price only when the options and futures contracts mature simultaneously, the futures price of $1.7326/£1 must be applicable to a three-month contract:

$$\$1.7326 = \$1.7500e^{(0.08-0.12)(0.25)}.$$

Of course, the corresponding European BP put futures option price must be $0.0909/£1:

$$\$0.0909 = 0.1228 + 1.700e^{-0.08(0.25)} - 1.7326e^{-0.08(0.25)}.$$

American Currency Futures Options

The currency futures options traded on the International Monetary Market division of the Chicago Mercantile Exchange are American, capable of being exercised prematurely. It may be optimal to prematurely exercise an American currency futures option. For calls (puts) the necessary condition is $F \ggg X$ ($F \lll X$). Thus, American currency futures options command an early exercise premium. Appendix 15.B provides a model for pricing American currency futures options.

Relating American Currency Spot and Futures Option Prices

Ogden and Tucker (1988) developed pricing conditions relating American currency spot and futures options under the assumptions that interest rates are constant and the interest rate parity theorem holds continuously. In particular, they showed that for premium currencies $C_F^A \geq C_A$ and $P_F^A \leq P^A$, and for discount currencies $C_F^A \leq C^A$ and $P_F^A \geq P^A$. These functional relations are illustrated in Exhibit 15.3. Shown are the differences in model prices of American currency spot and futures options for various parameter values. These prices are generated using the valuation models given in Appendix 15.B.

Exhibit 15.3

Differences In Model Prices of American Currency Spot and Futures Call (Put) Options

Panel A			Panel D		
$r - r_f$	$C^A - C_F^A$	$P^A - P_F^A$	T	$C^A - C_F^A$	$P^A - P_F^A$
-0.04	0.00204	-0.00057	30	0.00002	-0.00012
-0.02	0.00093	-0.00040	60	0.00039	-0.00013
0.00	0.00000	0.00000	90	0.00080	-0.00014
0.02	-0.00035	0.00077	180	0.00204	-0.00057
0.04	-0.00046	0.00173	270	0.0039	-0.00126

Panel B			Panel E		
S	$C^A - C_F^A$	$P^A - P_F^A$	T	$C^A - C_F^A$	$P^A - P_F^A$
0.80	0.00009	-0.00821	30	-0.00010	0.00001
0.90	0.00014	-0.00233	60	-0.00010	0.00031
1.00	0.00204	-0.00057	90	-0.00011	0.00073
1.10	0.00979	-0.00006	180	-0.00046	0.00173
1.20	0.02349	-0.00004	270	-0.00103	0.00276

Panel C		
S	$C^A - C_F^A$	$P^A - P_F^A$
0.80	-0.00003	0.01624
0.90	-0.00009	0.00876
1.00	-0.00046	0.00173
1.10	-0.00240	0.00013
1.20	-0.00747	0.00001

Notes: a. For all panels, base values are $\sigma = 0.15$, $T = 180$ days, $S = \$1.00$, and $X = \$1.00$. In panels B and D (C and E), $r = 0.08$ and $r_f = 0.12$ (0.04).

b. The differences in model prices are reported in U.S. dollars per unit of foreign exchange.

These relations are obtained from arbitrage restrictions. For example, assume $C_F^A > C^A$ for discount currency such that a violation occurs. The trading strategy used to exploit this violation is (a) purchase the spot call option, (b) write the futures call option, and (c) invest the proceeds in a riskless U.S. asset maturing at T, the options and futures contracts' common maturity. If the written futures call option is not exercised prematurely, then holding the spot call option until expiration provides a positive cash inflow of $(C_F^A - C^A)e^{rT}$ at T:

	Payoff at T	
	$F = S \leq X$	$F = S > X$
Purchase C^A	$-(C^A)e^{rT}$	$-(C^A)e^{rT} + (S - X)$
Write C_F^A	$(C_F^A)e^{rT}$	$(C_F^A)e^{rT} - (F - X)$
Total	$(C_F^A - C^A)e^{rT} > 0$	$(C_F^A - C^A)e^{rT} > 0$

Note that $F = S$ at T and the riskless profit earned is identical regardless of whether the options expire in the money.

Now suppose that the written futures call option is exercised prematurely at $t^* < T$. The trading strategy now provides a positive cash inflow of $(C_F^A - C^A)e^{rt^*} + (S - F)$ at t^*:

	Payoff at t^*
	$S > F > X$
Purchase C^A	$-(C^A)e^{rt^*} + (S - F)$
Write C_F^A	$(C_F^A)e^{rt^*} - (F - X)$
Total	$(C_F^A - C^A)e^{rt^*} + (S - F) > 0$

Note that the spot call option can be exercised to yield $S - X$, that both options must be in the money at t^* for premature exercise to occur, and that $S > F$ at t^* by interest rate parity and the assumption of constant interest rates.

Similar arbitrage strategies ensure the remaining pricing relations. Ogden and Tucker described these strategies and, empirically, reported that many violations of the relations are observed for options on the BP, DM, and SF for the calendar year 1986. They were unable to distinguish whether these unexploited profit opportunities are attributable to an inefficient market or to violation of the assumption of constant interest rates.

EMPIRICAL EVIDENCE

Most empirical studies involving options are concerned with one of the following two related issues: (1) market efficiency and (2) model accuracy. A market exhibits efficiency if no persistent abnormal profit opportunities exist. Tests of options market efficiency are of two types:

- Arbitrage tests, with which markets are examined for violations of pricing bounds like put-call parity. Here the market is said to be efficient if few violations are detected after controlling for the effects of market imperfections such as transaction costs, data nonsynchronization, execution lags, and the like.

- Hedge tests, with which trading rules based on differences between observed and model prices are examined for their ability to earn risk-adjusted abnormal returns. These hedge tests are said to be joint tests; the detection of abnormal profits may be attributable to model misspecification as well as market inefficiency.

Whether a model exhibits predictive accuracy often is a nebulous issue. Most studies concerning the accuracy of option pricing models pit one model against another more complex model. These models are compared for their ability to forecast actual market prices. Often the more complex model prevails. However, the improvement in pricing accuracy may be insufficient to justify the added costs of implementing the more complex pricing model. For instance, European models often can be used safely to value out-of-the-money, short-maturity American options since such options have a very low probability of premature exercise and, thus, a very small early exercise premium.

In this section we summarize a body of empirical literature regarding currency option market efficiency and currency option valuation. These studies support the notion of market efficiency, finding few violations of pricing bounds and no abnormal profits from trading rules after accounting for market imperfections. A few recent studies have found that more complex currency option pricing models, which allow for nonconstant interest rates or for deviations of lognormally distributed currency returns, offer improved pricing accuracy.

Arbitrage Tests of Market Efficiency

Bodurtha and Courtadon (1986) conducted the most extensive arbitrage tests of currency options market efficiency to date. They examined a total of 10 early exercise and put-call parity pricing boundaries applicable to American currency options. Their data consist of over 52,000 PHLX-traded calls and puts for the period February 1983 to September 1984. These are synchronous transactions data; that is, Bodurtha and Courtadon used intradaily data for which the underlying exchange rate is recorded at the time of each option trade. The authors also accounted for the relevant transaction costs exhibited by the least cost traders, namely, market makers at the PHLX.

Bodurtha and Courtadon found that the number and percentage of exploitable arbitrage opportunities are very small. Only 31 option trades out of 52,509 violate the early exercise arbitrage boundaries, and just one put-call pair out of 3,998 violates a put-call boundary. These results support currency option market efficiency. Similar tests and results are reported by Shastri and Tandon (1986b) and Tucker (1985).

Ogden and Tucker (1987) conducted analogous arbitrage tests of the efficiency of the currency futures option market. Their synchronous transactions data consist of over 125,000 option trades for the calendar year 1986. Options on BP, DM, and SF futures were investigated. The results support market efficiency, as less than 0.7% of the observations tested exhibit violations that exceed transaction costs for floor traders on the International Monetary Market division of the CME.

Hedge Tests of Market Efficiency

Tucker (1985) conducted a hedge test of the efficiency of the PHLX currency option market. He employed synchronous transactions data to determine if an active trading strategy could outperform a more passive trading strategy after accounting for risk and transaction costs. Tucker's active strategy was based on deviations between market prices and model prices, where model prices were given by eq. 15.3. Tucker used an ex ante test. At time t it was determined whether an option was undervalued or overvalued; undervalued options were bought and overvalued options were sold at the next available market prices. Both historical and implied currency return variances were used.

Although Tucker found that excess returns can be earned by his trading rule, such returns vanish once transaction costs are introduced. Thus we have the usual result that nonmember traders cannot beat the market. Option prices are efficiently determined down to the level of transaction costs.

Model Accuracy

A Black-Scholes type of currency option pricing model (OPM) is one in which the underlying returns are lognormally distributed with constant variance. Also, interest rates are assumed to be constant. Empirical studies have documented systematic pricing biases for such a model. For instance, Bodurtha and Courtadon (1987) reported that the model exhibits a definite time-to-maturity bias when applied to listed currency options. As time to maturity increases, the overpricing of in-the-money and at-the-money currency options first decreases and then increases slightly. This pattern of mispricing implies that currency returns may not be lognormally distributed with constant variance. Several studies—including Westerfield (1977); McFarland, Pettit, and Sung (1982); Friedman and Vandersteel (1982); and Tucker and Pond (1988)—document violations of lognormality for exchange return distributions.

Shastri and Wethyavivorn (1987) also documented systematic mispricing by a Black-Scholes type of OPM applied to listed currency options. Using a methodology developed by Rubinstein (1985), Shastri and Wethyavivorn examined the stability of currency return variances implied from currency option prices. They implied variances using observed market prices and a Black-Scholes type of OPM. They then categorized these implied variances by the maturities of the options and by the options' S/X ratios. Since the Black-Scholes type of OPM assumes constant variance, there should be no distinguishable pattern of implied variances across maturities or S/X ratios. However, Shastri and Wethyavivorn found that implied currency return variances first decrease and then increase as the S/X ratio climbs. They reported no distinguishable pattern with respect to maturities. The U-shaped pattern of implied variances reported by Shastri and Wethyavivorn suggests that currency returns are not lognormally distributed.

Alternative Option Pricing Models

The preceding studies, which document systematic biases for a Black-Scholes type of currency option pricing model, suggest that some alternative model may be superior. Three alternative models have been tested. First, Hilliard, Madura, and Tucker (1991) found that a stochastic interest rate model exhibits superior pricing accuracy than a constant interest rate currency option pricing model. Their stochastic rate model is detailed in Appendix 15.D. Using over 3,000 PHLX trades, the authors found that the stochastic rate model exhibits significantly smaller pricing errors across all currencies, S/X ratios, and maturities. The overall error reduction offered by the stochastic interest rate model is about 16%.

Second, Tucker, Peterson, and Scott (1988) reported that a *constant elasticity of variance* (CEV) currency option pricing model exhibits better forecast accuracy than the Black-Scholes type of model for predictive intervals of five or fewer trading days. The CEV model allows currency return variances to change over time. Specifically, return variances change as the level of exchange rates changes. The Black-Scholes model is a special case of the more general CEV model, as the former assumes constant variance.

Third, Tucker (1990) found that a currency option model that incorporates discrete jumps in exchange rate changes outperforms the Black-Scholes model for pricing PHLX-traded currency options. Tucker and Pond (1988) reported that daily currency returns exhibit such jumps, which may be caused by factors such as central bank intervention or exchange rate realignment by the European community. Tucker reports that the pricing improvement offered by the mixed-jump model can be substantial; the overall error reduction offered by the mixed-jump model is about 50%.

SUMMARY

Currency option prices exhibit certain bounds or limits that follow from arbitrage restrictions. Calls and puts have floors and ceilings and their values are related through parity conditions.

The valuation of currency options is complex, especially for American options that can be exercised prematurely. The factors affecting currency option prices are the exchange rate, the option's exercise price and maturity, the volatility of currency returns, and the U.S. and foreign riskless rates of interest.

The valuation of currency futures options also is complex, and under certain assumptions the relative valuation of currency spot and futures options is determined by arbitrage restrictions.

Empirical studies support the notion of efficiency for the currency option market. Recent empirical evidence finds that models that allow for nonconstant interest rates or more complex currency return distributions offer superior pricing accuracy than a Black-Scholes currency option model. We cannot determine whether this pricing improvement is sufficient to justify the added costs of employing the more complex models. However, these added costs are being reduced as technology improves.

Questions and Problems

1. What is an American currency put option's floor? What strategy would you undertake to exploit a violation of this floor?

2. What is an American currency call option's ceiling? What strategy would you undertake to exploit a violation of this ceiling?

3. Assume that a violation of put-call parity exists for two corresponding European currency options such that $P^E > C^E + Xe^{-rT} - Se^{-r_fT}$. What trading strategy would you undertake to exploit this violation? Provide a numerical example demonstrating your profit realized at T.

4. Suppose that a holder of an American currency put option is debating whether to prematurely exercise his option. Under what conditions would it be optimal for him to do so?

5. Demonstrate the necessary condition for premature exercise of an American call currency futures option.

6. Suppose $C_F^A < C^A$ for a premium currency. What trading strategy would you undertake to exploit this mispricing? And what is your cash inflow at T, assuming that interest rates are constant and interest rate parity holds continuously?

7. Figure 15.1 graphs the value of a currency call option as a function of the value of the underlying foreign exchange. What factors would cause an upward shift in this convex function?

8. Provide the price of a European currency option given the following parameters: $S = \$0.50$, $X = \$0.47$, $\sigma^2 = 0.15$, $T = 0.50$, $r = 0.08$, and $r_f = 0.05$.

9. What is the value of the corresponding European put?

10. Why is an implied currency return variance typically considered a superior measure of actual future variance than a historical currency return variance?

11. Provide the price of a European currency futures option given the following parameters: $F = \$1.25$, $X = \$1.25$, $\sigma^2 = 0.10$, $T = 0.25$, and $r = 0.10$.

12. Because foreign exchange rates are reciprocals (e.g., $\$2/£1$ or £.50/$1), a currency call option on a foreign currency may be considered a currency put option on the domestic currency. Show this using eq. 15.3 and 15.5 and the following parameters: $S = \$2/£1$, $X = \$2/£1$, $\sigma = 0.10$, $r = 0.08$, $r_f = 0.12$, and $T = 0.25$.

13. Using put-call parity, establish a fictitious range-forward contract that has a zero cost at contract inception.

References

Ball, C., and W. Torous. "Futures Options and the Volatility of Futures Prices," *Journal of Finance* (September 1986): 857–70.

Barone-Adesi, G., and R. Whaley. "Efficient Analytic Approximation of American Option Values." *Journal of Finance* (June 1987): 301–20.

Black, F. "The Pricing of Commodity Contracts," *Journal of Financial Economics* (January/March 1976): 167–79.

Black, F., and M. Scholes. "The Pricing of Options and Corporate Liabilities." *Journal of Political Economy* (May/June 1973): 637–59.

Bodurtha, J., and G. Courtadon. "Efficiency Tests of the Foreign Currency Options Market." *Journal of Finance* (March 1986): 151–62.

————. "Tests of an American Option Pricing Model on the Foreign Currency Options Market." *Journal of Financial and Quantitative Analysis* (June 1987): 153–67.

Cox, J., J. Ingersoll, and S. Ross. "The Relation Between Forward and Future Prices," *Journal of Financial Economics* (December 1981): 321–46.

Cox, J., and S. Ross. "The Valuation of Options for Alternative Stochastic Processes." *Journal of Financial Economics* (January/March 1976): 145–66.

Friedman, D., and S. Vandersteel. "Short-Run Fluctuations in Foreign Exchange Rates: Evidence from the Data 1973–79." *Journal of International Economics* (August 1982): 171–86.

Hilliard, J., J. Madura, and A. Tucker. "Pricing Foreign Currency Options with Stochastic Domestic and Foreign Interest Rates." *Journal of Financial and Quantitative Analysis*. Forthcoming, 1991.

Hsieh, D. "A Model of Foreign Currency Options with Random Interest Rates." Working Paper, University of Chicago (1988).

Itô, K. "On Stochastic Differential Equations." *Memoirs, American Mathematical Society* (December 1951): 1–51.

Jorion, P., and N. Stoughton. "The Valuation of the Early Exercise Premium in the Foreign Currency Options Market." In *Recent Developments In Inernational Banking and Finance*, eds. S. Khoury and A. Ghosh, Lexington Books, 1988.

McFarland, J., R. Pettit, and S. Sung. "The Distribution of Foreign Exchange Price Changes: Trading Day Effects and Risk Measurement." *Journal of Finance* (June 1982): 693–715.

Merton, R. "Theory of Rational Option Pricing," *Bell Journal of Economics* (Spring 1973): 141–83.

Ogden, J., and A. Tucker. "Empirical Tests of the Efficiency of the Currency Futures Options Market." *Journal of Futures Markets* (December 1987): 695–703.

————. "The Relative Valuation of American Currency Spot and Futures Options: Theory and Empirical Tests." *Journal of Financial and Quantitative Analysis* (December 1988): 351–68.

Rubinstein, M. "Nonparametric Tests of Alternative Option Pricing Models Using All Reported Trades and Quotes on the 30 Most Active CBOE Option Classes from August 23, 1976 through August 31, 1978," *Journal of Finance* (June 1985): 38–47.

Schwartz, E. "The Valuation of Warrants: Implementing a New Approach." *Journal of Financial Economics* (January 1977): 79–93.

Scott, E., and A. Tucker. "Predicting Currency Return Volatility." *Journal of Banking and Finance* (December 1989): 839–51.

Shastri, K., and K. Tandon, "On the Use of European Models to Price American Options on Foreign Currency." *Journal of Futures Markets* (Spring 1986a): 145–60.

————. "Valuation of Foreign Currency Options: Some Empirical Tests." *Journal of Financial and Quantitative Analysis* (June 1986b): 145–60.

Shastri, K., and K. Wethyavivorn. "The Valuation of Currency Options for Alternate Stochastic Processes." *Journal of Financial Research* (Winter 1987): 283–93.

Tucker, A. "Empirical Tests of the Efficiency of the Currency Option Market." *Journal of Financial Research* (Winter 1985): 275–85.

————. "Market-Determined Premia for American Currency Spot Options." Working Paper, Temple University (1989).

———. "Exchange Rate Jumps and Currency Options Pricing." In *Recent Developments in International Banking and Finance*, eds. S. Khoury and R. Haugen, Lexington Books, 1990.

Tucker, A., D. Peterson, and E. Scott. "Tests of the Black-Scholes and Constant Elasticity of Variance Currency Call Option Valuation Models." *Journal of Financial Research* (Fall 1988): 201–13.

Tucker, A., and L. Pond. "The Probability Distribution of Foreign Exchange Price Changes: Tests of Candidate Processes." *Review of Economics and Statistics* (November 1988): 638–47.

Tucker, A., and E. Scott. "A Study of Diffusion Processes for Foreign Exchange Rates." *Journal of International Money and Finance* (December 1987): 465–78.

Vasicek, O. "An Equilibrium Characterization of the Term Structure." *Journal of Financial Economics* (March 1982): 29–58.

Westerfield, J. "An Examination of Foreign Exchange Risk under Fixed and Floating Rate Regimes." *Journal of International Economics* (May 1977): 181–200.

Appendix 15.A

DERIVATION OF THE EUROPEAN CURRENCY OPTION PRICING MODEL

Assume that currency returns are described by the following diffusion process:

15.A.1
$$d\tilde{S}/S = (\mu - r_f)dt + \sigma d\tilde{Z},$$

where μ is the currency's instantaneous expected rate of return, r_f is the constant foreign riskless interest rate, σ is the instantaneous standard deviation of the rate of return, dt is a small increment of time, and $d\tilde{Z}$ is a standard Wiener process increment.

Applying Itô's (1951) lemma to eq. 15.A.1, we can express the change in the currency call option price, C^E, by the following stochastic differential equation:

15.A.2 $$d\tilde{C}^E = (\partial C^E/\partial S)d\tilde{S} + (\partial C^E/\partial t)dt + 1/2(\partial^2 C^E/\partial S^2)\sigma^2 S^2 dt.$$

Note that the only stochastic term in the expression for $d\tilde{C}^E$ is $d\tilde{S}$.

Next form a hedged portfolio, V_H, consisting of N_S units of the currency and N_{C^E} units of the option:

15.A.3
$$V_H = N_S S + N_{C^E} C^E.$$

The change in the value of this hedged portfolio is the total derivative of eq. 15.A.3:

15.A.4
$$d\tilde{V}_H = N_S d\tilde{S} + N_{C^E} dC^E.$$

Substituting eq. 15.A.2 into 15.A.4 gives

15.A.5
$$d\tilde{V}_H = N_S dS + N_{C^E}[(\partial C^E/\partial S)d\tilde{S} + (\partial C^E/\partial t)dt + 1/2(\partial^2 C^E/\partial S^2)\sigma^2 S^2 dt].$$

Notice that $d\tilde{V}_H$ is stochastic. However, by properly selecting N_S and N_{C^E} we can eliminate the stochastic element dS. In equilibrium the now riskless hedged portfolio should earn the domestic risk-free rate:

15.A.6 $dV_H/V_H \stackrel{e}{=} rdt.$

To eliminate $d\tilde{S}$ we set N_S and N_{C^E} equal to the following values:

15.A.7 $N_S = 1;\ N_{C^E} = -1/(\partial C^E/\partial S).$

Substituting eqs. 15.A.6 and 15.A.7 into 15.A.5 gives

15.A.8 $(\partial C^E/\partial t) = rV_H(-\partial C^E/\partial S) - 1/2(\partial^2 C^E/\partial^2 S)\sigma^2 S^2.$

Substituting eq. 15.A.3 for V_H and using eq. 15.A.7 gives

15.A.9 $(\partial C^E/\partial t) = rC^E - (r - r_f)S(\partial C^E/\partial S)$
$$- 1/2(\partial^2 C^E/\partial S^2)\sigma^2 S^2.$$

Equation 15.A.9 is a nonstochastic partial differential equation for the value of the currency call option. This partial differential equation can be solved subject to the following two boundary conditions:

15.A.10 $C^E(S,X,T = 0) = MAX(0,S - X);\ C^E(S = 0,X,T) = 0.$

The solution to eq. 15.A.9, subject to eq. 15.A.10, is the European currency call option pricing model:

15.A.11 $C^E = e^{-r_f T}SN(d) - e^{-rT}XN(d - \sigma\sqrt{T}),$

where

$$d = \frac{ln(S/X) + [r - r_f + (\sigma^2/2)]T}{\sigma\sqrt{T}}.$$

Unlike a European option that cannot be exercised prematurely, an American currency option is subject to a third boundary condition. Specifically:

15.A.12 $C^A(S,X,t^*) = MAX[C^A(S,X,t^*),\ S - X],$

where $C^A(S,X,t^*)$ is the value of an unexercised option at time t^*, an instant of time after t. Equation 15.A.12 is the boundary condition associated with the early exercise privilege of the American currency call option. At each time $t < T$ there exists a critical exchange rate, $\bar{S}(t)$, above which early exercise is optimal.

Unfortunately, this additional boundary condition precludes solving eq. 15.A.9 directly. That is, there exists no closed-form, analytic model for American currency options valuation, like eq. 15.A.11 for European pricing. Instead, the value of an American currency option must be obtained through numerical procedures or analytic approximations.

Appendix 15.B

AN AMERICAN CURRENCY OPTION PRICING MODEL

Barone-Adesi and Whaley (1987) provide a simple, quadratic approximation to value American options written on assets exhibiting continuous leakages. Their model is therefore applicable to currency options. For call options the model is

15.B.1 $\qquad C^A = C^E + A_2(S/\bar{S})^{q_2} \qquad$ where $S < \bar{S}$, and
$\qquad\qquad\qquad\quad C^A = S - X \qquad\qquad$ where $S \geq \bar{S}$,

and where

$$A_2 = (\bar{S}/q_2)\{1 - e^{-r_f T}N[d_2(\bar{S})]\}$$
$$d_2(\bar{S}) = \{[ln(\bar{S}/X) + (r - r_f + (\sigma^2/2))T]/\sigma\sqrt{T}\}$$
$$q_2 = (1 + \sqrt{1 + 4K})/2$$
$$K = 2r/[\sigma^2(1 - e^{-rT})]$$
$$\bar{S} = \text{the critical exchange rate above which the American currency}$$
$$\qquad\text{call option should be exercised immediately.}$$

$\bar{S}$ can be determined iteratively by solving eq. 15.B.2:

15.B.2 $\qquad \bar{S} - X = C^E + \{1 - e^{-r_f T}N[d_2(\bar{S})]\}\bar{S}/q_2.$

Equation 15.B.1 states that if the exchange rate is below $\bar{S}$, then the American call value is equal to its corresponding European value plus the early exercise premium, as approximated by $A_2(S/\bar{S})^{q_2}$. Above $\bar{S}$, the value of C^A is its exercisable proceeds, $S - X$.

Similarly, the value of the American currency put option is

15.B.3 $\qquad P^A = P^E + A_1(S/\bar{S})^{q_1} \qquad$ where $S > \bar{S}$,
$\qquad\qquad\qquad\quad P^A = X - S \qquad\qquad$ where $S \leq \bar{S}$,

and where

$$A_1 = (\bar{S}/q_1)\{1 - e^{-r_f T}N[-d_2(\bar{S})]\} \text{ and}$$
$$q_1 = (1 - \sqrt{1 + 4K})/2.$$

Here $\bar{S}$, the critical exchange rate below which the American currency put option should be exercised immediately, is determined iteratively by solving eq. 15.B.4:

15.B.4 $\qquad X - \bar{S} = P^E - \{1 - e^{-r_f T}N[-d_2(\bar{S})]\}\bar{S}/q_1.$

To generate American currency futures option prices, C_F^A and P_F^A, simply replace S with F, $\bar{S}$ with $\bar{F}$, and r_f with r everywhere in the preceding model developed by Barone-Adesi and Whaley.

Appendix 15.C

PROOF THAT THE INSTANTANEOUS VOLATILITIES OF CURRENCY SPOT AND FUTURES PRICE CHANGES ARE EQUAL

Define the instantaneous currency spot change relative by the following standard Itô process:

15.C.1
$$d\tilde{S} = \propto Sdt + \sigma Sd\tilde{Z}.$$

Also, let the currency futures price be given by interest rate parity:

15.C.2
$$F = Se^{(r-r_f)T},$$

where r and r_f are assumed constant. From Itô's lemma:

15.C.3
$$d\tilde{F} = [(\partial F/\partial S)\propto S + (\partial F/\partial t) + 1/2(\partial^2 F/\partial S^2)\sigma^2 S^2]dt + (\partial F/\partial S)\sigma Sd\tilde{Z},$$

where $\partial F/\partial S = e^{(r-r_f)T}$, $\partial F/\partial t = -(r - r_f)Se^{(r-r_f)T}$, and $\partial^2 F/\partial S^2 = 0$.

Substituting for the partial derivatives yields

15.C.4
$$\begin{aligned} d\tilde{F} &= [e^{(r-r_f)T}\propto S - (r - r_f)Se^{(r-r_f)T}]dt + e^{(r-r_f)T}\sigma Sd\tilde{Z} \\ &= (\mu - r + r_f)Fdt + \sigma Fd\tilde{Z}. \end{aligned}$$

Thus, the instantaneous volatility of currency spot price changes, σ, equals that of currency futures prices changes, σ. The instantaneous drifts differ by $(r - r_f)$.

Appendix 15.D

A EUROPEAN CURRENCY OPTION PRICING MODEL WITH NONCONSTANT DOMESTIC AND FOREIGN INTEREST RATES

Assume that domestic (r) and foreign (r_f) interest rates each follow an arithmetic Brownian motion:

15.D.1
$$d\tilde{r} = \mu_r dt + \sigma_r d\tilde{Z}_r; \text{ and}$$

15.D.2
$$d\tilde{r}_f = \mu_f dt + \sigma_f d\tilde{Z}_f.$$

Additionally, assume that

15.D.3 $$COV(\sigma_r d\tilde{Z}_r, \sigma_f d\tilde{Z}_f) = \sigma_{rf} dt;$$

15.D.4 $$COV(\sigma_r d\tilde{Z}_r, \sigma_f d\tilde{Z}_f) = \sigma_{rs} dt; \text{ and}$$

15.D.5 $$COV(\sigma_f d\tilde{Z}_f, \sigma_s d\tilde{Z}_S) = \sigma_{fs} dt.$$

Given these assumptions, the value of a European currency call option is

15.D.6 $$C^E = e^{-r_f T} SN(d) - e^{-rT} XN(d - \gamma),$$

where

$$d = \{[ln(S/X) + [r - r_f]T + .5\gamma^2/\gamma\} \text{ and}$$
$$\gamma^2 = \sigma_S^2 T + (1/3)T^3(\sigma_r^2 - 2\sigma_{rf} + \sigma_f^2) + T^2(\sigma_{rS} - \sigma_{fS}).$$

The value of a corresponding European currency put option is obtained from put-call parity:

15.D.7 $$P^E = C^E + Xe^{-rT} - Se^{-r_f T}.$$

For a derivation of eq. 15.D.6, see Hilliard, Madura and Tucker (1991). Also see Hsieh (1988).

CURRENCY AND INTEREST RATE SWAP MARKETS

A *currency swap* allows two firms to exchange currencies at recurrent intervals, and is usually used in conjunction with debt issues. For instance, each of two firms may issue fixed-rate debt in a unique currency, then swap the proceeds of the issues and assume each other's obligation to pay principal and interest payments. This swap of currencies can allow each firm to make payments without exposure to exchange rate risk.

As discussed briefly in Chapter 8, an *interest rate swap* occurs when a firm that has issued one form of debt agrees to swap interest payments with another firm that has issued a different form of debt denominated in the same currency. For instance, a firm that issued floating-rate dollar-denominated debt agrees in a swap to make fixed-rate payments to another firm that issued dollar-denominated fixed-rate debt. In return, the second firm makes floating-rate payments to the first. Such an interest rate swap may result in net interest savings and represents an efficient vehicle for transferring interest rate risk from one party to another.

The markets for currency and interest rate swaps grew substantially during the 1980s. For instance, although the first interest rate swaps appeared in 1982, U.S. dollar interest rate swaps exhibited volume estimated at $541 billion in 1987 alone. In this chapter we analyze these emerging derivative securities. Specifically, we undertake the following investigative issues: What are swaps and how did they evolve? What benefits do swaps provide? How are swap pricing schedules determined? How are swaps related to other securities, including forward contracts and default-free loans? And what lies ahead for this emerging market? Swaps are important financial instruments because they have meaningfully contributed to the integration of the world's capital markets.

CURRENCY SWAPS

A standard currency swap entails the exchange of debt denominated in one currency for debt denominated in another currency. For example, suppose a U.S. multinational corporation, MNC_{US}, wants to issue a

Figure 16.1   Currency Swap

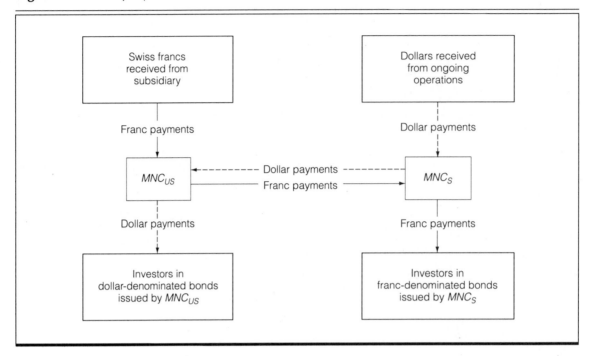

Swiss franc-denominated bond since it can make payments with franc inflows generated by a Swiss subsidiary. Also, suppose there exists a Swiss multinational, MNC$_S$, that seeks to issue dollar-denominated debt. MNC$_{US}$ could issue dollar debt while MNC$_S$ issues franc debt. MNC$_{US}$ could then provide franc payments, both principal and interest, to MNC$_S$ in exchange for dollar payments. This swap of currencies allows the two multinationals to make payments to their respective debtholders without having to repatriate foreign exchange. For instance, MNC$_{US}$ does not need to convert francs into dollars. Thus, the two MNC$_S$ have reduced their exchange exposure. Figure 16.1 illustrates this currency swap.

Currency swaps evolved from back-to-back loans and parallel loans, which came into popularity in the United Kingdom in the 1970s. These loans provided a means of circumventing foreign exchange controls implemented to prevent the outflow of U.K. capital. These controls were usually in the form of taxes imposed on foreign transactions, thereby discouraging the outflow of pounds and encouraging domestic investment. Back-to-back and parallel loans were created to avoid this tax. *Back-to-back loans* occur between two national firms, each making the other a loan in its respective currency. *Parallel loans* occur when each MNC makes a loan to the other's subsidiary; here each MNC makes the loan in its respective currency, and each subsidiary is located in the other's country. For instance, MNC$_{US}$ may loan dollars to a British MNC's U.S. subsidiary, while the British MNC, MNC$_{UK}$, loans pounds

A Currency Swap between IBM and the World Bank

International Business Machines and the World Bank engaged in the first-ever currency swap in August 1981. IBM exhibited outstanding debt in both West German marks and Swiss francs. The debt was fixed rate. The dollar had greatly appreciated against both foreign currencies earlier in the year. The management of IBM wanted to swap its foreign obligations for dollar obligations in order to reap the gain on its liabilities due to the dollar's appreciation. To do so, IBM engaged in a swap with the World Bank. This swap was arranged by Salomon Brothers. The World Bank issued two dollar Eurobonds, one with the same maturity as IBM's mark debt and one with the same maturity as IBM's franc debt. The World Bank paid all principal and periodic interest obligations on IBM's debt and, in return, IBM paid the World Bank's dollar obligations. This transaction introduced an entirely new financial innovation, the currency swap.

to the U.S.-MNC's subsidiary located in Britain. The principal and periodic interest payments on these loans are structured to coincide. Since the loans are repaid with foreign revenues from ongoing operations, we have avoided the tax on currency translations. The British MNC does not need to convert pounds into dollars. Also, note that we have achieved the basic structure of a currency swap, which minimizes the MNCs' exposure to exchange rate risk. Figure 16.2 illustrates the swap for the parallel loan.[1] Today's currency swaps evolved as simple extensions of such loan agreements.

Rationales for the Existence of Currency Swaps

Since foreign exchange controls are generally not applied by today's governments, why do currency swaps still exist? It is generally agreed that there are two (related) reasons for the existence and popularity of currency swaps today. The first is exchange rate risk reallocation, as exemplified by the swap arrangements described earlier. The second is regulatory barriers to capital flows. For instance, in the first currency swap described, MNC_{US} wanted to issue Swiss franc-denominated debt. Instead of issuing such debt directly, MNC_{US} issued dollar-denominated debt and engaged in a currency swap with MNC_S in order to reduce exchange exposure. Perhaps MNC_{US} was precluded from issuing franc debt directly. That is, the inability to issue debt in Switzerland, representing a barrier to capital flow, resulted in the swap arrangement. Thus, by engaging in the swap the U.S.-MNC circumvented the capital flow barrier. Also, MNC_{US} may have preferred to issue dollar-denominated debt because it is better known in the United States than in Switzerland. If issuing dollar-denominated debt reduces financing costs, the swap arrangement is attractive. This same argument holds from the

---

[1] The parallel loan agreement often contained an embedded futures contract. Should one currency have depreciated greatly relative to the other during the loan period, the lender of the devalued currency was required to increase its loan to offset its gain.

Figure 16.2   A Parallel Loan Swap

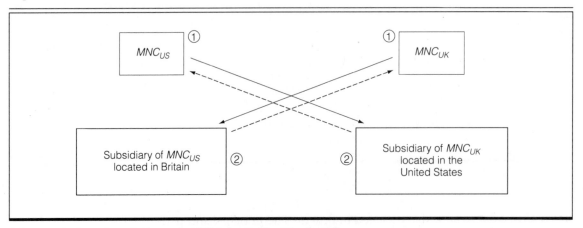

1. Loans are simultaneously provided by parents of MNCs to the subsidiary of the other MNC.
2. At contemporaneous times the principal and periodic interest payments are repaid in the same currency that was borrowed.

viewpoint of MNC$_S$.[2] Thus, currency swaps can be used to overcome barriers to international capital movements. For this reason, swaps have played an important role in integrating the world's capital markets.

INTEREST RATE SWAPS

Interest rate swaps evolved in the early 1980s as a special case of a currency swap in which all payments are made in the same currency. In the classical example of an interest rate swap, borrowers who are creditworthy with a cost advantage in both the fixed-rate and floating-rate debt markets, but exhibit a comparative advantage in the fixed-rate market, can borrow in that market and swap the fixed interest payments for floating payments with another less creditworthy borrower who issues floating-rate debt. Interest payments but not the principal are swapped, and payments are conditional in that if one party defaults then the other is absolved of its obligation. Since the principal is not swapped, we say that it is *notional*. The gains from this swap are allocated between the two parties and, typically, a financial intermediary who facilitates the swap.[3]

The parameters provided in Exhibit 16.1 can be used to illustrate a traditional interest rate swap. Firm A can issue U.S. dollar-denominated

---

[2] Recognize that not being well known in Switzerland really represents a form of capital flow barrier faced by MNC$_{US}$. Further, the foreign exchange controls originally implemented by the U.K. government merely represented a form of capital flow barrier.
[3] Swaps are not standardized contracts traded on organized exchanges. Commercial or investment banks acting as brokers facilitate the swap, often guaranteeing both sides of the contract. These banks maintain carefully guarded lists of debt issuers who may be potential parties to a swap. Also, banks will serve as a party to the swap, warehousing the swap until they can off-load it.

Exhibit 16.1

Parameters for an Interest
Rate Swap

	Firm A	Firm B	Differential
Fixed:	9.5%	10.2%	70 bps
Floating:	LIBOR + 15 bps	LIBOR + 30 bps	15 bps
		Net differential	55 bps

Note: The differential represents the relative credit risk premium. The relative credit risk premium for A for fixed-rate debt (70 bps) is greater than its relative credit risk premium for floating-rate debt (15 bps).

fixed-rate debt at 9.5%, or floating-rate debt at LIBOR plus 15 basis points (bps).[4] Firm B, which is less creditworthy, can issue dollar-denominated fixed-rate debt of the same maturity at 10.2% or floating-rate debt at LIBOR plus 30 bps. The difference in the credit risk premiums in the fixed and floating debt markets are 70 bps and 15 bps, respectively. Hence, the difference in the fixed-rate market is comparatively greater; firm A has a credit advantage in both markets, but a *comparative advantage* in the fixed debt market. The net difference in Exhibit 16.1 (55 bps) represents the gain from the swap, which is distributed among the two firms and the swap intermediary.

Assume that firm A issues fixed-rate debt at 9.5% and B issues floating-rate debt at LIBOR plus 30 bps. In the swap, A pays the intermediary a floating rate of LIBOR plus 5 bps and the intermediary pays firm A a fixed rate of 9.8%.[5] Firm B pays the intermediate a fixed rate of 10.05% and in return receives a floating rate of LIBOR plus 20 bps from the intermediary. The net payments to the two firms are shown in Figure 16.3.

The result of the swap is that A has effectively issued floating-rate debt at LIBOR minus 25 bps, saving 40 bps from issuing floating debt directly. Firm B has effectively issued fixed-rate debt at 10.15%, saving 5 bps from issuing fixed debt directly. The intermediary reaps 10 bps: +25 bps on the fixed-rate debt and −15 bps on the floating-rate debt. Hence, the total gain from the swap to all parties is 55 bps.[6]

---

[4] LIBOR is an acronym for the London Interbank Offer Rate, which is the interest rate earned on Eurodollar deposits. Eurodollar deposits are dollar-denominated deposits in European banks or a European branch of an American bank. The LIBOR is a variable rate, and it is typically used to establish the coupon payments on floating-rate Eurobonds. Eurobonds are bonds underwritten by international syndicates and sold outside the country of the currency that denominated the bonds. Here, firm A can issue Eurobonds, denominated in U.S. dollars but sold outside of the United States, at LIBOR plus 15 bps. The growth of interest rate swaps is linked to the increasing growth of the Eurobond market. For more on this subject, see Kidwell, Marr, and Thompson (1985).
[5] In practice these payments would be netted. Also, assume (for simplicity only) that all payments are made contemporaneously.
[6] The market for swaps has grown more competitive. As a result, the spreads earned by swap intermediaries have declined. Today a spread of about 5 to 10 bps earned by the intermediary is common.

Figure 16.3

An Interest Rate Swap

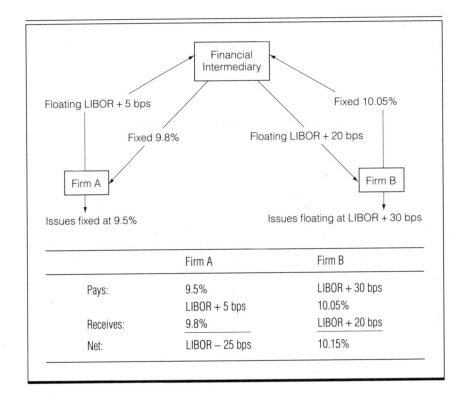

	Firm A	Firm B
Pays:	9.5%	LIBOR + 30 bps
	LIBOR + 5 bps	10.05%
Receives:	9.8%	LIBOR + 20 bps
Net:	LIBOR – 25 bps	10.15%

Rationales for the Existence of Interest Rate Swaps

Currently there exists some debate as to why interest rate swaps exist, and what benefits they provide. In the classical example of an interest rate swap, the swap itself results from a credit market comparative advantage. Firm A's comparative advantage in the fixed-rate debt market results in "gains from trade" similar to those gains arising from any specialization of trade arrangement.

This rationale has been criticized on two accounts, however. First, it is unusual that the creditworthy firm (A) exhibits a relative credit risk premium on floating debt (15 bps) that is lower than its relative credit risk premium on fixed debt (70 bps). Presumably, the lower-rated firm (B) should face a higher relative credit risk premium on floating-rate debt since it is less able to meet debt obligations should interest rates rise. Some have argued that this apparent underpricing of floating-rate credit risk may be the result of embedded option values. Specifically, the apparent savings from borrowing at a fixed rate via a swap may be attributable to a lost *prepayment option* that firm B would normally have if it issued fixed debt directly. This prepayment option is the call provision evident in the vast majority of standard corporate bonds. Therefore, in our example, firm B can borrow at a fixed rate more cheaply by swapping from floating because the borrowing-floating/swap-to-fixed alternative does not include the interest rate (i.e., prepayment) option contained in the borrow-fixed alternative. Firm B has effectively sold an interest rate option since interest rate swaps normally do not contain such an option. The apparent gains from trade therefore may not be genuine. These "gains" instead derive from a foregone option. The premium from this sold option is shared by the two firms and the intermediary.

The second criticism of the gains-from-trade argument is that if the gains from trade were genuine, then in an efficient credit market such gains would not be persistent, since arbitrageurs would rapidly exploit them. The comparative-advantage rationale neglects arbitrage. With no barriers to capital flows the comparative-advantage rationale cannot hold, because arbitrage eliminates any potential gains. Thus, the comparative-advantage argument cannot explain the persistent growth of the interest rate swap market, if credit markets operate efficiently.

From these two criticisms it is apparent that superficial interest rate savings may not be motivating interest rate swaps. So why are these swaps still so popular?

Another viable rationale focuses on the management of interest rate exposure. For example, a savings and loan or other thrift may employ an interest rate swap to help manage the gap between its asset and liability maturities. As an alternative to offering adjustable-rate mortgages or selling mortgages and reinvesting the proceeds in shorter-term assets, the thrift may engage in swaps to help reduce its interest rate exposure. By properly engaging in an interest rate swap, the thrift can convert its fixed-rate assets to floating-rate assets, convert its floating-rate liabilities to fixed-rate liabilities, or both. Thrifts and insurance companies are active participants in the interest rate swap market.

Further, these swaps may exist because of their usefulness in creating new financial instruments. Before the introduction of interest rate swaps, when the only instruments available to borrowers were long-term fixed-rate, long-term floating-rate, and short-term debt, there was no instrument that allowed a firm to achieve a fixed-base interest rate and a floating credit spread. A combination of short-term funding and a swap in which the borrower receives floating and pays fixed, however, achieves a fixed base and floating spread. A firm that anticipates an improved credit rating may employ this combination. Consequently, the existence of interest rate swaps allows issuers to separate interest rate risk and credit risk, and hedge the target amount of each. Interest rate swaps therefore provide for more complete markets, in the Arrow-Debrue sense.

As another example of a synthetic instrument created by interest rate swaps, consider the combination of a fixed-rate loan and interest rate swap where the firm pays fixed. This combination produces a reverse floating-rate loan. If interest rates rise, then the coupon payments on the loan actually fall.

SWAP INTERMEDIARIES

Investment banks, commercial banks, and independent brokers and dealers facilitate swap transactions. In the early days of the swap market, these intermediaries would act as brokers. That is, they would

Exhibit 16.2

Indication Pricing Schedule for
Interest Rate Swap Transactions

Maturity	Intermediary Pays Fixed Rate	Intermediary Receives Fixed Rate	U.S. Treasury Note Rate
2 years	2-yr. TN sa + 19 bps	2-yr. TN sa + 41 bps	8.50%
3 years	3-yr. TN sa + 23 bps	3-yr. TN sa + 49 bps	8.67%
4 years	4-yr. TN sa + 26 bps	4-yr. TN sa + 54 bps	8.79%
5 years	5-yr. TN sa + 31 bps	5-yr. TN sa + 56 bps	8.86%
6 years	6-yr. TN sa + 35 bps	6-yr. TN sa + 63 bps	8.91%
7 years	7-yr. TN sa + 40 bps	7-yr. TN sa + 69 bps	8.95%

simply serve as agents in matching the swap parties. For this service, an intermediary would charge a commission. Also, since the intermediary merely served as a broker, it incurred no risk exposure.

Today, however, most intermediaries in the swap market act as dealers. Thus, they serve as a counterparty to the swap and are consequently exposed to exchange rate, interest rate, or default risks. To limit these risks, the intermediary typically engages in an *offsetting swap* (also known as a *matched swap*), thereby laying off its swap risk. Like a futures market clearinghouse, by engaging in a matched swap, the intermediary's position is net zero in the market. The intermediary profits from the basis point spread (as illustrated in Figure 16.3), and may charge each client a front-end fee as well.

What if the intermediary has trouble finding a swap counterparty to lay off its risk? How can the intermediary protect itself during the interim period? The answer is that the intermediary must use the short-term debt market. For example, suppose that a client issues $10 million of floating-rate debt and then swaps this debt for fixed-rate debt with the intermediary. Ideally, the intermediary would like to swap with another client (serving as a counterparty) who seeks to issue fixed-rate debt and exchange it for floating. If such a counterparty cannot be found quickly, however, the intermediary will most likely short $10 million of longer-term fixed debt and employ the proceeds to purchase $10 million of T-bills. The intermediary is then paying a fixed rate and receiving a floating rate (i.e., the T-bill rate). Since the T-bill and LIBOR rates are highly correlated, however, the intermediary is hedging its interest rate risk. The intermediary will roll over its T-bill position until a counterparty can be found.

INDICATION PRICING SCHEDULES

Intermediaries who facilitate swap transactions regularly quote swap prices through the use of *indication pricing schedules*. Exhibit 16.2 provides such a schedule for interest rate swaps. The schedule was obtained from a leading swap dealer. It assumes semiannual rates and *bullet transactions,* meaning that the loan principal is repaid in full at maturity. For example, a T-bill represents a type of bullet transaction.

Notice two important aspects of this typical pricing schedule. First, there is a spread between the situations in which the intermediary pays a fixed rate and those in which it receives a fixed rate. For example, the spread for a maturity of five years is 25 basis points. The intermediary's revenue ultimately stems from this spread. Second, no floating rates appear in the schedule. When this occurs, the floating side is assumed to be the six-month LIBOR flat.

Suppose that a U.S. company decides to issue $10 million of five-year debt, at par, which is nonamortizing (a bullet transaction) and exhibits a semiannual coupon payment of 9.50%. The company then approaches our intermediary to arrange a swap in which the intermediary pays a fixed rate and receives a floating rate. In other words, the U.S. company seeks to swap its fixed-rate debt for floating. Since the intermediary will pay fixed and receive floating, it pays 9.17% (5-year TN rate + 31 bps) and receives six-month LIBOR flat. The intermediary then seeks a counterparty to offset this swap transaction. For the U.S. company, the resulting debt cost is approximately LIBOR + 0.33% (9.50% + LIBOR − 9.17%).[7] Presumably, this cost is lower than what the firm could have obtained by issuing floating-rate debt directly.

Exhibit 16.3 provides a typical indication price schedule for a fixed-for-floating-rate currency swap entailing the British pound and the U.S. dollar. Notice that prices are expressed as a midrate, with the intermediary adding or deducting basis points depending on whether it receives or pays a fixed rate. Here the spread is 10 bps, representing the source of revenues for the currency swap intermediary.

Suppose that a British firm seeks to convert £10,000,000 three-year semiannual fixed-rate debt into floating-rate dollar-denominated debt. The intermediary will exchange dollars for pounds at the prevailing spot exchange rate, which is $1.50/£1 (assumed). Consequently, the intermediary receives £10,000,000 and pays $16,000,000. The principals will be exchanged in three years at the same initial spot rate of $1.60/£1. These principals are assumed to be bullet transactions.

Since the intermediary is paying a fixed rate, the applicable rate is 6.22% (semiannual): 6.27% sa midrate − 5 bps. Thus, the British firm pays the swap intermediary the six-month LIBOR on a principal of $16,000,000, and the intermediary pays the British firm 6.22% sa on a principal of £10,000,000. Presumably, the British firm would have had to pay more to issue floating-rate dollar-denominated debt directly, or perhaps was precluded from issuing such debt at all because of capital flow barriers. Meanwhile, the intermediary will search for a swap counterparty to eliminate its exchange rate risk. Ideally, the counterparty would seek to exchange $16,000,000 three-year floating-rate debt for fixed-rate

---

[7] Actually, a slight adjustment must be made because the six-month LIBOR is quoted on the basis of a 360-day year, whereas bond yields assume a 365-day year. Since the LIBOR and coupon rates are both semiannual here, the adjustment is simply LIBOR + 0.33% (360/365) = LIBOR + 0.3255%.

Exhibit 16.3

Indication Pricing Schedule for
British Pound/U.S. Dollar Swaps

Maturity	Midrate[a]
2 years	6.05% sa
3 years	6.27% sa
4 years	6.44% sa
5 years	6.58% sa
6 years	6.68% sa
7 years	6.75% sa

[a] Deduct 5 bps if the intermediary is paying a fixed rate, and add 5 bps if it is receiving a fixed rate.

debt denominated in British pounds. Depending on market conditions, the intermediary may have to move its midrates or spread in order to attract such a counterparty. As with any security, the price of a swap must respond to supply and demand forces in the marketplace.

SWAPS AS A PORTFOLIO OF FORWARD CONTRACTS

It is interesting to relate swaps to other securities, including other derivative securities. For example, a traditional swap can be expressed as a portfolio of forward contracts. To illustrate this concept, consider the interest rate swap shown in Figure 16.3.[8] Suppose that this swap was based on the six-month LIBOR such that interest payments are exchanged every six months. One party simply sends a check covering the difference between the fixed and floating payments to the other. However, with a swap the rate that is used on the payment dates is (here) the six-month LIBOR that prevailed six months earlier. The first payment date occurs six months after the inception of the swap, so that the first payment is known at inception, the second payment is known six months after inception, and so on. For instance, suppose that the LIBOR is 11% six months before a payment date. From Figure 16.3 and assuming semiannual compounding for all interest rates, firm A would be required to pay the intermediary the following amount on the next payment date:

16.1 $0.50(0.1105 - 0.0980)NP = 0.00625NP,$

where NP is the notional principal of the swap. In turn, the intermediary would pay firm B the following amount:

16.2 $0.50(0.1120 - 0.1005)NP = 0.00575NP.$

Thus, the intermediary's profit is $0.0005NP$ per six months, or 10 bps per year.

---

[8] Using a similar analysis, it is possible to demonstrate that a currency swap can be represented by a portfolio of currency forward contracts.

To generalize this process, denote L as the six-month LIBOR on any previous payment (or inception) date. Thus, the payoff to firm A on each payment date is

16.3
$$NP/2[0.098 - (L + 5 \text{ bps})].$$

This expression is nothing more than a forward contract on six-month LIBOR that is settled up six months in arrears. Thus, for firm A the swap can be represented by a portfolio of these forward contracts. If the swap (debt instrument) has a 10-year maturity, then there are 20 of these in-arrears forward contracts.

For firm B, the payoff on each payment date is given by the following in-arrears forward contracts:

16.4
$$NP/2[(L + 20 \text{ bps}) - 0.1005].$$

At the swap's inception, the *sum* of the values of these forward contracts should be zero. But each forward contract's value is not necessarily equal to zero, as is the case for a normal forward contract. For example, suppose that the term structure of interest rates is upward sloping, which is common. As a consequence, for A the forward rate of interest is likely to be less than 9.8% when the forward contract's maturity is short, and vice versa. For firm A, the values of the shorter-maturity forward contracts are therefore likely to be negative, while the values of the longer-term forward contracts are likely to be positive. The opposite is true for firm B.

Cash flow patterns such as these have implications for default risk when considering swap arrangements. For instance, firm B is more likely to default later in the swap period if, as just described, the term structure is upward sloping. The preceding analysis of swaps as a portfolio of forward contracts implicitly assumes that the swap arrangement is free of default risk. We further discuss default risk in a following section.

SWAPS AS A PORTFOLIO OF DEFAULT-FREE BONDS

Swaps can also be expressed as a portfolio of default-free bonds, assuming no default risk exists. To illustrate this concept, consider the arrangement between firm A and the financial intermediary in Figure 16.3.[9] In this arrangement, firm A borrows the notional principal, NP, from the intermediary at a fixed rate of 9.8%. In turn, the swap intermediary borrows NP from firm A at LIBOR plus 5 bps. Define B_1 as the value of a fixed-rate, default-free bond that pays 9.8%. Define B_2 as the value of a default-free bond paying LIBOR plus 5 bps. Thus, the value of the interest rate swap to the intermediary is $B_1 - B_2$. In other words, the swap value can be expressed as a portfolio of the two default-free bonds.

---

[9] Using a similar analysis, it is possible to demonstrate that a currency swap can be represented as a portfolio of default-free bonds.

Should interest rates increase, the value of the swap to firm A increases. The value of the swap to firm B can be similarly decomposed into a portfolio of default-free bonds. By finding a swap counterparty, the intermediary eliminates its interest rate risk.

DEFAULT RISK AND REGULATION

Swaps are typically arranged by financial intermediaries that have entered into offsetting contracts with the two firms involved. These intermediaries are fully hedged if neither firm defaults. For instance, in the interest rate swap illustrated in Figure 16.1, the intermediary earns 10 bps annually if A and B do not default, regardless of how the six-month LIBOR varies over the swap period.

However, should one firm default, the intermediary is no longer fully hedged. The intermediary must honor the swap arrangement with the remaining firm and, thus, is exposed to risk. For instance, if B defaults and interest rates rise, the intermediary loses monies. This result is evident from the preceding discussion of interest rate swaps as portfolios of bond instruments.

Given the present competitive nature of the swap market, the smaller spreads being earned by intermediaries, the off-balance-sheet nature of swap arrangements, and the fact that commercial banks are becoming bigger players in swap intermediation, regulators of these banks are becoming more and more concerned with default risk as it relates to swaps.[10] Although bank supervisory authorities such as the Federal Reserve are just beginning to grapple with this issue, some regulatory recommendations are being given intense consideration:

- Risk weighting. In a risk-weighting scheme, now used widely in the United Kingdom, a bank's capital adequacy requirement is determined by assigning to each balance and off-balance-sheet item, including swaps, a weight reflecting the item's riskiness. The major determinants of this weight for asset items are the credit risk of the other party and the asset's maturity.

- Marking to the market. As explained earlier, swaps are akin to a series of forward contracts. From Chapter 12, we know that a significant difference between forwards and futures is that the latter require daily resettlement. This daily procedure of marking to the market helps to reduce the riskiness of a futures position relative to that of a forward position. Now notice that a swap entails a series of resettlements that fall somewhere between a listed futures contract and a normal forward contract. For example, the interest rate swap described earlier entailed resettlement every six months. By shortening the interval between payment dates, therefore, the swap is less risky to the intermediary. This is obvious when one thinks about a swap intermediary

---

[10] However, it should still be kept in mind that swap defaults have far lighter consequences to commercial bank intermediaries than do straight loan defaults. Recall that the principal on an interest rate swap is only notional.

as a type of futures market clearinghouse. Thus, shortening the resettlement window on swaps may help to reduce the intermediary's risk exposure.

- Performancing bonding. Margins in a futures or options market represent a type of performance bond. Similar performance bonding occurs in swaps markets, although it is not required by legislation. For example, a firm with a low credit rating may have to post collateral in the form of financial securities in order to engage in the swap arrangement. Also, performance bonding through insurance has been used. For instance, the World Bank established an arrangement in which the default risk of a swap is assumed by a private insurer, Aetna Casualty and Surety Co.

OTHER TYPES OF SWAPS

The currency and interest rate swaps we have thus far presented in this chapter can be called "straight" or "plain" swaps. We now briefly describe a number of more elaborate swap arrangements:

- Amortized swaps. Here the principal reduces over time, similar to the way that a home mortgage is amortized.
- Deferred swaps. Here interest payments do not begin until a more deferred future date.
- Circus swaps. These are combinations of currency and interest rate swaps. The parties exchange fixed-rate debt denominated in one currency for floating-rate debt denominated in another currency. The swap arrangement described earlier in connection with Exhibit 16.3 (in which a British firm swapped fixed-rate pound-denominated debt for floating-rate dollar-denominated debt) is an example of a circus swap.
- Extendable swaps. Here one of the parties has the option to extend the swap's life beyond the originally prescribed period.
- Puttable swaps. Here one party has the option to terminate the swap before its originally prescribed period.

THE FUTURE FOR SWAP MARKETS

In 1982, the combined value of dollar currency and interest rate swaps outstanding was about $5 billion. In 1984 the combined value grew to over $45 billion, and at year-end 1987 this value was over $703 billion. The swaps market has exhibited astonishingly rapid growth, attesting to its vital role in integrating international capital markets. Swaps have effectively created a single unified international capital market from what was earlier, due to restrictions on capital flows, a set of segmented capital markets.

Currently, the development of the swaps market is akin to the early development of the futures and options markets. That is, swaps are initiated through an informal network of brokers and dealers, are tailored contracts, and exhibit little secondary market trading. Recently, however, there has been a concentrated effort to offer more standardized swap contracts, known as *master agreements,* in order to reduce the time and costs associated with swap contracting and to enhance the trading liquidity of swaps in secondary markets.

Much of this effort has been initiated by the International Swap Dealers Association (ISDA), which is an organization of leading swap intermediaries originally founded in 1985. During that year, the ISDA published *The Code of Standard Wording, Assumptions, and Provisions for Swaps,* a document that has been revised and expanded annually since then. The purpose of the code was to establish master agreements, from which every swap transaction could be created as a supplement to these agreements. In other words, these master agreements provided a set of terms applicable to any swap transaction; the parties could then tailor the transaction by appending specific terms to the master agreement.

Today, two master agreements exist: the *Interest Rate Swap Agreement* and the *Interest Rate and Currency Exchange Agreement.* The former agreement relates to U.S. dollar-denominated interest rate swaps, and the second relates to currency and circus swap transactions. The actual swap contract negotiated between the parties typically represents some extension of these basic agreements. In this way, the costs of negotiation are limited to these extensions.

The swaps market will very likely continue to expand. Swaps provide for interest rate and exchange rate risk reallocations, help to create synthetic instruments that serve to complete the market, and play a major role in the integration of the world's capital markets. As this market expands, swap transactions are becoming more and more standardized. It appears that the market is moving toward standardization, in much the same way that the markets for futures and options did earlier in this century.

SUMMARY

Currency swaps enable multinational corporations to exchange currencies at periodic intervals and are typically used to complement debt issues in which payments are made in a foreign currency. The currency swap market is unorganized and growing, and its existence can be clearly linked to exchange exposure management and to international market segmentation, including regulatory barriers to capital flows.

An interest rate swap generally occurs when two firms agree to trade interest payments on each other's outstanding debt. The debt issues are denominated in the same currency, and the trade typically involves both fixed-rate and floating-rate debt. The interest rate swap market is growing very rapidly. In the classical example of this swap, a credit market comparative advantage gives rise to gains from trade. However, such gains should not persist because of arbitrage restrictions and may instead represent compensation for lost prepayment options. The existence and growth of this market most likely result from the ability of interest rate swaps to facilitate interest rate risk reallocation and to create synthetic financial instruments.

Both currency and interest rate swaps can be expressed as a portfolio of forward contracts or default-free bonds in the absence of default risk. Financial intermediaries who facilitate swaps, as well as their supervisory authorities, are currently grappling with the issue of default risk.

The organization of the swaps market is becoming more structured as parties seek standardized swap arrangements in order to reduce the costs of transacting. To this extent, the International Swap Dealers Association is playing a major role in the development of consistent swap terms.

Questions and Problems

1. Define a currency swap. Define an interest rate swap.
2. Define a back-to-back loan. Define a parallel loan.
3. Provide two reasons for the existence of currency swaps.
4. Provide two reasons for the existence of interest rate swaps.
5. Provide two criticisms of the credit market comparative advantage argument for the existence of interest rate swaps.
6. Given the following parameters, what are the potential "gains from trade" from an interest rate swap? Devise a swap in which both firms and a swap intermediary gain.

	Firm A	Firm B
Fixed:	10.0%	10.75%
Floating:	LIBOR + 10 bps	LIBOR + 30 bps

7. Discuss how swaps can be expressed as a portfolio of forward contracts in the absence of default risk.
8. Suppose that a firm can borrow at a fixed rate of 11.25%, or at a floating rate of LIBOR plus 60 bps. On the other hand, the firm can enter into a fixed-for-floating-interest-rate swap in which the intermediary would pay LIBOR flat while the firm would pay 10.00%. Should the firm issue fixed-rate debt directly, or issue floating and swap to fixed? Why?
9. Consider the indication pricing schedule for interest rate swap transactions appearing in Exhibit 16.2. Suppose that a U.S. corporation issues $25 million of seven-year debt (at par), which is nonamortizing and exhibits a semiannual coupon payment of 9.30%. If the corporation engages in a swap in which the intermediary pays fixed and receives floating, then: (a) What will be the floating rate cost to the corporation? (b) What rates will the intermediary receive and pay? (c) If the corporation could issue floating-rate debt directly at LIBOR + 0.25%, should it engage in the fixed-to-floating-interest-rate swap?
10. In question 9, how would the intermediary most likely try to offset the swap? In other words, describe the ideal swap counterparty.

11. Consider the following indication pricing schedule for Swiss franc/U.S. dollar swaps:

Maturity	Midrate[a]
3 years	6.19% sa
4 years	6.35% sa
5 years	6.49% sa

[a] Deduct 5 bps if the intermediary is paying fixed, and add 5 bps if it is receiving fixed.

Suppose that a Swiss firm wants to convert SF1,000,000 four-year semiannual fixed-rate debt into floating-rate dollar-denominated debt: (a) What does the Swiss firm pay the intermediary, and what does the intermediary pay the firm? (b) Why might the firm seek to undertake this circus swap?

12. In the preceding swap arrangement, describe the intermediary's ideal swap counterparty.

References

Arak, M., A. Estrella, L. Goodman, and A. Silver. "Interest Rate Swaps: An Alternative Explanation." *Financial Management* (Summer 1988): 12–18.

Arnold, T. "How to Do Interest Rate Swaps." *Harvard Business Review* (September/October 1984): 96–101.

Beckstrom, R. "The Development of the Swap Market." In *Swap Finance*, ed. B. Antl, vol. 1. London: Euromoney Publications, 1986.

Beidleman, C. *Financial Swaps*. Homewood, Ill.: Dow Jones-Irwin, 1985.

Bicksler, J., and A. Chen. "An Economic Analysis of Interest Rate Swaps." *Journal of Finance* (July 1986): 645–55.

Felgran, S. "Interest Rate Swaps: Use, Risk, and Prices." *New England Economic Review* (Federal Reserve Bank of Boston) (November 1987): 22–32.

Gary, R., W. Kruz, and C. Strupp. "Interest Rate Swaps." In *Swap Financing Techniques*, ed. B. Antl, 11–15. London: Euromoney Publications, 1983.

Kidwell, D., W. Marr, and R. Thompson. "Eurodollar Bonds: Alternative Financing for U.S. Companies." *Financial Management* (Winter 1985): 18–27.

Lipsky, J., and S. Elhalaski. "Swap-Driven Primary Insurance in the International Bond Market." Salomon Brothers Inc. (January 1986).

Park, Y. "Currency Swaps as a Long-Term International Financing Technique." *Journal of International Business Studies* 15, no. 3 (Winter 1984): 47–54.

Powers, J. "The Vortex of Finance." *Intermarket Magazine*, 3, no. 2 (February 1986): 27–38.

Price, J., J. Keller, and M. Nelson. "The Delicate Art of Swaps." *Euromoney* (April 1983): 118–25.

Shirreff, D. "The Fearsome Growth of Swaps." *Euromoney* (October 1985): 247–61.

Smith, C., C. Smithson, and L. Wakeman. "The Evolving Market for Swaps." *Midland Corporate Finance Journal* (Winter 1986): 20–32.

————. "The Market for Interest Rate Swaps." *Financial Management* (Winter 1988): 34–44.

Turnbull, S. "Swaps: A Zero Sum Game." *Financial Management* (Spring 1987): 15–22.

Wall, L. "Interest Rate Swaps in an Agency Theoretic Model with Uncertain Interest Rates." Working paper no. 86–6, Federal Reserve Bank of Atlanta (July 1986).

Wall, L., and J. Pringle. "Alternative Explanations of Interest Rate Swaps." Working paper no. 87–2, Federal Reserve Bank of Atlanta (April 1987).

Whittaker, J. "Interest Rate Swaps: Risk and Regulation." *Economic Review* (Federal Reserve Bank of Kansas City) 72, no. 3 (March 1987): 3–13.

Appendix A

INTEGRATION OF THE EUROPEAN ECONOMIC COMMUNITY

With the removal of import tariffs and a common agricultural policy of price supports and production management between member nations of the European Economic Community (EEC) in the late 1960s, the EEC completed an important step toward the creation of a unified or *common market*. The total integration of EEC trading and markets is scheduled for completion in 1992, when the last of all nontariff barriers are to be removed. Such nontariff barriers include divergent national product standards, differential rates of value-added taxes and excise duties, and other barriers such as customs controls.

The idea of a common market originated in 1952 with the *Treaty of Rome*. Today the twelve national economies that constitute the EEC, with their 323 million people, represent a substantial portion of world output and trade. A free market of 323 million West Europeans would represent a third capitalist economic power, bigger in population than Japan or North America. The current challenge facing these twelve nations is the removal of intra-EEC barriers and, thus, the creation of a single EEC home market. Such market integration may lead to enhanced economic prosperity and a strong and unified Western Europe.

After the removal of import tariffs in the 1960s, the EEC, under the direction of the Commission of the European Communities, set out to remove all nontariff barriers. Such barriers include a hodgepodge of national inspection laws, regulatory regimes, technical standards, and industrial policies that preclude British firms from selling phones to the French telecommunications monopoly, or German firms from marketing life insurance in Ireland. The barrier removal process had been slow and somewhat unsuccessful until 1985, when an EEC summit endorsed a European Commission's plan for full integration. This plan, detailed in the Commission's "White Paper on Completing the Internal Market" (Brussels, 1985), established a detailed legislative program consisting of over 300 acts to remove nontariff barriers. Currently over one-third of these acts have been adopted and, consequently, the EEC is making substantial progress toward its goal of full integration by year-end 1992.

This goal and the Commission's 1985 plan were affirmed by the *Single European Act* of 1987, the first and only amendment to the Treaty of Rome.

Yet, many nontariff barriers exist that currently preclude unification. For instance, several barriers are still in place that fragment what would otherwise be the world's largest automobile market. These include differential taxation levels on car sales across EEC countries; differential national vehicle equipment requirements; and differential fiscal incentives to promote emission standards. A report by Ford of Europe documents that ECU 285,000,000 could be saved as a result of eliminating divergent European specifications on the product development costs of passenger cars alone.[1] It is barriers such as these that integration seeks to tear down. Ultimately, the goal is to have community-wide standards and regulatory schemes to replace the national ones now in existence.

Integration of the banking sector is also a priority. Currently each EEC country is dominated by an oligopoly of big banks: three in France, three in Germany, and four in Britain. Each oligopoly's size and resources present a formidable barrier to competitive entry by cross-border banks.

To try to create one truly common banking market in the EEC, two steps have already been taken, and one step remains. First, an international deal has been struck concerning capital adequacy. In the Bank for International Settlements Act (December 1987), a set of rules and ratios has been established to ensure that no bank in Europe benefits from imprudent or lax capital requirements. Second, a draft titled "The Second Banking Coordination Directive" was produced by the Commission in January 1988. This draft effectively enacts a common law defining what a bank is and its scope of allowable operations. And the EEC has agreed to a very liberal scope of operations. For instance, EEC banks are now able to sell mutual funds. Third, work has begun on the remaining step of ensuring that all EEC countries have deposit insurance.

These three steps should establish a type of minimal regulatory climate for international banking operations within the EEC. Each bank will operate on a level playing field, so competition should eliminate all other inconsistencies such as tax differences and differences across countries as to whether current accounts can earn interest. Simply put, the EEC formula for integration in the banking sector is to establish a minimal regulatory framework that allows the market forces of competition to gradually create a unified banking market. This simple formula also underlies the integration of all EEC manufacturing and services.

Evidence of increasing integration in the EEC banking sector already exists. Banks are preparing for the expansive opportunities offered by 1992. For instance, in 1987 Deutsche Bank moved into Italy by purchasing BankAmerica's network of 100 branches for $603 million, and Munich-based Bayerische Vereinsbank acquired First National Bank of Chicago's Rome and Milan branches. In December of 1987, Credit Lyonnais

---

[1] See Motor Industry Research Unit, "A Study into the Economic Implications of a European Internal Market from the Perspective of the Volume Automotive Sector," a report commissioned by Ford of Europe for the EEC Commission, Brussels, 1988. European Currency Unit (ECU) at 1985 value.

bought Nederlandse Credietbank (NCB), the Dutch subsidiary of America's Chase Manhattan and Holland's sixth largest bank. Today some Danish banks advertise their deposit accounts in north German newspapers. Barclays Bank recently offered a personal line of credit, in French francs, to Parisians. The effect of EEC integration will be to promote more of such cross-border operations and competition.

The collective thought among EEC nations is that integration will result in a united and strong Europe because of the economic gains from the elimination of nontariff barriers. Such gains will take two basic forms: (1) savings from unnecessary costs and lost opportunities associated with barriers and fragmented markets, and (2) revenues from enhanced competitiveness in world markets and from synergies created by cooperative linkages.

The elimination of barriers should serve as a type of supply-side shock or injection, resulting in lower production costs and thus lower prices. Prices are assured to be lower because of pressures created by competitive entry, either by extant border competitors or by new rivals. This downward price pressure should stimulate demand, thereby leading to increased output, jobs creation, deficit reductions, and other benefits. Ideally such benefits can be achieved without spiraling demand-pull inflation.

Not everyone will benefit from integration, however, especially in the short run. The removal of protective barriers may offer new opportunities for some firms, but monopolistic national firms will exhibit a profit squeeze. Those firms best suited to exploit the advantages of integration are those recapitalizing to meet new demand. Successful market integration also will require careful management of currency flows and, at a macro level, a strong EEC monetary system.

Employing an econometric forecasting model (known as *HERMES*) for the EEC, Catinat (1988) recently estimated the potential gains from integration.[2,3] Highlights of his findings are

- An increase in EEC gross domestic product of 4.5%
- A reduction in consumer prices of over 6%
- The creation of 1.8 million new jobs

Such welfare gains are impressive. Indeed, the total gain potential of an integrated Europe is put at ECU 200 billion.[4] Such benefits could be magnified by complementary economic policy.

Of the total gain, about 10% (or ECU 21 billion) will accrue to the financial services sector alone. Still, a number of important barriers are preventing the integration of EEC financial markets and services. One important barrier is controls on capital movements. Such exchange con-

---

[2] Catinat, M. "Radioscope du grant marche interieur," *Economie Prospective Internationale* no. 33 (1988) CEPII, ler trimestre, Documentation francaise.

[3] For a detailed discussion of HERMES, see Commission of the EEC, "The Economics of 1992—An Assessment of the Potential Economic Effects of Completing the Internal Market of the EEC," Brussels (March 1988): Part C, p. 3.2.3.

[4] ECU at 1985 value.

trols are still in effect in Greece, Ireland, Portugal, and Spain. This barrier prevents the free movement of capital, and thus represents an important obstacle to intercountry investment and product development and competition. Current EEC legislation seeks to phase out capital controls and liberalize cross-border investment.

Current legislation also seeks to reform security markets. Rules presently allow discriminatory taxes on foreign securities purchased, differential listing requirements across national equity markets, and restrictions on holdings of foreign securities. Directives to integrate EEC security markets are now in effect.

Segmentation in the banking and insurance areas also still exists. Spain, for instance, has restrictions on foreign acquisitions of local banks. Some EEC countries prevent the cross-border solicitation of deposits as well as the sale of some banking services. Discriminatory taxes offer domestic insurance companies protection from border competition.

Yet, evidence of integration of EEC financial markets is beginning to appear. For instance, Spain and France now allow foreign financial institutions to purchase local brokerage firms. In October of 1987, French insurance company Cie du Mir bought British Insurance Equity and Law for $800 million. The effect of EEC financial market integration will be to promote more of such cross-border operations.

Another concern facing EEC leaders regards the distribution of these forecasted benefits. The EEC is commonly divided into the wealthy north (except Ireland) and the poor south (except emerging Italy). When Greece entered the EEC in 1981, meat traders from Holland and West Germany were outbidding local slaughterhouses to supply Athens supermarkets. And after two years in the EEC, Spain's intra-EEC trade balance fell from a surplus of $2 billion in 1985 to a deficit of $4 billion in 1987. Greece and Portugal have double-digit inflation. Unemployment in Spain and Ireland is about twice the community average. Greece, Ireland, Portugal, and Spain have a comparatively large farming work force.

Given these disparities, how will the benefits of EEC integration be divided among the member nations, and will the poorer member nations benefit?

This is a difficult question to tackle, but an answer appears to be emerging with the test case of Spain. Despite its current status as one of the four poorest EEC nations (with Greece, Ireland, and Portugal), Spain is quickly moving to prepare for 1992. The government is encouraging domestic industry to establish cooperative links with foreign industrial powers, including the Japanese and Americans and even other EEC nations. Spain wants to be a production center where foreign manufacturers can pay lower wages while penetrating the entire EEC market. Spain wants to attract foreign capital and investment in order to lower unemployment and to compete in a free-market community.

The recent strategy of Spain may serve as a model for development for other poor EEC nations. Through integration these poor nations may benefit greatly by serving as manufacturing centers. Clearly such a strategy appears warranted, since these poor countries cannot compete in the service sectors such as banking and insurance. Thus, it appears that integration can offer benefits to the poorer EEC nations in the form of industrialization.

Spain's proposed strategy to attract foreign capital investment and to serve as a springboard for foreign penetration of EEC markets has raised some concern in the community. EEC politicians and business leaders in many member nations feel that the early winners of 1992 may be U.S. and Japanese multinational firms with global marketing and manufacturing clout. As a result, signs are appearing that EEC integration may be ushered in with an escort of broad European protectionism. Currently such protectionist policies include the following:

- Denying foreign banks and brokerages houses access to the EEC unless their countries grant reciprocal rights
- Limiting Japanese car and light-truck imports to 9.5% of the EEC market, down from 11%
- Levying infant-industry tariffs on foreign imports of new technologies
- Launching grant programs for television and film production to counter the growing influence of U.S. entertainment groups

Although it is likely that some protectionist policies will be instituted, the degree of protectionism and its maturity are currently unknown. Protectionism tends to reduce the volume of world trade. Yet many non-EEC firms stand to benefit substantially through integration. For instance, Japanese auto firms plan to expand production in Europe. Provided they are made with a high proportion of European components, Japanese cars from Spain and other EEC nations can be sold as freely across Europe as can Fiats or BMWs. In December of 1987, Nissan began a five-year, $400 million expansion of its Sunderland, England, plant. American firms may also benefit. When the differential national standards for autos disappear, Ford of Europe should reap profits from lower production costs. And Philips estimates savings of over $300 million per year by 1992, from reduced inventories, warehouses, and clerical staff as a result of integration. Thus, despite some anticipated protectionist policies by the EEC, foreign firms can exhibit expansion and the net effect on world trade of integration should clearly be positive.

Although full EEC integration is not scheduled to occur until the end of 1992, nearly 150 acts to remove nontariff barriers have been adopted, and the expected effects of full integration are already being capitalized in securities markets. We now provide some early evidence concerning integration and its impact on the interrelationships between member nations' inflation rates, exchange rates, and stock markets. This evidence suggests that member economies are indeed more integrated now than in the past. Implications of this evidence for institutional portfolio management and multinational corporations are also discussed.

As cross-border restrictions are eliminated, the price levels of each member nation should become more susceptible to those of the other countries. As labor and capital become more transferable, and production and capital costs are exported across borders, prices will converge. Exhibit A.1 reports correlation coefficients of inflation rates across the

Exhibit A.1

Correlation Coefficients of Inflation
Rates across Member Nations

	B	D	F	GR	IT	IR	LUX	N	P	SP	UK
D	−0.05										
	0.35										
F	0.51	0.17									
	0.39	0.00									
GR	0.16	0.03	0.15								
	−0.17	−0.03	0.05								
IT	0.35	0.09	0.49	0.61							
	0.78	0.37	0.30	0.27							
IR	0.35	0.05	0.60	0.47	0.23						
	0.77	0.23	0.30	0.10	0.60						
LUX	0.53	0.00	0.59	0.52	0.49	0.55					
	0.81	0.36	0.16	−0.02	0.85	0.57					
N	0.18	0.24	0.74	0.27	0.40	0.58	0.49				
	0.44	0.52	−0.09	0.25	0.50	0.20	0.54				
P	−0.09	−0.02	0.12	0.15	−0.06	0.00	0.24	0.44			
	0.47	−0.08	0.37	−0.02	0.35	0.48	0.27	−0.13			
SP	0.04	0.01	−0.12	−0.51	−0.27	−0.43	−0.28	−0.16	−0.07		
	0.11	0.16	0.07	0.35	0.11	0.08	0.01	0.01	0.15		
UK	−0.15	0.45	0.46	0.27	0.30	0.46	0.22	0.40	0.05	−0.16	
	0.17	0.24	0.07	0.24	0.08	0.22	0.13	0.33	−0.02	0.22	
WGR	0.22	0.02	0.41	0.59	0.37	0.67	0.67	0.29	0.11	−0.33	0.53
	0.75	0.40	0.42	0.08	0.78	0.61	0.77	0.41	0.37	0.17	0.26

Notes: a. The country codes are Belgium (B), Denmark (D), France (F), Greece (GR), Italy (IT), Ireland (IR), Luxembourg (LUX), Netherlands (N), Portugal (P), Spain (SP), United Kingdom (UK), and West Germany (WGR).

b. The top number in each cell is the correlation coefficient for the period 1977–1982; the bottom number in each cell is that for the period 1983–1988. The overall average correlation coefficient for each subperiod is 0.2302 and 0.2858, respectively.

twelve member nations for two separate periods: 1977–1982 and 1983–1988. Quarterly data obtained from the *International Monetary Fund Statistical Yearbooks* are used. A comparison of inflation correlations over these two periods can indicate whether inflationary trends are becoming more similar among the twelve members. The coefficients reported suggest that this is the case. For the two periods, the overall average correlation coefficients are 0.230 and 0.286, respectively.

Presently, nine member nations participate in an exchange rate arrangement in which their home currency's value is tied to those of the other participants (see Chapter 2). Recently there has been some discussion regarding full participation by all twelve members in a similar exchange rate arrangement or, perhaps, the use of the ECU as a common medium of exchange for all cross-border transactions. But whichever arrangement is accepted, integration should result in higher correlations among member exchange rates as their economies become more interdependent. Exhibit A.2 presents correlations for rates of exchange among members. For the same two periods, the overall average correlations are 0.500 and 0.538, suggesting more common rate movements among EEC nations.

	B	D	F	GR	IT	IR	LUX	N	P	SP	UK
D	−0.95 0.99										
F	0.89 0.97	0.90 0.96									
GR	0.77 0.64	0.77 0.62	0.84 0.69								
IT	0.92 0.96	0.91 0.95	0.94 0.95	0.83 0.70							
IR	−0.92 −0.93	−0.93 −0.93	−0.89 −0.93	−0.83 −0.63	−0.91 −0.88						
LUX	0.99 0.99	0.95 0.99	0.90 0.97	0.77 0.64	0.92 0.97	−0.92 −0.93					
N	0.94 0.98	0.95 0.98	0.91 0.98	0.78 0.64	0.92 0.97	−0.92 −0.93	0.94 0.99				
P	0.65 0.89	0.60 0.89	0.68 0.88	0.62 0.56	0.59 0.86	−0.64 −0.86	0.66 0.90	0.64 0.88			
SP	0.62 0.77	0.66 0.73	0.60 0.77	0.59 0.55	0.61 0.78	−0.61 −0.69	0.62 0.77	0.63 0.78	0.47 0.79		
UK	0.69 0.66	0.68 0.64	0.67 0.70	0.67 0.63	0.68 0.62	−0.76 −0.79	0.69 0.66	0.71 0.68	0.64 0.60	0.53 0.61	
WGR	0.94 0.99	0.94 0.99	0.92 0.97	0.80 0.64	0.92 0.97	−0.93 −0.91	0.94 0.99	0.98 0.99	0.66 0.88	0.63 0.75	0.72 0.64

Exhibit A.2

Correlation Coefficients of Exchange Rates across Member Nations

Note: The top number in each cell is the correlation coefficient for the period 1977–1982; the bottom number in each cell is that for the period 1983–1988. The overall average correlation coefficients for each subperiod are 0.4996 and 0.5383, respectively.

To the extent that stock markets are affected by economic conditions, and member economies become more integrated, these stock markets should become more highly correlated. Also, increased capital mobility resulting from lessened capital restrictions should increase the influence of one member's stock market conditions on the others. Exhibit A.3 displays correlations of stock market returns, based on indices measured in local currency units, for some members over the same 1977–1982 and 1983–1988 periods. It appears that stock markets are more integrated; the overall average correlation coefficient in the later period (0.425) is much higher than that in the earlier period (0.074).

The preceding results suggest more highly correlated inflation rates, exchange rates, and stock market returns among EEC countries as a result of increased integration efforts and expectations. These findings have relevance for institutional portfolio management. First, the potential for geographical diversification may be limited. Yields on portfolios of money market securities, bonds, or stocks of different member nations may be too highly correlated to offer any substantial risk reduction benefits from cross-border diversification. Thus, portfolios may be revised to replace some EEC securities with non-EEC securities. Arguably, correlations of EEC and non-EEC securities may be lowered as a consequence of integration, if such integration results in EEC protectionism and increased segmentation.

Exhibit A.3

Correlation Coefficients of Stock
Market Index Returns across
Member Nations

	B	D	F	IR	IT	SP	UK
D	−0.26						
	0.27						
F	0.16	−0.37					
	0.68	0.35					
IR	−0.26	−0.08	0.07				
	0.66	0.39	0.62				
IT	−0.02	0.36	0.11	0.09			
	0.45	0.22	0.69	0.41			
SP	0.12	0.51	−0.01	−0.36	0.22		
	0.00	0.52	0.26	−0.07	0.08		
UK	0.12	0.25	−0.02	0.46	0.17	0.11	
	0.72	0.20	0.66	0.61	0.33	0.08	
WGR	−0.21	0.16	−0.22	0.51	−0.02	0.03	0.44
	0.65	0.52	0.66	0.46	0.52	0.29	0.66

Note: The top number in each cell is the correlation coefficient for the period 1977–1982; the bottom number in each cell is that for the period 1983–1988. The overall average correlation coefficient for each subperiod is 0.0736 and 0.4246, respectively.

Second, international diversification by institutional investors often is undertaken, in part, to reduce exchange rate risk. However, if member currencies are more closely tied to each other, they will be more highly correlated with respect to institutional investors in non-EEC nations such as the United States. Again, the implication is that investors may seek to rebalance their international holdings.

Multinational corporations (MNCs) that have already established a presence in EEC countries may benefit from integration, because they will be allowed to more easily cross EEC borders without excessive cost. However, those MNCs that have established foreign subsidiaries solely in EEC countries may experience greater risk, as geographic unification reduces diversification benefits. Because of differences in economic conditions across countries, MNCs focusing on a particular business may be able to stabilize cash flows by penetrating various geographic markets. Yet, if the EEC economies become more highly correlated as hypothesized earlier, the geographic diversification across EEC countries will be less effective in stabilizing cash flows.

U.S. multinational firms with a presence in Europe could benefit from European unification. The present inconsistencies create significant inefficiencies that will dissipate as rules for unification are implemented. Television ads have been subject to country-specific regulations. Standards for autos and other products have differed among members. As the differential product standards, border checks, and other frictions are eliminated, MNCs can benefit. And evidence exists that MNCs are positioning to exploit these benefits. 3M Company will now spend more on advertising to target all EEC nations. Gillette Company reorganized its European plants to target all members. Other companies like Colgate-Palmolive and Prime Computer now manufacture more homogeneous products that can be marketed in all EEC countries.

Nearly two decades ago, the EEC initiated the process of integrating member economies through the elimination of import tariffs. Today, the EEC is rapidly approaching its long-awaited goal of full integration as all nontariff barriers are being phased out. The early evidence reported here clearly suggests that member economies are growing more integrated.

With continuing market integration, the EEC hopes to unleash sustained and inflation-free economic growth stemming from lowered production costs, enhanced cross-border competition, and synergistic mergers. Current analyses and forecasts do suggest that such benefits may accrue to the citizens of an integrated and free-market Europe.

Still, much needs to be done before full integration and its benefits are realized. Significant barriers remain intact, and may be sustained by the self-interests of domestic nations and their specialized industries. And many questions remain unanswered, including these: Will integration result in truly inflation-free growth, or will attenuating demand-pull inflation occur? Who will reap the vast majority of the benefits of market integration? What will be the impact of integration on non-EEC nations and their economies?

Only time holds the answers to these difficult questions. Until then, suffice it to say that integration represents a bold economic experiment that, if successful, may serve as a model for the integration of other national economies and financial markets and services.

Appendix B

CURRENCIES AND SYMBOLS

Afghanistan	afghani	Af
Algeria	dinar	DA
Antigua and Barbuda	dollar	EC$
Argentina	austral	₳
Australia	dollar	A$
Austria	schilling	S
Bahamas	dollar	B$
Bahrain	dinar	BD
Bangladesh	taka	Tk
Barbados	dollar	BdS$
Belgium	franc	BF
Belize	dollar	BZ$
Benin	franc	CFAF
Bhutan	ngultrum	Nu
Bolivia	peso	$b
Botswana	pula	P
Brazil	cruzado	Cr$
Burkina Faso	franc	CFAF
Burma	kyat	K
Burundi	franc	FBu
Cameroon	franc	CFAF
Canada	dollar	Can$
Cape Verde	escudo	C.V.Esc.
Central African Republic	franc	CFAF
Chad	franc	CFAF
Chile	peso	Ch$
China (People's Republic)	renminbi	Cy
Colombia	peso	Col$
Comoros	franc	CF
Congo	franc	CFAF

343

Costa Rica	colon	₡
Cote d'Ivoire	franc	CFAF
Cyprus	pound	£C
Denmark	krone	Dkr
Djibouti	franc	DF
Dominica	dollar	EC$
Dominican Republic	peso	RD$
Ecuador	sucre	S/
Egypt	pound	£E
El Salvador	colon	₡
Ethiopia	birr	Br
Fiji	dollar	F$
Finland	markka	Fmk
France	franc	F
Gabon	franc	CFAF
Gambia	dalasi	D
Germany	deutsche mark	DM
Ghana	cedi	¢
Greece	drachma	Dr
Grenada	dollar	EC$
Guatemala	quetzal	Q
Guinea	franc	GS
Guinea-Bissau	peso	PG
Guyana	dollar	G$
Honduras	lempira	L
Hungary	forint	Ft
Iceland	krona	ISK
India	rupee	Rs
Indonesia	rupiah	Rp
Iran	rial	Rls
Iraq	dinar	ID
Ireland	pound	£Ir
Israel	new shekel	IS
Italy	lira	Lit
Jamaica	dollar	J$
Japan	yen	¥
Jordan	dinar	JD
Kampuchea	riel	KR
Kenya	shilling	K Sh
Korea	won	W
Kuwait	dinar	KD
Laos (People's Democratic Republic)	kip	KN
Lebanon	pound	LL
Lesotho	loti	M
Liberia	dollar	$
Libya	dinar	LD
Luxembourg	franc	Lux F
Madagascar	franc	FMG
Malawi	kwacha	MK
Malaysia	ringgit	M$

Maldives	rufiyaa	Rf
Mali	franc	CFAF
Malta	lira	Lm
Mauritania	ouguiya	UM
Mauritius	rupee	Mau Rs
Mexico	peso	Mex$
Morocco	dirham	DH
Mozambique	metical	Mt
Nepal	rupee	NRs
Netherlands	guilder	f.
New Zealand	dollar	$NZ
Nicaragua	cordoba	C$
Niger	franc	CFAF
Nigeria	naira	₦
Norway	krone	NKr
Oman	rial	RO
Pakistan	rupee	PRs
Panama	balboa	B
Papua New Guinea	kina	K
Paraguay	guarani	₲
Peru	inti	I/.
Philippines	peso	₱
Portugal	escudo	Esc
Qatar	riyal	QR
Romania	leu	—
Rwanda	franc	RF
St. Christopher-Nevis	dollar	EC$
St. Lucia	dollar	EC$
St. Vincent	dollar	EC$
Sao Tome' and Principe	dobra	Db
Saudi Arabia	riyal	SRls
Senegal	franc	CFAF
Seychelles	rupee	SR
Sierra Leone	leone	Le
Singapore	dollar	S$
Solomon Islands	dollar	Sl$
Somalia	shilling	So. Sh.
South Africa	rand	R
Spain	peseta	Ptas
Sri Lanka	rupee	SLRs
Sudan	pound	LSd
Suriname	guilder	Sf
Swaziland	ilangeni	E
Sweden	krona	Sk
Switzerland	franc	SwF
Syria	pound	LS
Tanzania	shilling	TSh
Thailand	baht	Bht or Bt
Togo	franc	CFAF
Tonga	pa'anga	PT

Trinidad and Tobago	dollar	TT$
Tunisia	dinar	D
Turkey	lira	LT
Uganda	shilling	USh
United Arab Emirates	dirham	Dh
United Kingdom	pound	£
United States	dollar	$
Uruguay	new peso	NUr$
Vanuatu	vatu	VT
Venezuela	bolivar	Bs
Viet Nam	dong	D
Western Samoa	tala	WS$
Yemen Arab Republic	rial	YRls
Yemen (People's Democratic Republic)	dinar	YD
Yugoslavia	dinar	Din
Zaire	zaire	Z
Zambia	kwacha	K
Zimbabwe	dollar	Z$

GLOSSARY

Absolute Purchasing Power Parity It postulates that the exchange rate is expressed in terms of the two nations' price levels.

Adaptive Expectations An approach that has been commonly used to model price behavior. Expectations of the future spot rate are formed from a weighted average of the current spot rate and the lagged expected rate.

Allocational Efficiency Resource allocation is in an optimal state and further rearrangement of resources would not improve the well-being of economic agents.

American Depository Receipts (ADRs) Certificates that represent the ownership of foreign stocks.

Appreciation An increase in the value of a currency.

Arbitrage Pricing Theory (APT) The use of relative pricing on a set of assets that adhere to a specific return-generating process.

Asset Allocation Determination of the optimal combination of stocks and bonds in which to invest.

ARIMA Model An Auto-Regressive Integrated Moving Average model, which is a time series model used for forecasting based on a systematic pattern of the variable. The pattern is derived from its history and shocks in finite order.

Autocorrelation Function (ACF) A statistic for calculating the correlation coefficients of each set of time series variable, separated by k orders.

Baker Plan Policy proposed to reduce the exposure of commercial banks to the debt of less developed countries.

Balance of Payments A measurement of all transactions between domestic and foreign residents over a specified period of time.

Bandwagon Expectations Market expectations of exchange rates are formed in such a way that a depreciation in the current spot rate will generate an expectation of further depreciation in the next period.

Big Bang Deregulatory event in London in 1986, in which the London exchange was opened to foreign investment firms, and the commission structure on stock transactions was allowed to be competitive.

Bilateral Exchange Rate The exchange ratio for two countries' currency trading is called the bilateral exchange rate. The trading may be made in either the spot market or the forward market.

Black Monday The day of the world stock market crash, October 19, 1987.

Brady Plan Policy to reduce the exposure of commercial banks to debt of less developed countries.

Capital Account A principal division of the balance of payments, it measures the flows of financial securities across national borders.

Capital Asset Pricing Model (CAPM) Model used to determine the required return by investors who invest in particular securities (or other assets).

Carrying Charge Model An arbitrage-based model for determining forward and futures prices that holds that such prices are equal to the current spot price of the underlying asset plus the costs of carrying it forward to delivery.

Cash and Carry Arbitrage The arbitrage trading strategy that ensures that the carrying charge model obtains.

Circus Swap A combination of a currency swap and an interest rate swap. The parties exchange fixed-rate debt denominated in one currency for floating-rate debt denominated in another currency.

Clearinghouse An entity related to a futures exchange through which trades must be matched, confirmed, and resettled daily.

Commodity Arbitrage A market behavior that describes buying a commodity in one market and reselling it in another market or buying a commodity today and selling it in the future by signing a contract or just holding it.

Composite Efficiency Hypothesis A hypothesis that the expectation of the future spot exchange rate is a weighted average of the current spot rate and the forward rate.

Conditional Variance The calculation of variance for an economic variable is conditioned on a given information set.

Country Risk From a bank perspective, the term can be broadly defined as any type of risk within a country that could adversely affect the cash flows of the lending bank.

Covered Interest Arbitrage An arbitrage strategy that ensures interest rate parity. It is the currency market's version of the general cash and carry arbitrage underlying the carrying charge model.

Covered Interest Parity The risk-free interest rate differential is matched by the forward exchange premium (discount).

Currency Cocktail Bonds Bonds denominated in a mix or portfolio of currencies.

Currency Forward Contract A contract, negotiated on the interbank market, that entails the trading of a designated amount of foreign exchange at a prescribed future date and price.

Currency Futures Contract A contract entailing the trading of a designated amount of foreign exchange at a prescribed future date and price, which is determined by an auction process on the floor of an organized futures exchange. Unlike a currency forward contract, it entails daily resettlement and the posting of margin.

Currency Futures Option A contract giving the buyer the right to trade a designated currency futures contract at a prescribed exercise price through contract expiration.

Currency Option A contract giving the buyer the right to trade a designated underlying currency at a prescribed exercise price through contract expiration.

Currency Swap A contract allowing two firms to exchange different currencies at recurrent intervals that is usually employed in conjunction with debt issues.

Current Account A principal division of the balance of payments, it is a record of all transactions entailing goods and services and unilateral transfers across national borders.

Daily Resettlement Also known as marking-to-the-market, it is a futures market requirement that traders realize losses (and gains) each trading day.

Debt-Equity Swaps Process whereby creditors return debt to debtors in exchange for an equity interest in assets owned by debtors; this activity has been frequently conducted by commercial banks holding debt of less developed countries.

Deficit Units Firms, governments, or individuals in need of funds.

Depreciation A decline in the value of a currency.

Devaluation A decrease in the official value of a national currency with respect to a foreign currency. This term is usually applied in the fixed exchange rate regime.

Distributed Lag Expectations Expectations of the exchange rates are formed on the basis of current and lagged spot rates.

Dividend Discount Model Model used to discount future cash flows in order to determine the present value of an asset.

Dual Trading Occurs when futures exchange members trade both for public clients and their own trading accounts within the same trading session.

Effective Financing Rate Cost of financing as a percentage of the funds borrrowed, after adjusting for exchange rate effects.

Efficient Market Hypothesis A hypothesis that asset prices reflect all market information. Since news by definition is unpredictable, changes in asset prices are unpredictable.

Elasticities Approach to the Balance of Trade A concept based on the idea that using the exchange rate as an instrument to improve the balance-of-trade position depends on the elasticities of goods, demands, and supplies.

Equity Risk Premia Excess returns for holding equity, measured by the excess amount of the equity market return over the risk-free rate.

Eurobanks Commercial banks that serve as intermediaries in the Eurocurrency market.

Eurobond Market Market designed to facilitate the transfer of long-term funds (in various currencies) from surplus units to deficit units.

Eurocommercial Paper Short-term security issued by large corporations that need short-term funds.

Eurocredit Market Market designed to provide medium-term funds (in various currencies) to deficit units, whereby commercial banks serve as intermediaries.

Eurocurrency Market Market designed to facilitate the transfer of short-term funds (in various currencies) from surplus units to deficit units, whereby commercial banks serve as intermediaries.

Eurodollar Deposit A dollar-denominated deposit in a non-U.S. bank or overseas branch of a U.S. bank.

Eurodollar Floating-Rate CDs (FRCDs) Certificates of deposit issued by commercial banks in the Eurocurrency market that offer a floating interest rate.

Euroequities Market Market in which stocks are

underwritten and distributed among investors in several countries.

European Currency Unit (ECU) Unit of account consisting of European currencies; several European countries maintain the value of their currency with respect to the ECU within boundaries.

European Economic Community Also known as the Common Market, it is a community of twelve European nations that is designed to promote the common economic and political interests of the region. The European Monetary System is an exchange rate arrangement formed in 1979 that entails most nations of the Common Market.

Exchange Rate The price of one country's currency in terms of another country's currency.

Extrapolative Approach Strategy used to construct a portfolio based on historical covariances of stock and bond returns.

Extrapolative Expectations Expectations formed such that current spot rate depreciation (appreciation) will lead to a further depreciation (appreciation) in the near future.

Filter Rule A mechanical trading rule which indicates that if an asset's price rises by x% (percent), the investor should buy and hold until the price drops at least x% from a previous high, in which case the asset will be sold.

Fisher Parity The nominal interest rate differential between countries equals the expected inflation-rate differential. This is also called Fisher closed hypothesis.

Fixed Exchange Rate System A system of exchange rates wherein rates are maintained within narrow ranges, usually through the trading of currency reserves by participating central banks.

Floating Exchange Rate System A system of exchange rates wherein currency values are determined by a competitive, open-market process—like the prices of most commodities. The system may be "managed" or "dirty" if participating central banks intervene to adjust their currency values.

Foreign Currency Market Market in which arrangements are made for trading major currencies.

Fortress Europe Name given to a strategy in which new barriers would be established to prevent firms outside of European countries from competing for business in Europe.

Forward Contracts Contracts offered by commercial banks that allow for the purchase or sale of a specified currency for a specified exchange rate at a specified point in time.

Forward Discount A term used for the case in which the forward exchange rate is less than the spot rate.

Forward Premium A term used for the case in which the forward exchange rate is greater than the spot rate.

Forward Rate Exchange rate for the exchange of currencies at a future date, negotiated between firms and commercial banks.

Fundamental Analysis Valuation of an asset is based on economic factors. These factors are relative inflation rates, relative money supplies, interest rate differentials, etc.

Glass-Steagall Act Separated securities and banking activities in the U.S.; prevented commercial banks from underwriting corporate bonds.

Hedging Premium Also known as a risk premium, it is a premium embedded in a currency forward or futures price that stems from the risk-averse nature of market participants and that is as function of the covariance between the participant's marginal rate of substitution and the exchange rate. Because of the hedging premium, the forward or futures price may be regarded as a biased estimator of the exchange rate expected to prevail at contract delivery.

Intercurrency Spread A futures spread constructed by assuming a long position in one currency futures contract and a short position in another futures contract exhibiting the same delivery date but different underlying currency.

Interest Rate Parity An arbitrage-based theorem that holds that the difference between spot and forward exchange rates is determined by the interest rate differential between the two nations. It is the currency market's version of the general carrying charge model.

Interest Rate Swap Occurs when a firm that has issued one form of debt agrees to swap interest payments with another firm that has issued a different form of debt denominated in the same currency.

International Banking Act Enacted in 1978 to make domestic and foreign banks in the U.S. subject to the same regulations.

International CAPM Model that accounts for the influence of domestic and world markets on the returns of securities.

International Fisher Parity The expected change in exchange rates is equal to the interest rate differential for the two trading countries. This is also called Fisher open hypothesis.

International Mutual Funds (IMFs) Internationally diversified portfolios of securities created by investment firms that pool investments of individual investors.

Intracurrency Spread A futures spread constructed by assuming a long position in one currency futures contract and a short position in another futures contract exhibiting the same underlying currency but different delivery date.

J-curve Effect A time pattern in the balance of trade in which, following a devaluation, initial decreases in the trade balance are followed by increases.

January Effect A phenomenon in which an asset is observed to yield a higher return during the month of January. Over the past ten years, the dollar has appreciated against a basket of foreign currencies every January.

Law of One Price   Commodity prices, once they are converted into a common currency unit, are everywhere equal.

London Interbank Offer Rate   The rate at which eurobanks in London offer to lend to other banks.

Margin   A performance bond consisting of cash and/or liquid securities that must be posted in order to engage in currency futures trading. Writers of currency options must also post margin.

Master Agreements   Provide a set of terms applicable to any swap transaction. Parties can tailor the transaction by appending specific terms to the master agreement.

Monetary Approach   An analysis of balance of payments or exchange rates which emphasizes the factors affecting money supply and money demand.

Operational Efficiency   A state in which transactions are carried out with minimum transaction costs.

Pegged Exchange Rate System   A system of exchange rates wherein a nation ties the value of its currency to that of some other currency or unit of exchange.

Portfolio Balance Approach   An analysis of the balance of payments or the exchange rate which emphasizes the stock equilibrium in asset supply and asset demand. It highlights the role of wealth and views assets as imperfect substitutes.

Price Indexes   Indexes that measure the value of representative commodity bundles. The most popular one is the Consumer Price Index (CPI).

Pricing Efficiency   A state of resource allocation in which the asset price is equal to its intrinsic economic value.

Production Subsidies   Provided by national governments to domestic industries in order to make their finished good prices more competitive on international markets.

Purchasing Power Parity (PPP)   A theory that relates the exchange rate to two countries' prices. The absolute version states that the exchange rate is equal to the ratio of the domestic and foreign prices levels. The relative version contends that the percentage change in the exchange rate is equal to the inflation differential between the two countries.

Put-Call Parity   An arbitrage-based condition that relates the values of corresponding European put and call options.

Q-statistic   A test for examining the randomness of the estimated coefficients as a group, which is chi-square distributed with k degrees of freedom. The Q-statistic is usually employed to test serial correlation with k order lags.

Quantity Theory of Money   The theory that a proportional increase in the money supply leads to a proportional increase in the price level.

Quota   Establishes an absolute limit on the number or quantity of a foreign-made good that can be imported over a prescribed period of time.

Random Walk Hypothesis   An asset price changes from period to period, usually day to day, at random. The changes are independent of each other and have an identical distribution.

Rational Expectations   Expectations of economic variables that fully reflect market information. In the currency market, the forward exchange rate is assumed to summarize the exchange rate determinants concerning the future variables.

Real Exchange Rate   The exchange rate is defined in real terms, that is, the exchange rate is adjusted by the two countries' prices.

Real Interest Rate Parity   A parity relation which states that the expected change in real exchange rates is equal to the real interest rate differential in two countries.

Regressive Expectations   Expectations of exchange rates are formed by a weighted average of the current and the equilibrium exchange rates.

Reinvestment Rate Premium   A premium embedded in a currency futures price that arises from daily resettlement and nonconstant interest rates.

Runs Test   A nonparametric test which is used for detecting the frequency of changes in direction in a series.

Semistrong Efficient Markets Hypothesis   A hypothesis which states that current asset prices fully reflect all historical and public information.

Single European Act   Enacted in order to promote the free flow of goods and funds across European countries.

Special Drawing Right   A reserve credit held on the books of the International Monetary Fund that could be used to settle international trade and balance of payments deficits under the Bretton Woods Agreement.

Speculative Bubbles   Speculative bubbles represent a deviation of the current market price of the asset from the value implied by market fundamentals. The price movements are likely generating of self-fulfilling prophecies.

Spot Rate   The exchange rate for immediate exchange of currencies.

Static Expectations   Market expectations are stable; the expectations of the future spot rate are nothing but the current spot rate.

Strong Efficient Markets Hypothesis   A hypothesis that the current asset prices (exchange rates) reflect all market information, including any useful "inside" information.

Surplus Units   Firms, governments, or individuals with excess funds.

Tariff   A type of tax levied on imports.

Technical Analysis   An analysis which involves the use of historical information (exchange rates) in order to derive a visible pattern to predict the future movements of an asset (foreign currency).

Term Premium   A premium embedded in a currency futures price that arises from liquidity premia in the term structure of interest rates when participants are risk-averse.

Triffin Paradox A theory contending that fixed exchange rate systems are inherently unstable due to the need for the reserve country to accumulate trade deficits.

Unbiased Forward Rate Hypothesis A hypothesis that the forward exchange rate is an unbiased predictor of the future spot rate.

Weak Efficient Markets Hypothesis The hypothesis that assets prices reflect all historical information.

INDEX